D0119592

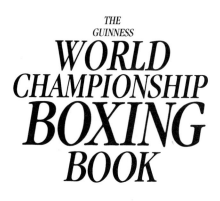

THE
GUINNESS
WORLD
CHAMPIONSHIP
BOXING
BOOK

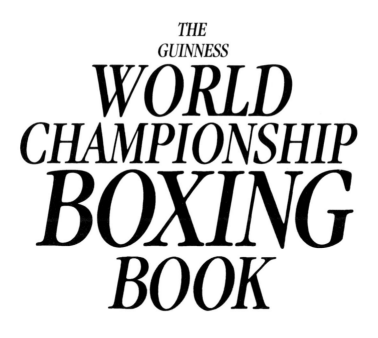

THE
GUINNESS
WORLD
CHAMPIONSHIP
BOXING
BOOK

Ian Morrison

GUINNESS PUBLISHING

EDITOR: Charles Richards
DESIGN AND LAYOUT: Edward Q. Botchway
PICTURE RESEARCH: Julie O'Leary

Copyright © Ian Morrison and
Guinness Publishing Ltd 1990

Published in Great Britain by Guinness Publishing Ltd,
33 London Road, Enfield, Middlesex

Typeset in Garamond Light and Garamond Book
by Ace Filmsetting Ltd, Frome, Somerset
Printed and bound in Great Britain by
The Bath Press, Bath

'Guinness' is a registered trade mark of
Guinness Superlatives Ltd

British Library Cataloguing in Publication Data

Morrison, Ian, 1947
   The Guinness book of world championship boxing
   1. Boxing. Biographies. Collections
   I. Title
   796.83092

ISBN 0-85112-900-5

1196

ACKNOWLEDGEMENTS

The author would like to thank his wife, Ann, for her invaluable time spent checking the mass of information in this book.

AUTHOR'S NOTE

With over 60 world champions in 17 weight divisions, one would think that sorting out the current state of world boxing must be a minefield. Well, it is! But there is nothing new in that. Throughout the last hundred years or so, boxing has posed a problem to historians and statisticians. Fighters claimed titles when they shouldn't have done, others were denied titles when, maybe, they had a good claim. Establishing a definitive list of world champions and world championship fights is a near-impossibility, but the lists on the following pages are as accurate as I believe any lists can be.

Regarding present-day contests it is not quite as difficult, it's just that there are more of them. If you accept the WBC, WBA and IBF as the three ruling bodies and accept their champions then the 'minefield' doesn't become too hazardous. But if you start delving into the realms of the WBO, and Intercontinental and Americas world champions then things quickly become decidedly hairy. The line has to be drawn somewhere and it has been – the three main bodies only are used for current record purposes. The WBO was going to be included, but then it was announced that several of its champions were relinquishing titles after only a few months because of 'reduced pay days'. So out came the WBO champions. Maybe it will be a different story in a year's time and their champions will be classed alongside those of the WBC, WBA and IBF. If that is the case then they will be included in the next edition.

Ian Morrison

CONTENTS

ABBREVIATIONS

WEIGHT DIVISIONS

SH	Super-heavyweight
H	Heavyweight
C	Cruiserweight
LH	Light-heavyweight
SM	Super-middleweight
M	Middleweight
LM	Light-middleweight/Junior-middleweight
W	Welterweight
LW	Light-welterweight/Junior-welterweight
L	Lightweight
JL	Junior-lightweight/Super-featherweight
Fe	Featherweight
SB	Super-bantamweight/Junior-featherweight
B	Bantamweight
SF	Super-flyweight/Junior-bantamweight
Fl	Flyweight
LF	Light-flyweight/Junior-flyweight
MF	Mini-flyweight/Strawweight

BOXING AUTHORITIES

EBU	European Boxing Union
IBF	International Boxing Federation
IBU	International Boxing Union
NBA	National Boxing Association
NY	New York State Athletic Commission
WBA	World Boxing Association
WBC	World Boxing Council

FINAL DECISIONS

D	Drew
DEF	Default
DIS	Disqualified
KO	Knock-out
NC	No contest
ND	No decision
PTS	Points
RSF	Referee stopped fight
RTD	Retired
TD	Technical decision
TKO	Technical knock-out

COUNTRIES

Alg	Algeria
Ant	Antigua
Arg	Argentina
Aus	Australia
Aut	Austria
Bah	Bahamas
Bar	Barbados
Bel	Belgium
Ber	Bermuda
Bra	Brazil
Bul	Bulgaria
CA	Costa Rica
Cam	Cameroon
Can	Canada
Cey	Ceylon
Chi	Chile
Chn	China
Col	Colombia
Cz	Czechoslovakia
Den	Denmark
Dom	Dominican Republic
Ecu	Ecuador
Eng	England
Est	Estonia
Fin	Finland
Fra	France
FRG	Federal Republic of Germany
GB	Great Britain
GDR	German Democratic Republic
Ger	Germany
Gha	Ghana
Gre	Greece
Guy	Guyana
Haw	Hawaii
Hol	Holland
IC	Ivory Coast
Ina	Indonesia
Ire	Ireland
Ita	Italy
Jam	Jamaica
Jap	Japan
Jor	Jordan
Ken	Kenya
Mex	Mexico
Mon	Mongolia
Mor	Morocco
NG	New Guinea
Ngr	Nigeria
Nic	Nicaragua
N. Kor	North Korea
Nor	Norway
NZ	New Zealand
Pan	Panama
Par	Paraguay
Phi	Philippines
PNG	Papua New Guinea
Por	Portugal
PR	Puerto Rico
Rho	Rhodesia
Rom	Romania
SA	South Africa
Sco	Scotland
Sen	Senegal
S. Kor	South Korea
Spa	Spain
St. Vin	St. Vincent
Swe	Sweden
Swi	Switzerland
Syr	Syria
Tha	Thailand
Ton	Tonga
Tri	Trinidad and Tobago
Tun	Tunisia
Uga	Uganda
Uru	Uruguay
USA	United States of America
USSR	Union of Soviet Socialist Republics
Ven	Venezuela
VI	Virgin Islands (US)
Wal	Wales
Yug	Yugoslavia
Zai	Zaire

HISTORY OF WORLD CHAMPIONSHIP BOXING

1

Man has always had the ability to hit his fellow man. And since the day when that ability was joined by the desire to do so, fisticuffs have been part of our life. Man still chooses to hit his fellow man, normally after a skinful of lager on a Saturday night. But in between the throwing of the first punch, in the days when a fig leaf covered one's dignity, and the present day, the throwing of punches at one another has, for some, been turned into the art of boxing.

Perhaps surprisingly, boxing did not become an organised sport until the early 18th century. The Chinese, Japanese and other Eastern nations had developed their own forms of fighting, armed or otherwise, hundreds of years before. But the simplest form of fighting, with fists, did not gain recognition until a little over 200 years ago.

The first person to open a boxing school was James Figg. Born in Oxfordshire, he was a leading swordsman and cudgel-fighter and in 1719 he opened his school of arms in London's Oxford Road. It became boxing's first home and in 1720 Figg accepted a challenge from Ned Sutton, a Gravesend pipefitter. Figg won, and became recognised as the sport's first champion.

A far cry from the multi-million dollar hype of world championship boxing today. This is boxing as it was in the 19th century (Mary Evans)

Two of the pioneers of pugilism, Jack Broughton (left) and James Figg, who was regarded as the sport's first champion (Hulton)

Boxing began to spread from Figg's amphitheatre, and not only to other parts of England, but also across the Channel into Europe. In 1733 Figg promoted the first international boxing contest when England's Bob Whittaker fought Tito Alberto di Carini of Italy. It was to become the foundation stone for international boxing.

Another leading exponent of the 'gentle art' in those early days was Jack Broughton, and it was he, after one of his opponents, George Stevenson, died following their bout in 1741, who devised a set of rules to make boxing safer. They were published in August 1743 and resulted in Broughton being widely acknowledged as the 'Father of Boxing'. His rules remained in force for nearly 100 years until superseded by the London Prize Ring rules.

The first boxing club, the Pugilistic Club, was opened in London in 1814 and the London Prize Ring rules were issued by the Pugilists' Protective Association in 1838. These new rules replaced the original ones drawn up by Broughton, and were subsequently revised in 1853 and 1866.

By the mid-19th century, prize fighting had taken a hold in the United States and as early as 1816 Jacob Hyer and Tom Beasley had engaged in the first fight billed as being for the American Championship. But it was in 1860 that the first steps towards a world championship were taken when Tom Sayers of England met John C. Heenan of the United States at Farnborough, Hampshire. The contest was declared a draw after 37 rounds. It was the first international contest of any significance and for all intents and purposes can be regarded as the first world title fight.

Two more early pugilists, Tom Johnson and Isaac Perrins. As you can see, they had none of the weight divisions that exist today (Mary Evans)

Their contest was held under the London Prize Ring rules which permitted wrestling. But in 1865 John Sholto Douglas, better known as the 8th Marquess of Queensberry, drew up his famous set of rules which were to become the foundation for the present-day rules of boxing. He spent time studying prize fighting in the United States, and then compared it with the sport in England before drawing up a set of rules which he felt to be in the best interests of the sport and its safety. He was successful in getting fighters on both sides of the Atlantic to adopt his new code.

Queensberry's rules contained 12 laws, the most important being (i) that fighters must wear gloves, (ii) each round should last for three minutes (previously a round ended when a fighter was floored) and (iii) wrestling, which was permitted in the London Rules, was outlawed.

Despite the new rules, to which many men fought, prize fighting to the London Rules still took place, but by the mid-1890s the transition to the new rules was complete and prize fighting had become virtually obsolete. The last bare-knuckle contest for the

world heavyweight title was between John L. Sullivan
(USA) and Jake Kilrain (USA) in 1889.

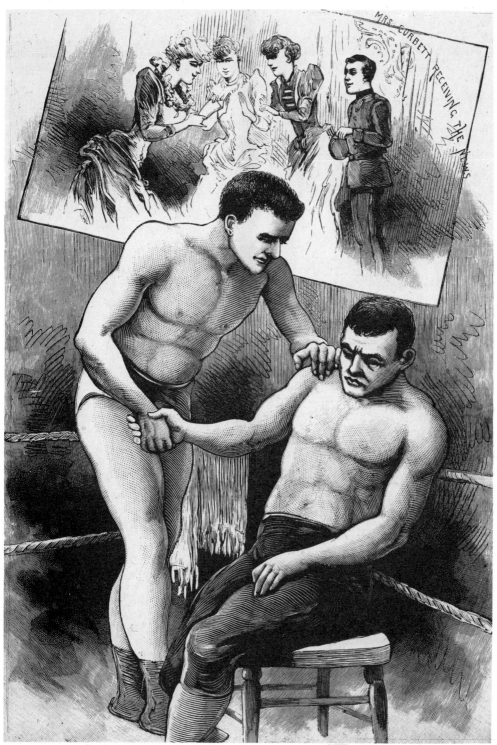

*James J. Corbett
shakes hands with
a dejected
John L. Sullivan
after becoming
the first generally
recognised world
heavyweight
champion under
Queensberry Rules in
1892 (Mary Evans)*

Queensberry's rules led to the formation of
many boxing organisations, notably the Amateur
Boxing Association (ABA) in 1881. The following year
Charley Mitchell was declared the first British
champion and in 1884 Irish-born American Jack
Dempsey was universally acknowledged as the first
world champion under Queensberry rules when he

beat George Fulljames (USA) in New York with a 22nd
round knock-out to win the middleweight crown.
James J. Corbett (USA) became the first generally
recognised heavyweight champion under
Queensberry Rules when he beat the last bare-knuckle
champion, Sullivan, at New Orleans in 1892. He won
with a 21st round knock-out.

As the 20th century arrived, so did the increased popularity of boxing as a spectator and participant sport. The Queensberry Rules were revised in 1909 and two years later the International Boxing Union (IBU) was formed in Paris. But the real growth period for boxing came in between the two world wars, particularly in the United States.

The New York State Athletic Commission was founded in 1920, and by the end of the decade boxing had attracted a great deal of media attention, including its first radio broadcasts, as million-dollar fights and six-figure crowds became commonplace. Big money was coming into the sport as thousands of fight fans filled halls and arenas across America and Britain. In 1921 the Jack Dempsey (USA)–Georges Carpentier (Fra) world heavyweight contest in New Jersey attracted the sport's first million-dollar gate, whilst in 1926 over 120,000 fans poured into the

Sesquicentennial Stadium, Philadelphia, for the all-American world heavyweight bout between Dempsey and Gene Tunney.

The National Boxing Association (NBA), the forerunner of the World Boxing Association (WBA), was established in 1921, although it did not start recognising its own world champions until 1927. It was set up by other US states where boxing was popular, as a direct result of their disgruntlement with the monopoly held by the boxing department of the New York Athletic Association over title fights. This brought inevitable problems, particularly after universally recognised champions retired. Both the New York Association and the NBA would hold their own world championship bouts, and sometimes the IBU would sanction a contest to which they gave 'world championship' status, to further add to the confusion. This confusion would be cleared up only

A sparring match at the Fives Courts. It looks as though hats were compulsory and you had to talk to the gentleman next to you instead of watching the contest. Mind you, it couldn't have been all that interesting, even the referee's half-asleep! (ET Archive)

Control, those US states not affiliated to the WBA, the EBU, Commonwealth countries, and more, formed the World Boxing Council (WBC) in Mexico on 14 February 1963. The new body also received support from the boxing department of the New York Athletic Association and thus renewed the rivalry between it and the NBA of the 1920s, albeit in different guises.

Until 1983, when the International Boxing Federation (IBF) was formed in the United States, all world championship fights were sanctioned by either the WBC or WBA. The IBF has grown in credibility since its formation and was helped by Larry Holmes becoming their heavyweight champion in 1984. Several attempts have been made over the years to form one governing body to control all world title fights, but to no avail.

To add even further to the confusion, a fourth organisation, the World Boxing Organization (WBO), was formed in 1988 and set about organising its own 'world championship' contests. Things seemed to be going smoothly for the WBO until the latter part of 1989 when two of its champions resigned on the grounds that they were being restricted from the big pay days the other recognised champions were getting. The WBO's challenge to the other three bodies seemed therefore to have dwindled after only twelve months. World championship boxing in the 1980s is further complicated by the fact that there are WBC and IBF Intercontinental world champions, Americas world champions, and so on.

As ever, the demands of television to cover title fights have put increasing pressure on the way in which the governing bodies run the sport. Title fights with the word 'world' in their billing are a big attraction to the TV companies and with the publicity TV generates for fights like Leonard v Duran, boxing finds itself in a similar position to many other sports in the 1990s of having to adopt an increasingly flexible approach towards accommodating the needs of TV.

Since the formation of the WBC in 1963 the number of weight divisions has risen from 10 to 17 with the introduction of many 'junior' weight divisions. The number of world champions has also risen dramatically, from 10 to more than 60. World championship boxing has grown out of all proportion. In 1958 there were a mere 10 world title fights. In 1989 there were well over 100. How many will there be in another 30 years?

when the two champions of the main bodies met for the universal title.

Prior to the formation of the NBA, and in some cases after its formation, several other State Associations in America occasionally recognised their own champions, as did other associations around the world. But their claims to titles have to be regarded as flimsy and dubious. The various bodies were often at loggerheads as to who the rightful champion was and that has made the life of boxing historians a nightmare over the years.

The IBU changed its name to the European Boxing Union (EBU) in 1946 and the NBA became the World Boxing Association (WBA) in 1962. However, because they were not happy with the WBA assuming 'world' control of the sport, several national associations, including the British Boxing Board of

THE WEIGHT DIVISIONS

Jim Watt, Britain's popular lightweight world champion from 1979–81. The Scot is now making a name for himself as a television summariser and after-dinner speaker (All Sport)

The first time weight divisions were introduced into boxing was in the mid-1850s when the following three divisions were introduced: Heavyweight (over 156lb), Middleweight (up to 156lb), Lightweight (up to 133lb). Two further categories, Featherweight (up to 119lb) and Bantamweight (up to 105lb) were added later. Even though different weight divisions existed, boxers were not restricted to fights within their own weight category and could challenge fighters from a different division.

Once world championship boxing became popular at the end of the last century there was a need to review and standardise the weight divisions on both sides of the Atlantic, and in 1910 the following revised weight categories were drawn up:

Heavyweight	– over 175lb
Light-heavyweight	– up to 175lb
Middleweight	– up to 154lb
Welterweight	– up to 142lb
Lightweight	– up to 133lb
Featherweight	– up to 122lb
Bantamweight	– up to 116lb
Flyweight	– up to 112lb
Paperweight	– up to 105lb

On 1 September 1970 the WBC, WBA and other authorities agreed to standardise the then 11 weight categories. Since then the number of divisions has increased to 17, as follows:

Heavyweight	over 190lb/86kg
Cruiserweight	up to 190lb/86kg
Light-heavyweight	up to 175lb/79kg
Super-middleweight	up to 168lb/76kg
Middleweight	up to 160lb/73kg
Junior-middleweight (WBC Super-welterweight)	up to 154lb/70kg
Welterweight	up to 147lb/67kg
Junior-welterweight (WBC Super-lightweight)	up to 140lb/64kg
Lightweight	up to 135lb/61kg
Junior-lightweight (WBC Super-featherweight)	up to 130lb/59kg
Featherweight	up to 126lb/57kg
Junior-featherweight (WBC Super-bantamweight)	up to 122lb/55kg
Bantamweight	up to 118lb/54kg
Junior-bantamweight (WBC Super-flyweight)	up to 115lb/52kg
Flyweight	up to 112lb/51kg
Junior-flyweight (WBC Light-flyweight)	up to 108lb/49kg
Strawweight (IBF and WBA Mini-flyweight)	up to 105lb/48kg

The first all-European world heavyweight title fight took place on 22 October 1933 when Italy's Primo Carnera fought Spain's Paulino Uzcudun.

The first world title fight in each weight division as officially recognised by each of the three major current boxing authorities (WBC, WBA and IBF) plus the first official undisputed (Und) champion in each category was as follows (winner's name first):

HEAVYWEIGHT
Und: 7 Sep 1892 James J. Corbett v John L. Sullivan (New Orleans, USA)
WBA: 5 Mar 1965 Ernie Terrell v Eddie Machen (Chicago, USA)
WBC: 10 Jun 1978 Larry Holmes v Ken Norton (Las Vegas, USA)
IBF: 9 Nov 1984 Larry Holmes v James Smith (Las Vegas, USA)

CRUISERWEIGHT
Und: 9 Apr 1988 Evander Holyfield v Carlos De Leon (Las Vegas, USA)
WBA: 13 Feb 1982 Ossie Ocasio v Robbie Williams (Johannesburg, S. Africa)
WBC: 8 Dec 1979 Marvin Camel v Mate Parlov (Split, Yugoslavia)
IBF: 13 Dec 1983 Marvin Camel v Roddy McDonald (Halifax, Canada)

LIGHT-HEAVYWEIGHT
Und: 22 Apr 1903 Jack Root v Charles 'Kid' McCoy (Detroit, USA)
WBA: 27 Feb 1971 Vicente Paul Rondon v Jimmy Dupree (Caracas, Venezuela)
WBC: 2 Mar 1971 Bob Foster v Hal Carroll (Scranton, USA)
IBF: 21 Dec 1985 Slobodan Kacar v Eddie Mustafa Mohammad (Pesaro, Italy)

SUPER-MIDDLEWEIGHT
Und: There has not been an undisputed champion
WBA: 6 Dec 1987 Chong-Pal Park v Jesus Gallardo (Pusan, South Korea)
WBC: 7 Nov 1988 Sugar Ray Leonard v Donny Lalonde (Las Vegas, USA)
IBF: 28 Mar 1984 Murray Sutherland v Ernie Singletary (Atlantic City, USA)

MIDDLEWEIGHT
Und: 30 Jul 1884 Jack Dempsey v George Fulljames (New York, USA)
WBA: 5 Oct 1974 Carlos Monzon v Tony Mundine (Buenos Aires, Argentina)
WBC: 25 May 1974 Rodrigo Valdez v Bennie Briscoe (Monte Carlo, Monaco)
IBF: 10 Oct 1987 Frank Tate v Michael Olijade (Las Vegas, USA)

JUNIOR-MIDDLEWEIGHT
Und: 19 Feb 1963 Denny Moyer v Stan Harrington (Honolulu, Hawaii, USA)
WBA: 20 Oct 1962 Denny Moyer v Joey Giambra (Portland, USA)

WBC: 7 May 1975 Miguel de Oliveira v Jose Duran (Madrid, Spain)
IBF: 11 Mar 1984 Mark Medal v Earl Hargrove (Atlantic City)

WELTERWEIGHT
Und: 30 Oct 1888 Paddy Duffy v William McMillan (Fort Foote, USA)
WBA: 24 Aug 1966 Curtis Cokes v Manuel Gonzalez (New Orleans, USA)
WBC: 12 Jul 1975 Jose Napoles v Armando Muniz (Mexico City, Mexico)
IBF: 22 Feb 1987 Lloyd Honeyghan v Johnny Bumphus (London, England)

JUNIOR-WELTERWEIGHT
Und: 21 Sep 1926 Mushy Callahan v Pinkey Mitchell (Vernon, USA)
WBA: 12 Dec 1968 Nicolino Loche v Paul Fuji (Tokyo, Japan)
WBC: 14 Dec 1968 Pedro Adigue v Adolph Pruitt (Manila, Philippines)
IBF: 22 Jun 1984 Aaron Pryor v Nicky Furlano (Toronto, Canada)

LIGHTWEIGHT
Und: 16 Nov 1887 Jack McAuliffe v Jem Carney (Revere, USA)
WBA: 28 Nov 1966 Carlos Ortiz v Flash Elorde (New York, USA)
WBC: 5 Nov 1971 Pedro Carrasco v Mando Ramos (Madrid, Spain)
IBF: 30 Jan 1984 Charlie Brown v Melvin Paul (Atlantic City, USA)

JUNIOR-LIGHTWEIGHT
Und: 18 Nov 1921 Johnny Dundee v George Chaney (New York, USA)
WBA: 6 Apr 1969 Hiroshi Kobayashi v Antonio Amaya (Tokyo, Japan)
WBC: 15 Feb 1969 Rene Barrientos v Ruben Navarro (Manila, Philippines)
IBF: 22 Apr 1984 Hwan-Kil Yuh v Rod Sequenan (Seoul, South Korea)

FEATHERWEIGHT
Und: 31 Mar 1889 Ike Weir v Frank Murphy (Kouts, USA)
WBA: 28 Mar 1968 Raul Rojas v Enrique Higgins (Los Angeles, USA)
WBC: 23 Jan 1968 Howard Winstone v Mitsunori Seki (London, England)
IBF: 4 Mar 1984 Min-Keum Oh v Joko Arter (Seoul, South Korea)

JUNIOR-FEATHERWEIGHT
Und: There has not been an undisputed champion
WBA: 26 Nov 1977 Soo-Hwan Hong v Hector Carrasquilla (Panama City, Panama)
WBC: 3 Apr 1976 Rigoberto Riasco v Waruinge Nakayama (Panama City, Panama)

IBF: 4 Dec 1983 Bobby Berna v Seung-Il Suh
(Seoul, South Korea)

BANTAMWEIGHT

Und: 27 Jun 1890 George Dixon v Nunc Wallace
(London, England)
WBA: 20 Jan 1973 Romeo Anaya v Enrique Pinder
(Panama City, Panama)
WBC: 14 Apr 1973 Rafael Herrera v Rodolfo
Martinez (Monterrey, Mexico)
IBF: 15 Apr 1984 Satoshi Shingaki v Elmer
Magallano (Kashiwara, Japan)

JUNIOR-BANTAMWEIGHT

Und: There has not been an undisputed champion
WBA: 12 Sep 1981 Gustavo Ballas v Suk-Chul Bae
(Buenos Aires, Argentina)
WBC: 2 Feb 1980 Rafael Orono v Seung-Hoon Lee
(Caracas, Venezuela)
IBF: 10 Dec 1983 Joo-Do Chun v Ken Kasugai
(Osaka, Japan)

FLYWEIGHT

Und: 18 Dec 1916 Jimmy Wilde v Young Zulu Kid
(London, England)

WBA: 1 Mar 1966 Horacio Accavallo v Katsuyoshi
Takayama (Tokyo, Japan)
WBC: 2 Dec 1965 Salvatore Burruni v Rocky
Gattelleri (Sydney, Australia)
IBF: 24 Dec 1983 Soo-Chun Kwon v Rene
Busayong (Seoul, South Korea)

JUNIOR-FLYWEIGHT

Und: There has not been an undisputed champion
WBA: 23 Aug 1975 Jaime Rios v Rigoberto Marcano
(Panama City, Panama)
WBC: 4 Apr 1975 Franco Udella v Valentine
Martinez (Milan, Italy)
IBF: 10 Dec 1983 Dodie Penalosa v Satoshi
Shingaki (Osaka, Japan)

STRAWWEIGHT

Und: There has not been an undisputed champion
WBA: 10 Jan 1988 Leo Gamez v Kim-Bong Jun
(Pusan, South Korea)
WBC: 18 Oct 1987 Hiroki Ioka v Mai Thonburifarm
(Osaka, Japan)
IBF: 14 Jun 1987 Kyung-Yun Lee v Masaharu
Kawakami (Bukok, South Korea)

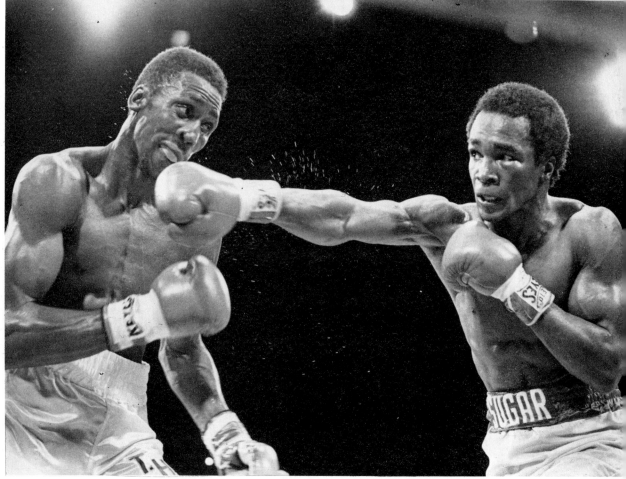

Tommy Hearns and Sugar Ray Leonard (right) have both won world titles at five different weights (Hulton-Deutsch)

THE WORLD CHAMPIONS

The following is an alphabetical list of all generally recognised world champions. Fighters with dubious claims to titles have not been included, nor have WBO champions.

Horacio Accavallo Born: Parque Patricios, Argentina, 14 October 1934
World title fights: 4 (all flyweight) won 4, lost 0

Pedro Adigue Born: Palanas, Masbate, Philippines, 22 December 1943
World title fights: 2 (both junior-welter) won 1, lost 1

Virgil Akins Born: St. Louis, Missouri, USA, 10 March 1928
World title fights: 3 (all welterweight) won 1, lost 2

Oscar Albarado Born: Pecos, Texas, USA, 15 September 1948
World title fights: 3 (all junior-middle) won 2, lost 1

Muhammad Ali Born: Louisville, Kentucky, USA, 17 January 1942
World title fights: 25 (all heavyweight) won 22, lost 3

Terry Allen Born: London, England, 18 June 1924
World title fights: 5 (all flyweight) won 1, lost 3, drew 1

Lou Ambers Born: Herkimer, New York, USA, 8 November 1913
World title fights: 7 (all lightweight) won 4, lost 3

Romeo Anaya Born: Chiapas, Mexico, 5 April 1946
World title fights: 5 (all bantamweight) won 3, lost 2

Dennis Andries Born: Georgetown, Guyana, 5 November 1953
World title fights: 5 (all light-heavy) won 3, lost 2

Sammy Angott Born: Washington, Pennsylvania, USA, 17 January 1915
Died: Cleveland, Ohio, USA, 22 October 1980
World title fights: 5 (all lightweight) won 4, lost 1

Vito Antuofermo Born: Bari, Italy, 9 February 1953
World title fights: 5 (all middleweight) won 1, lost 3, drew 1

Fred Apostoli Born: San Francisco, California, USA, 2 February 1913
Died: San Francisco, California, USA, 29 November 1973
World title fights: 3 (all middleweight) won 2, lost 1

Lupe Aquino Born: Chihuahua, Mexico, 23 January 1963
World title fights: 2 (both junior-middle) won 1, lost 1

Bruno Arcari Born: Latina Latinum, Italy, 1 January 1942
World title fights: 10 (all junior-welter) won 10, lost 0

Joey Archibald Born: Providence, Rhode Island, USA, 6 December 1915
World title fights: 6 (all featherweight) won 4, lost 2

Alexis Arguello Born: Managua, Nicaragua, 19 April 1952
World title fights: 22 (6 featherweight, 9 junior-light, 5 lightweight, 2 junior-welter) won 19, lost 3

Alberto 'Baby' Arizmendi Born: Coahila, Mexico, 17 March 1914
Died: Los Angeles, USA, 31 December 1963
World title fights: 3 (1 welterweight, 2 featherweight) won 1, lost 2

Henry Armstrong Born: Columbus, Mississippi, USA, 12 December 1912
Died: Los Angeles, USA, 23 October 1988
World title fights: 26 (1 featherweight, 22 welterweight, 2 lightweight, 1 middleweight) won 22, lost 3, drew 1

Rene Arredondo Born: Apatzingan, Mexico, 15 June 1961
World title fights: 4 (all junior-welter) won 2, lost 2

Ricardo Arredondo Born: Apatzingan, Mexico, 26 May 1949
World title fights: 8 (all junior-light) won 6, lost 2

Harry Arroyo Born: Youngstown, Ohio, USA, 25 October 1957
World title fights: 4 (all lightweight) won 3, lost 1

Abe Attell Born: San Francisco, California, USA, 22 February 1884
Died: New Paltz, New York, USA, 7 February 1970
World title fights: 14 (all featherweight) won 10, lost 1, drew 3

Antonio Avelar Born: Jalisco, Mexico, 25 August 1958
World title fights: 4 (all flyweight) won 2, lost 2

Billy Backus Born: Canastota, New York, USA, 5 March 1943
World title fights: 3 (all welterweight) won 1, lost 2

In-Chul Baek Born: Chun-Nam, South Korea, 20 December 1961
World title fights: 4 (1 junior-middle, 3 super-middle) won 3, lost 1

Max Baer Born: Omaha, Nebraska, USA, 11 February 1909
Died: Hollywood, California, USA, 21 November 1959
World title fights: 2 (both heavyweight) won 1, lost 1

Gustavo Ballas Born: Cordoba, Argentina, 10 February 1958
World title fights: 4 (all junior-bantam) won 1, lost 3

Mike Ballerino Born: Bayonne, New Jersey, USA, 10 April 1901
Died: Tampa, Florida, USA, 4 April 1965
World title fights: 3 (all junior-light) won 1, lost 2

Iran Barkley Born: Bronx, New York, USA, 9 May 1960
World title fights: 4 (all middleweight) won 1, lost 3

Rene Barrientos Born: Balite, Philippines, February 1942
World title fights: 4 (all junior-light) won 1, lost 2, drew 1

Jimmy Barry Born: Chicago, Illinois, USA, 7 March 1870
Died: Chicago, Illinois, USA, 4 April 1943
World title fights: 3 (all bantamweight) won 1, lost 0, drew 2

Sal Bartolo Born: Boston, Massachusetts, USA, 5 November 1917
World title fights: 6 (all featherweight) won 4, lost 2

Carmen Basilio Born: Canastota, New York, USA, 2 April 1927
World title fights: 11 (6 welterweight, 5 middleweight) won 5, lost 6

Benny Bass Born: Kiev, Russia, 4 December 1904
Died: Philadelphia, Pennsylvania, USA, 25 June 1925
World title fights: 4 (2 featherweight, 2 junior-light) won 2, lost 2

Fidel Bassa Born: El Reten-Magdalena, Colombia, 18 December 1962
World title fights: 8 (all flyweight) won 6, lost 1, drew 1

Hogan 'Kid' Bassey Born: Calabar, Nigeria, 3 June 1932
World title fights: 4 (all featherweight) won 2, lost 2

Battling Battalino Born: Hartford, Connecticut, USA, 18 February 1908
Died: Hartford, Connecticut, USA, 25 July 1977
World title fights: 6 (all featherweight) won 6, lost 0

Joe Becerra Born: Guadalajara, Mexico, 15 April 1936
World title fights: 3 (all bantamweight) won 3, lost 0

Albert 'Frenchie' Belanger Born: Toronto, Canada, 17 May 1906
World title fights: 4 (all flyweight) won 1, lost 3

Toufik Belbouli Born: Bovenzi, Mauritania, 10 December 1954
World title fights: 1 (cruiserweight) won 1, lost 0

Mike Belloise Born: New York City, USA, 18 February 1911
Died: New York City, USA, 2 June 1969
World title fights: 2 (both featherweight) won 1, lost 1

Fabrice Benichou Born: Madrid, Spain, 5 April 1965
World title fights: 4 (all junior-feather) won 3, lost 1

Wilfred Benitez (formerly Wilfredo Benitez) Born: Bronx, New York, USA, 12 September 1958
World title fights: 10 (7 junior-welter, 3 welterweight) won 8, lost 2

Bernard Benton Born: Toledo, Ohio, USA, 6 January 1957
World title fights: 2 (both cruiserweight) won 1, lost 1

Nino Benvenuti Born: Trieste, Italy, 26 April 1938
World title fights: 12 (3 junior-middle, 9 middleweight) won 8, lost 4

Trevor Berbick Born: Port Anthony, Jamaica, 1 August 1952
World title fights: 3 (all heavyweight) won 1, lost 2

Jack 'Kid' Berg Born: London, England, 28 June 1909
World title fights: 6 (4 junior-welter, 1
lightweight/junior-welter, 1 lightweight)
won 4, lost 2

Paul Berlenbach Born: New York City, USA, 18
February 1901
Died: Port Jefferson, New York, USA, 30
September 1985
World title fights: 5 (all light-heavy) won 4, lost 1

Bobby Berna Born: Philippines, 19 May 1961
World title fights: 4 (all junior-feather) won 1,
lost 3

Gabriel Bernal Born: Guerrero, Mexico, 24 March
1956
World title fights: 5 (all flyweight) won 2,
lost 2, drew 1

Jack Bernstein Born: New York City, USA, 5
November 1899
Died: Yonkers, New York, USA, 26 December
1945
World title fights: 2 (both junior-light) won 1,
lost 1

Melio Bettina Born: Bridgeport, Connecticut, USA, 18
November 1916
World title fights: 4 (all light-heavy) won 1,
lost 3

Rolando Bohol Born: Philippines, 25 December 1966
World title fights: 3 (all flyweight) won 2,
lost 1

Venice Borkorsor Born: Thailand, 1950
World title fights: 4 (2 flyweight, 2
bantamweight) won 2, lost 2

Carmelo Bossi Born: Milan, Italy, 15 October 1939
World title fights: 3 (all junior-middle) won 1,
lost 1, drew 1

Joe Bowker Born: Salford, England, 20 July 1883
Died: London, England, 22 October 1955
World title fights: 1 (bantamweight) won 1,
lost 0

Cornelius Boza-Edwards Born: Kampala, Uganda, 27
May 1956
World title fights: 6 (4 junior-light, 2
lightweight) won 2, lost 4

James J. Braddock Born: New York City, USA, 7 June
1906
Died: North Bergen, New Jersey, USA, 29
November 1974
World title fights: 3 (1 light-heavy, 2
heavyweight) won 1, lost 2

Livingstone Bramble Born: St Kitts, Windward Islands,
3 March 1960
World title fights: 4 (all lightweight) won 3, lost 1

Johnny Bratton Born: Little Rock, Arkansas, USA, 9
September 1927
World title fights: 3 (all welterweight) won 1,
lost 2

Mark Breland Born: Brooklyn, New York, USA, 11 May
1963
World title fights: 7 (all welterweight) won 5,
lost 1, drew 1

Jack Britton Born: Clinton, New York, USA, 14
October 1885
Died: Miami, Florida, USA, 27 March 1962
World title fights: 12 (all welterweight) won 6,
lost 4, drew 2

Mark Breland of the United States (light vest) on his way to victory in the welterweight division at the 1984 Olympics. Breland has since gone on to become the world welterweight champion (All Sport)

Lou Brouillard Born: St. Eugene, Quebec, Canada, 23 May 1911
    Died: Taunton, Massachusetts, USA, 14 September 1984
    World title fights: 5 (2 welterweight, 3 middleweight) won 2, lost 3

Charlie 'Choo Choo' Brown Born: Philadelphia, Pennsylvania, USA, 16 April 1958
    World title fights: 2 (both lightweight) won 1, lost 1

Jackie Brown Born: Manchester, England, 29 November 1909
    Died: Manchester, England, 15 March 1971
    World title fights: 6 (all flyweight) won 4, lost 1, drew 1

Joe Brown Born: New Orleans, Louisiana, USA, 18 May 1926
    World title fights: 13 (all lightweight) won 12, lost 1

Panama Al Brown Born: Colon, Panama, 5 July 1902
Died: New York City, USA, 11 April 1951
World title fights: 12 (all bantamweight)
won 11, lost 1

Simon Brown Born: Jamaica, 15 August 1963
World title fights: 7 (all welterweight) won 7,
lost 0

Ken Buchanan Born: Edinburgh, Scotland, 28 June
1945
World title fights: 5 (all lightweight) won 3,
lost 2

Johnny Buff Born: Perth Amboy, New Jersey, USA, 12
June 1888
Died: East Grange, New Jersey, USA, 14
January 1955
World title fights: 3 (all bantamweight) won 2,
lost 1

Johnny Bumphus Born: Tacoma, Washington, USA, 17
August 1960
World title fights: 3 (2 junior-welter, 1
welterweight) won 1, lost 2

Tommy Burns Born: Chelsey, Ontario, Canada, 17
June 1881
Died: Vancouver, Canada, 10 May 1955
World title fights: 13 (1 heavyweight/light-
heavy, 12 heavyweight) won 11, lost 1,
drew 1

Salvatore Burruni Born: Sardinia, Italy, 11 April 1933
World title fights: 3 (all flyweight) won 2,
lost 1

Johnny Caldwell Born: Belfast, Northern Ireland, 7
May 1938
World title fights: 3 (all bantamweight) won 2,
lost 1

Mushy Callahan Born: New York City, USA, 3
November 1905
Died: Los Angeles, California, USA, 16 June
1986
World title fights: 2 (both junior-welter)
won 1, lost 1

Victor Callejas Born: Guaynabo, Puerto Rico, 12
November 1960
World title fights: 4 (3 junior-feather, 1
featherweight) won 3, lost 1

Jackie Callura Born: Hamilton, Ontario, Canada, 24
September 1917
World title fights: 4 (all featherweight) won 2,
lost 2

Hector Camacho Born: Bayamon, Puerto Rico, 24
May 1962
World title fights: 5 (2 junior-light, 3
lightweight) won 5, lost 0

Marvin Camel Born: Missoula, Montana, USA, 24
December 1951
World title fights: 6 (all cruiserweight) won 2,
lost 3, drew 1

Gaby Canizales Born: Laredo, Texas, USA, 1 May 1960
World title fights: 4 (all bantamweight) won 1,
lost 3

Orlando Canizales Born: Laredo, Texas, USA, 25
November 1965
World title fights: 4 (all bantamweight) won 4,
lost 0

Miguel Canto Born: Yucatan, Mexico, 30 January 1949
World title fights: 18 (all flyweight) won 15,
lost 2, drew 1

Tony Canzoneri Born: Slidell, Louisiana, USA, 6
November 1908
Died: New York City, USA, 9 December 1959
World title fights: 22 (2 bantamweight, 3
featherweight, 9 lightweight, 3 junior-
welter/lightweight, 5 junior-welter) won
12, lost 9, drew 1

Prudencio Cardona Born: Bolivar, Colombia, 22
December 1951
World title fights: 3 (all flyweight) won 1,
lost 2

Ricardo Cardona Born: Bolivar, Colombia, 9
November 1952
World title fights: 8 (all junior-feather) won 6,
lost 2

Erubey 'Chango' Carmona Born: Mexico City, Mexico,
29 September 1944
World title fights: 2 (both lighweight) won 1,
lost 1

Primo Carnera Born: Sequals, Italy, 26 October 1906
Died: Sequals, Italy, 29 June 1967
World title fights: 4 (all heavyweight) won 3,
lost 1

Georges Carpentier Born: Lens, France, 12 January
1894
Died: Paris, France, 28 October 1975
World title fights: 5 (1 middleweight, 3 light-
heavy, 1 heavyweight) won 2, lost 3

Pedro Carrasco Born: Huelva, Spain, 11 July 1943
World title fights: 3 (all lightweight) won 1,
lost 2

Jimmy Carruthers Born: New South Wales, Australia, 5
July 1929
World title fights: 4 (all bantamweight) won 4,
lost 0

Jimmy Carter Born: Aiken, South Carolina, USA, 15
December 1923
World title fights: 12 (all lightweight) won 8,
lost 4

Miguel Angel Castellini Born: Santa Rosa, La Pampa,
Argentina, 26 January 1947
World title fights: 2 (both junior-middle)
won 1, lost 1

Freddie Castillo Born: Yucatan, Mexico, 15 June 1955
World title fights: 5 (2 junior-fly, 3 flyweight)
won 2, lost 3

Mexican Julio Cesar Chavez (left) has been world champion at junior-lightweight and lightweight since 1984. Despite taking this blow from the Brazilian Francisco da Cruz in 1987, Chavez still managed to stop his man in three rounds (AP)

Jesus 'Chucho' Castillo Born: Nuevo Valle de Moreno, Mexico, 17 June 1944
    World title fights: 4 (all bantamweight) won 1, lost 3
Frank Cedeno Born: Cebu, Philippines, 16 March 1958
    World title fights: 3 (2 flyweight, 1 junior-bantam) won 1, lost 2
Marcel Cerdan Born: Sidi Bel-Abbes, Algeria, 22 July 1916
    Died: Azores, 27 October 1949
    World title fights: 2 (both middleweight) won 1, lost 1
Antonio Cervantes Born: San Basilio de Palenque, Bolivar, Colombia, 23 December 1945
    World title fights: 21 (all junior-welter) won 18, lost 3
Bobby Chacon Born: Los Angeles, California, USA, 28 November 1951
    World title fights: 8 (3 featherweight, 4 junior-light, 1 lightweight) won 4, lost 4
Jeff Chandler Born: Philadelphia, Pennsylvania, USA, 3 September 1956
    World title fights: 12 (all bantamweight) won 10, lost 1, drew 1

Jung-Koo Chang Born: Pusan, South Korea, 4 February 1963
    World title fights: 18 (all junior-fly) won 16, lost 2
Tae-Il Chang Born: Damyang-Kun, South Korea, 10 April 1965
    World title fights: 3 (all junior-bantam) won 1, lost 2
Ezzard Charles Born: Lawrenceville, Georgia, USA, 7 July 1921
    Died: Chicago, Illinois, USA, 27 May 1975
    World title fights: 13 (all heavyweight) won 9, lost 4
Berkrerk Chartvanchai Born: Bangkok, Thailand, 1946
    World title fights: 2 (both flyweight) won 1, lost 1
Eric Chavez Born: Philippines, 4 September 1962
    World title fights: 2 (both strawweight) won 1, lost 1
Julio Cesar Chavez Born: Ciudad Obregon, Mexico, 12 July 1962
    World title fights: 15 (10 junior-light, 3 lightweight, 2 junior-welter) won 15, lost 0

Chartchai Chionoi Born: Bangkok, Thailand, 10 October 1942
World title fights: 13 (all flyweight) won 9, lost 4

George Chip Born: Scranton, Pennsylvania, USA, 25 August 1888
Died: New Castle, Pennsylvania, USA, 8 November 1960
World title fights: 4 (all middleweight) won 2, lost 1, ND 1

Sot Chitalada Born: Bangkok, Thailand, 24 May 1962
World title fights: 11 (1 junior-fly, 10 flyweight) won 8, lost 2, drew 1

Kid Chocolate Born: Cerro, Cuba, 6 January 1910
World title fights: 9 (5 featherweight, 3 junior-light, 1 junior-welter/lightweight) won 6, lost 3

Chang-Ho Choi Born: Seoul, South Korea, 10 February 1964
World title fights: 3 (2 flyweight, 1 junior-bantam) won 1, lost 2

Jum-Hwan Choi Born: Pusan, South Korea, 9 June 1963
World title fights: 7 (5 junior-fly, 2 strawweight) won 4, lost 3

Anton Christoforidis Born: Messina, Greece, 26 May 1917
Died: Athens, Greece, November 1986
World title fights: 2 (both light-heavy) won 1, lost 1

Joo-Do Chun Born: South Korea, 25 January 1964
World title fights: 7 (all junior-bantam) won 6, lost 1

Bi-Won Chung Born: Seoul, South Korea, 15 January 1960
World title fights: 2 (both flyweight) won 1, lost 1

Chong-Kwan Chung Born: South Korea, 30 November 1961
World title fights: 4 (all flyweight) won 1, lost 1, drew 2

Ki-Yung Chung Born: South Korea, 23 November 1959
World title fights: 4 (all featherweight) won 3, lost 1

Freddie 'Red' Cochrane Born: Elizabeth, New Jersey, USA, 6 May 1915
World title fights: 2 (both welterweight) won 1, lost 1

Gerrie Coetzee Born: Boksburg, Transvaal, South Africa, 4 August 1955
World title fights: 4 (all heavyweight) won 1, lost 3

Juan Martin Coggi Born: Figuera, Santa Fe, Argentina, 19 December 1961
World title fights: 4 (all junior-welter) won 4, lost 0

Robert Cohen Born: Bone, Algeria, 15 November 1930
World title fights: 3 (all bantamweight) won 1, lost 1, drew 1

Curtis Cokes Born: Dallas, Texas, USA, 15 June 1937
World title fights: 8 (all welterweight) won 6, lost 2

Billy Conn Born: East Liberty, Pittsburgh, Pennsylvania, USA, 8 October 1917
World title fights: 6 (4 light-heavy, 2 heavyweight) won 4, lost 2

John Conteh Born: Liverpool, England, 27 May 1951
World title fights: 7 (all light-heavy) won 4, lost 3

James J. Corbett Born: San Francisco, California, USA, 1 January 1866
Died: Bayside, New York, USA, 18 February 1933
World title fights: 5 (all heavyweight) won 2, lost 3

Young Corbett Born: Denver, Colorado, USA, 4 October 1880
Died: Denver, Colorado, USA, 10 April 1927
World title fights: 1 (featherweight) won 1, lost 0

Young Corbett III Born: Protenza, Campania, Italy, 27 May 1905
World title fights: 3 (2 welterweight, 1 middleweight) won 1, lost 2

Hugo Corro Born: San Carlos, Mendoza, Argentina, 5 November 1953
World title fights: 4 (all middleweight) won 3, lost 1

Billy Costello Born: Kingston, New York, USA, 10 April 1956
World title fights: 5 (all junior-welter) won 4, lost 1

Johnny Coulon Born: Toronto, Canada, 12 February 1889
World title fights: 6 (all bantamweight) won 4, lost 1, ND 1

Eugene Criqui Born: Belleville, France, 15 August 1893
Died: Villepinte, France, 7 March 1977
World title fights: 2 (both featherweight) won 1, lost 1

Piet Crous Born: Johannesburg, Transvaal, South Africa, 2 July 1955
World title fights: 3 (all cruiserweight) won 2, lost 1

Carlos Teo Cruz Born: Santiago de los Cabelleros, Dominican Republic, 4 November 1937
Died: Dominican Republic, 15 February 1970
World title fights: 3 (all lightweight) won 2, lost 1

Leonardo Cruz Born: Santiago, Dominican Republic, 17 January 1953
World title fights: 7 (all junior-feather) won 4, lost 3

Roberto Cruz Born: Baguilo, Philippines, 2 November 1941
World title fights: 2 (both junior-welter) won 1, lost 1

Steve Cruz Born: Fort Worth, Texas, USA, 2 November 1963
World title fights: 3 (all featherweight) won 1, lost 2

Miguel Angel Cuello Born: Elortondo, Santa Fe, Argentina, 27 February 1946
World title fights: 2 (both light-heavy) won 1, lost 1

Pipino Cuevas Born: Mexico City, Mexico, 27 December 1957
World title fights: 13 (all welterweight) won 12, lost 1

Bruce Curry Born: Marlin, Texas, USA, 29 March 1956
World title fights: 4 (all junior-welter) won 3, lost 1

Donald Curry Born: Fort Worth, Texas, USA, 7 September 1961
World title fights: 12 (9 welterweight, 3 junior-middle) won 9, lost 3

Bobby Czyz Born: Wanaque, New Jersey, USA, 10 February 1962
World title fights: 7 (all light-heavy) won 4, lost 3

Harold Dade Born: Chicago, Illinois, USA, 24 March 1923
Died: Los Angeles, California, USA, 17 July 1962
World title fights: 2 (both bantamweight) won 1, lost 1

Mario D'Agata Born: Arezzo, Tuscany, Italy, 29 May 1926
World title fights: 2 (both bantamweight) won 1, lost 1

Eckhard Dagge Born: Berlin, Germany, 27 February 1948
World title fights: 4 (all junior-middle) won 2, lost 1, drew 1

Alberto Davila Born: Olion, Texas, USA, 10 August 1954
World title fights: 7 (all bantamweight) won 2, lost 5

Esteban de Jesus Born: Carolina, Puerto Rico, 2 August 1951
Died: San Juan, Puerto Rico, 11 May 1989
World title fights: 8 (6 lightweight, 2 junior-welter) won 4, lost 4

Jack Delaney Born: St. Francis du Lac, Quebec, Canada, 18 March 1900

Died: Katonah, New York, USA, 27 November 1948
World title fights: 2 (both light-heavy) won 1, lost 1

Carlos De Leon Born: Rio Piedras, Puerto Rico, 3 May 1959
World title fights: 15 (all cruiserweight) won 11, lost 3, drew 1

Paddy de Marco Born: Brooklyn, New York, USA, 10 February 1928
World title fights: 2 (both lightweight) won 1, lost 1

Tony de Marco Born: Boston, Massachusetts, USA, 14 January 1932
World title fights: 3 (all welterweight) won 1, lost 2

Jack Dempsey Born: Manassa, Colorado, USA, 24 June 1895
Died: New York, USA, 31 May 1983
World title fights: 8 (all heavyweight) won 6, lost 2

Jack Dempsey, world heavyweight champion 1919–26 (Syndication International)

Jack Dempsey (Nonpareil) Born: County Kildare, Ireland, 15 December 1862
Died: Portland, Oregon, USA, 2 Nov 1895
World title fights: 8 (7 middleweight, 1 welterweight) won 5, lost 3

Miguel de Oliveira Born: São Paulo, Brazil, 30 September 1947
World title fights: 4 (all junior-middle) won 1, lost 2, drew 1

Jack Dillon Born: Frankfort, Indiana, USA, 2 February 1891
Died: Chattahoochee, Florida, USA, 7 August 1942
World title fights: 4 (all light-heavy) won 3, lost 1

George Dixon Born: Halifax, Nova Scotia, Canada, 29 July 1870
Died: New York City, USA, 6 January 1909
World title fights: 22 (3 bantamweight, 18 featherweight) won 19, lost 2, drew 2

Michael Dokes Born: Akron, Ohio, USA, 10 August 1958
World title fights: 3 (all heavyweight) won 1, lost 1, drew 1

James 'Buster' Douglas Born: Columbus, Ohio, USA, 7 April 1960
World title fights: 2 (both heavyweight) won 1, lost 1

Terry Downes Born: Paddington, London, England, 9 May 1936
World title fights: 4 (3 middleweight, 1 light-heavy) won 1, lost 3

Buster Drayton Born: Philadelphia, USA, 2 March 1953
World title fights: 4 (all junior-middle) won 2, lost 2

Paddy Duffy Born: Boston, Massachusetts, USA, 12 November 1864
Died: Boston, Massachusetts, USA, 19 July 1890
World title fights: 2 (both welterweight) won 2, lost 0

Joe Dundee Born: Rome, Italy, 16 August 1903
Died: Baltimore, Maryland, USA, 31 March 1982
World title fights: 3 (all welterweight) won 2, lost 1

Johnny Dundee Born: Sciacca, Sicily, 22 November 1893
Died: East Orange, New Jersey, USA, 22 April 1965
World title fights: 10 (4 featherweight, 6 junior-light) won 6, lost 3, drew 1

Vince Dundee Born: Baltimore, Maryland, USA, 22 October 1907
Died: Glendale, California, USA, 27 July 1949
World title fights: 5 (all middleweight) won 3, lost 1, drew 1

Ralph Dupas Born: New Orleans, Louisiana, USA, 14 October 1935
World title fights: 6 (1 lightweight, 1 welterweight, 4 junior-middle) won 2, lost 4

Jose Duran Born: Madrid, Spain, 9 October 1945
World title fights: 4 (all junior-middle) won 1, lost 3

Roberto Duran Born: Guarare, Panama, 16 June 1951
World title fights: 21 (13 lightweight, 2 welterweight, 3 junior-middle, 2 middleweight, 1 super-middleweight) won 16, lost 5

Hiroyuki Ebihara Born: Tokyo, Japan, 26 March 1940
World title fights: 6 (all flyweight) won 2, lost 4

Jimmy Ellis Born: Louisville, Kentucky, USA, 24 February 1940
World title fights: 3 (all heavyweight) won 2, lost 1

Two former world heavyweight champions attempting to rediscover past glories in 1976. It was George Foreman (right) who stopped the shaven-headed Joe Frazier in the 5th round of their non-title bout. Foreman is still fighting in 1990, but he's the one with the shaven head now! (AP)

Alfredo Escalera Born: Carolina, Puerto Rico, 21 March 1952
World title fights: 13 (all junior-light) won 10, lost 2, drew 1

Sixto Escobar Born: Barcelona, Puerto Rico, 23 March 1913
Died: Puerto Rico, 17 November 1979
World title fights: 10 (all bantamweight) won 8, lost 2

Angel Espada Born: Salinas, Puerto Rico, 2 February 1948
World title fights: 6 (all welterweight) won 3, lost 3

Gustavo 'Guty' Espadas Born: Yucatan, Mexico, 20 December 1954
World title fights: 8 (7 flyweight, 1 junior-bantam) won 5, lost 3

Ernesto Espana Born: Laflor, Venezuela, 7 November 1954
World title fights: 6 (all lightweight) won 2, lost 4

Antonio Esparragoza Born: Cumana, Venezuela, 2 September 1959
World title fights: 7 (all featherweight) won 6, lost 0, drew 1

Luisito Espinosa Born: Manila, Philippines
World title fights: 1 (bantamweight) won 1, lost 0

Louie Espinoza Born: Phoenix, Arizona, USA, 12 May 1962
World title fights: 5 (4 junior-feather, 1 featherweight) won 3, lost 1, drew 1

Luis Estaba Born: Sucre, Venezuela, 13 August 1941
World title fights: 14 (all junior-fly) won 12, lost 2

Juan Jose Estrada Born: Tijuana, Mexico, 28 November 1963
World title fights: 5 (all junior-feather) won 4, lost 1

Johnny Famechon Born: Paris, France, 28 March 1945
World title fights: 4 (all featherweight) won 3, lost 1

Jeff Fenech Born: Sydney, Australia, 28 May 1964
World title fights: 11 (4 bantamweight, 3 junior-feather, 4 featherweight) won 11, lost 0

Perico Fernandez Born: Zaragoza, Spain, 19 November 1952
World title fights: 4 (all junior-welter) won 2, lost 2

Rube Ferns Born: Pittsburg, Kansas, USA, 20 January 1874
Died: Pittsburg, Kansas, USA, 11 June 1952
World title fights: 5 (all welterweight) won 3, lost 2

Lester Ellis Born: Blackpool, England, 15 March 1965
World title fights: 3 (all junior-light) won 2, lost 1

Gabriel 'Flash' Elorde Born: Bogo, Cebu, Philippines, 22 March 1935
Died: Manila, Philippines, 2 January 1985
World title fights: 15 (1 featherweight, 12 junior-light, 2 lightweight) won 11, lost 4

Frank Erne Born: Zurich, Switzerland, 8 January 1875
Died: New York City, New York, USA, 17 September 1954
World title fights: 7 (1 featherweight, 5 lightweight, 1 welterweight) won 2, lost 3, drew 2

Jackie Fields Born: Chicago, Illinois, USA, 9 February 1908
World title fights: 5 (all welterweight) won 3, lost 2

Bob Fitzsimmons Born: Helston, Cornwall, England, 26 May 1863
Died: Chicago, USA, 22 October 1917
World title fights: 7 (5 heavyweight, 2 light-heavy) won 4, lost 3

Pedro Flores Born: Jalisco, Mexico, 14 January 1951
World title fights: 3 (all junior-fly) won 1, lost 2

Tiger Flowers Born: Camille, Georgia, USA, 5 August 1895
Died: New York City, USA, 16 November 1927
World title fights: 3 (all middleweight) won 2, lost 1

Harry Forbes Born: Rockford, Illinois, USA, 13 May 1879
Died: Chicago, Illinois, USA, 19 December 1946
World title fights: 11 (9 bantamweight, 2 featherweight) won 5, lost 5, drew 1

George Foreman Born: Marshall, Texas, USA, 22 January 1948
World title fights: 4 (all heavyweight) won 3, lost 1

Bob Foster Born: Albuquerque, New Mexico, USA, 15 December 1938
World title fights: 16 (15 light-heavy, 1 heavyweight) won 14, lost 1, drew 1

Alfonso Frazer Born: Panama City, Panama, 17 January 1948
World title fights: 4 (all junior-welter) won 2, lost 2

Joe Frazier Born: Beaufort, South Carolina, USA, 12 January 1944
World title fights: 12 (all heavyweight) won 10, lost 2

Tommy Freeman Born: Hot Springs, Arkansas, USA, 22 January 1904
Died: Little Rock, Arkansas, USA, 25 February 1986
World title fights: 7 (all welterweight) won 6, lost 1

Arturo Frias Born: Montebello, California, USA, 27 October 1956
World title fights: 3 (all lightweight) won 2, lost 1

Paul Fujii Born: Honolulu, Hawaii, 6 July 1940
World title fights: 3 (all junior-welter) won 2, lost 1

Gene Fullmer Born: West Jordan, Utah, USA, 21 July 1931
World title fights: 13 (all middleweight) won 7, lost 3, drew 3

Kaokar Galaxy Born: Petchaboon, Thailand, 15 May 1959
World title fights: 4 (all bantamweight) won 2, lost 2

Kaosai Galaxy Born: Petchaboon, Thailand, 15 May 1959
World title fights: 12 (all junior-bantam) won 12, lost 0

Victor Galindez Born: Vedia, Buenos Aires, Argentina, 2 November 1948
Died: De Mayo, Argentina, 26 October 1980
World title fights: 14 (all light-heavy) won 12, lost 2

Leo Gamez Born: Panama, 8 August 1963
World title fights: 2 (both strawweight) won 2, lost 0

Joe Gans Born: Baltimore, Maryland, USA, 25 November 1874
Died: Baltimore, Maryland, USA, 10 August 1910
World title fights: 13 (all lightweight) won 10, lost 3

Ceferino Garcia Born: Manila, Philippines, 26 August 1910
Died: San Diego, California, USA, 1 January 1981
World title fights: 6 (2 welterweight, 4 middleweight) won 2, lost 3, drew 1

George Gardner Born: Lindoonvarna, County Clare, Ireland, 17 March 1877
Died: Chicago, USA, 8 July 1954
World title fights: 2 (both light-heavy) won 1, lost 1

Jaime Garza Born: Santa Cruz, California, USA, 10 September 1959
World title fights: 3 (all junior-feather) won 2, lost 1

Kid Gavilan Born: Camaguey, Cuba, 6 January 1926
World title fights: 11 (all welterweight) won 8, lost 3

Eddie Gazo Born: San Lorenzo, Managua, Nicaragua, 12 September 1950
World title fights: 5 (all junior-middle) won 4, lost 1

Frankie Genaro Born: New York City, USA, 26 August 1901
Died: New York City, USA, 27 December 1966
World title fights: 13 (all flyweight) won 8, lost 3, drew 2

Julio Gervacio Born: La Romana, Dominican Republic, 17 October 1967
World title fights: 2 (both junior-feather) won 1, lost 1

Joey Giardello Born: Brooklyn, New York, USA, 16 July 1930
World title fights: 4 (all middleweight) won 2, lost 1, drew 1

Bob Godwin Born: Moultrie, Georgia, USA, 5 May 1911
  World title fights: 2 (both light-heavy) won 1, lost 1

Abe Goldstein Born: New York City, USA, 10 September 1898
  Died: St. Petersburg, Florida, USA, 12 February 1977
  World title fights: 5 (all bantamweight) won 4, lost 1

Harold Gomes Born: Providence, Rhode Island, USA, 22 August 1933
  World title fights: 3 (all junior-light) won 1, lost 2

Antonio Gomez Born: Cumana, Venezuela, 30 September 1945
  World title fights: 4 (all featherweight) won 2, lost 2

Wilfredo Gomez Born: Las Monjas, Puerto Rico, 29 October 1956
  World title fights: 23 (18 junior-feather, 3 featherweight, 2 junior-light) won 20, lost 3

Betulio Gonzalez Born: Maracaibo, Venezuela, 24 October 1949
  World title fights: 17 (all flyweight) won 7, lost 8, drew 2

Humberto Gonzalez Born: Mexico, 1967
  World title fights: 2 (both junior-fly) won 2, lost 0

Rodolfo Gonzalez Born: Zapopan, Jalisco, Mexico, 16 December 1945
  World title fights: 5 (all lightweight) won 3, lost 2

Jimmy Goodrich Born: Scranton, Pennsylvania, USA, 30 July 1900
  Died: Fort Myers, Florida, USA, 25 December 1982
  World title fights: 2 (both lightweight) won 1, lost 1

S. T. Gordon Born: Pascoe, Washington, USA, 18 April 1959
  World title fights: 3 (all cruiserweight) won 2, lost 1

Bushy Graham Born: Italy, 18 June 1903
  World title fights: 2 (both bantamweight) won 1, lost 1

Rocky Graziano Born: New York City, USA, 7 June 1922
  World title fights: 4 (all middleweight) won 1, lost 3

Harry Greb Born: Pittsburgh, Pennsylvania, USA, 6 June 1894
  Died: Atlantic City, New Jersey, USA, 22 October 1926
  World title fights: 9 (all middleweight) won 7, lost 2

Former world middleweight champion Harry Greb. In 1922 he beat Gene Tunney in an American light-heavyweight contest. It was former world heavyweight champion Tunney's only professional defeat (Hulton)

Emile Griffith Born: St. Thomas, Virgin Islands, 3 February 1938
  World title fights: 22 (13 welterweight, 8 middleweight, 1 junior-middle) won 14, lost 8

Calvin Grove Born: Pottstown, Philadelphia, USA, 5 August 1962
  World title fights: 4 (all featherweight) won 2, lost 2

Yoko Gushiken Born: Okinawa, Japan, 28 June 1955
  World title fights: 15 (all junior-fly) won 14, lost 1

Juan Guzman Born: Santiago, Dominican Republic, 21 August 1951
  World title fights: 2 (both junior-fly) won 1, lost 1

*They don't mess
around when it
comes to training at
The Kronk gym as
Tommy Hearns is
finding out
(All Sport/Dave
Cannon)*

Marvin Hagler Born: Newark, New Jersey, USA, 23

World title fights: 15 (all middleweight) won 13, lost 1, drew 1

Leroy Haley Born: Garland County, Arkansas, USA, 27 December 1954

World title fights: 6 (all junior-welter) won 3, lost 3

Alphonse Halimi Born: Constantine, Algeria, 18 June 1932

World title fights: 7 (all bantamweight) won 3, lost 4

Tsuyoshi Hamada Born: Nakagusuku, Okinawa, Japan, 29 November 1960

World title fights: 2 (both junior-welter) won 2, lost 0

Susumu Hanagata Born: Yokohama, Japan, 21 January 1946

World title fights: 8 (all flyweight) won 1, lost 7

Masahiko (Fighting) Harada Born: Tokyo, 5 April 1943

World title fights: 10 (2 flyweight, 6 bantamweight, 2 featherweight) won 6, lost 4

Jeff Harding Born: Australia, 5 February 1965

World title fights: 2 (both light-heavy) won 2, lost 0

Marvin Hart Born: Jefferson County, Kentucky, USA, 16 September 1876

Died: Fern Creek, Kentucky, USA, 17 September 1931

World title fights: 2 (both heavyweight) won 1, lost 1

Gene Hatcher Born: Fort Worth, Texas, USA, 28 June 1959

World title fights: 4 (3 junior-welter, 1 welterweight) won 2, lost 2

Greg Haugen Born: Aubern, Washington, USA, 31 August 1960

World title fights: 6 (all lightweight) won 4, lost 2

Thomas Hearns Born: Memphis, Tennessee, USA, 18 October 1958

World title fights: 15 (5 welterweight, 5 junior-middle, 3 middleweight, 1 light-heavy, 1 super-middle) won 11, lost 3, drew 1

Pete 'Kid' Herman Born: New Orleans, Louisiana, USA, 12 February 1896

Died: New Orleans, Louisiana, USA, 13 April 1973

World title fights: 6 (all bantamweight) won 3, lost 2, drew 1

Carlos Hernandez Born: Caracas, Venezuela, 22 April 1940

World title fights: 5 (all junior-welter) won 3, lost 2

Juan Herrera Born: Yucatan, Mexico, 12 January 1958
World title fights: 4 (all flyweight) won 2, lost 2

Rafael Herrera Born: Michoacan, Mexico, 7 January 1945
World title fights: 6 (all bantamweight) won 4, lost 2

Virgil Hill Born: Clinton, Missouri, USA, 18 January 1964
World title fights: 9 (all light-heavy) won 9, lost 0

Matthew Hilton Born: Port Credit, Ontario, Canada, 27 December 1965
World title fights: 3 (all junior-middle) won 2, lost 1

Robert Hines Born: Philadelphia, USA, 20 March 1962
World title fights: 2 (both junior-middle) won 1, lost 1

Garry Hinton Born: Philadelphia, Pennsylvania, USA, 29 August 1956
World title fights: 3 (all junior-welter) won 1, lost 2

Larry Holmes Born: Cuthbert, Georgia, USA, 3 November 1949
World title fights: 24 (all heavyweight) won 21, lost 3

Lindell Holmes: Born: Detroit, Michigan, USA, 15 October 1958
World title fights: 2 (both super-middleweight) won 1, lost 0, NC 1

Evander Holyfield Born: Atmore, Alabama, USA, 19 October 1962
World title fights: 6 (all cruiserweight) won 6, lost 0

Lloyd Honeyghan Born: St. Elizabeth, Jamaica, 22 April 1960
World title fights: 8 (all welterweight) won 6, lost 2

Soo-Hwan Hong Born: Seoul, South Korea, 26 May 1950
World title fights: 7 (4 bantamweight, 3 junior-feather) won 4, lost 3

Maurice Hope Born: Antigua, West Indies, 6 December 1951
World title fights: 6 (all junior-middle) won 4, lost 1, drew 1

Al Hostak Born: Minneapolis, Minnesota, USA, 7 January 1916
World title fights: 6 (all middleweight) won 3, lost 3

Luis Ibarra Born: Colon, Panama, 23 February 1953
World title fights: 4 (all flyweight) won 2, lost 2

Hiroki Ioka Born: Osaka, Japan, 8 January 1969
World title fights: 5 (all strawweight) won 2, lost 2, drew 1

Guts Ishimatsu (formerly Ishimatsu Suzuki) Born: Tochigi Prefecture, Japan, 5 June 1949
World title fights: 10 (9 lightweight, 1 junior-welter) won 5, lost 4, drew 1

Beau Jack Born: Augusta, Georgia, USA, 1 April 1921
World title fights: 5 (all lightweight) won 2, lost 3

Julian Jackson Born: St. Thomas, Virgin Islands, USA, 12 September 1960
World title fights: 5 (all junior-middle) won 4, lost 1

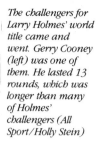

The challengers for Larry Holmes' world title came and went. Gerry Cooney (left) was one of them. He lasted 13 rounds, which was longer than many of Holmes' challengers (All Sport/Holly Stein)

Rene Jacquot Born: Toulouse, France, 28 July 1961
World title fights: 2 (both junior-middle) won 1, lost 1

Johnny Jadick Born: Philadelphia, Pennsylvania, USA, 16 June 1908
Died: Philadelphia, Pennsylvania, USA, 3 April 1970
World title fights: 3 (all junior-welter) won 2, lost 1

Ben Jeby Born: New York City, USA, 27 December 1909

World title fights: 5 (all middleweight) won 3, lost 1, drew 1

Harry Jeffra Born: Baltimore, Maryland, USA, 30 November 1914
World title fights: 7 (2 bantamweight, 5 featherweight) won 3, lost 4

James J. Jeffries Born: Carroll, Ohio, USA, 15 April 1875
Died: Burbank, California, USA, 3 March 1953
World title fights: 8 (all heavyweight) won 7, lost 1

Lew Jenkins Born: Milburn, Texas, USA, 4 December 1916
Died: Oakland, California, USA, 30 October 1981
World title fights: 3 (all lightweight) won 2, lost 1

Eder Jofre Born: São Paulo, Brazil, 26 March 1936
World title fights: 13 (11 bantamweight, 2 featherweight) won 11, lost 2

Ingemar Johansson Born: Gothenburg, Sweden, 16 October 1932
World title fights: 3 (all heavyweight) won 1, lost 2

Harold Johnson Born: Manayunk, Pennsylvania, USA, 9 August 1928
World title fights: 7 (all light-heavy) won 5, lost 2

Jack Johnson Born: Galveston, Texas, USA, 31 March 1878
Died: Raleigh, North Carolina, USA, 10 June 1946
World title fights: 8 (all heavyweight) won 7, lost 1

Marvin Johnson Born: Indianapolis, Indiana, USA, 12 April 1954
World title fights: 7 (all light-heavy) won 4, lost 3

Gorilla Jones Born: Memphis, Tennessee, USA, 4 May 1910
Died: Los Angeles, California, USA, 4 January 1982
World title fights: 6 (all middleweight) won 4, lost 2

Don Jordan Born: Los Angeles, California, USA, 22 June 1934
World title fights: 4 (all welterweight) won 3, lost 1

Kim-Bong Jun Born: South Korea
World title fights: 4 (all strawweight) won 3, lost 1

Slobodan Kacar Born: Belgrade, Yugoslavia, 15 September 1957
World title fights: 2 (both light-heavy) won 1, lost 1

Sumbu Kalambay Born: Lubunbashi, Zaire, 10 April 1956
World title fights: 5 (all middleweight) won 4, lost 1

The referee of the Benny Lynch–Peter Kane (both GB) world flyweight title fight in Glasgow in October 1937 was BBC radio commentator Barrington Dalby.

Ayub Kalule Born: Kampala, Uganda, 6 January 1954
World title fights: 7 (all junior-middle) won 5, lost 2

Peter Kane Born: Golborne, England, 28 February 1918
World title fights: 4 (all flyweight) won 1, lost 2, drew 1

Rocky Kansas Born: Buffalo, New York, USA, 21 April 1895
Died: Buffalo, New York, USA, 10 January 1954
World title fights: 4 (all lightweight) won 1, lost 3

Louis 'Kid' Kaplan Born: Russia, 15 October 1901
Died: Norwich, Connecticut, USA, 26 October 1970
World title fights: 3 (all featherweight) won 2, lost 0, drew 1

Hilmer Kenty Born: Austin, Texas, USA, 30 July 1955
World title fights: 5 (all lightweight) won 4, lost 1

Stanley Ketchel Born: Grand Rapids, Michigan, USA, 14 September 1886
Died: Conway, Missouri, USA, 15 October 1910
World title fights: 10 (9 middleweight, 1 heavyweight) won 8, lost 2

Napa Kiatwanchai Born: Nakonratchasima, Thailand, 27 July 1967
World title fights: 4 (all strawweight) won 3, lost 0, drew 1

Dixie Kid Born: Fulton, Missouri, USA, 23 December 1883
Died: Los Angeles, California, 3 October 1935
World title fights: 2 (both welterweight) won 1, lost 0, drew 1

Johnny Kilbane Born: Cleveland, Ohio, USA, 18 April 1889
Died: Cleveland, Ohio, USA, 31 May 1957
World title fights: 8 (7 featherweight, 1 lightweight) won 4, lost 2, drew 2

Chi-Won Kim Born: South Korea, 6 August 1959
World title fights: 5 (all junior-feather) won 5, lost 0

Chul-Ho Kim Born: Ohsan, South Korea, 3 March 1961
World title fights: 7 (all junior-bantam) won 5, drew 1, lost 1

Hwan-Jin Kim Born: Kyungnam, South Korea, 25 June 1955
World title fights: 4 (all junior-fly) won 2, lost 2

Ki-Soo Kim Born: Buk-Chong, Ham-kyongnamdo, Korea, 17 September 1939
World title fights: 4 (all junior-middle) won 3, lost 1

Sang-Hyun Kim Born: Pusan, South Korea, 18 January 1955
World title fights: 5 (all junior-welter) won 3, lost 2

Sung-Jun Kim Born: Seoul, South Korea, 3 June 1953
World title fights: 6 (5 junior-fly, 1 flyweight) won 3, lost 2, drew 1

Tae-Shik Kim Born: Kanwon-Do, South Korea, 4 July 1957
World title fights: 4 (all flyweight) won 2, lost 2

Yung-Kang Kim Born: Hwasoon Kun Chunnam, South Korea, 3 January 1965
World title fights: 4 (all flyweight) won 3, lost 1

Pone Kingpetch Born: Hui Hui, Thailand, 12 February 1936
Died: Bangkok, Thailand, 31 May 1982
World title fights: 9 (all flyweight) won 6, lost 3

Muangchai Kittikasem Born: Thailand, 6 May 1968
World title fights: 3 (both junior-fly) won 3, lost 0

Frankie Klaus Born: Pittsburgh, USA, 30 December 1887
Died: Pittsburgh, USA, 8 February 1948
World title fights: 3 (all middleweight) won 1, lost 2

Frankie Klick Born: San Francisco, California, USA, 5 May 1907
Died: San Francisco, 18 May 1982
World title fights: 3 (1 junior-light, 2 junior-welter) won 1, lost 1, drew 1

Hiroshi Kobayashi Born: Isesaki, Gumma, Japan, 23 August 1944
World title fights: 8 (all junior-light) won 6, lost 1, drew 1

Koji Kobayashi Born: Tokyo, Japan, 27 August 1957
World title fights: 2 (both flyweight) won 1, lost 1

Kazuo 'Royal' Kobayashi Born: Fukuoka, Japan, 10 October 1949
World title fights: 5 (2 featherweight, 3 junior-feather) won 1, lost 4

Nana Yan Konadu Born: Ghana
World title fights: 2 (both junior-bantamweight) won 1, lost 1

Juan La Porte of Puerto Rico stands with arms raised after beating Rocky Lockridge for the USBA featherweight title in 1981. La Porte later went on to capture the WBC version of the world title (AP)

Benny Leona[rd],
world lightwe[ight]
champion
1917–25. He
also had a cr[ack]
at Jack Britto[n's]
welterweight [title]
in 1922 but [was]
disqualified [in]
the 13th rou[nd]
(AP)

David 'Poison' Kotey Born: Accra, Ghana, 7
    December 1950
        World title fights: 5 (all featherweight) won 3,
        lost 2

Solly Kreiger Born: Brooklyn, New York, USA, 28
    March 1909
        Died: Las Vegas, USA, 24 September 1964
        World title fights: 2 (both middleweight)
        won 1, lost 1

Masashi Kudo Born: Gojome-cho, Akita-Gun, Japan,
    24 August 1951
        World title fights: 5 (all junior-middle) won 4,
        lost 1

Soo-Chun Kwon Born: Kyong-Ki Do, South Korea, 24
    April 1959
        World title fights: 9 (1 junior-bantam, 8
        flyweight) won 5, lost 2, drew 2

Fidel La Barba Born: New York City, USA, 29
    September 1905
        Died: Los Angeles, California, USA, 3 October
        1981
        World title fights: 4 (2 flyweight, 2
        featherweight) won 2, lost 2

Santos Laciar Born: Cordoba, Argentina, 31 January
    1959
        World title fights: 16 (12 flyweight, 4 junior-
        bantam) won 12, lost 3, drew 1

Ismael Laguna Born: Colon, Panama, 28 June 1943
        World title fights: 6 (all lightweight) won 3,
        lost 3

Donny Lalonde Born: Kitchener, Ontario, Canada, 12
    March 1960
        World title fights: 3 (2 light-heavy, 1 light-
        heavy/super-middle) won 2, lost 1

Jake La Motta Born: Bronx, New York, USA, 10 July
    1921
        World title fights: 4 (all middleweight) won 3,
        lost 1

Juan Laporte Born: Guyama, Puerto Rico, 24
    November 1959
        World title fights: 7 (6 featherweight, 1 junior-
        light) won 3, lost 4

Tippy Larkin Born: Garfield, New Jersey, USA, 11
    November 1917
        World title fights: 3 (1 lightweight, 2 junior-
        welter) won 2, lost 1

Cecilio Lastra Born: Monte, Santander, Spain, 12
    August 1951
        World title fights: 2 (both featherweight)
        won 1, lost 1

Pete Latzo Born: Coloraine, Pennsylvania, USA, 1
    August 1902
        Died: Atlantic City, New Jersey, USA, 7 July
        1968
        World title fights: 7 (5 welterweight, 2 light-
        heavy) won 3, lost 3, ND 1

George 'Kid' Lavigne Born: Bay City, Michigan,
    USA, 6 December 1869
        Died: Detroit, Michigan, USA, 9 March 1928
        World title fights: 10 (9 lightweight, 1
        welterweight) won 6, lost 2, drew 2)

Alfredo Layne Born: Panama City, Panama, 9 October
    1959
        World title fights: 2 (both junior-light) won 1,
        lost 1

Kyung-Yun Lee Born: Poongki-Kyungnam, South
    Korea, 4 December 1966
        World title fights: 2 (both strawweight) won 1,
        lost 1

Seung-Hoon Lee Born: Chunbuk, South Korea, 26 July
    1960
        World title fights: 8 (1 junior-bantam, 1
        bantamweight, 6 junior-feather) won 4,
        lost 3, drew 1

Yul-Woo Lee Born:
        World title fights: 2 (both junior-fly) won 1,
        lost 1

Jose Legra Born: Baracoa, Cuba, 19 April 1943
        World title fights: 4 (all featherweight) won 2,
        lost 2

Richie Lemos Born: Los Angeles, California, USA, 6
    February 1920
        World title fights: 3 (all featherweight) won 1,
        lost 2

Benny Leonard Born: New York City, USA, 7 April
    1896
        Died: New York City, USA, 18 April 1947
        World title fights: 9 (8 lightweight, 1
        welterweight) won 8, lost 1

Sugar Ray Leonard Born: Wilmington, South Carolina,
    USA, 17 May 1956
        World title fights: 12 (7 welterweight, 1 junior-
        middle, 1 middleweight, 1 light-heavy/
        super-middle, 2 super-middleweight) won
        10, lost 1, drew 1

Gus Lesnevich Born: Cliffside Park, New Jersey, USA,
    22 February 1915
        Died: Cliffside Park, New Jersey, USA, 28
        February 1964
        World title fights: 10 (9 light-heavy, 1
        heavyweight) won 6, lost 4

Battling Levinsky Born: Philadelphia, USA, 10 June
    1891
        Died: Philadelphia, USA, 12 February 1949
        World title fights: 3 (all light-heavy) won 1,
        lost 2

John Henry Lewis Born: Los Angeles, California, USA,
    1 May 1914
        Died: Berkeley, California, USA, 18 April 1974
        World title fights: 7 (6 light-heavy, 1
        heavyweight) won 6, lost 1

Ted 'Kid' Lewis Born: London, England, 24 October 1894

Died: London, England, 20 October 1970

World title fights: 11 (10 welterweight, 1 light-heavy) won 5, lost 4, ND 2

Rafael Limon Born: Mexico City, Mexico, 13 January 1954

World title fights: 7 (all junior-light) won 3, lost 4

Sonny Liston Born: St. Francis County, Arkansas, USA, 8 May 1932

Died: Las Vegas, Nevada, USA, 30 December 1970

World title fights: 4 (all heavyweight) won 2, lost 2

Freddie Little Born: Picayune, Mississippi, USA, 25 April 1936

World title fights: 6 (all junior-middle) won 3, lost 3

Nicolino Loche Born: Tunuyan, Mendoza, Argentina, 2 September 1939

World title fights: 8 (all junior-welter) won 6, lost 2

Rocky Lockridge Born: Dallas, Texas, USA, 10 January 1959

World title fights: 12 (2 featherweight, 10 junior-light) won 6, lost 6

Duilio Loi Born: Trieste, Italy, 19 April 1929

World title fights: 6 (all junior-welter) won 3, lost 2, drew 1

Alfonso Lopez Born: Taimiti, Panama, 8 January 1953

World title fights: 6 (4 flyweight, 2 junior-fly) won 2, lost 4

Danny Lopez Born: Fort Duchesne, Utah, USA, 6 July 1952

World title fights: 11 (all featherweight) won 9, lost 2

Tony Lopez Born: Sacramento, California, USA, 24 February 1963

World title fights: 5 (all junior-light) won 4, lost 1

Sandro Lopopolo Born: Milan, Italy, 18 December 1939

World title fights: 3 (all junior-welter) won 2, lost 1

The last bout under the Frawley Law, which prohibited the giving of points decisions in contests in New York, was the world middleweight title fight between Americans Mike O'Dowd and Al McCoy on 14 November 1917. The result: O'Dowd won with a sixth round knock-out.

Miguel 'Happy' Lora Born: Monteria, Cordoba, Colombia, 12 April 1961

World title fights: 9 (all bantamweight) won 8, lost 1

Tommy Loughran Born: Philadelphia, USA, 29 November 1902

Died: Altoona, Pennsylvania, USA, 7 July 1982

World title fights: 8 (7 light-heavy, 1 heavyweight) won 7, lost 1

Joe Louis Born: Lafayette, Alabama, USA, 13 May 1914

Died: Las Vegas, Nevada, USA, 12 April 1981

World title fights: 27 (all heavyweight) won 26, lost 1

Jorge Lujan Born: Colon, Panama, 18 March 1955

World title fights: 10 (8 bantamweight, 1 junior-feather, 1 featherweight) won 6, lost 4

Benny Lynch Born: Clydesdale, Scotland, 2 April 1913

Died: Glasgow, Scotland, 6 August 1946

World title fights: 5 (all flyweight) won 4, lost 0, drew 1

Joe Lynch Born: New York City, USA, 30 November 1898

Died: Brooklyn, New York, USA, 1 August 1965

World title fights: 5 (all bantamweight) won 3, lost 2

Dave McAuley Born: Larne, Northern Ireland, 15 June 1961

World title fights: 4 (all flyweight) won 2, lost 2

Jack McAuliffe Born: Cork, Ireland, 24 March 1866

Died: Forest Hills, New York, USA, 5 November 1937

World title fights: 3 (all lightweight) won 2, lost 0, drew 1

Mike McCallum Born: Kingston, Jamaica, 7 December 1956

World title fights: 10 (7 junior-middle, 3 middleweight) won 9, lost 1

Al McCoy Born: Rosenhayn, New Jersey, USA, 23 October 1894

Died: Los Angeles, California, USA, 22 August 1966

World title fights: 3 (all middleweight) won 1, lost 2

Charles 'Kid' McCoy Born: Rush County, Indiana, USA, 13 October 1872

Died: Detroit, Michigan, USA, 18 April 1940

World title fights: 2 (1 welterweight, 1 light-heavy) won 1, lost 1

Glenn McCrory Born: Stanley, Co. Durham, England, 23 September 1964

World title fights: 2 (both cruiserweight) won 2, lost 0

Charles 'Kid' McCoy (USA) can claim to be the most married of all world champions with ten marriages to his credit – three to the same woman.

McCoy is also famous for lending his name to a well-known saying. He was a master of tricking his opponents into believing he was ill or in difficulty. Consequently, his opponents were never sure whether he was 'real' or not. And so was born the saying: 'Is it the real McCoy?'

Milton McCrory Born: Detroit, Michigan, USA, 7 February 1962
World title fights: 8 (7 welterweight, 1 junior-middle) won 5, lost 2, drew 1

James Buddy McGirt Born: Brentwood, New York, USA, 17 January 1964
World title fights: 3 (all junior-welter) won 2, lost 1

Terry McGovern Born: Johnstown, Pennsylvania, USA, 9 March 1880
Died: Brooklyn, New York, USA, 26 February 1918
World title fights: 10 (2 bantamweight, 8 featherweight) won 9, lost 1

Walter McGowan Born: Burnbank, Scotland, 13 October 1942
World title fights: 3 (all flyweight) won 1, lost 2

Barry McGuigan Born: Clones, Monaghan, Ireland, 28 February 1961
World title fights: 4 (all featherweight) won 3, lost 1

Duke McKenzie Born: Croydon, England, 5 May 1963
World title fights: 3 (all flyweight) won 2, lost 1

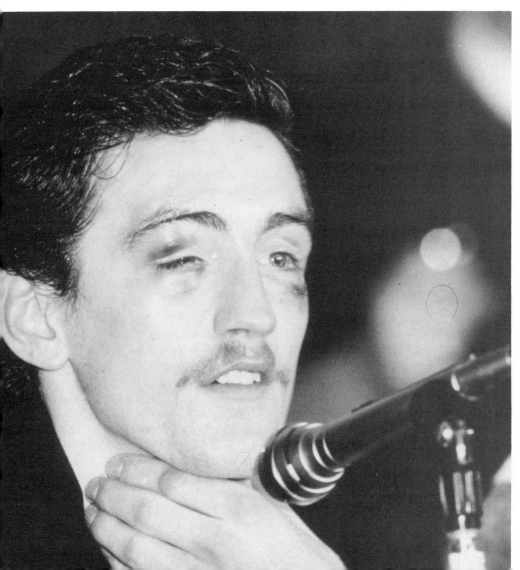

Battered and bruised, the not so smiling Irish eyes of Barry McGuigan (All Sport)

Jimmy McLarnin Born: Inchacore, Ireland, 19 December 1906
World title fights: 5 (1 lightweight, 4 welterweight) won 2, lost 3

Mike McTigue Born: Killmonaugh Parish, County Clare, Ireland, 26 November 1892
Died: New York, USA, 12 August 1966
World title fights: 3 (all light-heavy) won 1, lost 2

Tacy Macalos Born: Tanguan, Philippines, 28 October 1965
World title fights: 4 (all junior-fly) won 1, lost 3

Raton Macias Born: Mexico City, Mexico, 28 July 1934
World title fights: 4 (all bantamweight) won 3, lost 1

Lupe Madera Born: Yucatan, Mexico, 17 December 1952
World title fights: 5 (all junior-fly) won 2, lost 2, drew 1

Charlie Magri Born: Tunis, Tunisia, 20 July 1956
World title fights: 3 (all flyweight) won 1, lost 2

Saoul Mamby Born: Jamaica, West Indies, 4 June 1947
World title fights: 8 (all junior-welter) won 6, lost 2

Ray Mancini Born: Youngstown, Ohio, USA, 4 March 1961
World title fights: 8 (all lightweight) won 5, lost 3

Sammy Mandell Born: Rockford, Illinois, USA, 5 February 1904
Died: Oak Park, Illinois, USA, 7 November 1967
World title fights: 4 (all lightweight) won 3, lost 1

Joe Louis Manley Born: Lima, Ohio, USA, 11 June 1959
World title fights: 2 (both junior-welter) won 1, lost 1

Alfredo Marcano Born: Sucre, Venezuela, 17 January 1947
World title fights: 4 (3 junior-light, 1 featherweight) won 2, lost 2

Ernesto Marcel Born: Colon, Panama, 23 May 1948
World title fights: 6 (all featherweight) won 5, lost 0, drew 1

Rocky Marciano Born: Brockton, Massachusetts, USA, 1 September 1923
Died: Newton, Iowa, USA, 31 August 1969
World title fights: 7 (all heavyweight) won 7, lost 0

Dado Marino Born: Honolulu, Hawaii, 26 August 1916
World title fights: 6 (5 flyweight, 1 bantamweight) won 2, lost 4

Tony Marino Born: Pittsburgh, Pennsylvania, USA, 18 May 1912
Died: New York, USA, 1 February 1937
World title fights: 2 (both bantamweight) won 1, lost 1

Terry Marsh Born: Stepney, London, England, 7 February 1958
World title fights: 2 (both junior-welter) won 2, lost 0

Eddie 'Cannonball' Martin Born: Brooklyn, New York, USA, 3 March 1903
Died: Brooklyn, New York, USA, 27 August 1966
World title fights: 3 (2 bantamweight, 1 junior-light) won 1, lost 2

Rodolfo Martinez Born: Tepito, Mexico, 24 August 1946
World title fights: 6 (all bantamweight) won 4, lost 2

Peter Mathebula Born: Transvaal, South Africa, 3 July 1952
World title fights: 2 (both flyweight) won 1, lost 1

Matty Matthews Born: New York City, USA, 13 July 1873
Died: Brooklyn, New York, USA, 6 December 1948
World title fights: 4 (all welterweight) won 2, lost 2

Rocky Mattioli Born: Ripa Teatine, Italy, 20 July 1953
World title fights: 5 (all junior-middle) won 3, lost 2

Joey Maxim Born: Cleveland, Ohio, 28 March 1922
World title fights: 7 (6 light-heavy, 1 heavyweight) won 3, lost 4

Roger Mayweather Born: Grand Rapids, Michigan, USA, 24 April 1961
World title fights: 11 (5 junior-light, 6 junior-welter) won 8, lost 3

Sandro Mazzinghi Born: Pontedera, Italy, 3 October 1938
World title fights: 8 (all junior-middle) won 6, lost 2

Mark Medal Born: Jersey City, New Jersey, USA, 10 June 1957
World title fights: 3 (all junior-middle) won 1, lost 2

Honey Mellody Born: Charlestown, Massachusetts, USA, 15 January 1884
Died: Charlestown, Massachusetts, USA, 15 March 1919
World title fights: 2 (both welterweight) won 1, lost 1

Eleoncio Mercedes Born: La Romana, Dominican Republic, 12 September 1957
Died: La Romana, Dominican Republic, 22

December 1985
World title fights: 2 (both flyweight) won 1, lost 1

Juan 'Kid' Meza Born: Mexicali, Mexico, 18 March 1956
World title fights: 5 (all junior-feather) won 2, lost 3

Barry Michael Born: London, England, 2 June 1955
World title fights: 5 (all junior-light) won 4, lost 1

Tadashi Mihara Born: Gumma Prefecture, Japan, 3 March 1955
World title fights: 2 (both junior-middle) won 1, lost 1

Freddie Miller Born: Cincinnati, Ohio, USA, 3 April 1911
Died: Cincinnati, Ohio, USA, 8 May 1962
World title fights: 13 (all featherweight) won 10, lost 3

Freddie Mills Born: Parkstone, Dorset, England, 26 June 1919
Died: London, England, 25 July 1965
World title fights: 3 (all light-heavy) won 1, lost 2

Alan Minter Born: Crawley, Sussex, England, 17 August 1951
World title fights: 3 (all middleweight) won 2, lost 1

Brian Mitchell Born: Johannesburg, South Africa, 30 August 1961
World title fights: 11 (all junior-light) won 10, lost 0, drew 1

Juan 'John John' Molina Born: Puerto Rico, 7 March 1965
World title fights: 2 (both junior-light) won 1, lost 1

Tomas Molinares Born: Cartagena, Colombia, 6 April 1965
World title fights: 1 (welterweight) won 1, lost 0

Rinty Monaghan Born: Belfast, Northern Ireland, 21 August 1920
Died: Belfast, Northern Ireland, 3 March 1984
World title fights: 4 (all flyweight) won 3, lost 0, drew 1

Small Montana Born: Philippines, 24 February 1913
World title fights: 2 (both flyweight) won 1, lost 1

Bob Montgomery Born: Sumter, South Carolina, USA, 10 February 1919
World title fights: 6 (all lightweight) won 4, lost 2

Carlos Monzon Born: Santa Fe, Argentina, 7 August 1942
World title fights: 15 (all middleweight) won 15, lost 0

Sung-Kil Moon Born: Yeoung-Am, South Korea, 20 July 1963
World title fights: 5 (4 bantamweight, 1 junior-bantam) won 4, lost 1

Archie Moore Born: Benoit, Mississippi, USA, 13 December 1913 or 1916 (year uncertain)
World title fights: 11 (9 light-heavy, 2 heavyweight) won 9, lost 2

Davey Moore Born: Lexington, Kentucky, USA, 1 November 1933
World title fights: 7 (all featherweight) won 6, lost 1

Davey Moore Born: Bronx, New York, USA, 9 June 1959
Died: USA, 5 June 1988
World title fights: 5 (all junior-middle) won 4, lost 1

Tod Morgan Born: Seattle, Washington, USA, 25 December 1902
Died: Seattle, Washington, USA, 3 August 1953
World title fights: 6 (all junior-light) won 5, lost 1

Denny Moyer Born: Portland, Oregon, USA, 8 August 1939
World title fights: 6 (1 welterweight, 4 junior-middle, 1 middleweight) won 2, lost 4

Saensak Muangsurin Born: Phetchabun, Thailand, 13 August 1950
World title fights: 12 (all junior-welter) won 10, lost 2

John Mugabi Born: Kampala, Uganda, 4 March 1960
World title fights: 3 (1 middleweight, 2 junior-middle) won 1, lost 2

Takuya Muguruma Born: Osaka, Japan, 16 January 1961
World title fights: 4 (3 bantamweight, 1 junior-feather) won 1, lost 2, drew 1

Eddie Mustafa Muhammad (formerly Eddie Gregory) Born: Brooklyn, New York, USA, 30 April 1952
World title fights: 6 (all light-heavy) won 3, lost 3

Matthew Saad Muhammad (formerly Matt Franklin) Born: Philadelphia, Pennsylvania, USA, 5 August 1954
World title fights: 11 (all light-heavy) won 9, lost 2

Billy Murphy Born: Auckland, New Zealand, 3 November 1863
Died: Auckland, New Zealand, 26 July 1939
World title fights: 1 (featherweight) won 1, lost 0

Lee Roy Murphy Born: Chicago, Illinois, USA, 16 July 1958
World title fights: 5 (all cruiserweight) won 4, lost 1

Shigeo Nakajima Born: Ibaraki, Japan, 18 January 1954
  World title fights: 3 (all junior-fly) won 1, lost 2

Jose Napoles Born: Santiago de Cuba, Oriente, Cuba, 13 April 1940
  World title fights: 18 (17 welterweight, 1 middleweight) won 15, lost 3

Rolando Navarrete Born: Santos City, Philippines, 14 February 1957
  World title fights: 4 (all junior-light) won 2, lost 2

Frankie Neil Born: San Francisco, California, USA, 25 July 1883
  Died: Richmond, California, USA, 6 March 1970
  World title fights: 7 (6 bantamweight, 1 featherweight) won 3, lost 3, drew 1

Azumah Nelson Born: Accra, Ghana, 19 July 1958
  World title fights: 13 (8 featherweight, 5 junior-light) won 12, lost 1

Battling Nelson Born: Copenhagen, Denmark, 5 June 1882
  Died: Chicago, Illinois, USA, 7 February 1954
  World title fights: 6 (all lightweight) won 4, lost 2

George Nichols Born: Sandusky, Ohio, USA, 9 July 1908
  World title fights: 2 (both light-heavy) won 1, lost 1

Claude Noel Born: Port of Spain, Trinidad, 25 July 1948
  World title fights: 3 (all lightweight) won 1, lost 2

Ken Norton Born: Jacksonville, Illinois, USA, 9 August 1943
  World title fights: 3 (all heavyweight) won 0, lost 3

Yoshiaki Numata Born: Tomikawa-cho, Hokkaido, Japan, 19 April 1945
  World title fights: 8 (7 junior-light, 1 lightweight) won 5, lost 3

Michael Nunn Born: Sherman Oaks, California, USA, 14 April 1963
  World title fights: 4 (all middleweight) won 4, lost 0

Elisha Obed Born: Nassau, Bahamas, 21 February 1952
  World title fights: 5 (all junior-middle) won 3, lost 2

Fulgencio Obelmejias Born: San Jose de Rio Chico, Venezuela, 11 January 1953
  World title fights: 3 (1 middleweight, 2 super-middle) won 1, lost 2

Philadelphia Jack O'Brien Born: Philadelphia, USA, 17 January 1878
  Died: New York, USA, 12 November 1942
  World title fights: 3 (2 light-heavy, 1 heavyweight/light-heavy) won 1, lost 1, drew 1

Ossie Ocasio Born: Trujillo Alto, Puerto Rico, 12 August 1955
  World title fights: 7 (1 heavyweight, 6 cruiserweight) won 4, lost 3

Mike O'Dowd Born: St. Paul, Minnesota, USA, 5 April 1895
  Died: St. Paul, Minnesota, USA, 28 July 1957
  World title fights: 5 (all middleweight) won 3, lost 2

Sean O'Grady Born: Oklahoma City, USA, 10 February 1959
  World title fights: 2 (both lightweight) won 1, lost 1

Shoji Oguma Born: Fukushima, Japan, 22 July 1951
  World title fights: 13 (12 flyweight, 1 junior-bantam) won 5, lost 7, drew 1

Min-Kuem Oh Born: South Korea, 15 August 1962
  World title fights: 4 (all featherweight) won 3, lost 1

Hideyuki Ohashi Born: Yokohama, Japan, 8 March 1965
  World title fights: 3 (all strawweight) won 1, lost 2

Masao Ohba Born: Tokyo, Japan, 21 October 1949
  Died: Tokyo, Japan, 24 January 1973
  World title fights: 6 (all flyweight) won 6, lost 0

Bob Olin Born: New York, USA, 4 July 1908
  Died: New York, USA, 16 December 1956
  World title fights: 3 (all light-heavy) won 1, lost 2

Patrizio Oliva Born: Naples, Italy, 28 January 1959
  World title fights: 4 (all junior-welter) won 3, lost 1

Ruben Olivares Born: Mexico City, Mexico, 14 January 1947
  World title fights: 13 (8 bantamweight, 5 featherweight) won 8, lost 5

Joey Olivo Born: Los Angeles, California, USA, 25 January 1958
  World title fights: 4 (all junior-fly) won 2, lost 2

Carl 'Bobo' Olson Born: Honolulu, Oahu, Hawaiian Islands, 11 July 1928
  World title fights: 8 (7 middleweight, 1 light-heavy) won 4, lost 4

Rafael Orono Born: Sucre, Venezuela, 30 August 1958
  World title fights: 11 (all junior-bantam) won 7, drew 1, lost 3

Rafael Ortega Born: Panama City, Panama, 25 September 1950
  World title fights: 3 (all featherweight) won 2, lost 1

Carlos Ortiz Born: Ponce, Puerto Rico, 9 September 1936
World title fights: 18 (5 junior-welter, 13 lightweight) won 14, lost 4

Manuel Ortiz Born: Corona, California, USA, 2 July 1916
Died: San Diego, California, USA, 31 May 1970
World title fights: 23 (all bantamweight) won 21, lost 2

Ken Overlin Born: Decatur, Illinois, USA, 15 August 1910
Died: Reno, Nevada, USA, 24 July 1969
World title fights: 5 (all middleweight) won 3, lost 2

Jorge Paez Born: Mexicali, Mexico, 27 October 1965
World title fights: 7 (all featherweight) won 6, lost 0, drew 1

Greg Page Born: Louisville, Kentucky, USA, 25 October 1958
World title fights: 3 (all heavyweight) won 1, lost 2

Sergio Palma Born: La Tigra, Chaco, Argentina, 1 January 1956
World title fights: 8 (all junior-feather) won 6, lost 2

Carlos Palomino Born: San Luis, Mexico, 10 August 1949
World title fights: 9 (all welterweight) won 8, lost 1

Billy Papke Born: Spring Valley, Illinois, USA, 17 September 1886
Died: Newport, California, USA, 26 November 1936
World title fights: 11 (all middleweight) won 6, lost 5

George Bernard (Fra) suddenly fell asleep at the end of the sixth round of his world middleweight title fight with Billy Papke (USA) in 1912. He could not be revived in time to start the seventh round. He later alleged he had been drugged.

Benny 'Kid' Paret Born: Santa Clara, Las Villas, Cuba, 14 March 1937
Died: New York City, USA, 3 April 1962 (as a result of injuries received in bout versus Emile Griffith, 24 March)
World title fights: 6 (5 welterweight, 1 middleweight) won 3, lost 3

Chan-Hee Park Born: Pusan, South Korea, 23 March 1957
World title fights: 9 (all flyweight) won 5, lost 3, drew 1

Chan-Young Park Born: South Korea, 10 June 1963
World title fights: 3 (2 bantamweight, 1 junior-featherweight) won 1, lost 2

Chong-Pal Park Born: Chon-Ra, Seoul, South Korea, 11 August 1960
World title fights: 12 (all super-middle) won 10, lost 1, NC 1

Rickey Parkey Born: Morristown, Tennessee, USA, 7 November 1956
World title fights: 3 (all cruiserweight) won 2, lost 1

Mate Parlov Born: Split, Yugoslavia, 16 November 1948
World title fights: 5 (3 light-heavy, 2 cruiserweight) won 2, lost 2, drew 1

Willie Pastrano Born: New Orleans, Louisiana, USA, 27 November 1935
World title fights: 4 (all light-heavy) won, 3 lost 1

Jackie Paterson Born: Springfield, Ayrshire, Scotland, 5 September 1920
Died: South Africa, 19 November 1966
World title fights: 3 (all flyweight) won 2, lost 1

Floyd Patterson Born: Waco, North Carolina, USA, 4 January 1935
World title fights: 13 (all heavyweight) won 8, lost 5

Jimmy Paul Born: Great Falls, South Carolina, USA, 27 August 1959
World title fights: 5 (all lightweight) won 4, lost 1

Tommy Paul Born: Buffalo, New York, USA, 4 March 1909
World title fights: 2 (both featherweight) won 1, lost 1

Samart Payakaroon Born: Chacherngsao, Thailand, 5 December 1962
World title fights: 3 (all junior-feather) won 2, lost 1

Vinnie Pazienza Born: Rhode Island, USA, 16 December 1962
World title fights: 3 (2 lightweight, 1 junior-welter) won 1, lost 2

Eusebio Pedroza Born: Panama City, Panama, 2 March 1953
World title fights: 22 (21 featherweight, 1 bantamweight) won 19, lost 2, drew 1

Dodie Penalosa Born: San Carlos, Negros, Philippines, 19 November 1962
World title fights: 8 (4 junior-fly, 4 flyweight) won 5, lost 3

Rafael Pedroza Born: Colon, Panama, 3 July 1955
World title fights: 2 (both junior-bantam) won 1, lost 1

Paul Pender Born: Brookline, Massachusetts, USA, 20 June 1930

World title fights: 6 (all middleweight) won 5, lost 1

Willie Pep Born: Middletown, Connecticut, USA, 19 September 1922

World title fights: 14 (all featherweight) won 11, lost 3

Juan Polo Perez Born: Barranquilla, Colombia, 17 October 1963

World title fights: 1 (junior-bantam) won 1, lost 0

Pascual Perez Born: Mendoza, Argentina, 4 March 1926

Died: Argentina, 22 January 1977

World title fights: 11 (all flyweight) won 9, lost 2

Raul Perez Born: Tijuana, Mexico, 14 February 1967

World title fights: 5 (all bantamweight) won 5, lost 0

Victor 'Young' Perez Born: Tunis, Tunisia, 18 October 1911

Died: Auschwitz, Poland, 4 February 1943

World title fights: 4 (2 flyweight, 2 bantamweight) won 1, lost 3

Eddie Perkins Born: Clarksdale, Mississippi, USA, 3 March 1937

World title fights: 7 (all junior-welter) won 4, lost 2, drew 1

Ellyas Pical Born: Maluku, Indonesia, 24 March 1960

World title fights: 11 (all junior-bantam) won 8, lost 3

Bernardo Pinango Born: Caracas, Venezuela, 9 February 1960

World title fights: 6 (4 bantamweight, 2 junior-feather) won 5, lost 1

Enrique Pinder Born: Panama City, Panama, 7 August 1947

World title fights: 3 (all bantamweight) won 1, lost 2

Lupe Pintor Born: Cuajimalpa, Mexico, 13 April 1955

World title fights: 12 (9 bantamweight, 3 junior-feather) won 9, lost 2, drew 1

Emile Pladner Born: Clermont-Ferrand, France, 2 September 1906

Died: Auch, France, 15 March 1960

World title fights: 3 (2 flyweight, 1 bantamweight) won 1, lost 2

Cesar Polanco Born: Santiago, Dominican Republic, 29 November 1967

World title fights: 2 (both junior-bantam) won 1, lost 1

Payao Poontarat Born: Prachuap Khiri Khan, Thailand, 1956

World title fights: 4 (all junior-bantam) won 2, lost 2

Aaron Pryor Born: Cincinnati, Ohio, USA, 20 October 1955

World title fights: 11 (all junior-welter) won 11, lost 0

Dwight Muhammed Qawi (formerly Dwight Braxton) Born: Baltimore, Maryland, USA, 5 January 1953

World title fights: 9 (5 light-heavy, 4 cruiserweight) won 6, lost 3

Francisco Quiroz Born: Moca, Dominican Republic, 4 June 1957

World title fights: 3 (all junior-fly) won 2, lost 1

Jose Luis Ramirez Born: Huatabampo, Sonora, Mexico, 3 December 1958

World title fights: 8 (all lightweight) won 4, lost 4

Mando Ramos Born: Long Beach, California, USA, 15 November 1948

World title fights: 8 (all lightweight) won 4, lost 4

Ultiminio 'Sugar' Ramos Born: Matanzas, Cuba, 2 December 1941

World title fights: 7 (5 featherweight, 2 lightweight) won 4, lost 3

Leo Randolph Born: Tacoma, Washington, USA, 27 February 1958

World title fights: 2 (both junior-feather) won 1, lost 1

Alfonso Ratliff Born: Chicago, Illinois, USA, 18 February 1956

World title fights: 2 (both cruiserweight) won 1, lost 1

Rigoberto Riasco Born: Panama City, Panama, 11 January 1953

World title fights: 5 (1 featherweight, 4 junior-feather) won 3, lost 2

Jaime Rios Born: Panama City, Panama, 14 August 1953

World title fights: 5 (all junior-fly) won 2, lost 3

Ed 'Babe' Risko Born: Syracuse, New York, USA, 14 July 1911

Died: Syracuse, New York, USA, 7 March 1957

World title fights: 4 (all middleweight) won 2, lost 2

The 1989 IBF featherweight champion Jorge Paez (Mex) came from a circus family and used to be a trick cyclist, acrobat, trapeze artist and clown. The 1989 IBF junior-featherweight champion Fabrice Benichou also hailed from a circus family. He was born in Spain, brought up in France and won an Israeli amateur boxing title. His father was a magician, his mother a dancer and Fabrice worked as a circus contortionist!

One of the greatest pound-for-pound fighters was Sugar Ray Robinson, who died in 1989 (Syndication International)

Willie Ritchie Born: San Francisco, California, USA, 13 February 1891

Died: Burlingame, California, USA, 24 March 1975

World title fights: 4 (all lightweight) won 3, lost 1

Antonio Rivera Born: Rio Piedras, Puerto Rico, 5 December 1963

World title fights: 2 (both featherweight) won 1, lost 1

Sugar Ray Robinson Born: Detroit, Michigan, USA, 3 May 1921

Died: Los Angeles, USA, 12 April 1989

World title fights: 22 (6 welterweight, 15 middleweight, 1 light-heavy) won 14, lost 7, drew 1

Graciano Rocchigiani Born: Rheinhausen, West Germany, 29 December 1963

World title fights: 4 (all super-middle) won 4, lost 0

Leo Rodak Born: Chicago, Illinois, USA, 5 June 1913

World title fights: 2 (both featherweight) won 1, lost 1

Luis Rodriguez Born: Camaguey, Cuba, 17 June 1937

World title fights: 4 (all welterweight) won 1, lost 3

Baby Rojas Born: Barranquilla, Colombia, 1 February 1961

World title fights: 4 (all junior-bantam) won 2, lost 2

Jesus Rojas Born: Venezuela

World title fights: 1 (flyweight) won 1, lost 0

Raul Rojas Born: San Pedro, California, USA, 5 November 1941

World title fights: 4 (3 featherweight, 1 junior-lightweight) won 1, lost 3

Gilberto Roman Born: Mexicali, Mexico, 29 November 1961

World title fights: 14 (all junior-bantam) won 12, drew 1, lost 1

Vicente Paul Rondon Born: San Jose de Rio Chico, Miranda, Venezuela, 29 July 1938

World title fights: 6 (all light-heavy) won 5, lost 1

Jack Root Born: Austria, 26 May 1876

Died: Los Angeles, California, USA, 10 June 1963

World title fights: 3 (2 light-heavy, 1 heavyweight) won 1, lost 2

Edwin Rosario Born: San Juan, Puerto Rico, 15 March 1963

World title fights: 8 (all lightweight) won 5, lost 3

Lionel Rose Born: Victoria, New South Wales, Australia, 21 June 1948

World title fights: 6 (5 bantamweight, 1 junior-light) won 4, lost 2

Charley Phil Rosenberg Born: New York City, USA, 15 August 1902

Died: New York City, USA, 12 March 1976

World title fights: 3 (all bantamweight) won 3, lost 0

Dave Rosenberg Born: New York City, USA, 15 May 1901

World title fights: 2 (both middleweight) won 1, lost 1

Maxie Rosenbloom Born: Leonard's Bridge, New York, USA, 6 September 1904

Died: South Pasadena, California, USA, 6 March 1976

World title fights: 11 (all light-heavy) won 8, lost 2, drew 1

Gianfranco Rosi Born: Assisi, Italy, 5 August 1957

World title fights: 5 (all junior-middle) won 4, lost 1

Barney Ross Born: New York City, USA, 23 December 1909

Died: Chicago, Illinois, USA, 17 January 1967

World title fights: 14 (1 lightweight/junior-welter, 1 lightweight, 6 junior-welter, 6 welterweight) won 11, lost 2, drew 1

Mike Rossman Born: Turnersville, New Jersey, USA, 1 July 1956

World title fights: 3 (all light-heavy) won 2, lost 1

Andre Routis Born: Bordeaux, France, 16 July 1900

Died: Paris, France, 16 July 1969

World title fights: 3 (all featherweight) won 2, lost 1

Tommy Ryan Born: Redwood, New York, USA, 31 March 1870

Died: Van Nuys, California, USA, 3 August 1948

World title fights: 10 (4 welterweight, 6 middleweight) won 8, lost 1, drew 1

Ubaldo Sacco Born: Buenos Aires, Argentina, 28 July 1955

World title fights: 3 (all junior-welter) won 1, lost 2

Sandy Saddler Born: Boston, Massachusetts, USA, 23 June 1926

World title fights: 6 (all featherweight) won 5, lost 1

Sho Saijyo Born: Kit-adachi-Gun, Japan, 28 January 1947

World title fights: 7 (all featherweight) won 6, lost 1

Lauro Salas Born: Monterrey, Nuevo Leon, Mexico, 18 August 1928

World title fights: 3 (all lightweight) won 1, lost 2

Erbito Salavarria Born: Manila, Philippines, 20 January 1946

World title fights: 7 (all flyweight) won 4, lost 2, drew 1

Vicente Saldivar Born: Mexico City, Mexico, 3 May 1943
Died: Mexico, 18 July 1985
World title fights: 11 (all featherweight) won 9, lost 2

Lou Salica Born: New York, USA, 26 July 1913
World title fights: 10 (all bantamweight) won 5, lost 4, drew 1

Jesus Salud Born: Wainae, Hawaii, USA, 3 May 1963
World title fights: 1 (junior-featherweight) won 1, lost 0

Jose Sanabria Born: Mormon, Venezuela, 16 February 1963
World title fights: 6 (all junior-feather) won 4, lost 2

Clemente Sanchez Born: Monterrey, Mexico, 9 July 1947
Died: Monterrey, Mexico, 25 December 1978
World title fights: 2 (both featherweight) won 1, lost 1

Salvador Sanchez Born: Santiago Tianguistenco, Mexico, 26 January 1959
Died: Queretaro, Mexico, 12 August 1982
World title fights: 10 (all featherweight) won 10, lost 0

Richie Sandoval Born: Pomona, California, USA, 18 October 1960
World title fights: 4 (all bantamweight) won 3, lost 1

Baltazar Sangchilli Born: Valencia, Spain, 15 October 1911
World title fights: 2 (both bantamweight) won 1, lost 1

Carlos Santos Born: Santurce, Puerto Rico, 1 October 1955
World title fights: 4 (all junior-middle) won 2, lost 2

Petey Sarron Born: Birmingham, Alabama, USA, 1908
World title fights: 5 (all featherweight) won 3, lost 2

Johnny Saxton Born: Newark, New Jersey, USA, 4 July 1930
World title fights: 5 (all welterweight) won 2, lost 3

Petey Scalzo Born: New York City, USA, 1 August 1917
World title fights: 3 (all featherweight) won 2, lost 1

Max Schmeling Born: Klein Luckaw, Brandenburg, Germany, 28 September 1905
World title fights: 4 (all heavyweight) won 2, lost 2

Izzy Schwartz Born: New York City, USA, 23 October 1902
World title fights: 5 (4 flyweight, 1

bantamweight) won 4, lost 1

Kelvin Seabrooks Born: Charlotte, North Carolina, USA, 10 March 1963
World title fights: 6 (all bantamweight) won 4, lost 2

Sam Serrano Born: Toa Alta, Puerto Rico, 7 November 1952
World title fights: 18 (all junior-light) won 15, lost 2, drew 1

Marty Servo Born: Schenectady, New York, USA, 3 November 1919
Died: Pueblo, Colorado, USA, 9 February 1969
World title fights: 1 (welterweight) won 1, lost 0

Jack Sharkey Born: Binghampton, New York, USA, 26 October 1902
World title fights: 3 (all heavyweight) won 1, lost 2

Battling Shaw Born: Nuevo Laredo, Tampaulipas, Mexico, 21 October 1910
World title fights: 2 (both junior-welter) won 1, lost 1

Kuniaki Shibata Born: Hitachi, Ibaraki, Japan, 29 March 1947
World title fights: 12 (4 featherweight, 8 junior-light) won 8, lost 3, drew 1

Hi-Sup Shin Born: Seoul, South Korea, 29 July 1964
World title fights: 3 (all flyweight) won 2, lost 1

Satoshi Shingaki Born: Okinawa, Japan, 21 February 1964
World title fights: 5 (1 junior-fly, 4 bantamweight) won 2, lost 3

Yoshio Shirai Born: Tokyo, Japan, 23 November 1923
World title fights: 7 (all flyweight) won 5, lost 2

Battling Siki Born: St. Louis, Senegal, 16 September 1897
Died: New York, USA, 15 December 1925
World title fights: 2 (both light-heavy) won 1, lost 1

Al Singer Born: New York City, USA, 6 September 1909
Died: New York City, USA, 20 April 1961
World title fights: 2 (both lightweight) won 1, lost 1

Mahasamuth Sithnaruepol Born: Chonburi, Thailand, 17 May 1959
World title fights: 4 (all strawweight) won 2, lost 1, drew 1

Jimmy Slattery Born: Buffalo, New York, USA, 24 August 1904
Died: Buffalo, New York, USA, 30 August 1960
World title fights: 6 (all light-heavy) won 2, lost 4

James Smith Born: Magnolia, North Carolina, USA, 3

April 1955

World title fights: 3 (all heavyweight) won 1, lost 2

Lonnie Smith Born: Pueblo, Colorado, USA, 25 November 1962

World title fights: 2 (both junior-welter) won 1, lost 1

Mysterious Billy Smith Born: Nova Scotia, Canada, 15 May 1871

Died: Portland, Oregon, 15 October 1937

World title fights: 12 (all welterweight) won 8, lost 2, drew 2

Solly Smith Born: Los Angeles, California, USA, 1871

Died: Culver City, California, USA, 29 August 1933

World title fights: 3 (all featherweight) won 1, lost 2

Wallace 'Bud' Smith Born: Cincinnati, Ohio, USA, 2 April 1929

Died: Cincinnati, Ohio, USA, 11 July 1973

World title fights: 4 (all lightweight) won 2, lost 2

Julian Solis Born: Rio Piedras, Puerto Rico, 7 January 1957

World title fights: 3 (all bantamweight) won 1, lost 2

Billy Soose Born: Farrell, Pennsylvania, USA, 2 August 1915

World title fights: 1 (middleweight) won 1, lost 0

Leon Spinks Born: St. Louis, Missouri, USA, 11 July 1953

World title fights: 4 (3 heavyweight, 1 cruiserweight) won 1, lost 3

Michael Spinks Born: St. Louis, Missouri, USA, 13 July 1956

World title fights: 15 (11 light-heavy, 4 heavyweight) won 14, lost 1

Marlon Starling Born: Hartford, Connecticut, USA, 29 August 1958

World title fights: 7 (all welterweight) won 4, lost 2, drew 1

Loris Stecca Born: Romagna, Italy, 30 March 1960

World title fights: 3 (all junior-feather) won 1, lost 2

Freddie Steele Born: Tacoma, Washington, USA, 18 December 1912

Died: Aberdeen, Washington, USA, 23 August 1984

World title fights: 7 (all middleweight) won 6, lost 1

Leslie Stewart Born: Laventille, Trinidad, 21 March 1961

World title fights: 4 (all light-heavy) won 1, lost 3

John H. Stracey Born: Bethnal Green, London,

England, 22 September 1950

World title fights: 3 (all welterweight) won 2, lost 1

Seung-Il Suh Born: South Korea, 18 July 1959

World title fights: 5 (all junior-feather) won 2, lost 3

Dave Sullivan Born: Cork, Ireland, 19 May 1877

Died: Cork, Ireland, 1929

World title fights: 2 (both featherweight) won 1, lost 1

Mike 'Twin' Sullivan Born: Cambridge, Massachusetts, USA, 23 September 1878

Died: Cambridge, Massachusetts, USA, 31 October 1937

World title fights: 2 (1 welterweight, 1 middleweight) won 1, lost 1

Steve 'Kid' Sullivan Born: Brooklyn, New York, USA, 21 May 1897

World title fights: 3 (all junior-light) won 2, lost 1

Murray Sutherland Born: Edinburgh, Scotland, 10 April 1954

World title fights: 4 (2 light-heavy, 2 super-middle) won 1, lost 3

Frank Tate Born: Detroit, Michigan, USA, 27 August 1964

World title fights: 4 (3 middleweight, 1 super-middle) won 2, lost 2

John Tate Born: Marion City, Arkansas, USA, 29 January 1955

World title fights: 2 (both heavyweight) won 1, lost 1

The following fighters overcame physical disabilities to go on to win world titles:
Mario D'Agata (bantamweight 1956–7) was a deaf and dumb mute
Harry Greb (middleweight 1923–6) was virtually blind in one eye
Eugene Criqui (featherweight 1923) had no jaw bone. A silver plate, held together by wire, had been inserted in its place
Willie Pep (featherweight 1942–8 and 1949–50), although he did not suffer from any physical disability, was severely injured in a plane crash in January 1947. He was told he would never box again, and it was unlikely he would walk without crutches. Five months after the crash he was back in the ring, winning the first of 26 consecutive contests. And in August that year, he beat Jock Leslie to retain his world title.

Arnold Taylor Born: Johannesburg, South Africa, 21 July 1945
Died: Johannesburg, South Africa, 22 November 1981
World title fights: 2 (both bantamweight) won 1, lost 1

Charles 'Bud' Taylor Born: Terre Haute, Indiana, USA, 22 July 1903
Died: Los Angeles, California, USA, 8 March 1962
World title fights: 2 (both bantamweight) won 1, lost 0, drew 1

Meldrick Taylor Born: Philadelphia, USA, 19 October 1966
World title fights: 3 (all junior-welter) won 3, lost 0

Phil Terranova Born: New York City, USA, 4 September 1919
World title fights: 5 (all featherweight) won 2, lost 3

Ernie Terrell Born: Chicago, Illinois, USA, 4 April 1939
World title fights: 4 (all heavyweight) won 3, lost 1

Marcel Thil Born: Saint-Dizier, France, 25 May 1904
Died: Cannes, France, 14 August 1968
World title fights: 10 (all middleweight) won 9, lost 0, drew 1

Duane Thomas Born: Detroit, Michigan, USA, 1 February 1961
World title fights: 3 (all junior-middle) won 1, lost 2

Nico Thomas Born: Tonsco, Indonesia, 10 June 1966
World title fights: 3 (all strawweight) won 1, lost 1, drew 1

Pinklon Thomas Born: Pontiac, Michigan, USA, 10 February 1958
World title fights: 4 (all heavyweight) won 2, lost 2

Johnny 'Cyclone' Thompson Born: Ogle County, Illinois, USA, 20 June 1876
Died: Sycamore, Illinois, USA, 28 May 1951
World title fights: 1 (middleweight) won 1, lost 0

Young Jack Thompson Born: Los Angeles, California, USA, 17 August 1904
Died: Los Angeles, California, USA, 9 April 1946
World title fights: 5 (all welterweight) won 2, lost 3

Dick Tiger Born: Amaigbo, Orlu, Nigeria, 14 August 1929
Died: Nigeria, 14 December 1971
World title fights: 10 (6 middleweight, 4 light-heavy) won 6, lost 3, drew 1

Katsuo Tokashiki Born: Okinawa, Japan, 27 July 1960
World title fights: 9 (all junior-fly) won 5, lost 3, drew 1

Tadashi Tomori Born: Okinawa, Japan, 28 December 1959
World title fights: 3 (all junior-fly) won 1, lost 2

Efren Torres Born: Michoacan, Mexico, 29 November 1943
World title fights: 5 (all flyweight) won 2, lost 3

German Torres Born: Celeya Guanajato, Mexico, 28 May 1957
World title fights: 6 (all junior-fly) won 1, lost 5

Jose Torres Born: Playa Ponce, Puerto Rico, 3 May 1936
World title fights: 6 (all light-heavy) won 4, lost 2

Vic Toweel Born: Benoni, Transvaal, South Africa, 12 January 1928
World title fights: 6 (all bantamweight) won 4, lost 2

Tony Tubbs Born: Cincinnati, Ohio, USA, 15 February 1959
World title fights: 3 (all heavyweight) won 1, lost 2

Tony Tucker Born: Grand Rapids, Michigan, USA, 27 December 1958
World title fights: 2 (both heavyweight) won 1, lost 1

Gene Tunney Born: New York City, USA, 25 May 1897
Died: Greenwich, Connecticut, USA, 7 November 1978
World title fights: 3 (all heavyweight) won 3, lost 0

Randolph Turpin Born: Leamington, Warwickshire, England, 7 June 1928
Died: Leamington, Warwickshire, England, 17 May 1966
World title fights: 3 (all middleweight) won 1, lost 2

Mike Tyson Born: Brooklyn, New York, USA, 30 June 1966
World title fights: 11 (all heavyweight) won 10, lost 1

Franco Udella Born: Cagliari, Italy, 25 February 1947
World title fights: 3 (1 flyweight, 2 junior-fly) won 1, lost 2

The last man to beat Mike Tyson before James 'Buster' Douglas was Henry Tillman in the trials for the 1984 Olympics. In 1987 Hillman married Gina Hemphill, grand-daughter of Jesse Owens who carried the Olympic torch into the stadium at the 1984 Los Angeles Games.

A smiling
Mike Tyson outside
the ring.
Put him in
the ring and
that smile
turns to
a sinister snarl
(All Sport/
Bob Martin)

Yasutsune Uehara Born: Okinawa, Japan, 12 October 1949
World title fights: 6 (4 junior-light, 2 featherweight) won 2, lost 4

Amado Ursua Born: Mexico City, Mexico, 13 September 1956
World title fights: 2 (both junior-fly) won 1, lost 1

Jorge Vaca Born: Guadalajara, Mexico, 14 December 1959
World title fights: 3 (all welterweight) won 1, lost 2

Rodrigo Valdez Born: Rocha, Bolivar, Colombia, 22 December 1946
World title fights: 10 (all middleweight) won 6, lost 4

Darrin Van Horn Born: Morgan City, Louisiana, USA, 7 September 1968
World title fights: 2 (both junior-middle) won 1, lost 1

Wilfredo Vasquez Born: Rio Piedras, Puerto Rico, 2 August 1960
World title fights: 4 (all bantamweight) won 1, lost 2, drew 1

Miguel Velasquez Born: Santa Cruz de Tenerife, Spain, 27 December 1944
World title fights: 2 (both junior-welter) won 1, lost 1

Pancho Villa Born: Illoilo, Philippines, 1 August 1901
Died: California, USA, 14 July 1925
World title fights: 3 (all flyweight) won 3, lost 0

Bernabe Villacampo Born: Toledo, Philippines, 6 June 1943
World title fights: 3 (all flyweight) won 1, lost 2

Ben Villaflor Born: Negros, Philippines, 10 November 1952
World title fights: 10 (all junior-light) won 5, lost 2, drew 3

Netrnoi Vorasingh Born: Bangkok, Thailand, 22 April 1959
Died: Thailand, 2 December 1982
World title fights: 5 (all junior-fly) won 2, lost 3

Koichi Wajima Born: Hoikkaido, Japan, 21 April 1943
World title fights: 13 (all junior-middle) won 8, lost 4, drew 1

Jersey Joe Walcott Born: Merchantville, New Jersey, USA, 31 January 1914
World title fights: 8 (all heavyweight) won 2, lost 6

Joe Walcott Born: Barbados, British West Indies, 13 March 1873
Died: Massillon, Ohio, USA, October 1935
World title fights: 7 (1 lightweight, 6 welterweight) won 2, lost 4, drew 1

Mickey Walker Born: Elizabeth, New Jersey, USA, 13 July 1901
Died: Freehold, New Jersey, USA, 28 April 1981
World title fights: 13 (6 welterweight, 5 middleweight, 2 light-heavy) won 9, lost 4

Jimmy Walsh Born: Newton, Massachusetts, USA, 18 July 1886
Died: Newton, Massachusetts, USA, 23 November 1964
World title fights: 3 (1 bantamweight, 2 featherweight) won 1, lost 1, drew 1

Jiro Watanabe Born: Osaka, Japan, 16 March 1955
World title fights: 14 (all junior-bantam) won 12, lost 2

Jim Watt Born: Glasgow, Scotland, 18 July 1948
World title fights: 6 (all lightweight) won 5, lost 1

Mike Weaver Born: Gatesville, Texas, USA, 14 June 1952
World title fights: 7 (all heavyweight) won 3, lost 3, drew 1

Freddie Welsh Born: Pontypridd, Wales, 5 March 1886
Died: New York City, USA, 29 July 1929
World title fights: 4 (all lightweight) won 3, lost 1

Pernell Whitaker Born: Norfolk, Virginia, USA, 2 January 1964
World title fights: 5 (all lightweight) won 4, lost 1

Jimmy Wilde Born: Tylorstown, Wales, 15 May 1892
Died: Cardiff, Wales, 10 March 1969
World title fights: 3 (all flyweight) won 2, lost 1

Jess Willard Born: Pottawatomie County, Kansas, USA, 29 December 1881
Died: Los Angeles, California, USA, 15 December 1968
World title fights: 3 (all heavyweight) won 2, lost 1

Ike Williams Born: Brunswick, Georgia, USA, 2 August 1923
World title fights: 9 (all lightweight) won 8, lost 1

Kid Williams Born: Copenhagen, Denmark, 5 December 1893
Died: Baltimore, Maryland, USA, 18 October 1963
World title fights: 6 (all bantamweight) won 1, lost 2, drew 2, ND 1

Prince Charles Williams Born: Columbus, Mississippi, USA, 2 June 1962
World title fights: 5 (all light-heavy) won 5, lost 0

When
Tim Witherspoon
came to England
to fight
Frank Bruno
in 1986
he took in
some tennis
at Wimbledon
(All Sport/
Simon Bruty)

J. B. Williamson Born: Indianapolis, Indiana, USA, 18 December 1956

World title fights: 2 (both light-heavy) won 1, lost 1

Jackie Wilson Born: Arkansas, USA, 1909

World title fights: 4 (all featherweight) won 2, lost 2

Johnny Wilson Born: New York City, USA, 23 March 1893

Died: Boston, Massachusetts, USA, 8 December 1985

World title fights: 6 (all middleweight) won 2, lost 2, ND 2

Howard Winstone Born: Merthyr Tydfil, Wales, 15 April 1939

World title fights: 5 (all featheweight) won 1, lost 4

Tim Witherspoon Born: Philadelphia, USA, 27 December 1957

World title fights: 6 (all heavyweight) won 3, lost 3

Ad Wolgast Born: Cadillac, Michigan, USA, 8 February 1888

Died: Camarillo, California, USA, 14 April 1955

World title fights: 6 (all lightweight) won 4, lost 2

Midget Wolgast Born: Philadelphia, Pennsylvania, USA, 18 July 1910

Died: Philadelphia, Pennsylvania, USA, 19 October 1955

World title fights: 5 (all flyweight) won 3, lost 1, drew 1

Albert 'Chalky' Wright Born: Durango, Mexico, 10 February 1912

Died: Los Angeles, California, USA, 12 August 1957

World title fights: 5 (all featherweight) won 3, lost 2

Teddy Yarosz Born: Pittsburgh, Pennsylvania, USA, 24 June 1910

Died: Monaca, Pennsylvania, USA, 29 March 1974

World title fights: 2 (both middleweight) won 1, lost 1

Hwan-Kil Yuh Born: Kyongnam, South Korea, 23 September 1962

World title fights: 3 (all junior-light) won 2, lost 1

Jae-Do Yuh Born: Chumra-Nam-Do, South Korea, 25 April 1948

World title fights: 3 (all junior-middle) won 2, lost 1

Myung-Woo Yuh Born: Seoul, South Korea, 10 January 1964

World title fights: 15 (all junior-fly) won 15, lost 0

Dong-Kyun Yum Born: Chung-Buk-Do, South Korea, 17 January 1952

World title fights: 4 (all junior-feather) won 2, lost 2

Tony Zale Born: Gary, Indiana, USA, 29 May 1913

World title fights: 8 (all middleweight) won 6, lost 2

Alfonso Zamora Born: Mexico City, Mexico, 9 February 1954

World title fights: 7 (all bantamweight) won 6, lost 1

Hilario Zapata Born: Colon, Panama, 19 August 1958

World title fights: 23 (14 junior-fly, 9 flyweight) won 18, lost 4, drew 1

Daniel Zaragoza Born: Mexico City, Mexico, 11 December 1959

World title fights: 8 (2 bantamweight, 6 junior-feather) won 6, lost 1, drew 1

Carlos Zarate Born: Tepito, Mexico, 23 May 1951

World title fights: 14 (11 bantamweight, 3 junior-feather) won 10, lost 4

Fritzie Zivic Born: Pittsburgh, Pennsylvania, USA, 8 May 1913

Died: Pittsburgh, Pennsylvania, USA, 16 May 1984

World title fights: 3 (all welterweight) won 2, lost 1

Juan Zurita Born: Guadalajara, Mexico, 12 May 1914

World title fights: 2 (both lightweight) won 1, lost 1

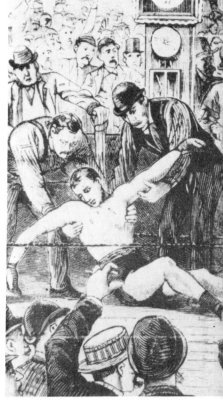

After beating Abe Willis in San Francisco in 1891 George Dixon, seen leaping out of the ring, became the first man to win two world titles. He added the featherweight crown to his bantamweight title (The Mansell Collection)

WORLD TITLE FIGHTS

The following is a list of all title fights generally accepted as being for world titles. Nationalities after fighters' names indicate their country of birth. Details of other claims to world titles are on pp. 121–4.

30 Jul 1884 *M* Jack Dempsey (Ire) KO–22 George Fulljames (USA) New York, USA
3 Feb 1886 *M* Jack Dempsey (Ire) KO–27 Jack Fogarty (USA) New York, USA
4 Mar 1886 *M* Jack Dempsey (Ire) KO–13 George LaBlanche (Can) New York, USA
16 Nov 1887 *L* Jack McAuliffe (Ire) D–74 Jem Carney (GB) Revere, USA. (Declared a draw after the ring had been invaded by spectators who tried to prevent Carney from knocking out McAuliffe.)
13 Dec 1887 *M* Jack Dempsey (Ire) KO–15 Johnny Reagan (USA) Long Island, USA
10 Oct 1888 *L* Jack McAuliffe (Ire) KO–10 Bill Dacey (USA) Dover, USA

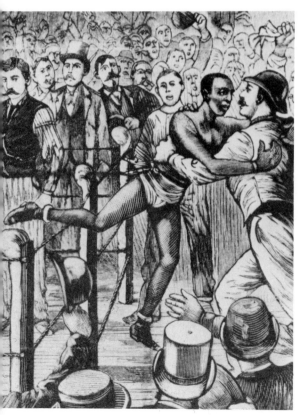

30 Oct 1888 *W* Paddy Duffy (USA) KO–17 William McMillan (GB) Forte Foote, USA
29 Mar 1889 *W* Paddy Duffy (USA) DIS–45 Tom Meadows (Aus) San Francisco, USA
31 Mar 1889 *Fe* Ike Weir (GB) D–80 Frank Murphy (GB) Kouts, USA. (Police stopped fight.)
27 Aug 1889 *M* George LaBlanche (Can) KO–32 Jack Dempsey (Ire) San Francisco, USA. (LaBlanche knocked out Dempsey with illegal pivot blow. He was also over the weight limit. Consequently, Dempsey was deemed not to have lost his title.)
13 Jan 1890 *Fe* Billy Murphy (NZ) KO–14 Ike Weir (GB) San Francisco, USA
18 Feb 1890 *M* Jack Dempsey (Ire) KO–28 Billy McCarthy (Aus) San Francisco, USA
27 Jun 1890 *B* George Dixon (Can) KO–18 Nunc Wallace (GB) London, England
3 Sept 1890 *Fe* Young Griffo (Aus) PTS–15 Billy Murphy (NZ) Sydney, Australia
23 Oct 1890 *B* George Dixon (Can) PTS–40 Johnny Murphy (USA) Providence, USA
14 Jan 1891 *M* Bob Fitzsimmons (GB) RSF–15 Jack Dempsey (Ire) New Orleans, USA
31 Mar 1891 *B* George Dixon (Can) RSF–22 Cal McCarthy (USA) Troy, USA
28 Jul 1891 *Fe* George Dixon (Can) KO–5 Abe Willis (Aus) San Francisco, USA
27 Jun 1892 *Fe* George Dixon (Can) KO–14 Fred Johnson (USA) Coney Island, USA
5 Sep 1892 *L* Jack McAuliffe (Ire) KO–15 Billy Myer (USA) New Orleans, USA
6 Sep 1892 *Fe* George Dixon (Can) KO–8 Jack Skelly (USA) New Orleans, USA
7 Sep 1892 *H* James J. Corbett (USA) KO–21 John L. Sullivan (USA) New Orleans, USA
14 Dec 1892 *W* Mysterious Billy Smith (USA) KO–14 Danny Needham (USA) San Francisco, USA
17 Apr 1893 *W* Mysterious Billy Smith (USA) KO–2 Tom Williams (Aus) New York, USA
8 Aug 1893 *Fe* George Dixon (Can) KO–3 Eddie Pierce (USA) Coney Island, USA
25 Sep 1893 *Fe* George Dixon (Can) KO–7 Solly Smith (USA) Coney Island, USA
25 Jan 1894 *H* James J. Corbett (USA) KO–3 Charlie Mitchell (GB) Jacksonville, USA
26 Jul 1894 *W* Tommy Ryan (USA) PTS–20 Mysterious Billy Smith (USA) Minneapolis, USA
26 Sep 1894 *M* Bob Fitzsimmons (GB) KO–2 Dan Creedon (Aus) New Orleans, USA

26 Sep 1894 *Fe* George Dixon (Can) D–20 Young Griffo (Aus) Boston, USA

18 Jan 1895 *W* Tommy Ryan (USA) KO–3 Jack Dempsey (Ire) New York, USA

27 May 1895 *W* Tommy Ryan (USA) D–18 Mysterious Billy Smith (USA) New York, USA. (Police stopped fight.)

27 Aug 1895 *Fe* George Dixon (Can) PTS–25 Johnny Griffin (USA) Boston, USA

2 Mar 1896 *W* Charles 'Kid' McCoy (USA) KO–15 Tommy Ryan (USA) Long Island, USA

1 Jun 1896 *L* George 'Kid' Lavigne (USA) KO–17 Dick Burge (GB) London, England

27 Oct 1896 *L* George 'Kid' Lavigne (USA) KO–24 Jack Everhardt (USA) New York, USA

8 Feb 1897 *L* George 'Kid' Lavigne (USA) PTS–25 Kid McPartland (USA) New York, USA

17 Mar 1897 *H* Bob Fitzsimmons (GB) KO–14 James J. Corbett (USA) Carson City, USA

7 Apr 1897 *Fe* George Dixon (Can) PTS–25 Frank Erne (Swi) New York, USA

28 Apr 1897 *L* George 'Kid' Lavigne (USA) KO–11 Eddie Connolly (USA) New York, USA

4 Oct 1897 *Fe* Solly Smith (USA) PTS–20 George Dixon (Can) San Francisco, USA

29 Oct 1897 *L* George 'Kid' Lavigne (USA) PTS–12 Joe Walcott (Bar) San Francisco, USA

6 Dec 1897 *B* Jimmy Barry (USA) KO–20 Walter Croot (GB) London, England

25 Feb 1898 *M* Tommy Ryan (USA) KO–18 George Green (USA) San Francisco, USA

17 Mar 1898 *L* George 'Kid' Lavigne (USA) D–20 Jack Daly (USA) Cleveland, USA

30 May 1898 *B* Jimmy Barry (USA) D–20 Casper Leon (Ita) New York, USA

25 Aug 1898 *W* Mysterious Billy Smith (USA) PTS–25 Matty Matthews (USA) New York, USA

26 Sep 1898 *Fe* Dave Sullivan (Ire) RTD–5 Solly Smith (USA) Coney Island, USA

28 Sep 1898 *Fe* George 'Kid' Lavigne (USA) D–20 Frank Erne (Swi) Coney Island, USA

7 Oct 1898 *W* Mysterious Billy Smith (USA) PTS–25 Charley McKeever (USA) New York, USA

24 Oct 1898 *M* Tommy Ryan (USA) PTS–20 Jack Bonner (USA) Coney Island, USA

11 Nov 1898 *Fe* George Dixon (Can) DIS–10 Dave Sullivan (Ire) New York, USA

25 Nov 1898 *L* George 'Kid' Lavigne (USA) PTS–20 Tom Tracy (USA) San Francisco, USA

29 Nov 1898 *Fe* George Dixon (Can) PTS–25 Oscar Gardner (USA) New York, USA

6 Dec 1898 *W* Mysterious Billy Smith (USA) PTS–20 Joe Walcott (Bar) New York, USA

29 Dec 1898 *B* Jimmy Barry (USA) D–20 Casper Leon (Ita) Davenport, USA

17 Jan 1899 *Fe* George Dixon (Can) KO–10 Young Pluto (USA) New York, USA

23 Jan 1899 *W* Mysterious Billy Smith (USA) KO–15 Billy Edwards (Aus) New York, USA

10 Mar 1899 *W* Mysterious Billy Smith (USA) RSF–14 George 'Kid' Lavigne (USA) San Francisco, USA

15 May 1899 *Fe* George Dixon (Can) PTS–20 Kid Broad (USA) Buffalo, USA

2 Jun 1899 *Fe* George Dixon (Can) PTS–25 Joe Bernstein (USA) New York, USA

9 Jun 1899 *H* James J. Jeffries (USA) KO–11 Bob Fitzsimmons (GB) Coney Island, USA

30 Jun 1899 *W* Mysterious Billy Smith (USA) D–20 Charley McKeever (USA) New York, USA

1 Jul 1899 *Fe* George Dixon (Can) PTS–20 Tommy White (USA) Denver, USA

3 Jul 1899 *L* Frank Erne (Swi) PTS–20 George 'Kid' Lavigne (USA) Buffalo, USA

11 Aug 1899 *Fe* George Dixon (Can) D–20 Eddie Santry (USA) New York, USA

12 Sep 1899 *B* Terry McGovern (USA) KO–1 Pedlar Palmer (GB) New York, USA

18 Sep 1899 *M* Tommy Ryan (USA) KO–10 Frank Craig (USA) Coney Island, USA

2 Nov 1899 *Fe* George Dixon (Can) PTS–25 Will Curley (USA) New York, USA

3 Nov 1899 *H* James J. Jeffries (USA) PTS–25 Tom Sharkey (Ire) Coney Island, USA

8 Nov 1899 *W* Mysterious Billy Smith (USA) PTS–20 Charley McKeever (USA) New York, USA

21 Nov 1899 *Fe* George Dixon (Can) PTS–25 Eddie Lenny (USA) New York, USA

4 Dec 1899 *L* Frank Erne (Swi) D–25 Jack O'Brien (USA) Coney Island, USA

22 Dec 1899 *B* Terry McGovern (USA) KO–2 Harry Forbes (USA) New York, USA

9 Jan 1900 *Fe* Terry McGovern (USA) KO–8 George Dixon (Can) New York, USA

15 Jan 1900 *W* Rube Ferns (USA) DIS–21 Mysterious Billy Smith (USA) Buffalo, USA

1 Feb 1900 *Fe* Terry McGovern (USA) KO–5 Eddie Santry (USA) Chicago, USA

9 Mar 1900 *Fe* Terry McGovern (USA) KO–3 Oscar Gardner (USA) New York, USA

23 Mar 1900 *L* Frank Erne (Swi) KO–12 Joe Gans (USA) New York, USA

11 May 1900 *H* James J. Jeffries (USA) KO–23 James J. Corbett (USA) Coney Island, USA

12 Jun 1900 *Fe* Terry McGovern (USA) KO–3 Tommy White (USA) Coney Island, USA

6 Sep 1900 *B* Harry Forbes (USA) D–20 Casper Leon (Ita) St Joseph, USA

16 Oct 1900 *W* Matty Matthews (USA) PTS–15 Rube Ferns (USA) Detroit, USA

2 Nov 1900 *Fe* Terry McGovern (USA) KO–7 Joe Bernstein (USA) Louisville, USA

4 Mar 1901 *Fe* Tommy Ryan (USA) KO–17 Tommy West (USA) Louisville, USA

2 Apr 1901 *B* Harry Forbes (USA) PTS–15 Casper Leon (Ita) Memphis, USA

29 Apr 1901 *W* Matty Matthews (USA) PTS–20 Tom Couhig (USA) Louisville, USA

30 Apr 1901 *Fe* Terry McGovern (USA) KO–4 Oscar Gardner (USA) San Francisco, USA

24 May 1901 *W* Rube Ferns (USA) KO–10 Matty Matthews (USA) Toronto, Canada

29 May 1901 *Fe* Terry McGovern (USA) KO–5 Aurelio Herrera (USA) San Francisco, USA

23 Sep 1901 *W* Rube Ferns (USA) KO–9 Frank Erne (Swi) Fort Erie, USA

15 Nov 1901 *H* James J. Jeffries (USA) RTD–5 Gus Ruthlin (USA) San Francisco, USA

28 Nov 1901 *Fe* Young Corbett (USA) KO–2 Terry McGovern (USA) Hartford, USA

18 Dec 1901 *W* Joe Walcott (Bar) KO–5 Rube Ferns (USA) Fort Erie, USA

23 Jan 1902 *B* Harry Forbes (USA) KO–4 Dan Dougherty (USA) St Louis, USA

27 Feb 1902 *B* Harry Forbes (USA) PTS–15 Tommy Feltz (USA) St Louis, USA

12 May 1902 *L* Joe Gans (USA) KO–1 Frank Erne (Swi) For Erie, USA

*Many thought
that the giant
Jess Willard
was invincible.
But then along
came Jack Dempsey,
here stood
watching over
Willard during
their
world title fight
at Toledo
in 1919.
Dempsey won
in three rounds
(Hulton-Deutsch)*

23 Jun 1902 *W* Joe Walcott (Bar) PTS–15 Tommy West
(GB) London, England
25 Jul 1902 *H* James J. Jeffries (USA) KO–8 Bob
Fitzsimmons (GB) San Francisco, USA
15 Sep 1902 *M* Tommy Ryan (USA) KO–6 Kid Carter (USA)
Fort Erie, USA
17 Sep 1902 *L* Joe Gans (USA) KO–5 Gus Gardner (USA)
Baltimore, USA
23 Dec 1902 *B* Harry Forbes (USA) RSF–7 Frankie Neil
(USA) Oakland, USA
27 Feb 1903 *B* Harry Forbes (USA) PTS–10 Andy Tokell
(GB) Detroit, USA
11 Mar 1903 *L* Joe Gans (USA) KO–11 Steve Crosby (USA)
Hot Springs, USA
22 Apr 1903 *LH* Jack Root (Aut) PTS–10 Charles 'Kid'
McCoy (USA) Detroit, USA
4 Jul 1903 *LH* George Gardner (Ire) KO–12 Jack Root (Aut)
Fort Erie, USA
13 Aug 1903 *B* Frankie Neil (USA) KO–2 Harry Forbes
(USA) San Francisco, USA
14 Aug 1903 *H* James J. Jeffries (USA) KO–10 James J.
Corbett (USA) San Francisco, USA
4 Sep 1903 *B* Frankie Neil (USA) KO–15 Billy de Coursey
(USA) Los Angeles, USA

16 Oct 1903 *B* Frankie Neil (USA) D–20 Johnny Reagan
(USA) Los Angeles, USA
9 Nov 1903 *M* Tommy Ryan (USA) KO–3 Johnny Gorman
(GB) London, England
25 Nov 1903 *LH* Bob Fitzsimmons (GB) PTS–20 George
Gardner (Ire) San Francisco, USA
1 Feb 1904 *Fe* Abe Attell (USA) KO–4 Harry Forbes (USA)
St Louis, USA
28 Mar 1904 *L* Joe Gans (USA) PTS–10 Gus Gardner (USA)
Saginaw, USA
30 Apr 1904 *W* Dixie Kid (USA) DIS–20 Joe Walcott (Bar)
San Francisco, USA
12 May 1904 *W* Dixie Kid (USA) D–20 Joe Walcott (Bar)
San Francisco, USA
17 Jun 1904 *B* Frankie Neil (USA) KO–3 Harry Forbes
(USA) Chicago, USA
26 Aug 1904 *H* James J. Jeffries (USA) KO–2 Jack Munro
(USA) San Francisco, USA
17 Oct 1904 *B* Joe Bowker (GB) PTS–20 Frankie Neil
(USA) London, England
31 Oct 1904 *B* Joe Gans (USA) DIS–5 Jimmy Britt (USA)
San Francisco, USA
22 Feb 1905 *Fe* Abe Attell (USA) D–15 Kid Goodman (USA)
Boston, USA

3 Jul 1905 *H* Marvin Hart (USA) RSF–12 Jack Root (Aut) Reno, USA

20 Oct 1905 *B* Jimmy Walsh (USA) PTS–15 Digger Stanley (GB) Chelsea, USA

20 Dec 1905 *LH* Philadelphia Jack O'Brien (USA) KO–13 Bob Fitzsimmons (GB) San Francisco, USA

23 Feb 1906 *H* Tommy Burns (Can) PTS–20 Marvin Hart (USA) Los Angeles, USA

4 Jul 1906 *Fe* Abe Attell (USA) PTS–20 Frankie Neil (USA) Los Angeles, USA

3 Sep 1906 *L* Joe Gans (USA) DIS–42 Battling Nelson (Den) Goldfield, USA

2 Oct 1906 *H* Tommy Burns (Can) KO–15 Jim Flynn (USA) Los Angeles, USA

16 Oct 1906 *W* Honey Mellody (USA) PTS–15 Joe Walcott (Bar) Chelsea, USA

30 Oct 1906 *Fe* Abe Attell (USA) PTS–20 Harry Baker (USA) Los Angeles, USA

28 Nov 1906 *H/LH* Tommy Burns (Can) D–20 Philadelphia Jack O'Brien (USA) Los Angeles, USA

7 Dec 1906 *Fe* Abe Attell (USA) KO–8 Jimmy Walsh (USA) Los Angeles, USA

18 Jan 1907 *Fe* Abe Attell (USA) KO–8 Harry Baker (USA) Los Angeles, USA

23 Apr 1907 *W* Mike 'Twin' Sullivan (USA) PTS–20 Honey Mellody (USA) Los Angeles, USA

8 May 1907 *H* Tommy Burns (Can) PTS–20 Philadelphia Jack O'Brien (USA) Los Angeles, USA

24 May 1907 *Fe* Abe Attell (USA) PTS–20 Kid Solomon (USA) Los Angeles, USA

4 Jul 1907 *H* Tommy Burns (Can) KO–1 Bill Squires (Aus) Colma, USA

2 Sep 1907 *M* Stanley Ketchel (USA) KO–32 Joe Thomas (USA) Colma, USA

9 Sep 1907 *L* Joe Gans (USA) KO–6 Jimmy Britt (USA) San Francisco, USA

27 Sep 1907 *L* Joe Gans (USA) PTS–20 George Memsic (USA) Los Angeles, USA

29 Oct 1907 *Fe* Abe Attell (USA) KO–4 Freddie Weekes (USA) Los Angeles, USA

2 Dec 1907 *H* Tommy Burns (Can) KO–10 Gunner Moir (GB) London, England

12 Dec 1907 *M* Stanley Ketchel (USA) PTS–20 Joe Thomas (USA) San Francisco, USA

1 Jan 1908 *Fe* Abe Attell (USA) D–25 Owen Moran (GB) San Francisco, USA

10 Feb 1908 *H* Tommy Burns (Can) KO–4 Jack Palmer (GB) London, England

22 Feb 1908 *M* Stanley Ketchel (USA) KO–1 Mike 'Twin' Sullivan (USA) Colma, USA

17 Mar 1908 *H* Tommy Burns (Can) KO–1 Jem Roche (Ire) Dublin, Ireland

1 Apr 1908 *L* Joe Gans (USA) KO–3 Spike Robson (GB) London, England

18 Apr 1908 *H* Tommy Burns (Can) KO–5 Jewey Smith (GB) Paris, France

14 May 1908 *L* Joe Gans (USA) KO–11 Rudy Unholz (USA) San Francisco, USA

4 Jun 1908 *M* Stanley Ketchel (USA) PTS–10 Billy Papke (USA) Milwaukee, USA

13 Jun 1908 *H* Tommy Burns (Can) KO–8 Bill Squires (Aus) Paris, France

4 Jul 1908 *L* Battling Nelson (Den) KO–17 Joe Gans (USA) San Francisco, USA

31 Jul 1908 *M* Stanley Ketchel (USA) KO–3 Hugo Kelly (USA) San Francisco, USA

18 Aug 1908 *M* Stanley Ketchel (USA) KO–2 Joe Thomas (USA) San Francisco, USA

24 Aug 1908 *H* Tommy Burns (Can) KO–13 Bill Squires (Aus) Sydney, Australia

2 Sep 1908 *H* Tommy Burns (Can) KO–6 Bill Lang (Aus) Sydney, Australia

7 Sep 1908 *M* Billy Papke (USA) KO–12 Stanley Ketchel (USA) Vernon, USA

7 Sep 1908 *Fe* Abe Attell (USA) D–23 Owen Moran (GB) San Francisco, USA

9 Sep 1908 *L* Battling Nelson (Den) KO–21 Joe Gans (USA) Colma, USA

26 Nov 1908 *M* Stanley Ketchel (USA) KO–11 Billy Papke (USA) Colma, USA

26 Dec 1908 *H* Jack Johnson (USA) RSF–14 Tommy Burns (Can) Sydney, Australia

26 Mar 1909 *Fe* Abe Attell (USA) KO–8 Frankie White (USA) Dayton, USA

29 May 1909 *L* Battling Nelson (Den) KO–23 Dick Hyland (USA) Colma, USA

22 Jun 1909 *L* Battling Nelson (Den) KO–5 Jack Clifford (USA) Oklahoma, USA

5 Jul 1909 *M* Stanley Ketchel (USA) PTS–20 Billy Papke (USA) Colma, USA

16 Oct 1909 *H* Jack Johnson (USA) KO–12 Stanley Ketchel (USA) Colma, USA

22 Feb 1910 *L* Ad Wolgast (USA) KO–40 Battling Nelson (Den) Port Richmond, USA

28 Feb 1910 *Fe* Abe Attell (USA) KO–6 Harry Forbes (USA) New York, USA

6 Mar 1910 *B* Johnny Coulon (Can) KO–19 Jim Kendrick (GB) New Orleans, USA

19 Mar 1910 *M* Billy Papke (USA) KO–3 Willie Lewis (USA) Paris, France

4 Jul 1910 *H* Jack Johnson (USA) RSF–15 James J. Jeffries (USA) Reno, USA

19 Dec 1910 *B* Johnny Coulon (Can) PTS–15 Earl Denning (USA) Memphis, USA

11 Feb 1911 *M* Cyclone Johnny Thompson (USA) PTS–20 Billy Papke (USA) Sydney, Australia

7 Mar 1911 *L* Ad Wolgast (USA) KO–9 George Memsic (USA) Los Angeles, USA

27 May 1911 *L* Ad Wolgast (USA) KO–16 Frankie Burns (USA) San Francisco, USA

8 Jun 1911 *M* Billy Papke (USA) KO–9 Jim Sullivan (GB) London, England

4 Jul 1911 *L* Ad Wolgast (USA) KO–13 Owen Moran (GB) San Francisco, USA

3 Feb 1912 *B* Johnny Coulon (Can) PTS–20 Frankie Conley (USA) Vernon, USA

18 Feb 1912 *B* Johnny Coulon (Can) PTS–20 Frankie Burns (USA) New Orleans, USA

22 Feb 1912 *Fe* Johnny Kilbane (USA) PTS–20 Abe Attell (USA) Vernon, USA

21 May 1912 *Fe* Johnny Kilbane (USA) D–12 Jimmy Walsh (USA) Boston, USA

29 Jun 1912 *M* Billy Papke (USA) RTD–15 Marcel Moreau (Fra) Paris, France

4 Jul 1912 *H* Jack Johnson (USA) KO–9 Jim Flynn (USA) Las Vegas, USA

4 Jul 1912 *L* Ad Wolgast (USA) KO–13 Joe Rivers (Mex) Vernon, USA

18 Oct 1912 *B* Johnny Coulon (Can) ND–10 Kid Williams (Den) New York, USA

23 Oct 1912 *M* Billy Papke (USA) RTD–17 Georges Carpentier (Fra) Paris, France

28 Nov 1912 *L* Willie Ritchie (USA) DIS–16 Ad Wolgast(USA) Daly City, USA

4 Dec 1912 *M* Billy Papke (USA) RTD–6 George Bernard (Fra) Paris, France

London-born Ted 'Kid' Lewis was born as Gershon Mendeloff . . . little wonder he changed it. His world welterweight contests with Jack Britton are among the most legendary series of contests in boxing history (Hulton)

5 Mar 1913 *M* Frank Klaus (USA) DIS–15 Billy Papke (USA) Paris, France

29 Apr 1913 *Fe* Johnny Kilbane (USA) D–20 Johnny Dundee (Ita) Vernon, USA

4 Jul 1913 *L* Willie Ritchie (USA) KO–11 Joe Rivers (Mex) San Francisco, USA

11 Oct 1913 *M* George Chip (USA) KO–6 Frank Klaus (USA) Pittsburgh, USA

28 Nov 1913 *H* Jack Johnson (USA) KO–2 Andre Sproul (Fra) Paris, France

19 Dec 1913 *H* Jack Johnson (USA) D–20 Jim Johnson (USA) Paris, France

23 Dec 1913 *M* George Chip (USA) KO–5 Frankie Klaus (USA) Pittsburgh, USA

7 Apr 1914 *M* Al McCoy (USA) KO–1 George Chip (USA) Brooklyn, USA

17 Apr 1914 *L* Willie Ritchie (USA) PTS–20 Harlem Tommy Murphy (USA) San Francisco, USA

28 Apr 1914 *LH* Jack Dillon (USA) PTS–10 Al Norton (USA) Kansas City, USA

3 Jun 1914 *B* Kid Williams (Den) KO–3 Johnny Coulon (Can) Los Angeles, USA

27 Jun 1914 *H* Jack Johnson (USA) PTS–20 Frank Moran (USA) Paris, France

7 Jul 1914 *L* Freddie Welsh (GB) PTS–20 Willie Ritchie (USA) London, England

5 Apr 1915 *H* Jess Willard (USA) KO–26 Jack Johnson (USA) Havana, Cuba

31 Aug 1915 *W* Ted 'Kid' Lewis (GB) PTS–12 Jack Britton (USA) Boston, USA

10 Sep 1915 *B* Johnny Ertle (Aut) DIS–5 Kid Williams (Den) St Paul, USA. Williams argued that the bout took place in a town where decisions were prohibited. Consequently he claimed he could not be disqualified. He continued to be regarded as the champion.

27 Sep 1915 *W* Ted 'Kid' Lewis (GB) PTS–12 Jack Britton (USA) Boston, USA

6 Dec 1915 *B* Kid Williams (Den) D–20 Frankie Burns (USA) New Orleans, USA

France's best known fighter, Georges Carpentier, is depicted here knocking out Marcel Nilles in the 1st round of their French heavyweight title bout in Paris in 1923 (ADPC Sport)

7 Feb 1916 *B* Kid Williams (Den) D–20 Pete Herman (USA) New Orleans, USA

25 Mar 1916 *H* Jess Willard (USA) ND–10 Frank Moran (USA) New York, USA

24 Apr 1916 *W* Jack Britton (USA) PTS–20 Ted 'Kid' Lewis (GB) New Orleans, USA

25 Apr 1916 *LH* Jack Dillon (USA) PTS–15 Battling Levinsky (USA) Kansas City, USA

4 Jul 1916 *L* Freddie Welsh (GB) DIS–11 Ad Wolgast (USA) Denver, USA

4 Sep 1916 *L* Freddie Welsh (GB) PTS–20 Charlie White (GB) Colorado Springs, USA

4 Sep 1916 *Fe* Johnny Kilbane (USA) KO–3 George 'Kayo' Chaney (USA) Cedar Point, USA

17 Oct 1916 *LH* Jack Dillon (USA) PTS–10 Tim O'Neill (USA) New York, USA

24 Oct 1916 *LH* Battling Levinsky (USA) PTS–12 Jack Dillon (USA) Boston, USA

18 Dec 1916 *Fl* Jimmy Wilde (GB) KO–11 Young Zulu Kid (Ita) London, England

9 Jan 1917 *B* Pete Herman (USA) PTS–20 Kid Williams (Den) New Orleans, USA

12 Mar 1917 *Fl* Jimmy Wilde (GB) RTD–4 George Clark (GB) London, England

28 May 1917 *L* Benny Leonard (USA) KO–9 Freddie Welsh (GB) New York, USA

25 Jun 1917 *W* Ted 'Kid' Lewis (GB) PTS–20 Jack Britton (USA) Dayton, USA

4 Jul 1917 *W* Ted 'Kid' Lewis (GB) ND–15 Johnny Griffiths (USA) Akron, USA

25 Jul 1917 *L* Benny Leonard (USA) RTD–3 Johnny Kilbane (USA) Philadelphia, USA

31 Aug 1917 *W* Ted 'Kid' Lewis (GB) KO–1 Albert Badoud (Swe) New York, USA

5 Nov 1917 *B* Pete Herman (USA) PTS–20 Frankie Burns (USA) New Orleans, USA

14 Nov 1917 *M* Mike O'Dowd (USA) KO–6 Al McCoy (USA) Brooklyn, USA

17 May 1918 *W* Ted 'Kid' Lewis (GB) RTD–20 Johnny Tillman (USA) Denver, USA

4 Jul 1918 *W* Ted 'Kid' Lewis (GB) ND–20 Johnny Griffiths (USA) Akron, USA

17 Mar 1919 *W* Jack Britton (USA) KO–9 Ted 'Kid' Lewis (GB) Canton, USA

5 May 1919 *W* Jack Britton (USA) PTS–15 Johnny Griffiths (USA) Buffalo, USA

4 Jul 1919 *H* Jack Dempsey (USA) RTD–3 Jess Willard (USA) Toledo, USA

17 Jul 1919 *M* Mike O'Dowd (USA) KO–3 Al McCoy (USA) St Paul, USA

21 Apr 1920 *Fe* Johnny Kilbane (USA) KO–7 Alvie Miller (USA) Lorian, USA

6 May 1920 *M* Johnny Wilson (USA) PTS–12 Mike O'Dowd (USA) Boston, USA

31 May 1920 *W* Jack Britton (USA) PTS–15 Johnny Griffiths (USA) Akron, USA

5 Jul 1920 *L* Benny Leonard (USA) KO–8 Charlie White (USA) Benton Harbor, USA

23 Aug 1920 *W* Jack Britton (USA) D–12 Lou Bogash (USA) Bridgeport, USA

6 Sep 1920 *H* Jack Dempsey (USA) KO–3 Billy Miske (USA) Benton Harbor, USA

12 Oct 1920 *LH* Georges Carpentier (Fra) KO–4 Battling Levinsky (USA) Jersey City, USA

26 Nov 1920 *L* Benny Leonard (USA) RSF–14 Joe Welling (USA) New York, USA

14 Dec 1920 *H* Jack Dempsey (USA) KO–12 Bill Brennan (USA) New York, USA

22 Dec 1920 *B* Joe Lynch (USA) PTS–15 Pete Herman (USA) New York, USA

14 Jan 1921 *L* Benny Leonard (USA) RSF–6 Ritchie Mitchell (USA) New York, USA

17 Jan 1921 *M* Johnny Wilson (USA) ND–12 George Chip (USA) Pittsburgh, USA

7 Feb 1921 *W* Jack Britton (USA) PTS–15 Ted 'Kid' Lewis (GB) New York, USA

17 Mar 1921 *M* Johnny Wilson (USA) PTS–15 Mike O'Dowd (USA) New York, USA

2 Jul 1921 *H* Jack Dempsey (USA) KO–4 Georges Carpentier (Fra) New Jersey, USA

25 Jul 1921 *B* Pete Herman (USA) PTS–15 Joe Lynch (USA) Brooklyn, USA

5 Sep 1921 *M* Johnny Wilson (USA) ND–12 Bryan Downey (USA) Jersey City, USA

17 Sep 1921 *Fe* Johnny Kilbane (USA) KO–7 Danny Frush (GB) Cleveland, USA

23 Sep 1921 *B* Johnny Buff (USA) PTS–15 Pete Herman (USA) New York, USA

10 Nov 1921 *B* Johnny Buff (USA) PTS–15 Little Jack Sharkey (Ita) New York, USA

18 Nov 1921 *JL* Johnny Dundee (Ita) DIS–5 George Chaney (USA) New York, USA

10 Feb 1922 *L* Benny Leonard (USA) PTS–15 Rocky Kansas (USA) New York, USA

17 Feb 1922 *W* Jack Britton (USA) D–15 Dave Shade (USA) New York, USA

11 May 1922 *LH* Georges Carpentier (Fra) KO–1 Ted 'Kid' Lewis (GB) London, England

26 Jun 1922 *W* Jack Britton (USA) DIS–13 Benny Leonard (USA) New York, USA

4 Jul 1922 *L* Benny Leonard (USA) RTD–8 Rocky Kansas (USA) Michigan, USA

8 Jul 1922 *JL* Johnny Dundee (Ita) PTS–15 Little Jack Sharkey (Ita) New York, USA

10 Jul 1922 *B* Joe Lynch (USA) RTD–14 Johnny Buff (USA) New York, USA

14 Aug 1922 *M(NY)* Dave Rosenberg (USA) PTS–15 Phil Krug (USA) New York, USA

15 Aug 1922 *Fe(NY)* Johnny Dundee (Ita) KO–9 Danny Frush (GB) Brooklyn, USA

24 Sep 1922 *LH* Battling Siki (Sen) KO–6 Georges Carpentier (Fra) Paris, France

1 Nov 1922 *W* Mickey Walker (USA) PTS–15 Jack Britton (USA) New York, USA

30 Nov 1922 *M(NY)* Mike O'Dowd (USA) DIS–8 Dave Rosenberg (USA) New York, USA

22 Dec 1922 *B* Joe Lynch (USA) PTS–15 Midget Smith (USA) New York, USA

2 Feb 1923 *JL* Johnny Dundee (Ita) PTS–15 Elino Flores (Phi) New York, USA

17 Mar 1923 *LH* Mike McTigue (Ire) PTS–20 Battling Siki (Sen) Dublin, Ireland

22 Mar 1923 *W* Mickey Walker (USA) ND–12 Pete Latzo (USA) Newark, USA

30 May 1923 *JL* Jack Bernstein (USA) PTS–15 Johnny Dundee (Ita) New York, USA

2 Jun 1923 *Fe* Eugene Criqui (Fra) KO–6 Johnny Kilbane (USA) New York, USA

18 Jun 1923 *Fl* Pancho Villa (Phi) KO–7 Jimmy Wilde (GB) New York, USA

4 Jul 1923 *H* Jack Dempsey (USA) PTS–15 Tom Gibbons (USA) Shelby, USA

24 Jul 1923 *L* Benny Leonard (USA) PTS–15 Lew Tendler (USA) New York, USA

26 Jul 1923 *Fe* Johnny Dundee (Ita) PTS–15 Eugene Criqui (Fra) New York, USA

31 Aug 1923 *M* Harry Greb (USA) PTS–15 Johnny Wilson (USA) New York, USA

14 Sep 1923 *H* Jack Dempsey (USA) KO–2 Luis 'Angel' Firpo (Arg) New York, USA

13 Oct 1923 *Fl* Pancho Villa (Phi) PTS–15 Benny Schwartz (USA) Baltimore, USA

19 Oct 1923 *B(NY)* Abe Goldstein (USA) PTS–12 Joe Burman (USA) New York, USA

3 Dec 1923 *M* Harry Greb (USA) PTS–10 Bryan Downey (USA) Pittsburgh, USA

17 Dec 1923 *JL* Johnny Dundee (Ita) PTS–15 Jack Bernstein (USA) New York, USA

18 Jan 1924 *M* Harry Greb (USA) PTS–15 Johnny Wilson (USA) New York, USA

21 Mar 1924 *B* Abe Goldstein (USA) PTS–15 Joe Lynch (USA) New York, USA

24 Mar 1924 *M* Harry Greb (USA) KO–12 Fay Kaiser (USA) Baltimore, USA

30 May 1924 *Fl* Pancho Villa (Phi) PTS–15 Frankie Ash (USA) Brooklyn, USA

2 Jun 1924 *W* Mickey Walker (USA) PTS–10 Lew Tendler (USA) Philadelphia, USA

20 Jun 1924 *JL* Steve 'Kid' Sullivan (USA) PTS–15 Johnny Dundee (Ita) New York, USA

26 Jun 1924 *M* Harry Greb (USA) PTS–15 Ted Moore (GB) New York, USA

16 Jul 1924 *B* Abe Goldstein (USA) PTS–15 Charles Ledoux (Fra) New York, USA

8 Sep 1924 *B* Abe Goldstein (USA) PTS–15 Tommy Ryan (USA) New York, USA

12 Oct 1924 *W* Mickey Walker (USA) KO–6 Bobby Barrett (USA) Philadelphia, USA

15 Oct 1924 *JL* Steve 'Kid' Sullivan (USA) KO–5 Mike Ballerino (USA) New York, USA

19 Dec 1924 *B* Eddie 'Cannonball' Martin (USA) PTS–15 Abe Goldstein (USA) New York, USA

2 Jan 1925 *Fe* Louis 'Kid' Kaplan (USSR) RTD–9 Danny Kramer (USA) New York, USA

20 Mar 1925 *B* Charley Phil Rosenberg (USA) PTS–15 Eddie 'Cannonball' Martin (USA) New York, USA

1 Apr 1925 *JL* Mike Ballerino (USA) PTS–10 Steve 'Kid' Sullivan (USA) Philadelphia, USA

31 May 1925 *LH* Paul Berlenbach (USA) PTS–15 Mike McTigue (Ire) New York, USA

2 Jul 1925 *M* Harry Greb (USA) PTS–15 Mickey Walker (USA) New York, USA

13 Jul 1925 *L* Jimmy Goodrich (USA) KO–2 Stanislaus Loayza (Chi) Long Island, USA

23 Jul 1925 *B* Charley Phil Rosenberg (USA) KO–4 Eddie Shea (USA) New York, USA

22 Aug 1925 *Fl* Fidel La Barba (USA) PTS–10 Frankie Genaro (USA) Los Angeles, USA

27 Aug 1925 *Fe* Louis 'Kid' Kaplan (USSR) D–15 Babe Herman (Por) Waterbury, USA

11 Sep 1925 *LH* Paul Berlenbach (USA) PTS–15 Jimmy Slattery (USA) New York, USA

12 Sep 1925 *W* Mickey Walker (USA) PTS–15 Dave Shade (USA) New York, USA

13 Nov 1925 *M* Harry Greb (USA) PTS–15 Tony Marullo (USA) New Orleans, USA

2 Dec 1925 *JL* Tod Morgan (USA) KO–10 Mike Ballerino (USA) Los Angeles, USA

8 Dec 1925 *L* Rocky Kansas (USA) PTS–15 Jimmy Goodrich (USA) New York, USA

11 Dec 1925 *LH* Paul Berlenbach (USA) PTS–15 Jack Delaney (Can) New York, USA

18 Dec 1925 *Fe* Louis 'Kid' Kaplan (USSR) PTS–15 Babe Herman (Por) New York, USA

26 Feb 1926 *M* Tiger Flowers (USA) PTS–15 Harry Greb (USA) New York, USA

2 Mar 1926 *B* Charley Phil Rosenberg (USA) PTS–10 George Butch (USA) St Louis, USA

20 May 1926 *W* Pete Latzo (USA) PTS–10 Mickey Walker (USA) Scranton, USA

10 Jun 1926 *LH* Paul Berlenbach (USA) PTS–15 Young Stribling (USA) New York, USA

29 Jun 1926 *W* Pete Latzo (USA) KO–5 Willie Harmon (USA) Newark, USA

3 Jul 1926 *L* Sammy Mandell (USA) PTS–10 Rocky Kansas (USA) Chicago, USA

9 Jul 1926 *W* Pete Latzo (USA) DIS–4 George Levine (USA) New York, USA

16 Jul 1926 *LH* Jack Delaney (Can) PTS–15 Paul Berlenbach (USA) New York, USA

19 Aug 1926 *M* Tiger Flowers (USA) PTS–15 Harry Greb (USA) New York, USA

21 Sep 1926 *LW* Mushy Callahan (USA) PTS–10 Pinkey Mitchell (USA) Vernon, USA

23 Sep 1926 *H* Gene Tunney (USA) PTS–10 Jack Dempsey (USA) Philadelphia, USA

19 Nov 1926 *JL* Tod Morgan (USA) PTS–15 Carl Duane (USA) New York, USA

3 Dec 1926 *M* Mickey Walker (USA) PTS–10 Tiger Flowers (USA) Chicago, USA

21 Jan 1927 *Fl* Fidel La Barba (USA) PTS–12 Elky Clark (GB) New York, USA

Luis Angel Firpo of Argentina knocks the defending champion Jack Dempsey through the ropes in the 1st round, in New York in 1923. It was a remarkable contest; Dempsey was floored twice in the opening round and Firpo seven times. The fight ended in the 2nd round with Dempsey retaining his title (Hulton)

4 Feb 1927 *B* Charley Phil Rosenberg (USA) PTS–15 Bushy Graham (Ita) New York, USA

26 Mar 1927 *B(NBA)* Bud Taylor (USA) D–10 Tony Canzoneri (USA) Chicago, USA

3 Jun 1927 *W* Joe Dundee (Ita) PTS–15 Pete Latzo (USA) New York, USA

24 Jun 1927 *B(NBA)* Bud Taylor (USA) PTS–10 Tony Canzoneri (USA) Chicago,USA

30 Jun 1927 *M* Mickey Walker (USA) KO–10 Tommy Milligan (GB) London, England

30 Aug 1927 *LH(NBA)* Jimmy Slattery (USA) PTS–10 Maxie Rosenbloom (USA) Hartford, USA

19 Sep 1927 *Fe* Benny Bass (USSR) PTS–10 Red Chapman (USA) Philadelphia, USA

22 Sep 1927 *H* Gene Tunney (USA) PTS–10 Jack Dempsey (USA) Chicago, USA

7 Oct 1927 *LH* Tommy Loughran (USA) PTS–15 Mike McTigue (Ire) New York, USA

24 Oct 1927 *Fe(NY)* Tony Canzoneri (USA) PTS–15 Johnny Dundee (Ita) New York, USA

28 Nov 1927 *Fl(NBA)* Albert 'Frenchie' Belanger (Can) PTS–10 Frankie Genaro (USA) Toronto, Canada

12 Dec 1927 *LH* Tommy Loughran (USA) PTS–15 Jimmy Slattery (USA) New York, USA

16 Dec 1927 *Fl(NY)* Corporal Izzy Schwartz (USA) PTS–15 Newsboy Brown (USSR) New York, USA

19 Dec 1927 *Fl(NBA)* Albert 'Frenchie' Belanger (Can) PTS–10 Ernie Jarvis (GB) Toronto, Canada

6 Jan 1928 *LH* Tommy Loughran (USA) PTS–15 Leo Lomski (USA) New York, USA

6 Feb 1928 *Fl(NBA)* Frankie Genaro (USA) PTS–10 Albert 'Frenchie' Belanger (Can) Toronto, Canada

10 Feb 1928 *Fe* Tony Canzoneri (USA) PTS–15 Benny Bass (USSR) New York, USA

9 Apr 1928 *Fl(NY)* Corporal Izzy Schwartz (USA) PTS–15 Routier Parra (Arg) New York, USA

21 May 1928 *L* Sammy Mandell (USA) PTS–15 Jimmy McLarnin (Ire) New York, USA

23 May 1928 *B(NY)* Bushy Graham (Ita) PTS–15 Corporal Izzy Schwartz (USA) Brooklyn, USA

1 Jun 1928 *LH* Tommy Loughran (USA) PTS–15 Pete Latzo (USA) Brooklyn, USA

21 Jun 1928 *M* Mickey Walker (USA) PTS–10 Ace Hudkins (USA) Chicago, USA

7 Jul 1928 *W* Joe Dundee (Ita) KO–8 Hilario Martinez (Spa) Barcelona, Spain

16 Jul 1928 *LH* Tommy Loughran (USA) PTS–10 Pete Latzo (USA) Wilkes-Barre, USA

18 Jul 1928 *JL* Tod Morgan (USA) PTS–15 Eddie 'Cannonball' Martin (USA) New York, USA

20 Jul 1928 *Fl(NY)* Corporal Izzy Schwartz (USA) DIS–4 Frisco Grande (Phi) New York, USA

23 Jul 1928 *H* Gene Tunney (USA) RSF–11 Tom Heeney (NZ) New York, USA

28 Sep 1928 *Fe* Andre Routis (Fra) PTS–15 Tony Canzoneri (USA) New York, USA

2 Mar 1929 *Fl(NBA)* Emile Pladner (Fra) KO–1 Frankie Genaro (USA) Paris, France

12 Mar 1929 *Fl(NY)* Corporal Izzy Schwartz (USA) PTS–12 Albert 'Frenchie' Belanger (Can) Toronto, Canada

25 Mar 1929 *W* Jackie Fields (USA) PTS–10 Young Jack Thompson (USA) Chicago, USA

28 Mar 1929 *LH* Tommy Loughran (USA) PTS–10 Mickey Walker (USA) Chicago, USA

5 Apr 1929 *JL* Tod Morgan (USA) PTS–10 Santiago Zorilla (Pan) Los Angeles, USA

18 Apr 1929 *Fl(NBA)* Frankie Genaro (USA) DIS–5 Emile Pladner (Fra) Paris, France

20 May 1929 *JL* Tod Morgan (USA) PTS–10 Baby Salsario (Mex) Los Angeles, USA

25 May 1929 *Fe* Andre Routis (Fra) KO–3 Buster Brown (USA) Baltimore, USA

18 Jun 1929 *B* Panama Al Brown (Pan) PTS–15 Vidal Gregorio (Spa) New York, USA

18 Jul 1929 *LH* Tommy Loughran (USA) PTS–15 Jimmy Braddock (USA) New York, USA

25 Jul 1929 *W* Jackie Fields (USA) DIS–2 Joe Dundee (Ita) Detroit, USA

2 Aug 1929 *L* Sammy Mandell (USA) PTS–10 Tony Canzoneri (USA) Chicago, USA

23 Sep 1929 *Fe* Battling Battalino (USA) PTS–15 Andre Routis (Fra) Hartford, USA

17 Oct 1929 *Fl(NBA)* Frankie Genaro (USA) PTS–15 Ernie Jarvis (GB) London, England

29 Oct 1929 *M* Mickey Walker (USA) PTS–10 Ace Hudkins (USA) Los Angeles, USA

19 Dec 1929 *JL* Benny Bass (USSR) KO–2 Tod Morgan (USA) New York, USA

18 Jan 1930 *Fl(NBA)* Frankie Genaro (USA) RTD–12 Yvon Trevidic (Fra) Paris, France

10 Feb 1930 *LH(NY)* Jimmy Slattery (USA) PTS–15 Lou Scozza (USA) Buffalo, USA

18 Feb 1930 *LW(NY)* Jack 'Kid' Berg (GB) RTD–10 Mushy Callahan (USA) London, England

21 Mar 1930 *Fl(NY)* Midget Wolgast (USA) PTS–15 Black Bill (USA) New York, USA

9 May 1930 *W* Young Jack Thompson (USA) PTS–15 Jackie Fields (USA) Detroit, USA

16 May 1930 *Fl(NY)* Midget Wolgast (USA) RTD–5 Willie La Morte (USA) New York, USA

10 Jun 1930 *Fl(NBA)* Frankie Genaro (USA) PTS–10 Albert 'Frenchie' Belanger (Can) Toronto, Canada

12 Jun 1930 *H* Max Schmeling (Ger) DIS–4 Jack Sharkey (USA) New York, USA

12 Jun 1930 *LW(NY)* Jack 'Kid' Berg (GB) RSF–10 Herman Perlick (USA) New York, USA

25 Jun 1930 *LH(NY)* Maxie Rosenbloom (USA) PTS–15 Jimmy Slattery (USA) Buffalo, USA

17 Jul 1930 *L* Al Singer (USA) KO–1 Sammy Mandell (USA) New York, USA

6 Aug 1930 *Fl(NBA)* Frankie Genaro (USA) PTS–10 Willie La Morte (USA) Newark, USA

3 Sep 1930 *LW(NY)* Jack 'Kid' Berg (GB) PTS–10 Buster Brown (USA) Newark, USA

5 Sep 1930 *W* Tommy Freeman (USA) PTS–15 Young Jack Thompson (USA) Cleveland, USA

4 Oct 1930 *B* Panama Al Brown (Pan) PTS–15 Eugene Huat (Fra) Paris, France

22 Oct 1930 *LH(NY)* Maxie Rosenbloom (USA) KO–11 Abe Bain (USA) New York, USA

14 Nov 1930 *L* Tony Canzoneri (USA) KO–1 Al Singer (USA) New York, USA

12 Dec 1930 *Fe* Battling Battalino (USA) PTS–15 Kid Chocolate (Cuba) New York, USA

26 Dec 1930 *Fl* Frankie Genaro (USA) D–15 Midget Wolgast (USA) New York, USA

9 Jan 1931 *W* Tommy Freeman (USA) PTS–10 Pete August (USA) Hot Springs, USA

23 Jan 1931 *LW* Jack 'Kid' Berg (GB) PTS–10 Goldie Hess (Nor) Chicago, USA

26 Jan 1931 *W* Tommy Freeman (USA) PTS–10 Eddie Murdock (USA) Oklahoma, USA

5 Feb 1931 *W* Tommy Freeman (USA) KO–5 Duke
      Trammel (USA) Memphis, USA

9 Feb 1931 *W* Tommy Freeman (USA) KO–5 Al 'Kid' Kober
      (USA) New Orleans, USA

11 Feb 1931 *B* Panama Al Brown (Pan) PTS–10 Nick Bensa
      (Fra) Paris, France

1 Mar 1931 *W* Tommy Freeman (USA) KO–12 Alfredo
      Gaona (Mex) Mexico City, Mexico

25 Mar 1931 *Fl(NBA)* Frankie Genaro (USA) D–15 Victor
      Ferrand (Spa) Barcelona, Spain

14 Apr 1931 *W* Young Jack Thompson(USA) KO–12
      Tommy Freeman (USA) Cleveland, USA

23 Apr 1931 *LW/L* Tony Canzoneri (USA) KO–3 Jack 'Kid'
      Berg (GB) Chicago, USA

22 May 1931 *Fe* Battling Battalino (USA) PTS–15 Fidel La
      Barba (USA) New York, USA

1 Jul 1931 *Fe* Battling Battalino (USA) PTS–10 Irish Bobby
      Brady (USA) Jersey City, USA

3 Jul 1931 *H* Max Schmeling (Ger) RSF–15 Young Tribling
      (USA) Cleveland, USA

13 Jul 1931 *LW* Tony Canzoneri (USA) PTS–10 Cecil Payne
      (USA) Los Angeles, USA

13 Jul 1931 *Fl(NY)* Midget Wolgast (USA) PTS–15 Ruby
      Bradley (USA) New York, USA

15 Jul 1931 *JL* Kid Chocolate (Cuba) RSF–7 Benny Bass
      (USSR) Philadelphia, USA

23 Jul 1931 *Fe* Battling Battalino (USA) PTS–15 Freddie
      Miller (USA) Cincinnati, USA

30 Jul 1931 *Fl(NBA)* Frankie Genaro (USA) KO–6 Jackie
      Harmon (USA) Waterbury, USA

5 Aug 1931 *LH(NY)* Maxie Rosenbloom (USA) PTS–15
      Jimmy Slattery (USA) New York, USA

25 Aug 1931 *M(NBA)* Gorilla Jones (USA) PTS–10 Tiger
      Thomas (USA) Milwaukee, USA

25 Aug 1931 *B* Panama Al Brown (Pan) PTS–15 Pete
      Sanstol (Nor) Montreal, Canada

10 Sep 1931 *L* Tony Canzoneri (USA) PTS–15 Jack 'Kid'
      Berg (GB) New York, USA

3 Oct 1931 *Fl(NBA)* Frankie Genaro (USA) PTS–15 Valentin
      Angelmann (Fra) Paris, France

23 Oct 1931 *W* Lou Brouillard (Can) PTS–15 Young Jack
      Thompson (USA) Boston, USA

27 Oct 1931 *B* Panama Al Brown (Pan) PTS–15 Eugene
      Huat (Fra) Montreal, Canada

27 Oct 1931 *Fl(NBA)* Young Perez (Tun) KO–2 Frankie
      Genaro (USA) Paris, France

29 Oct 1931 *LW* Tony Canzoneri (USA) PTS–10 Phillie
      Griffin (USA) Newark, USA

4 Nov 1931 *Fe* Battling Battalino (USA) PTS–10 Eddie
      Mastro (USA) Chicago, USA

20 Nov 1931 *LW/L* Tony Canzoneri (USA) PTS–15 Kid
      Chocolate (Cuba) New York, USA

18 Jan 1932 *LW* Johnny Jadick (USA) PTS–10 Tony
      Canzoneri (USA) Philadelphia, USA

25 Jan 1932 *M(NBA)* Gorilla Jones (USA) KO–6 Oddone
      Piazza (Ita) Milwaukee, USA

28 Jan 1932 *W* Jackie Fields (USA) PTS–10 Lou Brouillard
      (Can) Chicago, USA

18 Mar 1932 *LH(NBA)* George Nichols (USA) PTS–10 Dave
      Maier (USA) Chicago, USA

26 Apr 1932 *M(NBA)* Gorilla Jones (USA) PTS–12 Young
      Terry (USA) Trenton, USA

26 May 1932 *Fe(NBA)* Tommy Paul (USA) PTS–15 Johnny
      Pena (USA) Detroit, USA

31 May 1932 *LH(NBA)* Lou Scozza (USA) PTS–10 George
      Nichols (USA) Buffalo, USA

11 Jun 1932 *M(NBA)* Marcel Thil (Fra) DIS–11 Gorilla
      Jones (USA) Paris, France

21 Jun 1932 *H* Jack Sharkey (USA) PTS–15 Max
      Schmeling (Ger) Long Island, USA

4 Jul 1932 *M(NBA)* Marcel Thil (Fra) PTS–15 Len Harvey
      (GB) London, England

10 Jul 1932 *B* Panama Al Brown (Pan) PTS–15 Kid Francis
      (Fra) Marseilles, France

14 Jul 1932 *LH* Maxie Rosenbloom (USA) PTS–15 Lou
      Scozza (USA) Buffalo, USA

18 Jul 1932 *LW* Johnny Jadick (USA) PTS–10 Tony
      Canzoneri (USA) Philadelphia, USA

4 Aug 1932 *Fe(NY)* Kid Chocolate (Cuba) PTS–10 Eddie
      Shea (USA) Chicago, USA

19 Sep 1932 *B* Panama Al Brown (Pan) KO–1 Emile
      Pladner (Fra) Toronto, Canada

13 Oct 1932 *Fe(NY)* Kid Chocolate (Cuba) KO–12 Lew
      Feldman (USA) New York, USA

31 Oct 1932 *Fl(NBA)* Jackie Brown (GB) RSF–13 Young
      Perez (Tun) Manchester, England

4 Nov 1932 *L* Tony Canzoneri (USA) PTS–15 Billy Petrolle
      (USA) New York, USA

21 Nov 1932 *M(NY)* Ben Jeby (USA) PTS–15 Chick Devlin
      (USA) New York, USA

9 Dec 1932 *Fe(NY)* Kid Chocolate (Cuba) PTS–15 Fidel La
      Barba (USA) New York, USA

13 Jan 1933 *M(NY)* Ben Jeby (USA) KO–12 Frank Battaglia
      (Can) New York, USA

13 Jan 1933 *Fe(NBA)* Freddie Miller (USA) PTS–10 Tommy
      Paul (USA) Chicago, USA

30 Jan 1933 *M(NBA)* Gorilla Jones (USA) KO–7 Sammy
      Slaughter (USA) Cleveland, USA

20 Feb 1933 *LW* Battling Shaw (Mex) PTS–10 Johnny Jadick
      (USA) New Orleans, USA

22 Feb 1933 *LH* Maxie Rosenbloom (USA) PTS–10 Al
      Stillman (USA) St Louis, USA

22 Feb 1933 *W* Young Corbett III (Ita) PTS–10 Jackie Fields
      (USA) San Francisco, USA

24 Feb 1933 *Fe(NBA)* Freddie Miller (USA) PTS–10 Baby
      Arizmendi (Mex) Los Angeles, USA

10 Mar 1933 *LH* Maxie Rosenbloom (USA) PTS–15 Ad
      Heuser (Ger) New York, USA

17 Mar 1933 *M(NY)* Ben Jeby (USA) D–15 Vince Dundee
      (Ita) New York, USA

18 Mar 1933 *B* Panama Al Brown (Pan) PTS–12 Dom
      Bernasconi (Ita) Milan, Italy

21 Mar 1933 *Fe(NBA)* Freddie Miller (USA) PTS–10 Speedy
      Dado (Phi) Los Angeles, USA

24 Mar 1933 *LH* Maxie Rosenbloom (USA) KO–4 Bob
      Godwin (USA) New York, USA

9 May 1933 *Fe(NY)* Kid Chocolate (Cuba) PTS–15 Seaman
      Tommy Watson (GB) New York, USA

21 May 1933 *LW* Tony Canzoneri (USA) PTS–10 Battling
      Shaw (Mex) New Orleans, USA

29 May 1933 *W* Jimmy McLarnin (Ire) KO–1 Young Corbett
      III (Ita) Los Angeles, USA

12 Jun 1933 *Fl(NBA)* Jackie Brown (GB) PTS–15 Valentin
      Angelmann (Fra) London, England

23 Jun 1933 *LW/L* Barney Ross (USA) PTS–10 Tony
      Canzoneri (USA) Chicago, USA

29 Jun 1933 *H* Primo Carnera (Ita) KO–6 Jack Sharkey
      (USA) Long Island, USA

3 Jul 1933 *B* Panama Al Brown (Pan) PTS–15 Johnny King
      (GB) Manchester, England

10 Jul 1933 *M(NY)* Ben Jeby (USA) PTS–15 Young Terry
      (USA) Newark, USA

9 Aug 1933 *M(NY)* Lou Brouillard (Can) KO–7 Ben Jeby
      (USA) New York, USA

11 Sep 1933 *Fl(NBA)* Jackie Brown (GB) PTS–15 Valentin
      Angelmann (Fra) Manchester, England

12 Sep 1933 *L* Barney Rodd (USA) PTS–15 Tony Canzoneri (USA) New York, USA

2 Oct 1933 *M(NBA)* Marcel Thil (Fra) PTS–15 Kid Tunero (Cuba) Paris, France

22 Oct 1933 *H* Primo Carnera (Ita) PTS–15 Paulino Uzcudun (Spa) Rome, Italy

30 Oct 1933 *M(NY)* Vince Dundee (Ita) PTS–15 Lou Brouillard (Can) Boston, USA

3 Nov 1933 *LH* Maxie Rosenbloom (USA) PTS–15 Mickey Walker (USA) New York, USA

17 Nov 1933 *LW* Barney Ross (USA) PTS–10 Sammy Fuller (USA) Chicago, USA

8 Dec 1933 *M(NY)* Vince Dundee (Ita) PTS–15 Andy Callahan (USA) Boston, USA

11 Dec 1933 *Fl(NBA)* Jackie Brown (GB) PTS–15 Ginger Foran (GB) Manchester, England

26 Dec 1933 *JL* Frankie Klick (USA) KO–7 Kid Chocolate (Cuba) Philadelphia, USA

1 Jan 1934 *Fe(NBA)* Freddie Miller (USA) PTS–10 Little Jack Sharkey (USA) Chicago, USA

5 Feb 1934 *LH* Maxie Rosenbloom (USA) D–15 Joe Knight (USA) Miami, USA

7 Feb 1934 *LW* Barney Ross (USA) PTS–12 Pete Nebo (USA) Kansas City, USA

19 Feb 1934 *B* Panama Al Brown (Pan) PTS–15 Young Perez (Tun) Paris, France

26 Feb 1934 *M(NBA)* Marcel Thil (Fra) PTS–15 Ignacio Ara (Spa) Paris, France

1 Mar 1934 *H* Primo Carnera (Ita) PTS–15 Tommy Loughran (USA) Miami, USA

5 Mar 1934 *LW* Barney Ross (USA) D–10 Frankie Klick (USA) San Francisco, USA

1 May 1934 *M(NY)* Vince Dundee (Ita) PTS–15 Al Diamond (USA) Paterson, USA

3 May 1934 *M(NBA)* Marcel Thil (Fra) PTS–15 Gustave Roth (Bel) Paris, France

28 May 1934 *W* Barney Ross (USA) PTS–15 Jimmy McLarnin (Ire) New York, USA

2 Jun 1934 *B(NBA)* Sixto Escobar (PR) KO–9 Baby Casanova (Mex) Montreal, Canada

14 Jun 1934 *H* Max Baer (USA) KO–11 Primo Carnera (Ita) Long Island, USA

18 Jun 1934 *Fl(NBA)* Jackie Brown (GB) D–15 Valentin Angelmann (Fra) Manchester, England

8 Aug 1934 *B(NBA)* Sixto Escobar (PR) PTS–15 Eugene Huat (Fra) Montreal, Canada

30 Aug 1934 *Fe(NY)* Baby Arizmendi (Mex) PTS–15 Mike Belloise (USA) New York, USA

11 Sep 1934 *M(NY)* Teddy Yarosz (USA) PTS–15 Vince Dundee (Ita) Pittsburgh, USA

17 Sep 1934 *W* Jimmy McLarnin (Ire) PTS–15 Barney Ross (USA) New York, USA

21 Sep 1934 *Fe(NBA)* Freddie Miller (USA) PTS–15 Nel Tarleton (GB) Liverpool, England

15 Oct 1934 *M(NBA)* Marcel Thil (Fra) D–15 Carmelo Candel (Fra) Paris, France

1 Nov 1934 *B* Panama Al Brown (Pan) KO–10 Young Perez (Tun) Tunis, Tunisia

16 Nov 1934 *LH* Bob Olin (USA) PTS–15 Maxie Rosenbloom (USA) New York, USA

10 Dec 1934 *LW* Barney Ross (USA) PTS–12 Bobby Pacho (Mex) Cleveland, USA

28 Jan 1935 *LW* Barney Ross (USA) PTS–10 Frankie Klick (USA) Miami, USA

17 Feb 1935 *Fe(NBA)* Freddie Miller (USA) KO–1 Jose Girones (Spa) Barcelona, Spain

9 Apr 1935 *LW* Barney Ross (USA) PTS–12 Henry Woods (USA) Seattle, USA

10 May 1935 *L* Tony Canzoneri (USA) PTS–15 Lou Ambers (USA) New York, USA

28 May 1935 *W* Barney Ross (USA) PTS–15 Jimmy McLarnin (Ire) New York, USA

1 Jun 1935 *B(NY)* Baltazar Sangchilli (Spa) PTS–15 Panama Al Brown (Pan) Valencia, Spain

2 Jun 1935 *M(NBA)* Marcel Thil (Fra) PTS–15 Ignacio Ara (Spa) Madrid, Spain

12 Jun 1935 *Fe(NBA)* Freddie Miller (USA) PTS–15 Nel Tarleton (GB) Liverpool, England

Joe Louis lies on the canvas, beaten by the former world champion Max Schmeling of Germany in a 12th round knock-out in 1936. This was Louis' only defeat before capturing the world heavyweight crown the following year (AP)

3 Jun 1935 *H* James J. Braddock (USA) PTS–15 Max Baer (USA) Long Island, USA

28 Jun 1935 *M(NBA)* Marcel Thil (Fra) PTS–10 Carmelo Candel (Fra) Paris, France

26 Aug 1935 *B(NBA)* Lou Salica (USA) PTS–15 Sixto Escobar (PR) New York, USA

9 Sep 1935 *Fl(NBA)* Benny Lynch (GB) RTD–2 Jackie Brown (GB) Manchester, England

16 Sep 1935 *Fl(NY)* Small Montana (Phi) PTS–10 Midget Wolgast (USA) Oakland, USA

19 Sep 1935 *M(NY)* Ed 'Babe' Risko (USA) PTS–15 Teddy Yarosz (USA) Pittsburgh, USA

4 Oct 1935 *L* Tony Canzoneri (USA) PTS–15 Al Roth (USA) New York, USA

22 Oct 1935 *Fe(NBA)* Freddie Miller (USA) PTS–15 Vernon Cormier (USA) Boston, USA

31 Oct 1935 *LH* John Henry Lewis (USA) PTS–15 Bob Olin (USA) St Louis, USA

15 Nov 1935 *B(NBA)* Sixto Escobar (PR) PTS–15 Lou Salica (USA) New York, USA

20 Jan 1936 *M(NBA)* Marcel Thil (Fra) DIS–4 Lou Brouillard (Can) Paris, France
10 Feb 1936 *M(NY)* Ed 'Babe' Risko (USA) PTS–15 Tony Fisher (USA) Newark, USA
18 Feb 1936 *Fe(NBA)* Freddie Miller (USA) PTS–12 Johnny Pena (USA) Seattle, USA
2 Mar 1936 *Fe(NBA)* Freddie Miller (USA) PTS–15 Petey Sarron (USA) Miami, USA
13 Mar 1936 *LH* John Henry Lewis (USA) PTS–15 Jock McAvoy (GB) New York, USA
11 May 1936 *Fe(NBA)* Petey Sarron (USA) PTS–15 Freddie Miller (USA) Washington, USA
29 Jun 1936 *B(NY)* Tony Marino (USA) KO–14 Baltazar Sangchilli (Spa) New York, USA
11 Jul 1936 *M(NY)* Freddie Steele (USA) PTS–15 Ed 'Babe' Risko (USA) Seattle, USA
22 Jul 1936 *Fe(NBA)* Petey Sarron (USA) PTS–15 Baby Manuel (Spa) Dallas, USA
31 Aug 1936 *B* Sixto Escobar (PR) RSF–13 Tony Marino (USA) New York, USA
3 Sep 1936 *L* Lou Ambers (USA) PTS–15 Tony Canzoneri (USA) New York, USA
4 Sep 1936 *Fe(NY)* Mike Belloise (USA) KO–9 Dave Crowley (GB) New York, USA
16 Sep 1936 *Fl(NBA)* Benny Lynch (GB) KO–8 Pat Palmer (GB) Glasgow, Scotland
13 Oct 1936 *B* Sixto Escobar (PR) KO–1 Carlos 'Indian' Quintana (Pan) New York, USA
9 Nov 1936 *LH* John Henry Lewis (USA) PTS–15 Len Harvey (GB) London, England
27 Nov 1936 *W* Barney Ross (USA) PTS–15 Izzy Jannazzo (USA) New York, USA
1 Jan 1937 *M* Freddie Steele (USA) PTS–10 Gorilla Jones (USA) New York, USA
19 Jan 1937 *Fl* Benny Lynch (GB) PTS–15 Small Montana (USA) London, England
19 Feb 1937 *M* Freddie Steele (USA) PTS–15 Ed 'Babe' Risko (USA) New York, USA
21 Feb 1937 *B* Sixto Escobar (PR) PTS–15 Lou Salica (USA) San Juan, Puerto Rico
7 May 1937 *L* Lou Ambers (USA) PTS–15 Tony Canzoneri (USA) New York, USA
11 May 1937 *M* Freddie Steele (USA) KO–3 Frank Battaglia (Can) Seattle, USA
3 Jun 1937 *LH* John Henry Lewis (USA) KO–8 Bob Olin (USA) St Louis, USA
22 Jun 1937 *H* Joe Louis (USA) KO–8 James J. Braddock (USA) Chicago, USA
30 Aug 1937 *H* Joe Louis (USA) PTS–15 Tommy Farr (GB) New York, USA
4 Sep 1937 *Fe(NBA)* Petey Sarron (USA) PTS–12 Freddie Miller (USA) Johannesburg, South Africa
11 Sep 1937 *M* Freddie Steele (USA) KO–4 Ken Overlin (USA) Seattle, USA
23 Sep 1937 *W* Barney Ross (USA) PTS–15 Ceferino Garcia (Phi) New York, USA
23 Sep 1937 *L* Lou Ambers (USA) PTS–15 Pedro Montanez (PR) New York, USA
23 Sep 1937 *B* Harry Jeffra (USA) PTS–15 Sixto Escobar (PR) New York, USA
13 Oct 1937 *Fl* Benny Lynch (GB) KO–13 Peter Kane (GB) Glasgow, Scotland
29 Oct 1937 *Fe* Henry Armstrong (USA) KO–6 Petey Sarron (USA) New York, USA
19 Feb 1938 *M* Freddie Steele (USA) KO–7 Carmen Barth (USA) Cleveland, USA
20 Feb 1938 *B* Sixto Escobar (PR) PTS–15 Harry Jeffra (USA) San Juan, Puerto Rico

23 Feb 1938 *H* Joe Louis (USA) KO–3 Nathan Mann (USA) New York, USA
24 Mar 1938 *Fl* Benny Lynch (GB) D–15 Peter Kane (GB) Liverpool, England
1 Apr 1938 *H* Joe Louis (USA) KO–5 Harry Thomas (USA) Chicago, USA
1 Apr 1938 *M(NY)* Fred Apostoli (USA) PTS–15 Glen Lee (USA) New York, USA
25 Apr 1938 *LH* John Henry Lewis (USA) KO–4 Emilio Martinez (USA) Minneapolis, USA
31 May 1938 *W* Henry Armstrong (USA) PTS–15 Barney Ross (USA) New York, USA
22 Jun 1938 *H* Joe Louis (USA) KO–1 Max Schmeling (Ger) New York, USA
26 Jul 1938 *M(NBA)* Al Hostak (USA) KO–1 Freddie Steele (USA) Seattle, USA
17 Aug 1938 *L* Henry Armstrong (USA) PTS–15 Lou Ambers (USA) New York, USA
22 Sep 1938 *Fl* Peter Kane (GB) PTS–15 Jackie Jurich (USA) Liverpool, England
17 Oct 1938 *Fe(NY)* Joey Archibald (USA) PTS–15 Mike Belloise (USA) New York, USA
28 Oct 1938 *LH* John Henry Lewis (USA) PTS–15 Al Gainer (USA) New Haven, USA
1 Nov 1938 *M(NBA)* Sol Kreiger (USA) PTS–15 Al Hostak (USA) Seattle, USA
18 Nov 1938 *M(NY)* Fred Apostoli (USA) KO–8 Young Corbett III (Ita) New York, USA
25 Nov 1938 *W* Henry Armstrong (USA) PTS–15 Ceferino Garcia (Phi) New York, USA
28 Nov 1938 *LH(NY)* Tiger Jack Fox (USA) PTS–15 Al Gainer (USA) New York, USA
5 Dec 1938 *W* Henry Armstrong (USA) KO–3 Al Manfredo (USA) Cleveland, USA
29 Dec 1938 *Fe(NBA)* Leo Rodak (USA) PTS–10 Leone Efrati (Ita) Chicago, USA
10 Jan 1939 *W* Henry Armstrong (USA) PTS–10 Baby Arizmendi (Mex) Los Angeles, USA
25 Jan 1939 *H* Joe Louis (USA) RSF–1 John Henry Lewis (USA) New York, USA
3 Feb 1939 *LH(NY)* Melio Bettina (USA) RSF–9 Tiger Jack Fox (USA) New York, USA
14 Mar 1939 *W* Henry Armstrong (USA) KO–4 Bobby Pacho (Mex) Havana, Cuba
16 Mar 1939 *W* Henry Armstrong (USA) KO–1 Lew Feldman (USA) St Louis, USA
31 Mar 1939 *W* Henry Armstrong (USA) KO–12 Davey Day (USA) New York, USA
2 Apr 1939 *B* Sixto Escobar (PR) PTS–15 Johnny 'Kayo' Morgan (USA) San Juan, Puerto Rico
17 Apr 1939 *H* Joe Louis (USA) KO–1 Jack Roper (USA) Los Angeles, USA
18 Apr 1939 *Fe* Joey Archibald (USA) PTS–15 Leo Rodak (USA) Rhode Island, USA
25 May 1939 *W* Henry Armstrong (USA) PTS–15 Ernie Roderick (GB) London, England
27 Jun 1939 *M(NBA)* Al Hostak (USA) KO–4 Solly Kreiger (USA) Seattle, USA
28 Jun 1939 *H* Joe Louis (USA) RSF–4 Tony Galento (USA) New York, USA
13 Jul 1939 *LH* Billy Conn (USA) PTS–15 Melio Bettina (USA) New York, USA
22 Aug 1939 *L* Lou Ambers (USA) PTS–15 Henry Armstrong (USA) New York, USA
20 Sep 1939 *H* Joe Louis (USA) KO–11 Bob Pastor (USA) Detroit, USA
25 Sep 1939 *LH* Billy Conn (USA) PTA–15 Melio Bettina (USA) Pittsburgh, USA

28 Sep 1939 *Fe* Joey Archibald (USA) PTS–15 Harry Jeffra (USA) Washington, USA

2 Oct 1939 *M(NY)* Ceferino Garcia (Phi) KO–7 Fred Apostoli (USA) New York, USA

9 Oct 1939 *W* Henry Armstrong (USA) KO–4 Al Manfredo (USA) Des Moines, USA

13 Oct 1939 *W* Henry Armstrong (USA) KO–2 Howard Scott (USA) Minneapolis, USA

20 Oct 1939 *W* Henry Armstrong (USA) KO–3 Ritchie Fontaine (USA) Seattle, USA

24 Oct 1939 *W* Henry Armstrong (USA) PTS–10 Jimmy Garrison (USA) Los Angeles, USA

30 Oct 1939 *W* Henry Armstrong (USA) KO–4 Bobby Pacho (Mex) Denver, USA

17 Nov 1939 *LH* Billy Conn (USA) PTS–15 Gus Lesnevich (USA) New York, USA

11 Dec 1939 *M(NBA)* Al Hostak (USA) KO–1 Eric Seelig (Ger) Cleveland, USA

11 Dec 1939 *W* Henry Armstrong (USA) KO–7 Jimmy Garrison (USA) Cleveland, USA

23 Dec 1939 *M(NY)* Ceferino Garcia (Phi) KO–13 Glen Lee (USA) Manila, Philippines

4 Jan 1940 *W* Henry Armstrong (USA) KO–5 Joe Ghnouly (USA) St Louis, USA

24 Jan 1940 *W* Henry Armstrong (USA) KO–9 Pedro Montanez (PR) New York, USA

9 Feb 1940 *H* Joe Louis (USA) PTS–15 Arturo Godoy (Chi) New York, USA

1 Mar 1940 *M(NY)* Ceferino Garcia (Phi) D–10 Henry Armstrong (USA) Los Angeles, USA

4 Mar 1940 *B(NBA)* Georgie Pace (USA) D–15 Lou Salica (USA) Toronto, Canada

29 Mar 1940 *H* Joe Louis (USA) KO–2 Johnny Paycheck (USA) New York, USA

26 Apr 1940 *W* Henry Armstrong (USA) KO–7 Paul Junior (USA) Boston, USA

3 May 1940 *L(NBA)* Sammy Angott (USA) PTS–15 Davey Day (USA) Louisville, USA

10 May 1940 *L(NY)* Lew Jenkins (USA) RSF–3 Lou Ambers (USA) New York, USA

20 May 1940 *Fe(NY)* Harry Jeffra (USA) PTS–15 Joey Archibald (USA) Baltimore, USA

23 May 1940 *M(NY)* Ken Overlin (USA) PTS–15 Ceferino Garcia (Phi) New York, USA

24 May 1940 *W* Henry Armstrong (USA) KO–5 Ralph Zanelli (USA) Boston, USA

5 Jun 1940 *LH* Billy Conn (USA) PTS–15 Gus Lesnevich (USA) Detroit, USA

20 Jun 1940 *H* Joe Louis (USA) RSF–8 Arturo Godoy (Chi) New York, USA

21 Jun 1940 *W* Henry Armstrong (USA) KO–3 Paul Junior (USA) Portland, USA

10 Jul 1940 *Fe(NBA)* Petey Scalzo (USA) RSF–15 Bobby 'Poison' Ivy (USA) Hartford, USA

19 Jul 1940 *M(NBA)* Tony Zale (USA) KO–13 Al Hostak (USA) Seattle, USA

29 Jul 1940 *Fe(NY)* Harry Jeffra (USA) PTS–15 Spider Armstrong (Can) Baltimore, USA

23 Sep 1940 *W* Henry Armstrong (USA) KO–4 Phil Furr (USA) Washington, USA

24 Sep 1940 *B* Lou Salica (USA) PTS–15 Georgie Pace (USA) New York, USA

4 Oct 1940 *W* Fritzie Zivic (USA) PTS–15 Henry Armstrong (USA) New York, USA

1 Nov 1940 *M(NY)* Ken Overlin (USA) PTS–15 Steve Belloise (USA) New York, USA

22 Nov 1940 *L(NY)* Lou Jenkins (USA) RSF–2 Pete Lello (USA) New York, USA

13 Dec 1940 *M(NY)* Ken Overlin (USA) PTS–15 Steve Belloise (USA) New York, USA

16 Dec 1940 *H* Joe Louis (USA) RTD–6 Al McCoy (USA) Boston, USA

13 Jan 1941 *LH(NBA)* Anton Christoforidis (Gre) PTS–15 Melio Bettina (USA) Cleveland, USA

13 Jan 1941 *B* Lou Salica (USA) PTS–15 Tommy Forte (USA) Philadelphia, USA

17 Jan 1941 *W* Fritzie Zivic (USA) KO–12 Henry Armstrong (USA) New York, USA

31 Jan 1941 *H* Joe Louis (USA) KO–5 Red Burman (USA) New York, USA

17 Feb 1941 *H* Joe Louis (USA) KO–2 Gus Dorazio (USA) Philadelphia, USA

21 Feb 1941 *M(NBA)* Tony Zale (USA) KO–14 Steve Mamakos (Gre) Chicago, USA

21 Mar 1941 *H* Joe Louis (USA) KO–13 Abe Simon (USA) Detroit, USA

8 Apr 1941 *H* Joe Louis (USA) RSF–9 Tony Musto (USA) St Louis, USA

25 Apr 1941 *B* Lou Salica (USA) PTS–15 Lou Transparenti (USA) Baltimore, USA

9 May 1941 *M(NY)* Billy Soose (USA) PTS–15 Ken Overlin (USA) New York, USA

12 May 1941 *Fe(NY)* Joey Archibald (USA) PTS–15 Harry Jeffra (USA) Washington, USA

19 May 1941 *Fe(NBA)* Petey Scalzo (USA) PTS–15 Phil Zwick (USA) Milwaukee, USA

22 May 1941 *LH* Gus Lesnevich (USA) PTS–15 Anton Christoforidis (Gre) New York, USA

23 May 1941 *H* Joe Louis (USA) DIS–7 Buddy Baer (USA) Washington, USA

28 May 1941 *M(NBA)* Tony Zale (USA) KO–2 Al Hostak (USA) Chicago, USA

16 Jun 1941 *B* Lou Salica (USA) PTS–15 Tommy Forte (USA) Philadelphia, USA

18 Jun 1941 *H* Joe Louis (USA) KO–13 Billy Conn (USA) New York, USA

1 Jul 1941 *Fe(NBA)* Ritchie Lemos (USA) KO–5 Petey Scalzo (USA) Los Angeles, USA

21 Jul 1941 *W* Freddie 'Red' Cochrane (USA) PTS–15 Fritzie Zivic (USA) Newark, USA

26 Aug 1941 *LH* Gus Lesnevich (USA) PTS–15 Tami Mauriello (USA) New York, USA

11 Sep 1941 *Fe(NY)* Chalky Wright (Mex) KO–11 Joey Archibald (USA) Washington, USA

29 Sep 1941 *H* Joe Louis (USA) RSF–6 Lou Nova (USA) New York, USA

14 Nov 1941 *LH* Gus Lesnevich (USA) PTS–15 Tami Mauriello (USA) New York, USA

18 Nov 1941 *Fe(NBA)* Jackie Wilson (USA) PTS–12 Ritchie Lemos (USA) Los Angeles, USA

28 Nov 1941 *M* Tony Zale (USA) PTS–15 Georgie Abrams (USA) New York, USA

12 Dec 1941 *Fe(NBA)* Jackie Wilson (USA) PTS–12 Ritchie Lemos (USA) Los Angeles, USA

19 Dec 1941 *L* Sammy Angott (USA) PTS–15 Lew Jenkins (USA) New York, USA

9 Jan 1942 *H* Joe Louis (USA) KO–1 Buddy Baer (USA) New York, USA

27 Mar 1942 *H* Joe Louis (USA) KO–6 Abe Simon (USA) New York, USA

15 May 1942 *L* Sammy Angott (USA) PTS–15 Allie Stolz (USA) New York, USA

19 Jun 1942 *Fe(NY)* Chalky Wright (Mex) KO–10 Harry Jeffra (USA) Baltimore, USA

7 Aug 1942 *B* Manuel Ortiz (USA) PTS–12 Lou Salica (USA) Hollywood, USA

Jersey Joe
Walcott with [a]
special belt
presented to h[im]
by the 'Police
Gazette', who
claimed that
despite his los[ing]
a split decisio[n]
to Joe Louis in
December 19[ ]
he was the
actual winner
and so
presented him
with the belt
(AP)

25 Sep 1942 *Fe(NY)* Chalky Wright (Mex) PTS–15 Charlie Constantino (USA) New York, USA

20 Nov 1942 *Fe(NY)* Willie Pep (USA) PTS–15 Chalky Wright (Mex) New York, USA

18 Dec 1942 *L(NY)* Beau Jack (USA) KO–3 Tippy Larkin (USA) New York

1 Jan 1943 *B* Manuel Ortiz (USA) PTS–10 Kenny Lindsay (Can) Portland, USA

18 Jan 1943 *Fe(NBA)* Jackie Callura (Can) PTS–15 Jackie Wilson (USA) Providence, USA

27 Jan 1943 *B* Manuel Ortiz (USA) RSF–10 George Freitas (USA) Oakland, USA

10 Mar 1943 *B* Manuel Ortiz (USA) RSF–11 Lou Salica (USA) Oakland, USA

18 Mar 1943 *Fe(NBA)* Jackie Callura (Can) PTS–15 Jackie Wilson (USA) Boston, USA

28 Apr 1943 *B* Manuel Ortiz (USA) KO–6 Lupe Cordoza (USA) Fort Worth, USA

21 May 1943 *L(NY)* Bob Montgomery (USA) PTS–15 Beau Jack (USA) New York, USA

26 May 1943 *B* Manuel Ortiz (USA) PTS–15 Joe Robleto (USA) Long Beach, USA

8 Jun 1943 *Fe(NY)* Willie Pep (USA) PTS–15 Sal Bartolo (USA) Boston, USA

19 Jun 1943 *Fl* Jackie Paterson (GB) KO–1 Peter Kane (GB) Glasgow, Scotland

12 Jul 1943 *B* Manuel Ortiz (USA) KO–7 Joe Robleto (USA) Seattle, USA

16 Aug 1943 *Fe(NBA)* Phil Terranova (USA) KO–8 Jackie Callura (Can) New Orleans, USA

1 Oct 1943 *B* Manuel Ortiz (USA) KO–4 Leonardo Lopez (Mex) Hollywood, USA

27 Oct 1943 *L(NBA)* Sammy Angott (USA) PTS–15 Luther 'Slugger' White (USA) Hollywood, USA

19 Nov 1943 *L(NY)* Beau Jack (USA) PTS–15 Bob Montgomery (USA) New York, USA

23 Nov 1943 *B* Manuel Ortiz (USA) PTS–15 Benny Goldberg (USA) Los Angeles, USA

27 Dec 1943 *Fe(NBA)* Phil Terranova (USA) KO–6 Jackie Callura (Can) New Orleans, USA

3 Mar 1944 *L(NY)* Bob Montgomery (USA) PTS–15 Beau Jack (USA) New York, USA

8 Mar 1944 *L(NBA)* Juan Zurita (Mex) PTS–15 Sammy Angott (USA) Hollywood, USA

10 Mar 1944 *Fe(NBA)* Sal Bartolo (USA) PTS–15 Phil Terranova (USA) Boston, USA

14 Mar 1944 *B* Manuel Ortiz (USA) PTS–15 Ernesto Aguilar (Mex) Los Angeles, USA

4 Apr 1944 *B* Manuel Ortiz (USA) PTS–15 Tony Olivera (USA) Los Angeles, USA

5 May 1944 *Fe(NBA)* Sal Bartolo (USA) PTS–15 Phil Terranova (USA) Boston, USA

12 Sep 1944 *B* Manuel Ortiz (USA) RSF–4 Luis Castello (Mex) Los Angeles, USA

29 Sep 1944 *Fe(NY)* Willie Pep (USA) PTS–15 Chalky Wright (Mex) New York, USA

14 Nov 1944 *B* Manuel Ortiz (USA) RSF–9 Luis Castello (Mex) Los Angeles, USA

15 Dec 1944 *Fe(NBA)* Sal Bartolo (USA) PTS–15 Willie Roche (USA) Boston, USA

19 Feb 1945 *Fe(NY)* Willie Pep (USA) PTS–15 Phil Terranova (USA) New York, USA

18 Apr 1945 *L(NBA)* Ike Williams (USA) KO–2 Juan Zurita (Mex) Mexico City, Mexico

1 Feb 1946 *W* Marty Servo (USA) KO–4 Freddie 'Red' Cochrane (USA) New York, USA

25 Feb 1946 *B* Manuel Ortiz (USA) KO–13 Luis Castello (Mex) San Francisco, USA

29 Apr 1946 *LW* Tippy Larkin (USA) PTS–12 Willie Joyce (USA) Boston, USA

3 May 1946 *Fe(NBA)* Sal Bartolo (USA) KO–6 Spider Armstrong (Can) Boston, USA

14 May 1946 *LH* Gus Lesnevich (USA) RSF–10 Freddie Mills (GB) London, England

26 May 1946 *B* Manuel Ortiz (USA) KO–5 Kenny Lindsay (Can) Los Angeles, USA

7 Jun 1946 *Fe* Willie Pep (USA) KO–12 Sal Bartolo (USA) New York, USA

10 Jun 1946 *B* Manuel Ortiz (USA) KO–11 Jackie Jurich (USA) San Francisco, USA

19 Jun 1946 *H* Joe Louis (USA) KO–8 Billy Conn (USA) New York, USA

28 Jun 1946 *L(NY)* Bob Montgomery (USA) KO–13 Allie Stolz (USA) New York, USA

10 Jul 1946 *Fl* Jackie Paterson (GB) PTS–15 Joe Curran (GB) Glasgow, Scotland

4 Sep 1946 *L(NBA)* Ike Williams (USA) KO–9 Ronnie James (GB) Cardiff, Wales

13 Sep 1946 *LW* Tippy Larkin (USA) PTS–12 Willie Joyce (USA) New York, USA

18 Sep 1946 *H* Joe Louis (USA) KO–1 Tami Mauriello (USA) New York, USA

27 Sep 1946 *M* Tony Zale (USA) KO–6 Rocky Graziano (USA) New York, USA

26 Nov 1946 *L(NY)* Bob Montgomery (USA) KO–8 Wesley Mouzon (USA) Philadelphia, USA

20 Dec 1946 *W* Sugar Ray Robinson (USA) PTS–15 Tommy Bell (USA) New York, USA

6 Jan 1947 *B* Harold Dade (USA) PTS–15 Manuel Ortiz (USA) San Francisco, USA

28 Feb 1947 *LH* Gus Lesnevich (USA) KO–10 Billy Fox (USA) New York, USA

11 Mar 1947 *B* Manuel Ortiz (USA) PTS–15 Harold Dade (USA) Los Angeles, USA

30 May 1947 *B* Manuel Ortiz (USA) PTS–15 David Kui Kong Young (Haw) Honolulu, Hawaii

24 Jun 1947 *W* Sugar Ray Robinson (USA) KO–8 Jimmy Doyle (USA) Cleveland, USA

16 Jul 1947 *M* Rocky Graziano (USA) KO–6 Tony Zale (USA) Chicago, USA

4 Aug 1947 *L* Ike Williams (USA) KO–6 Bob Montgomery (USA) Philadelphia, USA

22 Aug 1947 *Fe* Willie Pep (USA) KO–12 Jock Leslie (USA) Flint, USA

20 Oct 1947 *Fl(NBA)* Rinty Monaghan (GB) PTS–15 Dado Marino (Haw) London, England

5 Dec 1947 *H* Joe Louis (USA) PTS–15 Jersey Joe Walcott (USA) New York, USA

19 Dec 1947 *W* Sugar Ray Robinson (USA) KO–6 Chuck Taylor (USA) Detroit, USA

20 Dec 1947 *B* Manuel Ortiz (USA) PTS–15 Tirso Del Rosario (Phi) Manila, Philippines

24 Feb 1948 *Fe* Willie Pep (USA) RSF–10 Humberto Sierra (Cuba) Miami, USA

5 Mar 1948 *LH* Gus Lesnevich (USA) KO–1 Billy Fox (USA) New York, USA

23 Mar 1948 *Fl* Rinty Monaghan (GB) KO–7 Jackie Paterson (GB) Belfast, Northern Ireland

25 May 1948 *L* Ike Williams (USA) PTS–15 Enrique Bolanos (USA) Los Angeles, USA

10 Jun 1948 *M* Tony Zale (USA) KO–3 Rocky Graziano (USA) Newark, USA

25 Jun 1948 *H* Joe Louis (USA) KO–11 Jersey Joe Walcott (USA) New York, USA

28 Jun 1948 *W* Sugar Ray Robinson (USA) PTS–15 Bernard Docusen (Phi) Chicago, USA

In his first defence of the world middleweight title in 1948, Rocky Graziano was knocked out in the 3rd round by Tony Zale, who regained the title (AP)

4 Jul 1948 *B* Manuel Ortiz (USA) KO–8 Memo Valero (Mex) Mexicali, Mexico

12 Jul 1948 *L* Ike Williams (USA) KO–6 Beau Jack (USA) Philadelphia, USA

26 Jul 1948 *LH* Freddie Mills (GB) PTS–15 Gus Lesnevich (USA) London, England

21 Sep 1948 *M* Marcel Cerdan (Alg) KO–12 Tony Zale (USA) Jersey City, USA

23 Sep 1948 *L* Ike Williams (USA) KO–10 Jesse Flores (USA) New York, USA

29 Oct 1948 *Fe* Sandy Saddler (USA) KO–4 Willie Pep (USA) New York, USA

11 Feb 1949 *Fe* Willie Pep (USA) PTS–15 Sandy Saddler (USA) New York, USA

1 Mar 1949 *B* Manuel Ortiz (USA) PTS–15 Dado Marino (Haw) Honolulu, Hawaii

5 Apr 1949 *Fl* Rinty Monaghan (GB) PTS–15 Maurice Sandeyron (Fra) Belfast, Northern Ireland

16 Jun 1949 *M* Jake La Motta (USA) RTD–10 Marcel Cerdan (Alg) Detroit, USA

22 Jun 1949 *H(NBA)* Ezzard Charles (USA) PTS–15 Jersey Joe Walcott (USA) Chicago, USA

11 Jul 1949 *W* Sugar Ray Robinson (USA) PTS–15 Kid Gavilan (Cuba) Philadelphia, USA

21 Jul 1949 *L* Ike Williams (USA) KO–4 Enrique Bolanos (USA) Los Angeles, USA

10 Aug 1949 *H(NBA)* Ezzard Charles (USA) RSF–7 Gus Lesnevich (USA) New York, USA

20 Sep 1949 *Fe* Willie Pep (USA) RSF–7 Eddie Compo (USA) Waterbury, USA

30 Sep 1949 *Fl* Rinty Monaghan (GB) D–15 Terry Allen (GB) Belfast, Northern Ireland

14 Oct 1949 *H(NBA)* Ezzard Charles (USA) KO–8 Pat Velentino (USA) San Francisco, USA

5 Dec 1949 *L* Ike Williams (USA) PTS–15 Freddie Dawson (USA) Philadelphia, USA

16 Jan 1950 *Fe* Willie Pep (USA) KO–5 Charley Riley (USA) St Louis, USA

24 Jan 1950 *LH* Joey Maxim (USA) KO–10 Freddie Mills (GB) London, England

17 Mar 1950 *Fe* Willie Pep (USA) PTS–15 Ray Famechon (Fra) New York, USA

25 Apr 1950 *Fl* Terry Allen (GB) PTS–15 Honore Pratesi (Fra) London, England

31 May 1950 *B* Vic Toweel (SA) PTS–15 Manuel Ortiz (USA) Johannesburg, South Africa

12 Jul 1950 *M* Jake La Motta (USA) PTS–15 Tiberio Mitri (Ita) New York, USA

1 Aug 1950 *Fl* Dado Marino (Haw) PTS–15 Terry Allen (GB) Honolulu, Hawaii

9 Aug 1950 *W* Sugar Ray Robinson (USA) PTS–15 Charley Fusari (USA) Jersey City, USA

15 Aug 1950 *H(NBA)* Ezzard Charles (USA) RSF–14 Freddy Beshore (USA) Buffalo, USA

8 Sep 1950 *Fe* Sandy Saddler (USA) RTD–7 Willie Pep (USA) New York, USA

13 Sep 1950 *M* Jake La Motta (USA) KO–15 Laurent Dauthuille (Fra) Detroit, USA

27 Sep 1950 *H* Ezzard Charles (USA) PTS–15 Joe Louis (USA) New York, USA

2 Dec 1950 *B* Vic Toweel (SA) RTD–10 Danny O'Sullivan (GB) Johannesburg, South Africa

5 Dec 1950 *H* Ezzard Charles (USA) KO–11 Nick Barone (USA) Cincinnati, USA

12 Jan 1951 *H* Ezzard Charles (USA) RSF–10 Lee Oma (USA) New York, USA

14 Feb 1951 *M* Sugar Ray Robinson (USA) RSF–13 Jake La Motta (USA) Chicago, USA

7 Mar 1951 *H* Ezzard Charles (USA) PTS–15 Jersey Joe Walcott (USA) Detroit, USA

14 Mar 1951 *W(NBA)* Johnny Bratton (USA) PTS–15 Charley Fusari (USA) Chicago, USA

18 May 1951 *W* Kid Gavilan (Cuba) PTS–15 Johnny Bratton (USA) New York, USA

25 May 1951 *L* Jimmy Carter (USA) RSF–14 Ike Williams (USA) New York, USA

30 May 1951 *H* Ezzard Charles (USA) PTS–15 Joey Maxim (USA) Chicago, USA

10 Jul 1951 *M* Randolph Turpin (GB) PTS–15 Sugar Ray Robinson (USA) London, England

18 Jul 1951 *H* Jersey Joe Walcott (USA) KO–7 Ezzard Charles (USA) Pittsburgh, USA

22 Aug 1951 *LH* Joey Maxim (USA) PTS–15 Irish Bob Murphy (USA) New York, USA

29 Aug 1951 *W* Kid Gavilan (Cuba) PTS–15 Billy Graham (USA) New York, USA

12 Sep 1951 *M* Sugar Ray Robinson (USA) RSF–10 Randolph Turpin (GB) New York, USA

26 Sep 1951 *Fe* Sandy Saddler (USA) RTD–9 Willie Pep (USA) New York, USA

1 Nov 1951 *Fl* Dado Marino (Haw) PTS–15 Terry Allen (GB) Honolulu, Hawaii

14 Nov 1951 *L* Jimmy Carter (USA) PTS–15 Art Aragon (USA) Los Angeles, USA

17 Nov 1951 *B* Vic Toweel (SA) PTS–15 Luis Romero (Spa) Johannesburg, South Africa

26 Jan 1952 *B* Vic Toweel (SA) PTS–15 Peter Keenan (GB) Johannesburg, South Africa

4 Feb 1952 *W* Kid Gavilan (Cuba) PTS–15 Bobby Dykes (USA) Miami, USA

13 Mar 1952 *M* Sugar Ray Robinson (USA) PTS–15 Carl 'Bobo' Olson (Haw) San Francisco, USA

1 Apr 1952 *L* Jimmy Carter (USA) PTS–15 Lauro Salas (Mex) Los Angeles,.USA

16 Apr 1952 *M* Sugar Ray Robinson (USA) KO–3 Rocky Graziano (USA) Chicago, USA

14 May 1952 *L* Lauro Salas (Mex) PTS–15 Jimmy Carter (USA) Los Angeles, USA

19 May 1952 *Fl* Yoshio Shirai (Jap) PTS–15 Dado Marino (Haw) Tokyo, Japan

5 Jun 1952 *H* Jersey Joe Walcott (USA) PTS–15 Ezzard Charles (USA) Philadelphia, USA

25 Jun 1952 *LH* Joey Maxim (USA) RTD–14 Sugar Ray Robinson (USA) New York, USA

7 Jul 1952 *W* Kid Gavilan (Cuba) KO–11 Gil Turner (USA) Philadelphia, USA

23 Sep 1952 *H* Rocky Marciano (USA) KO–13 Jersey Joe Walcott (USA) Philadelphia, USA

5 Oct 1952 *W* Kid Gavilan (Cuba) PTS–15 Billy Graham (USA) Havana, Cuba

15 Oct 1952 *L* Jimmy Carter (USA) PTS–15 Lauro Salas (Mex) Chicago, USA

15 Nov 1952 *B* Jimmy Carruthers (Aus) KO–1 Vic Toweel (SA) Johannesburg, South Africa

15 Nov 1952 *Fl* Yoshio Shirai (Jap) PTS–15 Dado Marino (Haw) Tokyo, Japan

17 Dec 1952 *LH* Archie Moore (USA) PTS–15 Joey Maxim (USA) St Louis, USA

11 Feb 1953 *W* Kid Gavilan (Cuba) KO–10 Chuck Davey (USA) Chicago, USA

21 Mar 1953 *B* Jimmy Carruthers (Aus) KO–10 Vic Toweel (SA) Johannesburg, South Africa

24 Apr 1953 *L* Jimmy Carter (USA) RSF–4 Tommy Collins (USA) Boston, USA

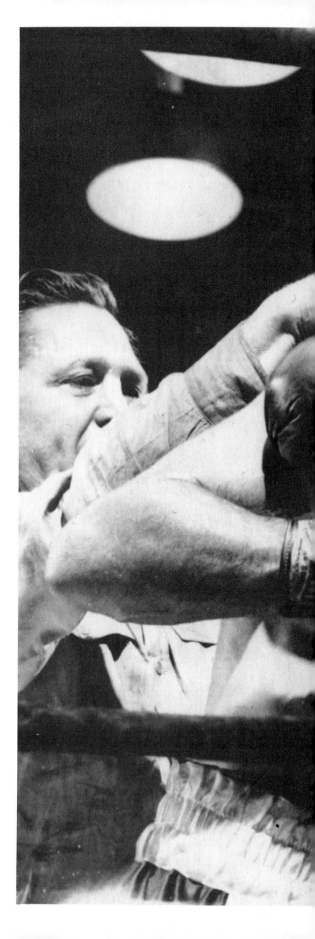

The scars of a bruising 1951 battle are clearly visible on the faces of Willie Pep (left) and Sandy Saddler. It was the fourth time they had met in a world featherweight title bout. Saddler retained his title with a technical knock-out in the 9th round (AP)

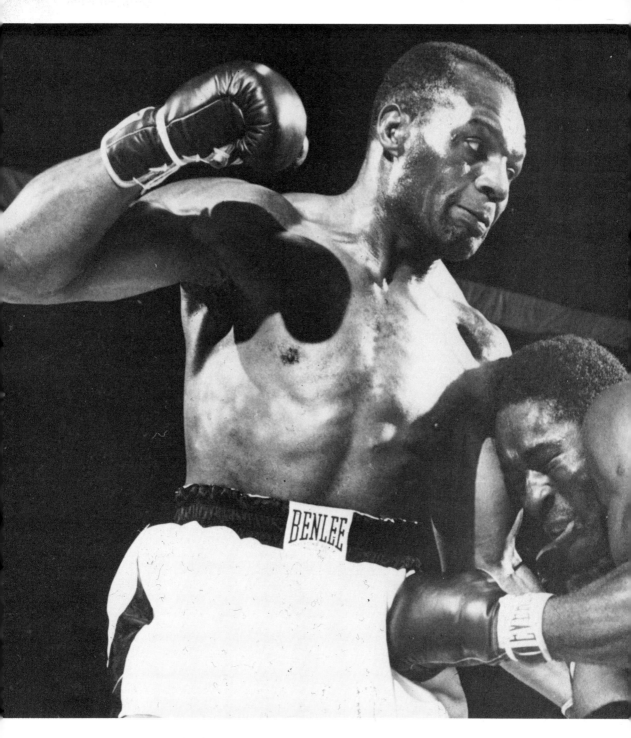

15 May 1953 *H* Rocky Marciano (USA) KO–1 Jersey Joe
Walcott (USA) Chicago, USA

18 May 1953 *Fl* Yoshio Shirai (Jap) PTS–15 Tanny Campo
(Phi) Tokyo, Japan

12 Jun 1953 *L* Jimmy Carter (USA) RSF–15 George Araujo
(USA) New York, USA

24 Jun 1953 *LH* Archie Moore (USA) PTS–15 Joey Maxim
(USA) Ogden, USA

18 Sep 1953 *W* Kid Gavilan (Cuba) PTS–15 Carmen Basilio
(USA) Syracuse, USA

24 Sep 1953 *H* Rocky Marciano (USA) RSF–11 Roland
LaStarza (USA) New York, USA

21 Oct 1953 *M* Carl 'Bobo' Olson (Haw) PTS–15 Randolph
Turpin (GB) New York, USA

27 Oct 1953 *Fl* Yoshio Shirai (Jap) PTS–15 Terry Allen (GB)
Tokyo, Japan

11 Nov 1953 *L* Jimmy Carter (USA) KO–5 Armand Savoi
(Can) Montreal, Canada

13 Nov 1953 *W* Kid Gavilan (Cuba) PTS–15 Johnny Bratton
(USA) Chicago, USA

13 Nov 1953 *B* Jimmy Carruthers (Aus) PTS–15 Henry
'Pappy' Gault (USA) Sydney, Australia

27 Jan 1954 *LH* Archie Moore (USA) PTS–15 Joey Maxim
(USA) Miami, USA

5 Mar 1954 *L* Paddy de Marco (USA) PTS–15 Jimmy Carter
(USA) New York, USA

2 Apr 1954 *M* Carl 'Bobo' Olson (Haw) PTS–15 Kid Gavilan
(Cuba) Chicago, USA

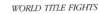

Defending champion Ezzard Charles takes cover as Jersey Joe Walcott gets ready to unleash another right. Walcott went on to win with a 7th round knock-out. It was one of the biggest surprises in heavyweight history and at the age of 37 Walcott became the oldest man to capture the crown (AP)

During their world bantamweight contest at Bangkok in 1954 both Jimmy Carruthers and Chamrern Songkitrat fought the entire 15 rounds barefooted because the ring was saturated after heavy rain.

---

2 May 1954 *B* Jimmy Carruthers (Aus) PTS–12 Chamrern Songkitrat (Tha) Bangkok, Thailand

24 May 1954 *Fl* Yoshio Shirai (Jap) PTS–15 Leo Espinosa (Phi) Tokyo, Japan

17 Jun 1954 *H* Rocky Marciano (USA) PTS–15 Ezzard Charles (USA) New York, USA

11 Aug 1954 *LH* Archie Moore (USA) KO–14 Harold Johnson (USA) New York, USA

20 Aug 1954 *M* Carl 'Bobo' Olson (Haw) PTS–15 Rocky Castellani (USA) San Francisco, USA

17 Sep 1954 *H* Rocky Marciano (USA) KO–8 Ezzard Charles (USA) New York, USA

19 Sep 1954 *B* Robert Cohen (Alg) PTS–15 Chamrern Songkitrat (Tha) Bangkok, Thailand

20 Oct 1954 *W* Johny Saxton (USA) PTS–15 Kid Gavilan (Cuba) Philadelphia, USA

17 Nov 1954 *L* Jimmy Carter (USA) RSF–15 Paddy de Marco (USA) San Francisco, USA

26 Nov 1954 *Fl* Pascual Perez (Arg) PTS–15 Yoshio Shirai (Jap) Tokyo, Japan

15 Dec 1954 *M* Carl 'Bobo' Olson (Haw) KO–11 Pierre Langlois (Fra) San Francisco, USA

25 Feb 1955 *Fe* Sandy Saddler (USA) PTS–15 Teddy 'Red Top' Davis (USA) New York, USA

9 Mar 1955 *B(NBA)* Raton Macias (Mex) KO–11 Chamrern Songkitrat (Tha) San Francisco, USA

1 Apr 1955 *W* Tony de Marco (USA) RSF–14 Johnny Saxton (USA) Boston, USA

16 May 1955 *H* Rocky Marciano (USA) RSF–9 Don Cockell (GB) San Francisco, USA

30 May 1955 *Fl* Pascual Perez (Arg) KO–5 Yoshio Shirai (Jap) Tokyo, Japan

10 Jun 1955 *W* Carmen Basilio (USA) RSF–12 Tony de Marco (USA) Syracuse, USA

22 Jun 1955 *LH* Archie Moore (USA) KO–3 Carl 'Bobo' Olson (Haw) New York, USA

29 Jun 1955 *L* Wallace 'Bud' Smith (USA) PTS–15 Jimmy Carter (USA) Boston, USA

3 Sep 1955 *B(NY)* Robert Cohen (Alg) D–15 Willie Toweel (SA) Johannesburg, South Africa

21 Sep 1955 *H* Rocky Marciano (USA) KO–9 Archie Moore (USA) New York, USA

19 Oct 1955 *L* Wallace 'Bud' Smith (USA) PTS–15 Jimmy Carter (USA) Cincinnati, USA

30 Nov 1955 *W* Carmen Basilio (USA) KO–12 Tony de Marco (USA) Boston, USA

9 Dec 1955 *M* Sugar Ray Robinson (USA) KO–2 Carl 'Bobo' Olson (Haw) Chicago, USA

11 Jan 1956 *Fl* Pascual Perez (Arg) PTS–15 Leo Espinosa (Phil) Buenos Aires, Argentina

18 Jan 1956 *Fe* Sandy Saddler (USA) RSF–13 Flash Elorde (Phi) San Francisco, USA

14 Mar 1956 *W* Johnny Saxton (USA) PTS–15 Carmen Basilio (USA) Chicago, USA

25 Mar 1956 *B(NBA)* Raton Macias (Mex) KO–10 Leo Espinosa (Phi) Mexico City, Mexico

18 May 1956 *M* Sugar Ray Robinson (USA) KO–4 Carl 'Bobo' Olson (Haw) Los Angeles, USA

5 Jun 1956 *LH* Archie Moore (USA) RSF–10 Yolande Pompey (Tri) London, England

29 Jun 1956 *B(NY)* Mario D'Agata (Ita) RTD–6 Robert Cohen (Alg) Rome, Italy

30 Jun 1956 *Fl* Pascual Perez (Arg) RTD–11 Oscar Suarez (Cuba) Montevideo, Uruguay

24 Aug 1956 *L* Joe Brown (USA) PTS–15 Wallace 'Bud' Smith (USA) New Orleans, USA

12 Sep 1956 *W* Carmen Basilio (USA) KO–9 Johnny Saxton (USA) Syracuse, USA

30 Nov 1956 *H* Floyd Patterson (USA) KO–5 Archie Moore (USA) Chicago, USA

2 Jan 1957 *M* Gene Fullmer (USA) PTS–15 Sugar Ray Robinson (USA) New York, USA

13 Feb 1957 *L* Joe Brown (USA) RSF–10 Wallace 'Bud' Smith (USA) Miami, USA

22 Feb 1957 *W* Carmen Basilio (USA) KO–2 Johnny Saxton (USA) Cleveland, USA

30 Mar 1957 *Fl* Pascual Perez (Arg) KO–1 Dai Dower (GB) Buenos Aires, Argentina

1 Apr 1957 *B(NY)* Alphonse Halimi (Alg) PTS–15 Mario D'Agata (Ita) Paris, France

1 May 1957 *M* Sugar Ray Robinson (USA) KO–5 Gene Fullmer (USA) Chicago, USA

15 Jun 1957 *B(NBA)* Raton Macias (Mex) RSF–11 Dommy Ursua (Phi) San Francisco, USA

19 Jun 1957 *L* Joe Brown (USA) RSF–15 Orlando Zulueta (Cuba) Denver, USA

24 Jun 1957 *Fe* Hogan 'Kid' Bassey (Ngr) RSF–10 Cherif Hamia (Alg) Paris, France

29 Jul 1957 *H* Floyd Patterson (USA) RSF–10 Tommy Jackson (USA) New York, USA

22 Aug 1957 *H* Floyd Patterson (USA) KO–6 Pete Rademacher (USA) Seattle, USA

Pete Rademacher (USA), the 1956 Olympic heavyweight champion, was knocked out by Floyd Patterson (USA) when he challenged Patterson for the world heavyweight title in 1957. It was Rademacher's first professional fight.

---

20 Sep 1957 *LH* Archie Moore (USA) KO–7 Tony Anthony (USA) Los Angeles, USA

23 Sep 1957 *M* Carmen Basilio (USA) PTS–15 Sugar Ray Robinson (USA) New York, USA

6 Nov 1957 *B* Alphonse Halimi (Alg) PTS–15 Raton Macias (Mex) Los Angeles, USA

4 Dec 1957 *L* Joe Brown (USA) RSF–11 Joey Lopes (USA) Chicago, USA

7 Dec 1957 *Fl* Pascual Perez (Arg) KO–3 Young Martin (Spa) Buenos Aires, Argentina

25 Mar 1958 *M* Sugar Ray Robinson (USA) PTS–15 Carmen Basilio (USA) Chicago, USA

1 Apr 1958 *Fe* Hogan 'Kid' Bassey (Ngr) KO–3 Ricardo Moreno (Mex) Los Angeles, USA

19 Apr 1958 *Fl* Pascual Perez (Arg) PTS–15 Ramon Arias (Ven) Caracas, Venezuela

7 May 1958 *L* Joe Brown (USA) RSF–8 Ralph Dupas (USA) Houston, USA

6 Jun 1958 *W* Virgil Atkins (USA) RSF–4 Vince Martinez (USA) Los Angeles, USA

23 Jul 1958 *L* Joe Brown (USA) PTS–15 Kenny Lane (USA) Houston, USA

18 Aug 1958 *H* Floyd Patterson (USA) RTD–12 Roy Harris (USA) Los Angeles, USA

5 Dec 1958 *W* Don Jordan (USA) PTS–15 Virgil Atkins (USA) Los Angeles, USA

10 Dec 1958 *LH* Archie Moore (USA) KO–11 Yvon Durelle (Can) Montreal, Canada

15 Dec 1958 *Fl* Pascual Perez (Arg) PTS–15 Dommy Ursua (Phi) Manila, Philippines

11 Feb 1959 *L* Joe Brown (USA) PTS–15 Johnny Busso (USA) Houston, USA

18 Mar 1959 *Fe* Davey Moore (USA) RTD–13 Hogan 'Kid' Bassey (Ngr) Los Angeles, USA

24 Apr 1959 *W* Don Jordan (USA) PTS–15 Virgil Atkins (USA) St Louis, USA

1 May 1959 *H* Floyd Patterson (USA) KO–11 Brian London (GB) Indianapolis, USA

3 Jun 1959 *L* Joe Brown (USA) RTD–8 Paolo Rosi (Ita) Washington, USA

12 Jun 1959 *LW* Carlos Ortiz (PR) RSF–12 Kenny Lane (USA) New York, USA

26 Jun 1959 *H* Ingemar Johansson (Swe) RSF–3 Floyd Patterson (USA) New York, USA

Britain's Freddie Mills rocks Joey Maxim with a right. However, the American won this 1950 bout with a 10th-round knockout to take the light-heavyweight title from the Englishman. It was to be Mills' last fight (Hulton-Deutsch)

8 Jul 1959 *B* Joe Becerra (Mex) KO–8 Alphonse Halimi (Alg) Los Angeles, USA

10 Jul 1959 *W* Don Jordan (USA) PTS–15 Denny Moyer (USA) Portland, USA

20 Jul 1959 *JL* Harold Gomes (USA) PTS–15 Paul Jorgensen (USA) Providence, USA

10 Aug 1959 *Fl* Pascual Perez (Arg) PTS–15 Kenji Yonekura (Jap) Tokyo, Japan

12 Aug 1959 *LH* Archie Moore (USA) KO–3 Yvon Durelle (Can) Montreal, Canada

19 Aug 1959 *Fe* Davey Moore (USA) RTD–10 Hogan 'Kid' Bassey (Ngr) Los Angeles, USA

28 Aug 1959 *M(NBA)* Gene Fullmer (USA) KO–14 Carmen Basilio (USA) San Francisco, USA

5 Nov 1959 *Fl* Pascual Perez (Arg) KO–13 Sadao Yaoita (Jap) Osaka, Japan

2 Dec 1959 *L* Joe Brown (USA) RTD-5 Dave Charnley (GB) Houston, USA

4 Dec 1959 *M(NBA)* Gene Fullmer (USA) PTS-15 Spider Webb (USA) Logan, USA

22 Jan 1960 *M* Paul Pender (USA) PTS-15 Sugar Ray Robinson (USA) Boston, USA

4 Feb 1960 *LW* Carlos Ortiz (PR) KO-10 Battling Torres (Mex) Los Angeles, USA

4 Feb 1960 *B* Joe Becerra (Mex) KO-9 Alphonse Halimi (Alg) Los Angeles, USA

16 Mar 1960 *JL* Flash Elorde (Phi) RSF-7 Harold Gomes (USA) Manila, Philippines

16 Apr 1960 *Fl* Pone Kingpetch (Tha) PTS-15 Pascual Perez (Arg) Bangkok, Thailand

20 Apr 1960 *M(NBA)* Gene Fullmer (USA) D-15 Joey Giardello (USA) Bozeman, USA

23 May 1960 *B* Joe Becerra (Mex) PTS-15 Kenji Yonekura (Jap) Tokyo, Japan

27 May 1960 *W* Benny 'Kid' Paret (Cuba) PTS-15 Don Jordan (USA) Las Vegas, USA

10 Jun 1960 *M* Paul Pender (USA) PTS-15 Sugar Ray Robinson (USA) Boston, USA

15 Jun 1960 *LW* Carlos Ortiz (PR) PTS-15 Duilio Loi (Ita) San Francisco, USA

20 Jun 1960 *H* Floyd Patterson (USA) KO-5 Ingemar Johansson (Swe) New York, USA

29 Jun 1960 *M(NBA)* Gene Fullmer (USA) KO-12 Carmen Basilio (USA) Salt Lake City, USA

17 Aug 1960 *JL* Flash Elorde (Phi) KO-1 Harold Gomes (USA) San Francisco, USA

29 Aug 1960 *Fe* Davey Moore (USA) PTS-15 Kazuo Takayama (Jap) Tokyo, Japan

1 Sep 1960 *LW* Duilio Loi (Ita) PTS-15 Carlos Ortiz (PR) Milan, Italy

22 Sep 1960 *Fl* Pone Kingpetch (Tha) RSF-8 Pascual Perez (Arg) Los Angeles, USA

25 Oct 1960 *B(EBU)* Alphonse Halimi (Alg) PTS-15 Freddie Gilroy (GB) London, England

28 Oct 1960 *L* Joe Brown (USA) PTS-15 Cisco Andrade (USA) Los Angeles, USA

18 Nov 1960 *B(NBA)* Eder Jofre (Bra) KO-6 Eloy Sanchez (Mex) Los Angeles, USA

3 Dec 1960 *M(NBA)* Gene Fullmer (USA) D-15 Sugar Ray Robinson (USA) Los Angeles, USA

10 Dec 1960 *W* Benny 'Kid' Paret (Cuba) PTS-15 Frederico Thompson (Pan) New York, USA

14 Jan 1961 *M* Paul Pender (USA) RSF-7 Terry Downes (GB) Boston, USA

7 Feb 1961 *LH(NBA)* Harold Johnson (USA) KO-9 Jesse Bowdry (USA) Miami, USA

4 Mar 1961 *M(NBA)* Gene Fullmer (USA) PTS-15 Sugar Ray Robinson (USA) Las Vegas, USA

13 Mar 1961 *H* Floyd Patterson (USA) KO-6 Ingemar Johansson (Swe) Miami, USA

19 Mar 1961 *JL* Flash Elorde (Phi) PTS-15 Joey Lopes (USA) Manila, Philippines

25 Mar 1961 *B(NBA)* Eder Jofre (Bra) RTD-9 Piero Rollo (Ita) Rio de Janeiro, Brazil

1 Apr 1961 *W* Emile Griffith (VI) KO-13 Benny 'Kid' Paret (Cuba) Miami, USA

8 Apr 1961 *Fe* Davey Moore (USA) KO-1 Danny Valdez (USA) Los Angeles, USA

18 Apr 1961 *L* Joe Brown (USA) PTS-15 Dave Charnley (GB) London, England

22 Apr 1961 *M* Paul Pender (USA) PTS-15 Carmen Basilio (USA) Boston, USA

24 Apr 1961 *LH(NBA)* Harold Johnson (USA) KO-2 Von Clay (USA) Philadelphia, USA

10 May 1961 *LW* Duilio Loi (Ita) PTS-15 Carlos Ortiz (PR) Milan, Italy

27 May 1961 *B(EBU)* Johnny Caldwell (GB) PTS-15 Alphonse Halimi (Alg) London, England

3 Jun 1961 *W* Emile Griffith (VI) RSF-12 Gaspar 'Indian' Ortega (Mex) Los Angeles, USA

10 Jun 1961 *LH* Archie Moore (USA) PTS-15 Giulio Rinaldi (Ita) New York, USA

27 Jun 1961 *Fl* Pone Kingpetch (Tha) PTS-15 Mitsunori Seki (Jap) Tokyo, Japan

11 Jul 1961 *M* Terry Downes (GB) RTD-9 Paul Pender (USA) London, England

5 Aug 1961 *M(NBA)* Gene Fullmer (USA) PTS-15 Florentino Fernandez (Cuba) Ogden, USA

19 Aug 1961 *B(NBA)* Eder Jofre (Bra) RTD-7 Ramon Arias (Ven) Caracas, Venezuela

29 Aug 1961 *LH(NBA)* Harold Johnson (USA) PTS-15 Eddie Cotton (USA) Seattle, USA

30 Sep 1961 *W* Benny 'Kid' Paret (Cuba) PTS-15 Emile Griffith (VI) New York, USA

21 Oct 1961 *LW* Duilio Loi (Ita) D-15 Eddie Perkins (USA) Milan, Italy

28 Oct 1961 *L* Joe Brown (USA) PTS-15 Bert Somodio (Phi) Quezon City, Philippines

31 Oct 1961 *B(EBU)* Johnny Caldwell (GB) PTS-15 Alphonse Halimi (Alg) London, England

13 Nov 1961 *Fe* Davey Moore (USA) PTS-15 Kazuo Takayama (Jap) Tokyo, Japan

4 Dec 1961 *H* Floyd Patterson (USA) KO-4 Tom McNeeley (USA) Toronto, Canada

9 Dec 1961 *M(NBA)* Gene Fullmer (USA) KO-10 Benny 'Kid' Paret (Cuba) Las Vegas, USA

16 Dec 1961 *JL* Flash Elorde (Phi) KO-1 Sergio Caprari (Ita) Manila, Philippines

18 Jan 1962 *B* Eder Jofre (Bra) RTD-10 Johnny Caldwell (GB) Sao Paulo, Brazil

24 Mar 1962 *W* Emile Griffith (VI) RSF-12 Benny 'Kid' Paret (Cuba) New York, USA

7 Apr 1962 *M* Paul Pender (USA) PTS-15 Terry Downes (GB) Boston, USA

21 Apr 1962 *L* Carlos Ortiz (PR) PTS-15 Joe Brown (USA) Las Vegas, USA

4 May 1962 *B* Eder Jofre (Bra) RSF-10 Herman Marques (USA) San Francisco, USA

12 May 1962 *LH* Harold Johnson (USA) PTS-15 Doug Jones (USA) Philadelphia, USA

30 May 1962 *Fl* Pone Kingpetch (Tha) PTS-15 Kyo Noguchi (Jap) Tokyo, Japan

23 Jun 1962 *LH* Harold Johnson (USA) PTS-15 Gustav Scholz (FRG) Berlin, West Germany

23 Jun 1962 *JL* Flash Elorde (Phi) PTS-15 Auburn Copeland (USA) Manila, Philippines

13 Jul 1962 *W* Emile Griffith (VI) PTS-15 Ralph Dupas (USA) Las Vegas, USA

17 Aug 1962 *Fe* Davey Moore (USA) RSF-2 Olli Makim (Fin) Helsinki, Finland

11 Sep 1962 *B* Eder Jofre (Bra) KO-6 Joe Medel (Mex) Sao Paulo, Brazil

14 Sep 1962 *LW* Eddie Perkins (USA) PTS-15 Duilio Loi (Ita) Milan, Italy

25 Sep 1962 *H* Sonny Liston (USA) KO-1 Floyd Patterson (USA) Chicago, USA

10 Oct 1962 *Fl* Fighting Harada (Jap) KO-11 Pone Kingpetch (Tha) Tokyo, Japan

20 Oct 1962 *LM* Denny Moyer (USA) PTS-15 Joey Giambra (USA) Portland, USA

23 Oct 1962 *M(NBA)* Dick Tiger (Ngr) PTS-15 Gene Fullmer (USA) San Francisco, USA

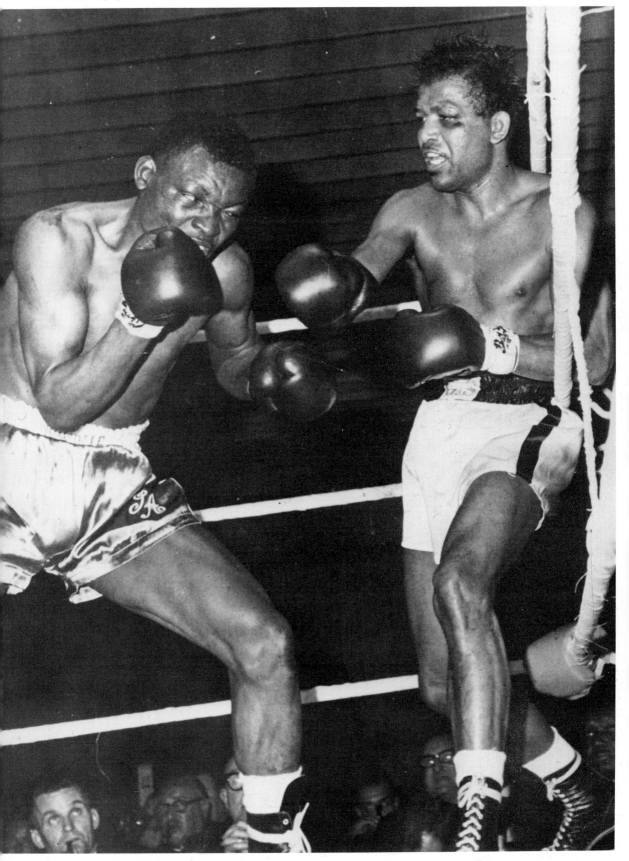

Sugar Ray Robinson (right) was 43 years of age when he came to London to fight Johnny Angel in 1964. Nevertheless, he was still too good for Angel and won in the 6th round (AP)

2 Dec 1962 *L* Carlos Ortiz (PR) KO–5 Teruo Kosaka (Jap) Tokyo, Japan

8 Dec 1962 *W* Emile Griffith (VI) RSF–9 Jorge Fernandez (Arg) Las Vegas, USA

15 Dec 1962 *LW* Duilio Loi (Ita) PTS–15 Eddie Perkins (USA) Milan, Italy

12 Jan 1963 *Fl* Pone Kingpetch (Tha) PTS–15 Fighting Harada (Jap) Bangkok, Thailand

16 Feb 1963 *JL* Flash Elorde (Phi) PTS–15 Johnny Bizzaro (USA) Manila, Philippines

19 Feb 1963 *LM* Denny Moyer (USA) PTS–15 Stan Harrington (USA) Honolulu, Hawaii

23 Feb 1963 *M* Dick Tiger (Ngr) D–15 Gene Fullmer (USA) Las Vegas, USA

21 Mar 1963 *W* Luis Rodriguez (Cuba) PTS–15 Emile Griffith (VI) Los Angeles, USA

21 Mar 1963 *LW* Roberto Cruz (Phi) KO–1 Battling Torres (Mex) Los Angeles, USA

21 Mar 1963 *Fe* Ultiminio 'Sugar' Ramos (Cuba) RTD–10 Davey Moore (USA) Los Angeles, USA

4 Apr 1963 *B* Eder Jofre (Bra) KO–3 Katsutoshi Aoki (Jap) Tokyo, Japan

7 Apr 1963 *L* Carlos Ortiz (PR) RSF–13 Doug Vaillant (Cuba) San Juan, Puerto Rico

29 Apr 1963 *LM* Ralph Dupas (USA) PTS–15 Denny Moyer (USA) New Orleans, USA

18 May 1963 *B* Eder Jofre (Bra) RTD–11 Johnny Jamito (Phi) Manila, Philippines

1 Jun 1963 *LH* Willie Pastrano (USA) PTS–15 Harold Johnson (USA) Las Vegas, USA

8 Jun 1963 *W* Emile Griffith (VI) PTS–15 Luis Rodriguez (Cuba) New York, USA

15 Jun 1963 *LW* Eddie Perkins (USA) PTS–15 Roberto Cruz (Phi) Manila, Philippines

17 Jun 1963 *LM* Ralph Dupas (USA) PTS–15 Denny Moyer (USA) Baltimore, USA

13 Jul 1963 *Fe* Ultiminio 'Sugar' Ramos (Cuba) PTS–15 Rafiu King (Ngr) Mexico City, Mexico

22 Jul 1963 *H* Sonny Liston (USA) KO–1 Floyd Patterson (USA) Las Vegas, USA

10 Aug 1963 *M* Dick Tiger (Ngr) KO–7 Gene Fullmer (USA) Ibadan, Nigeria

7 Sep 1963 *LM* Sandro Mazzinghi (Ita) KO–9 Ralph Dupas (USA) Milan, Italy

18 Sep 1963 *Fl* Hiroyuki Ebihara (Jap) KO–1 Pone Kingpetch (Tha) Tokyo, Japan

16 Nov 1963 *JL* Flash Elorde (Phi) DIS–11 Love Allotey (Gha) Manila, Philippines

2 Dec 1963 *LM* Sandro Mazzinghi (Ita) KO–13 Ralph Dupas (USA) Sydney, Australia

7 Dec 1963 *M* Joey Giardello (USA) PTS–15 Dick Tiger (Ngr) New York, USA

4 Jan 1964 *LW* Eddie Perkins (USA) RSF–13 Yoshinori Takahashi (Jap) Tokyo, Japan

23 Jan 1964 *Fl* Pone Kingpetch (Tha) PTS–15 Hiroyuki Ebihara (Jap) Bangkok, Thailand

15 Feb 1964 *L* Carlos Ortiz (PR) RSF–14 Flash Elorde (Phi) Manila, Philippines

25 Feb 1964 *H* Cassius Clay (USA) RTD–6 Sonny Liston (USA) Miami, USA

28 Feb 1964 *Fe* Ultiminio 'Sugar' Ramos (Cuba) RTD–6 Mitsonuri Seki (Jap) Tokyo, Japan

10 Apr 1964 *LH* Willie Pastrano (USA) KO–6 Gregorio Peralta (Arg) New Orleans, USA

11 Apr 1964 *L* Carlos Ortiz (PR) PTS–15 Kenny Lane (USA) San Juan, Puerto Rico

19 Apr 1964 *LW* Eddie Perkins (USA) PTS–15 Bunny Grant (Jam) Kingston, Jamaica

9 May 1964 *Fe* Ultiminio 'Sugar' Ramos (Cuba) PTS–15 Floyd Robertson (Gha) Accra, Ghana

12 Jun 1964 *W* Emile Griffith (VI) PTS–15 Luis Rodriguez (Cuba) Las Vegas, USA

27 Jul 1964 *JL* Flash Elorde (Phi) RSF–12 Teruo Kosaka (Jap) Tokyo, Japan

22 Sep 1964 *W* Emile Griffith (VI) PTS–15 Brian Curvis (GB) London, England

26 Sep 1964 *Fe* Vicente Saldivar (Mex) RTD–11 Ultiminio 'Sugar' Ramos (Cuba) Mexico City, Mexico

3 Oct 1964 *LM* Sandro Mazzinghi (Ita) RSF–12 Tony Montano (USA) Genoa, Italy

27 Nov 1964 *B* Eder Jofre (Bra) KO–7 Bernardo Carabello (Col) Bogotá, Colombia

30 Nov 1964 *LH* Willie Pastrano (USA) RSF–11 Terry Downes (GB) Manchester, England

11 Dec 1964 *LM* Sandro Mazzinghi (Ita) PTS–15 Fortunato Manca (Ita) Rome, Italy

14 Dec 1964 *M* Joey Giardello (USA) PTS–15 Rubin Carter (USA) Philadelphia, USA

18 Jan 1965 *LW* Carlos Hernandez (Ven) PTS–15 Eddie Perkins (USA) Caracas, Venezuela

5 Mar 1965 *H(WBA)* Ernie Terrell (USA) PTS–15 Eddie Machen (USA) Chicago, USA

30 Mar 1965 *LH* Jose Torres (PR) KO–9 Willie Pastrano (USA) New York, USA

30 Mar 1965 *W* Emile Griffith (VI) PTS–15 Jose Stable (Cuba) New York, USA

10 Apr 1965 *L* Ismael Laguna (Pan) PTS–15 Carlos Ortiz (PR) Panama City, Panama

23 Apr 1965 *Fl* Salvatore Burruni (Ita) PTS–15 Pone Kingpetch (Tha) Rome, Italy

7 May 1965 *Fe* Vicente Saldivar (Mex) RSF–15 Raul Rojas (USA) Los Angeles, USA

16 May 1965 *LW* Carlos Hernandez (Ven) RSF–4 Mario Rossito (Col) Maracaibo, Venezuela

18 May 1965 *B* Fighting Harada (Jap) PTS–15 Eder Jofre (Bra) Nagoya, Japan

25 May 1965 *H* Muhammad Ali (USA) KO–1 Sonny Liston (USA) Lewiston, USA

5 Jun 1965 *JL* Flash Elorde (Phi) KO–13 Teruo Kosaka (Jap) Manila, Philippines

18 Jun 1965 *LM* Nino Benvenuti (Ita) KO–6 Sandro Mazzinghi (Ita) Milan, Italy

10 Jul 1965 *LW* Carlos Hernandez (Ven) KO–3 Percy Hayles (Jam) Kingston, Jamaica

7 Sep 1965 *Fe* Vicente Saldivar (Mex) PTS–15 Howard Winstone (GB) London, England

21 Oct 1965 *M* Dick Tiger (Ngr) PTS–15 Joey Giardello (USA) New York, USA

1 Nov 1965 *H(WBA)* Ernie Terrell (USA) PTS–15 George Chuvalo (Can) Toronto, Canada

13 Nov 1965 *L* Carlos Ortiz (PR) PTS–15 Ismael Laguna (Pan) San Juan, Puerto Rico

22 Nov 1965 *H* Muhammad Ali (USA) RSF–12 Floyd Patterson (USA) Las Vegas, USA

30 Nov 1965 *B* Fighting Harada (Jap) PTS–15 Alan Rudkin (GB) Tokyo, Japan

2 Dec 1965 *Fl(WBC)* Salvatore Burruni (Ita) KO–13 Rocky Gattelleri (Ita) Sydney, Australia

4 Dec 1965 *JL* Flash Elorde (Phi) PTS–15 Kang-ll Suh (S. Kor) Manila, Philippines

10 Dec 1965 *W* Emile Griffith (VI) PTS–15 Manuel Gonzalez (USA) New York, USA

17 Dec 1965 *LM* Nino Benvenuti (Ita) PTS–15 Sandro Mazzinghi (Ita) Rome, Italy

12 Feb 1966 *Fe* Vicente Saldivar (Mex) KO–2 Floyd Robertson (Gha) Mexico City, Mexico

1 Mar 1966 *Fl(WBA)* Horacio Accavallo (Arg) PTS–15 Katsuyoshi Takayama (Jap) Tokyo, Japan

29 Mar 1966 *H* Muhammad Ali (USA) PTS–15 George Chuvalo (Can) Toronto, Canada

25 Apr 1966 *M* Emile Griffith (VI) PTS–15 Dick Tiger (Ngr) New York, USA

29 Apr 1966 *LW* Sandro Lopopolo (Ita) PTS–15 Carlos Hernandez (Ven) Rome, Italy

21 May 1966 *H* Muhammad Ali (USA) RSF–6 Henry Cooper (GB) London, England

21 May 1966 *LH* Jose Torres (PR) PTS–15 Wayne Thornton (USA) New York, USA

1 Jun 1966 *B* Fighting Harada (Jap) PTS–15 Eder Jofre (Bra) Tokyo, Japan

14 Jun 1966 *Fl(WBC)* Walter McGowan (GB) PTS–15 Salvatore Burruni (Ita) London, England

20 Jun 1966 *L* Carlos Ortiz (PR) RSF–12 Johnny Bizzaro (USA) Pittsburgh, USA

25 Jun 1966 *LM* Ki-Soo Kim (S. Kor) PTS–15 Nino Benvenuti (Ita) Seoul, South Korea

28 Jun 1966 *H(WBA)* Ernie Terrell (USA) PTS–15 Doug Jones (USA) Houston, USA

13 Jul 1966 *M* Emile Griffith (VI) PTS–15 Joey Archer (USA) New York, USA

15 Jul 1966 *Fl(WBA)* Horacio Accavallo (Arg) PTS–15 Hiroyuki Ebihara (Jap) Buenos Aires, Argentina

6 Aug 1966 *H* Muhammad Ali (USA) KO–3 Brian London (GB) London, England

7 Aug 1966 *Fe* Vicente Saldivar (Mex) PTS–15 Mitsunori Seki (Jap) Mexico City, Mexico

15 Aug 1966 *LH* Jose Torres (PR) PTS–15 Eddie Cotton (USA) Las Vegas, USA

24 Aug 1966 *W(WBA)* Curtis Cokes (USA) PTS–15 Manuel Gonzalez (USA) New Orleans, USA

10 Sep 1966 *H* Muhammad Ali (USA) RSF–12 Karl Mildenberger (FRG) Frankfurt, West Germany

15 Oct 1966 *LH* Jose Torres (PR) KO–2 Chic Calderwood (GB) San Juan, Puerto Rico

21 Oct 1966 *LW* Sandro Lopopolo (Ita) RSF–7 Vicente Rivas (Ven) Rome, Italy

22 Oct 1966 *L* Carlos Ortiz (PR) RSF–5 Ultiminio 'Sugar' Ramos (Cuba) Mexico City, Mexico

23 Oct 1966 *JL* Flash Elorde (Phi) PTS–15 Vicente Derado (Arg) Manila, Philippines

14 Nov 1966 *H* Muhammad Ali (USA) RSF–3 Cleveland Williams (USA) Houston, USA

28 Nov 1966 *W* Curtis Cokes (USA) PTS–15 Jean Josselin (Fra) Dallas, USA

28 Nov 1966 *L(WBA)* Carlos Ortiz (PR) KO–14 Flash Elorde (Phi) New York, USA

10 Dec 1966 *Fl(WBA)* Horacio Accavallo (Arg) PTS–15 Efren Torres (Mex) Buenos Aires, Argentina

16 Dec 1966 *LH* Dick Tiger (Ngr) PTS–15 Jose Torres (PR) New York, USA

17 Dec 1966 *LM* Ki-Soo Kim (S. Kor) PTS–15 Stan Harrington (USA) Seoul, South Korea

30 Dec 1966 *Fl(WBC)* Chartchai Chionoi (Tha) RSF–9 Walter McGowan (GB) Bangkok, Thailand

3 Jan 1967 *B* Fighting Harada (Jap) PTS–15 Joe Medel (Mex) Nagoya, Japan

23 Jan 1967 *M* Emile Griffith (VI) PTS–15 Joey Archer (USA) New York, USA

29 Jan 1967 *Fe* Vicente Saldivar (Mex) RSF–7 Mitsunori Seki (Jap) Mexico City, Mexico

6 Feb 1967 *H* Muhammad Ali (USA) PTS–15 Ernie Terrell (USA) Houston, USA

22 Mar 1967 *H* Muhammad Ali (USA) KO–7 Zora Folley (USA) New York, USA

17 Apr 1967 *M* Nino Benvenuti (Ita) PTS–15 Emile Griffith (VI) New York, USA

30 Apr 1967 *LW* Paul Fuji (Haw) RTD–2 Sandro Lopopolo (Ita) Tokyo, Japan

16 May 1967 *LH* Dick Tiger (Ngr) PTS–15 Jose Torres (PR) New York, USA

19 May 1967 *W* Curtis Cokes (USA) RSF–10 François Pavilla (Fra) Dallas, USA

15 Jun 1967 *JL* Yoshiaki Numata (Jap) PTS–15 Flash Elorde (Phi) Tokyo, Japan

15 Jun 1967 *Fe* Vicente Saldivar (Mex) PTS–15 Howard Winstone (GB) Cardiff, Wales

1 Jul 1967 *L* Carlos Ortiz (PR) RSF–4 Ultiminio 'Sugar' Ramos (Cuba) Mexico City, Mexico

4 Jul 1967 *B* Fighting Harada (Jap) PTS–15 Bernardo Carabello (Col) Tokyo, Japan

26 Jul 1967 *Fl(WBC)* Chartchai Chionoi (Tha) KO–3 Puntip Keosuriya (Tha) Bangkok, Thailand

13 Aug 1967 *Fl(WBA)* Horacio Accavallo (Arg) PTS–15 Hiroyuki Ebihara (Jap) Buenos Aires, Argentina

16 Aug 1967 *L* Carlos Ortiz (PR) PTS–15 Ismael Laguna (Pan) New York, USA

19 Sep 1967 *Fl(WBC)* Chartchai Chionoi (Tha) RSF–7 Walter McGowan (GB) London, England

29 Sep 1967 *M* Emile Griffith (VI) PTS–15 Nino Benvenuti (Ita) New York, USA

2 Oct 1967 *W* Curtis Cokes (USA) RSF–8 Charley Shipes (USA) Oakland, USA

14 Oct 1967 *Fe* Vicente Saldivar (Mex) RTD–12 Howard Winstone (GB) Mexico City, Mexico

31 Oct 1967 *LM* Ki-Soo Kim (S. Kor) PTS–15 Freddie Little (USA) Seoul, South Korea

16 Nov 1967 *LW* Paul Fuji (Haw) KO–4 Willi Quator (FRG) Tokyo, Japan

17 Nov 1967 *LH* Dick Tiger (Ngr) KO–12 Roger Rouse (USA) Las Vegas, USA

14 Dec 1967 *JL* Hiroshi Kobayashi (Jap) KO–12 Yoshiaki Numata (Jap) Tokyo, Japan

23 Jan 1968 *Fe(WBC)* Howard Winstone (GB) RSF–9 Mitsunori Seki (Jap) London, England

28 Jan 1968 *Fl(WBC)* Chartchai Chionoi (Tha) RSF–13 Efren Torres (Mex) Mexico City, Mexico

27 Feb 1968 *B* Lionel Rose (Aus) PTS–15 Fighting Harada (Jap) Tokyo, Japan

4 Mar 1968 *H(NY)* Joe Frazier (USA) RSF–11 Buster Mathis (USA) New York, USA

4 Mar 1968 *M* Nino Benvenuti (Ita) PTS–15 Emile Griffith (VI) New York, USA

28 Mar 1968 *Fe(WBA)* Raul Rojas (USA) PTS–15 Enrique Higgins (Col) Los Angeles, USA

30 Mar 1968 *JL* Hiroshi Kobayashi (Jap) D–15 Rene Barrientos (Phi) Tokyo, Japan

16 Apr 1968 *W* Curtis Cokes (USA) RSF–5 Willie Ludick (SA) Dallas, USA

27 Apr 1968 *H(WBA)* Jimmy Ellis (USA) PTS–15 Jerry Quarry (USA) Oakland, USA

24 May 1968 *LH* Bob Foster (USA) KO–4 Dick Tiger (Ngr) New York, USA

26 May 1968 *LM* Sandro Mazzinghi (Ita) PTS–15 Ki-Soo Kim (S. Kor) Milan, Italy

24 Jun 1968 *H(NY)* Joe Frazier (USA) RTD–2 Manuel Ramos (Mex) New York, USA

29 Jun 1968 *L* Carlos Cruz (Dom) PTS–15 Carlos Ortiz (PR) Santo Domingo, Dominican Republic

2 Jul 1968 *B* Lionel Rose (Aus) PTS–15 Takao Sakurai (Jap) Tokyo, Japan

24 July 1968 *Fe(WBC)* Jose Legra (Cuba) RSF–5 Howard Winstone (GB) Porthcawl, Wales

14 Sep 1968 *H(WBA)* Jimmy Ellis (USA) PTS–15 Floyd Patterson (USA) Stockholm, Sweden

27 Sep 1968 *L* Carlos Cruz (Dom) PTS–15 Mando Ramos (USA) Los Angeles, USA

28 Sep 1968 *Fe(WBA)* Sho Saijyo (Jap) PTS–15 Raul Rojas (USA) Los Angeles, USA

15 Oct 1968 *JL* Hiroshi Kobayashi (Jap) PTS–15 Jaime Valladares (Ecu) Tokyo, Japan

21 Oct 1968 *W* Curtis Cokes (USA) PTS–15 Ramon LaCruz (Arg) New Orleans, USA

25 Oct 1968 *LM* Sandro Mazzinghi (Ita) NC–8 Freddie Little (USA) Rome, Italy

10 Nov 1968 *Fl(WBC)* Chartchai Chionoi (Tha) PTS–15 Bernabe Villacampo (Phi) Bangkok, Thailand

6 Dec 1968 *H(NY)* Joe Frazier (USA) PTS–15 Oscar Bonavena (Arg) Philadelphia, USA

6 Dec 1968 *B* Lionel Rose (Aus) PTS–15 Chucho Castillo (Mex) Inglewood, USA

12 Dec 1968 *LW(WBA)* Nicolino Loche (Arg) RTD–9 Paul Fuji (Haw) Tokyo, Japan

14 Dec 1968 *M* Nino Benvenuti (Ita) PTS–15 Don Fullmer (USA) San Remo, Italy

14 Dec 1968 *LW(WBC)* Pedro Adigue (Phi) PTS–15 Adolph Pruitt (USA) Manila, Philippines

12 Jan 1969 *Fe(WBC)* Johnny Famechon (Fra) PTS–15 Jose Legra (Cuba) London, England

22 Jan 1969 *LH* Bob Foster (USA) KO–1 Frank de Paula (USA) New York, USA

9 Feb 1969 *Fe(WBA)* Sho Saijyo (Jap) PTS–15 Pedro Gomez (Ven) Tokyo, Japan

15 Feb 1969 *JL(WBC)* Rene Barrientos (Phi) PTS–15 Ruben Navarro (Mex) Manila, Philippines

18 Feb 1969 *L* Mando Ramos (USA) RSF–11 Carlos Cruz (Dom) Los Angeles, USA

23 Feb 1969 *Fl(WBC)* Efren Torres (Mex) RSF–8 Chartchai Chionoi (Tha) Mexico City, Mexico

8 Mar 1969 *B* Lionel Rose (Aus) PTS–15 Alan Rudkin (GB) Melbourne, Australia

17 Mar 1969 *LM* Freddie Little (USA) PTS–15 Stan Hayward (USA) Las Vegas, USA

30 Mar 1969 *Fl(WBA)* Hiroyuki Ebihara (Jap) PTS–15 Jose Severino (Bra) Sapporo, Japan

6 Apr 1969 *JL(WBA)* Hiroshi Kobayashi (Jap) PTS–15 Antonio Amaya (Pan) Tokyo, Japan

18 Apr 1969 *W* Jose Napoles (Cuba) RSF–13 Curtis Cokes (USA) Los Angeles, USA

22 Apr 1969 *H(NY)* Joe Frazier (USA) KO–1 Dave Zyglewicz (USA) Houston, USA

3 May 1969 *LW(WBA)* Nicolino Loche (Arg) PTS–15 Carlos Hernandez (Ven) Buenos Aires, Argentina

24 May 1969 *LH* Bob Foster (USA) KO–4 Andy Kendall (USA) West Springfield, USA

23 Jun 1969 *H(NY)* Joe Frazier (USA) RSF–7 Jerry Quarry (USA) New York, USA

29 Jun 1969 *W* Jose Napoles (Cuba) RTD–10 Curtis Cokes (USA) Mexico City, Mexico

28 Jul 1969 *Fe(WBC)* Johnny Famechon (Fra) PTS–15 Fighting Harada (Jap) Sydney, Australia

22 Aug 1969 *B* Ruben Olivares (Mex) KO–5 Lionel Rose (Aus) Inglewood, USA

7 Sep 1969 *Fe(WBA)* Sho Saijyo (Jap) KO–2 Jose Luis Pimente (Mex) Sapporo, Japan

9 Sep 1969 *LM* Freddie Little (USA) KO–2 Hisao Minami (Jap) Osaka, Japan

4 Oct 1969 *M* Nino Benvenuti (Ita) DIS–7 Fraser Scott (USA) Naples, Italy

4 Oct 1969 *L* Mando Ramos (USA) KO–6 Yoshiaki Numata (Jap) Los Angeles, USA

11 Oct 1969 *LW(WBA)* Nicolino Loche (Arg) PTS–15 Joao Henrique (Bra) Buenos Aires, Argentina

17 Oct 1969 *W* Jose Napoles (Cuba) PTS–15 Emile Griffith (VI) Los Angeles, USA

19 Oct 1969 *Fl(WBA)* Bernabe Villacampo (Phi) PTS–15 Hiroyuki Ebihara (Jap) Osaka, Japan

9 Nov 1969 *JL(WBA)* Hiroshi Kobayashi (Jap) PTS–15 Carlos Canete (Arg) Tokyo, Japan

22 Nov 1969 *M* Nino Benvenuti (Ita) KO–11 Luis Rodriguez (Cuba) Rome, Italy

28 Nov 1969 *Fl(WBC)* Efren Torres (Mex) PTS–15 Susumu Hanagata (Jap) Guadalajara, Mexico

12 Dec 1969 *B* Ruben Olivares (Mex) RSF–2 Alan Rudkin (GB) Inglewood, USA

6 Jan 1970 *Fe(WBC)* Johnny Famechon (Fra) KO–14 Fighting Harada (Jap) Tokyo, Japan

31 Jan 1970 *LW(WBC)* Bruno Arcari (Ita) PTS–15 Pedro Adigue (Phi) Rome, Italy

8 Feb 1970 *Fe(WBA)* Sho Saijyo (Jap) PTS–15 Godfrey Stevens (Chi) Tokyo, Japan

14 Feb 1970 *W* Jose Napoles (Cuba) RSF–15 Ernie Lopez (USA) Inglewood, USA

16 Feb 1970 *H* Joe Frazier (USA) RTD–4 Jimmy Ellis (USA) New York, USA

3 Mar 1970 *L* Ismael Laguna (Pan) RTD–9 Mando Ramos (USA) Los Angeles, USA

20 Mar 1970 *LM* Freddie Little (USA) PTS–15 Gerhard Piaskowy (FRG) Berlin, West Germany

20 Mar 1970 *Fl(WBC)* Chartchai Chionoi (Tha) PTS–15 Efren Torres (Mex) Bangkok, Thailand

4 Apr 1970 *LH* Bob Foster (USA) RSF–3 Roger Rouse (USA) Missoula, USA

5 Apr 1970 *JL(WBC)* Yoshiaki Numata (Jap) PTS–15 Rene Barrientos (Phi) Tokyo, Japan

14 Apr 1970 *Fl(WBA)* Berkrerk Chartvanchai (Tha) PTS–15 Bernabe Villacampo (Phi) Bangkok, Thailand

18 Apr 1970 *B* Ruben Olivares (Mex) PTS–15 Jesus Chucho Castillo (Mex) Los Angeles, USA

9 May 1970 *Fe(WBC)* Vicente Saldivar (Mex) PTS–15 Johnny Famechon (Fra) Rome, Italy

16 May 1970 *LW(WBA)* Nicolino Loche (Arg) PTS–15 Adolph Pruitt (USA) Buenos Aires, Argentina

23 May 1970 *M* Nino Benvenuti (Ita) KO–8 Tom Bethea (USA) Umag, Yugoslavia

6 Jun 1970 *L* Ismael Laguna (Pan) RSF–13 Ishimatsu Susuki (Jap) Panama City, Panama

27 Jun 1970 *LH* Bob Foster (USA) KO–10 Mark Tessman (USA) Baltimore, USA

5 Jul 1970 *Fe(WBA)* Sho Saijyo (Jap) PTS–15 Frankie Crawford (USA) Sendai, Japan

9 July 1970 *LM* Carmen Bossi (Ita) PTS–15 Freddie Little (USA) Monza, Italy

10 Jul 1970 *LW(WBC)* Bruno Arcari (Ita) DIS–6 Rene Roque (Fra) Lignano Sabbiadoro, Italy

23 Aug 1970 *JL(WBA)* Hiroshi Kobayashi (Jap) PTS–15 Antonio Amaya (Pan) Tokyo, Japan

26 Sep 1970 *L* Ken Buchanan (GB) PTS–15 Ismael Laguna (Pan) San Juan, Puerto Rico

27 Sep 1970 *JL(WBC)* Yoshiaki Numata (Jap) KO–5 Raul Rojas (USA) Tokyo, Japan

16 Oct 1970 *B* Jesus Chucho Castillo (Mex) RSF–14 Ruben Olivares (Mex) Inglewood, USA

21 Oct 1970 *Fl(WBA)* Masao Ohba (Jap) RSF–13 Berkrerk Chartvanchai (Tha) Tokyo, Japan

30 Oct 1970 *LW(WBC)* Bruno Arcari (Ita) KO–3 Raimundo Dias (Bra) Genoa, Italy

7 Nov 1970 *M* Carlos Monzon (Arg) KO–12 Nino Benvenuti (Ita) Rome, Italy

18 Nov 1970 *H* Joe Frazier (USA) KO–2 Bob Foster (USA) Detroit, USA

3 Dec 1970 *W* Billy Backus (USA) RSF–4 Jose Napoles (Cuba) Syracuse, USA

7 Dec 1970 *Fl(WBC)* Erbito Salavarria (Phi) RSF–2 Chartchai Chionoi (Tha) Bangkok, Thailand

11 Dec 1970 *Fe(WBC)* Kuniaki Shibata (Jap) RSF–12 Vicente Saldivar (Mex) Tijuana, Mexico

3 Jan 1971 *JL(WBC)* Yoshiaki Numata (Jap) PTS–15 Rene Barrientos (Phi) Shizuoka, Japan

12 Feb 1971 *L* Ken Buchanan (GB) PTS–15 Ruben Navarro (USA) Los Angeles, USA

27 Feb 1971 *LH(WBA)* Vicente Paul Rondon (Ven) RSF–6 Jimmy Dupree (USA) Caracas, Venezuela

28 Feb 1971 *Fe(WBA)* Sho Saijyo (Jap) PTS–15 Frankie Crawford (USA) Utsunomija, Japan

2 Mar 1971 *LH(WBC)* Bob Foster (USA) KO–4 Hal Carroll (USA) Scranton, USA

4 Mar 1971 *JL(WBA)* Hiroshi Kobayashi (Jap) PTS–15 Ricardo Arredondo (Mex) Utsunomija, Japan

6 Mar 1971 *LW(WBC)* Bruno Arcari (Ita) PTS–15 Joao Henrique (Bra) Genoa, Italy

8 Mar 1971 *H* Joe Frazier (USA) PTS–15 Muhammad Ali (USA) New York, USA

1 Apr 1971 *Fl(WBA)* Masao Ohba (Jap) PTS–15 Betulio Gonzalez (Ven) Tokyo, Japan

2 Apr 1971 *B* Ruben Olivares (Mex) PTS–15 Jesus Chucho Castillo (Mex) Inglewood, USA

3 Apr 1971 *LW(WBA)* Nicolino Loche (Arg) PTS–15 Domingo Barrera (Spa) Buenos Aires, Argentina

24 April 1971 *LH(WBC)* Bob Foster (USA) PTS–15 Ray Anderson (USA) Tampa, USA

29 Apr 1971 *LM* Carmen Bossi (Ita) D–15 Jose Hernandez (Spa) Madrid, Spain

30 Apr 1971 *Fl(WBC)* Erbito Salavarria (Phi) PTS–15 Susumu Hanagata (Jap) Manila, Philippines

8 May 1971 *M* Carlos Monzon (Arg) RSF–3 Nino Benvenuti (Ita) Monte Carlo, Monaco

31 May 1971 *JL(WBC)* Yoshiaki Numata (Jap) PTS–15 Lionel Rose (Aus) Hiroshima, Japan

Carlos Monzon of Argentina sends Italy's Nino Benvenuti to the canvas during Monzon's first defence of his world middleweight title in 1971 (AP)

3 Jun 1971 *Fe(WBC)* Kuniaki Shibata (Jap) KO–1 Raul Cruz (Mex) Tokyo, Japan

4 Jun 1971 *W* Jose Napoles (Cuba) RSF–8 Billy Backus (USA) Inglewood, USA

5 Jun 1971 *LH(WBA)* Vicente Paul Rondon (Ven) KO–1 Piero del Papa (Ita) Caracas, Venezuela

26 Jun 1971 *LW(WBC)* Bruno Arcari (Ita) RSF–9 Enrique Jana (Arg) Palermo, Italy

29 Jul 1971 *JL(WBA)* Alfredo Marcano (Ven) RTD–10 Hiroshi Kobayashi (Jap) Aomoni, Japan

21 Aug 1971 *LH(WBA)* Vicente Paul Rondon (Ven) PTS–15 Eddie Jones (USA) Caracas, Venezuela

2 Sep 1971 *Fe(WBA)* Antonio Gomez (Ven) RSF–5 Sho Saijyo (Jap) Tokyo, Japan

13 Sep 1971 *L* Ken Buchanan (GB) PTS–15 Ismael Laguna (Pan) New York, USA

25 Sep 1971 *M* Carlos Monzon (Arg) RSF–14 Emile Griffith (VI) Buenos Aires, Argentina

9 Oct 1971 *LW(WBC)* Bruno Arcari (Ita) KO–10 Domingo Barrera Corpas (Spa) Genoa, Italy

10 Oct 1971 *JL(WBC)* Ricardo Arredondo (Mex) KO–10 Yoshiaki Numata (Jap) Sendai, Japan

23 Oct 1971 *Fl(WBA)* Masao Ohba (Jap) PTS–15 Fernando Cabanela (Phi) Tokyo, Japan

25 Oct 1971 *B* Ruben Olivares (Mex) RSF–14 Kazuyoshi Kanazawa (Jap) Nagoya, Japan

26 Oct 1971 *LH(WBA)* Vincente Paul Rondon (Ven) RSF–12 Gomeo Brennan (Bah) Miami, USA

30 Oct 1971 *LH(WBC)* Bob Foster (USA) RSF–8 Tommy Hicks (USA) Scranton USA

31 Oct 1971 *LM* Koichi Wajima (Jap) PTS–15 Carmen Bossi (Ita) Tokyo, Japan

5 Nov 1971 *L(WBC)* Pedro Carrasco (Spa) DIS–11 Mando Ramos (USA) Madrid, Spain

6 Nov 1971 *JL(WBA)* Alfredo Marcano (Ven) RSF–4 Kenji Iwata (Jap) Caracas, Venezuela

11 Nov 1971 *Fe(WBC)* Kuniaki Shibata (Jap) D–15 Ernesto Marcel (Pan) Matsuyama, Japan

20 Nov 1971 *Fl(WBC)* Erbito Salavarria (Phi) D–15 Betulio Gonzalez (Ven) Maracaibo, Venezuela

11 Dec 1971 *LW(WBA)* Nicolino Loche (Arg) PTS–15 Antonio Cervantes (Col) Buenos Aires, Argentina

14 Dec 1971 *W* Jose Napoles (Cuba) PTS–15 Hedgemon Lewis (USA) Inglewood, USA

14 Dec 1971 *B* Ruben Olivares (Mex) RSF–11 Jesus Pimentel (Mex) Inglewood, USA

15 Dec 1971 *LH(WBA)* Vicente Paul Rondon (Ven) KO–8 Doyle Baird (USA) Cleveland, USA

16 Dec 1971 *LH(WBC)* Bob Foster (USA) RSF–4 Brian Kelly (USA) Oklahoma City, USA

15 Jan 1972 *H* Joe Frazier (USA) RSF–4 Terry Daniels (USA) New Orleans, USA

29 Jan 1972 *JL(WBC)* Ricardo Arredondo (Mex) PTS–15 Jose Isaac Marin (CR) San Jose, Costa Rica

5 Feb 1972 *Fe(WBA)* Antonio Gomez (Ven) KO–7 Raul Martinez (Mex) Maracay, Venezuela

18 Feb 1972 *L(WBC)* Mando Ramos (USA) PTS–15 Pedro Carrasco (Spa) Los Angeles, USA

4 Mar 1972 *M* Carlos Monzon (Arg) RSF–5 Denny Moyer (USA) Rome, Italy

4 Mar 1972 *Fl(WBA)* Masao Ohba (Jap) PTS–15 Susumu Hanagata (Jap) Tokyo, Japan

10 Mar 1972 *LW(WBA)* Alfonso Frazer (Pan) PTS–15 Nicolino Loche (Arg) Panama City, Panama

19 Mar 1972 *B* Rafael Herrera (Mex) KO–8 Ruben Olivares (Mex) Mexico City, Mexico

28 Mar 1972 *W* Jose Napoles (Cuba) KO–7 Ralph Charles (GB) London, England

7 Apr 1972 *LH* Bob Foster (USA) KO–2 Vicente Paul Rondon (Ven) Miami, USA

22 Apr 1972 *JL(WBC)* Ricardo Arredondo (Mex) KO–5 William Martinez (Nic) Mexico City, Mexico

25 Apr 1972 *JL(WBA)* Ben Villaflor (Phi) PTS–15 Alfredo Marcano (Ven) Honolulu, USA

7 May 1972 *LM* Koichi Wajima (Jap) KO–1 Domenico Tiberia (Ita) Fukuoka, Japan

9 May 1972 *Fe(WBC)* Clemente Sanchez (Mex) KO–3 Kuniaki Shibata (Jap) Tokyo, Japan

25 May 1972 *H* Joe Frazier (USA) RSF–4 Ron Stander (USA) Omaha, USA

3 Jun 1972 *Fl(WBC)* Betulio Gonzalez (Ven) KO–4 Socrates Batoto (Phi) Caracas, Venezuela

10 Jun 1972 *W* Jose Napoles (Cuba) RSF–2 Adolph Pruitt (USA) Monterrey, Mexico

10 Jun 1972 *LW(WBC)* Bruno Arcari (Ita) KO–12 Joao Henrique (Bra) Genoa, Italy

17 Jun 1972 *M* Carlos Monzon (Arg) RTD–12 Jean-Claude Boutier (Fra) Paris, France

20 Jun 1972 *Fl(WBA)* Masao Ohba (Jap) KO–5 Orlando Amores (Pan) Tokyo, Japan

26 Jun 1972 *L(WBA)* Roberto Duran (Pan) RSF–13 Ken Buchanan (GB) New York, USA

27 Jun 1972 *LH* Bob Foster (USA) KO–4 Mike Quarry (USA) Las Vegas, USA

28 Jun 1972 *L(WBC)* Mando Ramos (USA) PTS–15 Pedro Carrasco (Spa) Madrid, Spain

29 Jul 1972 *B* Enrique Pinder (Pan) PTS–15 Rafael Herrera (Mex) Panama City, Panama

19 Aug 1972 *M* Carlos Monzon (Arg) RSF–5 Tom Bogs (Den) Copenhagen, Denmark

19 Aug 1972 *Fe(WBA)* Ernesto Marcel (Pan) PTS–15 Antonio Gomez (Ven) Maracay, Venezuela

5 Sep 1972 *JL(WBA)* Ben Villaflor (Phi) D–15 Victor Echegaray (Arg) Honolulu, USA

15 Sep 1972 *L(WBC)* Erubey 'Chango' Carmona (Mex) RSF–8 Mando Ramos (USA) Los Angeles, USA

15 Sep 1972 *JL(WBC)* Ricardo Arredondo (Mex) KO–12 Susumu Okabe (Jap) Tokyo, Japan

26 Sep 1972 *LH* Bob Foster (USA) KO–14 Chris Finnegan (GB) London, England

29 Sep 1972 *Fl(WBC)* Venice Borkorsor (Tha) RTD–10 Betulio Gonzalez (Ven) Bangkok, Thailand

3 Oct 1972 *LM* Koichi Wajima (Jap) KO–3 Matt Donovan (Tri) Tokyo, Japan

29 Oct 1972 *LW(WBA)* Antonio Cervantes (Col) KO–10 Alfonso Frazer (Pan) Panama City, Panama

10 Nov 1972 *L(WBC)* Rodolfo Gonzalez (Mex) RTD–12 Erubey 'Chango' Carmona (Mex) Los Angeles, USA

11 Nov 1972 *M* Carlos Monzon (Arg) PTS–15 Bennie Briscoe (USA) Buenos Aires, Argentina

2 Dec 1972 *LW(WBC)* Bruno Arcari (Ita) PTS–15 Everaldo Costa Azevedo (Bra) Turin, Italy

16 Dec 1972 *Fe(WBC)* Jose Legra (Cuba) RSF–10 Clemente Sanchez (Mex) Monterrey, Mexico

21 Dec 1972 *Fe(WBA)* Ernesto Marcel (Pan) RSF–6 Enrique Garcia (Mex) Panama City, Panama

2 Jan 1973 *Fl(WBA)* Masao Ohba (Jap) RSF–12 Chartchai Chionoi (Tha) Tokyo, Japan

9 Jan 1973 *LM* Koichi Wajima (Jap) D–15 Miguel de Oliveira (Bra) Tokyo, Japan

20 Jan 1973 *L(WBA)* Roberto Duran (Pan) KO–5 Jimmy Robertson (USA) Panama City, Panama

20 Jan 1973 *B(WBA)* Romeo Anaya (Mex) KO–3 Enrique Pinder (Pan) Panama City, Panama

22 Jan 1973 *H* George Foreman (USA) RSF–2 Joe Frazier (USA) Kingston, Jamaica

9 Feb 1973 *Fl(WBC)* Venice Borkorsor (Tha) PTS–15 Erbito Salavarria (Phi) Bangkok, Thailand

15 Feb 1973 *LW(WBA)* Antonio Cervantes (Col) PTS–15 Jose Marquez (PR) San Juan, Puerto Rico

28 Feb 1973 *W* Jose Napoles (Cuba) KO–7 Ernie Lopez (USA) Inglewood, USA

6 Mar 1973 *JL(WBC)* Ricardo Arredondo (Mex) PTS–15 Apollo Yoshio (Jap) Fukuoka, Japan

12 Mar 1973 *JL(WBA)* Kuniaki Shibata (Jap) PTS–15 Ben Villaflor (Phi) Honolulu, USA

17 Mar 1973 *LW(WBA)* Antonio Cervantes (Col) RTD–9 Nicolino Loche (Arg) Maracay, Venezuela

17 Mar 1973 *L(WBC)* Rodolfo Gonzalez (Mex) RSF–9 Ruben Navarro (USA) Los Angeles, USA

14 Apr 1973 *B(WBC)* Rafael Herrera (Mex) RSF–12 Rodolfo Martinez (Mex) Monterrey, Mexico

20 Apr 1973 *LM* Koichi Wajima (Jap) PTS–15 Ryu Sorimachi (Jap) Tokyo, Japan

28 Apr 1973 *B(WBA)* Romeo Anaya (Mex) PTS–15 Rogelio Lara (Mex) Inglewood, USA

5 May 1973 *Fe(WBC)* Eder Jofre (Bra) PTS–15 Jose Legra (Cuba) Brasilia, Brazil

17 May 1973 *Fl(WBA)* Chartchai Chionoi (Tha) RSF–4 Fritz Chervet (Swi) Bangkok, Thailand

19 May 1973 *LW(WBA)* Antonio Cervantes (Col) RSF–5 Alfonso Frazer (Pan) Panama City, Panama

2 Jun 1973 *M* Carlos Monzon (Arg) PTS–15 Emile Griffith (VI) Monte Carlo, Monaco

2 Jun 1973 *L(WBA)* Roberto Duran (Pan) RSF–8 Hector Thompson (Aus) Panama City, Panama

19 Jun 1973 *JL(WBA)* Kuniaki Shibata (Jap) PTS–15 Victor Echegaray (Arg) Tokyo, Japan

23 Jun 1973 *W* Jose Napoles (Cuba) PTS–15 Roger Menetrey (Fra) Grenoble, France

14 Jul 1973 *Fe(WBA)* Ernesto Marcel (Pan) RTD–11 Antonio Gomez (Ven) Panama City, Panama

4 Aug 1973 *Fl(WBC)* Betulio Gonzalez (Ven) PTS–15 Miguel Canto (Mex) Maracaibo, Venezuela

14 Aug 1973 *LM* Koichi Wajima (Jap) RTD–12 Silvano Bertini (Ita) Sapporo, Japan

18 Aug 1973 *B(WBA)* Romeo Anaya (Mex) KO–3 Enrique Pinder (Pan) Inglewood, USA

21 Aug 1973 *LH* Bob Foster (USA) PTS–15 Pierre Fourie (SA) Albuquerque, USA

1 Sep 1973 *H* George Foreman (USA) KO–1 Joe Roman (PR) Tokyo, Japan

1 Sep 1973 *JL(WBC)* Ricardo Arredondo (Mex) RSF–6 Morita Kashiwaba (Jap) Tokyo, Japan

8 Sep 1973 *LW(WBA)* Antonio Cervantes (Col) RSF–5 Carlos Giminez (Arg) Bogotá, Colombia

8 Sep 1973 *L(WBA)* Roberto Duran (Pan) RSF–10 Ishimatsu Susuki (Jap) Panama City, Panama

8 Sep 1973 *Fe(WBA)* Ernesto Marcel (Pan) KO–9 Shig Nemoto (Jap) Panama City, Panama

22 Sep 1973 *W* Jose Napoles (Cuba) PTS–15 Clyde Gray (Can) Toronto, Canada

29 Sep 1973 *M* Carlos Monzon (Arg) PTS–15 Jean-Claude Boutier (Fra) Paris, France

13 Oct 1973 *B(WBC)* Rafael Herrera (Mex) PTS–15 Venice Borkorsor (Tha) Inglewood, USA

17 Oct 1973 *JL(WBA)* Ben Villaflor (Phi) KO–1 Kuniaki Shibata (Jap) Honolulu, USA

21 Oct 1973 *Fe(WBC)* Eder Jofre (Bra) KO–4 Vicente Saldivar (Mex) Salvador, Brazil

27 Oct 1973 *L(WBC)* Rodolfo Gonzalez (Mex) RTD–10 Antonio Puddu (Ita) Los Angeles, USA

27 Oct 1973 *Fl(WBA)* Chartchai Chionoi (Tha) PTS–15 Susumu Hanagata (Jap) Bangkok, Thailand

1 Nov 1973 *LW(WBC)* Bruno Arcari (Ita) KO–5 Jorgen Hansen (Den) Copenhagen, Denmark

3 Nov 1973 *B(WBA)* Arnold Taylor (SA) KO–14 Romeo Anaya (Mex) Johannesburg, South Africa

17 Nov 1973 *Fl(WBC)* Betulio Gonzalez (Ven) RSF–11 Alberto Morales (Mex) Caracas, Venezuela

1 Dec 1973 *LH* Bob Foster (USA) PTS–15 Pierre Fourie (SA) Johannesburg, South Africa

5 Dec 1973 *LW(WBA)* Antonio Cervantes (Col) PTS–15 Tetsuo Furuyama (Jap) Panama City, Panama

5 Feb 1974 *LM* Koichi Wajima (Jap) PTS–15 Miguel de Oliveira (Bra) Tokyo, Japan

9 Feb 1974 *M* Carlos Monzon (Arg) RTD–7 Jose Napoles (Cuba) Paris, France

16 Feb 1974 *LW(WBC)* Bruno Arcari (Ita) DIS–8 Tony Ortiz (Spa) Turin, Italy

16 Feb 1974 *Fe(WBA)* Ernesto Marcel (Pan) PTS–15 Alexis Arguello (Nic) Panama City, Panama

28 Feb 1974 *JL(WBA)* Kuniaki Shibata (Jap) PTS–15 Ricardo Arredondo (Mex) Tokyo, Japan

2 Mar 1974 *LW(WBA)* Antonio Cervantes (Col) KO–6 Chang Kil-Lee (S. Kor) Cartagena, Colombia

14 Mar 1974 *JL(WBA)* Ben Villaflor (Phi) D–15 Apollo Yoshio (Jap) Toyama, Japan

16 Mar 1974 *L(WBA)* Roberto Duran (Pan) KO–11 Esteban de Jesus (PR) Panama City, Panama

26 Mar 1974 *H* George Foreman (USA) RSF–2 Ken Norton (USA) Caracas, Venezuela

11 Apr 1974 *L(WBC)* Guts Ishimatsu (Jap) KO–8 Rodolfo Gonzalez (Mex) Tokyo, Japan

27 Apr 1974 *Fl(WBA)* Chartchai Chionoi (Tha) PTS–15 Fritz Chervet (Swi) Zurich, Switzerland

25 May 1974 *M(WBC)* Rodrigo Valdez (Col) KO–7 Bennie Briscoe (USA) Monte Carlo, Monaco

25 May 1974 *B(WBC)* Rafael Herrera (Mex) KO–6 Romeo Anaya (Mex) Mexico City, Mexico

4 Jun 1974 *LM* Oscar Albarado (USA) KO–15 Koichi Wajima (Jap) Tokyo, Japan

17 Jun 1974 *LH* Bob Foster (USA) D–15 Jorge Ahumada (Arg) Albuquerque, USA

27 Jun 1974 *JL(WBC)* Kuniaki Shibata (Jap) PTS–15 Antonio Amaya (Pan) Tokyo, Japan

3 Jul 1974 *B(WBA)* Soo-Hwan Hong (S. Kor) PTS–15 Arnold Taylor (SA) Durban, South Africa

9 Jul 1974 *Fe(WBA)* Ruben Olivares (Mex) RSF–7 Zensuke Utagawa (Jap) Inglewood, USA

20 Jul 1974 *Fl(WBC)* Betulio Gonzalez (Ven) RSF–10 Franco Udella (Ita) Sabbiardoro, Italy

27 July 1974 *LW(WBA)* Antonio Cervantes (Col) KO–2 Victor Ortiz (PR) Cartagena, Colombia

3 Aug 1974 *W* Jose Napoles (Cuba) RSF–9 Hedgemon Lewis (USA) Mexico City, Mexico

24 Aug 1974 *JL(WBA)* Ben Villaflor (Phi) RSF–2 Yasatsune Uehara (Jap) Honolulu, USA

7 Sep 1974 *Fe(WBC)* Bobby Chacon (USA) RSF–9 Alfredo Marcano (Ven) Los Angeles, USA

12 Sep 1974 *L(WBC)* Guts Ishimatsu (Jap) D–15 Arturo Pineda (USA) Nagoya, Japan

21 Sep 1974 *LW(WBC)* Perico Fernandez (Spa) PTS–15 Lion Furuyama (Jap) Rome, Italy

1 Oct 1974 *LH(WBC)* John Conteh (GB) PTS–15 Jorge Ahumada (Arg) London, England

1 Oct 1974 *Fl(WBC)* Shoji Oguma (Jap) PTS–15 Betulio Gonzalez (Ven) Tokyo, Japan

3 Oct 1974 *JL(WBC)* Kuniaki Shibata (Jap) RSF–15 Ramiro Clay Bolanos (Ecu) Tokyo, Japan

5 Oct 1974 *M(WBA)* Carlos Monzon (Arg) KO–7 Tony Mundine (Aus) Buenos Aires, Argentina

8 Oct 1974 *LM* Oscar Albarado (USA) RSF–7 Ryu Sorimachi (Jap) Tokyo, Japan

18 Oct 1974 *Fl(WBA)* Susumu Hanagata (Jap) RSF–6 Chartchai Chionoi (Tha) Yokohama, Japan

26 Oct 1974 *LW(WBA)* Antonio Cervantes (Col) KO–8 Yasuaki Kadota (Jap) Tokyo, Japan

30 Oct 1974 *H* Muhammad Ali (USA) KO–8 George Foreman (USA) Kinshasa, Zaire

13 Nov 1974 *M(WBC)* Rodrigo Valdez (Col) KO–11 Gratien Tonna (Fra) Paris, France

23 Nov 1974 *Fe(WBA)* Alexis Arguello (Nic) KO–13 Ruben Olivares (Mex) Inglewood, USA

28 Nov 1974 *L(WBC)* Guts Ishimatsu (Jap) KO–12 Rodolfo Gonzalez (Mex) Osaka, Japan

7 Dec 1974 *LH(WBA)* Victor Galindez (Arg) RTD–12 Len Hutchins (USA) Buenos Aires, Argentina

7 Dec 1974 *B(WBC)* Rodolfo Martinez (Mex) RSF–4 Rafael Herrera (Mex) Merida, Mexico

14 Dec 1974 *W* Jose Napoles (Cuba) KO–3 Horacio Saldano (Arg) Mexico City, Mexico

21 Dec 1974 *L(WBA)* Roberto Duran (Pan) RSF–1 Mastaka Takayama (Jap) San Jose, Costa Rica

28 Dec 1974 *B(WBA)* Soo-Hwan Hong (S. Kor) PTS–15 Fernando Cabanela (Phi) Seoul, South Korea

8 Jan 1975 *Fl(WBC)* Miguel Canto (Mex) PTS–15 Shoji Oguma (Jap) Sendai, Japan

21 Jan 1975 *LM* Koichi Wajima (Jap) PTS–15 Oscar Albarado (USA) Tokyo, Japan

27 Feb 1975 *L(WBC)* Guts Ishimatsu (Jap) PTS–15 Ken Buchanan (GB) Tokyo, Japan

1 Mar 1975 *Fe(WBC)* Bobby Chacon (USA) KO–2 Jesus Estrada (Mex) Los Angeles, USA

2 Mar 1975 *L(WBA)* Roberto Duran (Pan) KO–14 Ray Lampkin (USA) Panama City, Panama

11 Mar 1975 *LH(WBC)* John Conteh (GB) RSF–5 Lonnie Bennett (USA) London, England

14 Mar 1975 *JL(WBA)* Ben Villaflor (Phi) PTS–15 Hyun-Chi Kim (S. Kor) Manila, Philippines

14 Mar 1975 *B(WBA)* Alfonso Zamora (Mex) KO–4 Soo-Hwan Hong (S. Kor) Inglewood, USA

15 Mar 1975 *Fe(WBA)* Alexis Arguello (Nic) RSF–8 Leonel Hernandez (Ven) Caracas, Venezuela

23 Mar 1975 *JL(WBC)* Kuniaki Shibata (Jap) PTS–15 Ould Makloufi (Alg) Fukuoka, Japan

24 Mar 1975 *H* Muhammad Ali (USA) RSF–15 Chuck Wepner (USA) Cleveland, USA

29 Mar 1975 *W* Jose Napoles (Cuba) TD–12 Armando Muniz (Mex) Acapulco, Mexico

1 Apr 1975 *Fl(WBA)* Erbito Salavarria (Phi) PTS–15 Susumu Hanagata (Jap) Toyama, Japan

4 Apr 1975 *LF(WBC)* Franco Udella (Ita) DIS–12 Valentine Martinez (Mex) Milan, Italy

7 Apr 1975 *LH(WBA)* Victor Galindez (Arg) PTS–15 Pierre Fourie (SA) Johannesburg, South Africa

19 Apr 1975 *LW(WBC)* Perico Fernandez (Spa) KO–9 Joao Henrique (Bra) Barcelona, Spain

3 May 1975 *B(WBC)* Rodolfo Martinez (Mex) RSF–7 Nestor Jiminez (Col) Bogotá, Colombia

7 May 1975 *LM(WBC)* Miguel de Oliveira (Bra) PTS–15 Jose Duran (Spa) Madrid, Spain

16 May 1975 *H* Muhammad Ali (USA) RSF–11 Ron Lyle (USA) Las Vegas, USA

17 May 1975 *LW(WBA)* Antonio Cervantes (Col) PTS–15 Esteban de Jesus (PR) Panama City, Panama

24 May 1975 *Fl(WBC)* Miguel Canto (Mex) PTS–15 Betulio Gonzalez (Ven) Monterrey, Mexico

31 May 1975 *M(WBC)* Rodrigo Valdez (Col) KO–8 Ramon Mendez (Arg) Cali, Colombia

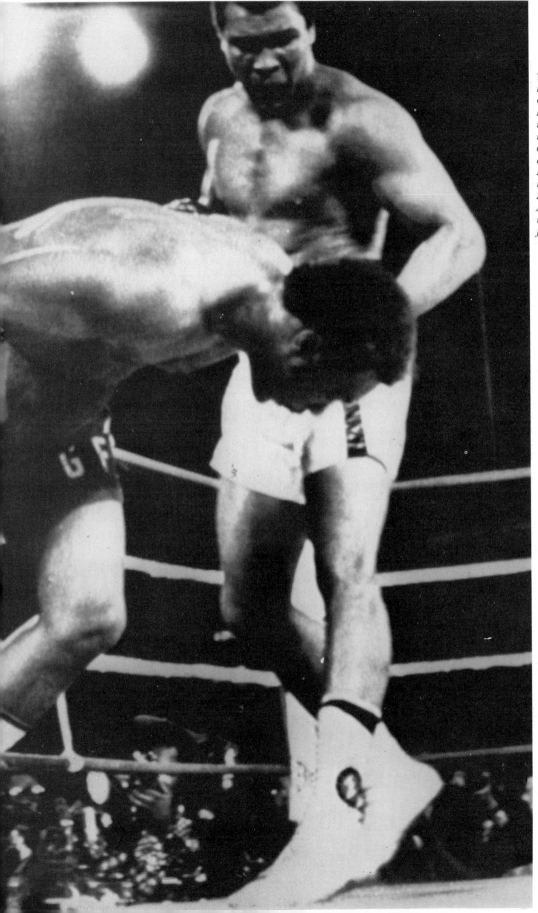

The beginning of the end for George Foreman. He was counted out in the 8th round of his world title defence against Muhammad Ali in Kinshasha, Zaire in 1974. Ali regained the world title for the first time (AP)

31 May 1975 *Fe(WBA)* Alexis Arguello (Nic) RSF–2
Rigoberto Riasco (Pan) Granada, Nicaragua

5 Jun 1975 *L(WBC)* Guts Ishimatsu (Jap) PTS–15 Arturo
Pineda (Mex) Osaka, Japan

7 Jun 1975 *LM(WBA)* Jae-Do Yuh (S. Kor) KO–7 Koichi
Wajima (Jap) Kitsakyushu, Japan

20 Jun 1975 *Fe(WBC)* Ruben Olivares (Mex) RSF–2 Bobby
Chacon (USA) Inglewood, USA

28 Jun 1975 *W(WBA)* Angel Espada (PR) PTS–15 Clyde
Gray (Can) San Juan, Puerto Rico

30 Jun 1975 *LH(WBA)* Victor Galindez (Arg) PTS–15 Jorge
Ahumada (Arg) New York, USA

30 Jun 1975 *M(WBA)* Carlos Monzon (Arg) KO–10 Tony
Licata (USA) New York, USA

1 Jul 1975 *H* Muhammad Ali (USA) PTS–15 Joe Bugner
(GB) Kuala Lumpur, Malaysia

5 Jul 1975 *JL(WBC)* Alfredo Escalera (PR) KO–2 Kuniaki
Shibata (Jap) Mito, Japan

12 Jul 1975 *W(WBC)* Jose Napoles (Cuba) PTS–15
Armando Muniz (Mex) Mexico City, Mexico

15 Jul 1975 *LW(WBC)* Saensak Muangsurin (Tha) RTD–8
Perico Fernandez (Spa) Bangkok, Thailand

16 Aug 1975 *M(WBC)* Rodrigo Valdez (Col) PTS–15 Rudy
Robles (Mex) Cartagena, Colombia

23 Aug 1975 *Fl(WBC)* Miguel Canto (Mex) RSF–11 Jiro
Takada (Jap) Merida, Mexico

23 Aug 1975 *LF(WBA)* Jaime Rios (Pan) PTS–15 Rigoberto
Marcano (Ven) Panama City, Panama

30 Aug 1975 *B(WBA)* Alfonso Zamora (Mex) KO–4
Thanomjit Sukothai (Tha) Anaheim, USA

13 Sep 1975 *LF(WBC)* Luis Estaba (Ven) KO–4 Rafael
Lovera (Par) Caracas, Venezuela

---

*In September 1975 the WBC declared the
light-flyweight title vacant and matched
Luis Estaba (Ven) and Rafael Lovera (Par)
for the vacant title. The Venezuelan won
with a fourth-round knock-out. It was later
learned that Lovera had never previously
boxed as a professional.*

---

13 Sep 1975 *LH(WBA)* Victor Galindez (Arg) PTS–15 Pierre
Fourie (SA) Johannesburg, South Africa

20 Sep 1975 *JL(WBC)* Alfredo Escalera (PR) D–15 Leonel
Hernandez (Ven) Caracas, Venezuela

20 Sep 1975 *Fe(WBC)* David Kotey (Gha) PTS–15 Ruben
Olivares (Mex) Inglewood, USA

1 Oct 1975 *H* Muhammad Ali (USA) RTD–14 Joe Frazier
(USA) Manila, Philippines

8 Oct 1975 *B(WBC)* Rodolfo Martinez (Mex) PTS–15
Hisami Numata (Jap) Sendai, Japan

11 Oct 1975 *W(WBA)* Angel Espada (PR) PTS–15 Johnny
Gant (USA) San Juan, Puerto Rico

12 Oct 1975 *Fe(WBA)* Alexis Arguello (Nic) KO–5 Royal
Kobayashi (Jap) Tokyo, Japan

17 Oct 1975 *Fl(WBA)* Erbito Salavarria (Phi) PTS–15
Susumu Hanagata (Jap) Yokohama, Japan

11 Nov 1975 *LM(WBA)* Jae-Do Yuh (S. Kor) KO–6
Masahiro Misako (Jap) Shizuoko, Japan

13 Nov 1975 *LM(WBC)* Elisha Obed (Bah) RTD–10 Miguel
de Oliveira (Bra) Paris, France

15 Nov 1975 *LW(WBA)* Antonio Cervantes (Col) RTD–7
Hector Thompson (Aus) Panama City, Panama

4 Dec 1975 *L(WBC)* Guts Ishimatsu (Jap) KO–14 Alvaro
Rojas (CR) Tokyo, Japan

6 Dec 1975 *W(WBC)* John H. Stracey (GB) RSF–6 Jose
Napoles (Cuba) Mexico City, Mexico

6 Dec 1975 *B(WBA)* Alfonso Zamora (Mex) KO–2 Socrates
Batoto (Phi) Mexico City, Mexico

12 Dec 1975 *JL(WBC)* Alfredo Escalera (PR) RSF–9 Svein-
Erik Paulsen (Nor) Oslo, Norway

13 Dec 1975 *M(WBA)* Carlos Monzon (Arg) KO–5 Gratien
Tonna (Fra) Paris, France

13 Dec 1975 *Fl(WBC)* Miguel Canto (Mex) PTS–15 Ignacio
Espnial (Dom) Merida, Mexico

17 Dec 1975 *LF(WBC)* Luis Estaba (Ven) RSF–10 Takenobu
Shimabukuro (Jap) Okinawa, Japan

20 Dec 1975 *L(WBA)* Roberto Duran (Pan) KO–15 Leoncio
Ortiz (Mex) San Juan, Puerto Rico

3 Jan 1976 *LF(WBA)* Jaime Rios (Pan) PTS–15 Kazunori
Tenryu (Jap) Kagoshima, Japan

12 Jan 1976 *JL(WBA)* Ben Villaflor (Phi) RSF–13 Morito
Kashiwaba (Jap) Tokyo, Japan

25 Jan 1976 *LW(WBC)* Saensak Muangsurin (Tha) PTS–15
Lion Furuyama (Jap) Tokyo, Japan

30 Jan 1976 *B(WBC)* Rodolfo Martinez (Mex) PTS–15
Venice Borkorsor (Tha) Bangkok, Thailand

14 Feb 1976 *LF(WBC)* Luis Estaba (Ven) PTS–15 Leo
Palacios (Mex) Caracas, Venezuela

17 Feb 1976 *LM(WBA)* Kiochi Wajima (Jap) KO–15 Jae-Do
Yuh (S. Kor) Tokyo, Japan

20 Feb 1976 *H* Muhammad Ali (USA) KO–5 Jean-Pierre
Coopman (Bel) San Juan, Puerto Rico

20 Feb 1976 *JL(WBC)* Alfredo Escalera (PR) KO–13 Jose
Fernandez (Dom) San Juan, Puerto Rico

27 Feb 1976 *Fl(WBA)* Alfonso Lopez (Pan) RSF–15 Erbito
Salavarria (Phi) Manila, Philippines

28 Feb 1976 *LM(WBC)* Elisha Obed (Bah) KO–2 Tony
Gardner (USA) Nassau, Bahamas

6 Mar 1976 *LW(WBA)* Wilfredo Benitez (USA) PTS–15
Antonio Cervantes (Col) San Juan, Puerto Rico

6 Mar 1976 *Fe(WBC)* David Kotey (Gha) RSF–12 Flipper
Uehara (Jap) Accra, Ghana

28 Mar 1976 *LH(WBA)* Victor Galindez (Arg) RTD–3 Harald
Skog (Nor) Oslo, Norway

28 Mar 1976 *M(WBC)* Rodrigo Valdez (Col) KO–4 Max
Cohen (Mor) Paris, France

30 Mar 1976 *W(WBC)* John H. Stracey (GB) RSF–10
Hedgemon Lewis (USA) London, England

1 Apr 1976 *JL(WBC)* Alfredo Escalera (PR) RSF–6 Buzzsaw
Yamabe (Jap) Nara, Japan

3 Apr 1976 *SB(WBC)* Rigoberto Riasco (Pan) RTD–8
Waruinge Nakayama (Ken) Panama City, Panama

3 Apr 1976 *B(WBA)* Alfonso Zamora (Mex) KO–2 Eusebio
Pedroza (Pan) Mexicali, Mexico

13 Apr 1976 *JL(WBA)* Ben Villaflor (Phi) D–15 Sam Serrano
(PR) Honolulu, USA

21 Apr 1976 *Fl(WBA)* Alfonso Lopez (Pan) PTS–15 Shoji
Oguma (Jap) Tokyo, Japan

24 Apr 1976 *LM(WBC)* Elisha Obed (Bah) PTS–15 Sea
Robinson (IC) Abidjan, Ivory Coast

27 Apr 1976 *W(WBA)* Angel Espada (PR) RSF–8 Alfonso
Hayman (USA) San Juan, Puerto Rico

30 Apr 1976 *H* Muhammad Ali (USA) PTS–15 Jimmy Young
(USA) Landover, USA

1 May 1976 *LF(WBC)* Luis Estaba (Ven) PTS–15 Juan
Alvarez (Mex) Caracas, Venezuela

8 May 1976 *L(WBC)* Esteban de Jesus (PR) PTS–15 Guts
Ishimatsu (Jap) San Juan, Puerto Rico

8 May 1976 *B(WBC)* Carlos Zarate (Mex) KO–9 Rodolfo
Martinez (Mex) Inglewood, USA

15 May 1976 *Fl(WBC)* Miguel Canto (Mex) PTS–15 Susumu Hanagata (Jap) Merida, Mexico

18 May 1976 *LM(WBA)* Jose Duran (Spa) KO–14 Koichi Wajima (Jap) Tokyo, Japan

22 May 1976 *LH(WBA)* Victor Galindez (Arg) KO–15 Richie Kates (USA) Johannesburg, South Africa

23 May 1976 *L(WBA)* Roberto Duran (Pan) KO–14 Lou Bizzaro (USA) Erie, USA

24 May 1976 *H* Muhammad Ali (USA) KO–5 Richard Dunn (GB) Munich, West Germany

31 May 1976 *LW(WBA)* Wilfredo Benitez (USA) PTS–15 Emiliano Villa (Col) San Juan, Puerto Rico

12 Jun 1976 *SB(WBC)* Rigoberto Riasco (Pan) RSF–10 Livio Nolasco (Dom) Panama City, Panama

18 Jun 1976 *LM(WBC)* Eckhard Dagge (FRG) RTD–10 Elisha Obed (Bah) Berlin, West Germany

19 Jun 1976 *Fe(WBA)* Alexis Arguello (Nic) KO–3 Salvador Torres (Mex) Inglewood, USA

22 Jun 1976 *W(WBC)* Carlos Palomino (Mex) RSF–12 John H. Stracey (GB) London, England

26 Jun 1976 *M* Carlos Monzon (Arg) PTS–15 Rodrigo Valdez (Col) Monte Carlo, Monaco

30 Jun 1976 *LW(WBC)* Miguel Velasquez (Spa) DIS–4 Saensak Muangsurin (Tha) Madrid, Spain

1 Jul 1976 *JL(WBC)* Alfredo Escalera (PR) PTS–15 Buzzsaw Yamabe (Jap) Nara, Japan

1 Jul 1976 *LF(WBA)* Juan Jose Guzman (Dom) PTS–15 Jaime Rios (Pan) Santo Domingo, Dominican Republic

10 Jul 1976 *B(WBA)* Alfonso Zamora (Mex) KO–3 Gilberto Illueca (Pan) Juarez, Mexico

16 Jul 1976 *Fe(WBC)* David Kotey (Gha) RSF–3 Shig Fukuyama (Jap) Tokyo, Japan

17 Jul 1976 *W(WBA)* Jose Pipino Cuevas (Mex) RSF–2 Angel Espada (PR) Mexicali, Mexico

18 Jul 1976 *LF(WBC)* Luis Estaba (Ven) KO–3 Franco Udella (Ita) Caracas, Venezuela

1 Aug 1976 *SB(WBC)* Rigoberto Riasco (Pan) PTS–15 Dong-Kyun Yum (S. Kor) Pusan, South Korea

28 Aug 1976 *B(WBC)* Carlos Zarate (Mex) RSF–12 Paul Ferreri (Ita) Inglewood, USA

11 Sep 1976 *L(WBC)* Esteban de Jesus (PR) KO–7 Hector Medina (Dom) Bayamon, Puerto Rico

18 Sep 1976 *LM(WBC)* Eckhard Dagge (FRG) PTS–15 Emile Griffith (VI) Berlin, West Germany

18 Sep 1976 *JL(WBC)* Alfredo Escalera (PR) RTD–12 Ray Lunny (USA) San Juan, Puerto Rico

26 Sep 1976 *LF(WBC)* Luis Estaba (Ven) RTD–10 Rodolfo Rodriguez (Arg) Caracas, Venezuela

28 Sep 1976 *H* Muhammad Ali (USA) PTS–15 Ken Norton (USA) New York, USA

2 Oct 1976 *Fl(WBA)* Guty Espadas (Mex) RSF–13 Alfonso Lopez (Pan) Los Angeles, USA

3 Oct 1976 *Fl(WBC)* Miguel Canto (Mex) PTS–15 Betulio Gonzalez (Ven) Caracas, Venezuela

5 Oct 1976 *LH(WBA)* Victor Galindez (Arg) PTS–15 Kosie Smith (SA) Johannesburg, South Africa

8 Oct 1976 *LM(WBA)* Miguel Angel Castellini (Arg) PTS–15 Jose Duran (Spa) Madrid, Spain

9 Oct 1976 *LH(WBC)* John Conteh (GB) PTS–15 Alvaro Lopez (Mex) Copenhagen, Denmark

9 Oct 1976 *SB(WBC)* Royal Kobayashi (Jap) RSF–8 Rigoberto Riasco (Pan) Tokyo, Japan

10 Oct 1976 *LF(WBA)* Yoko Gushiken (Jap) KO–7 Juan Jose Guzman (Dom) Kofu, Japan

15 Oct 1976 *L(WBA)* Roberto Duran (Pan) KO–1 Alvaro Rojas (CR) Hollywood, USA

16 Oct 1976 *LW(WBA)* Wilfredo Benitez (USA) RSF–3 Tony Petronelli (USA) San Juan, Puerto Rico

16 Oct 1976 *JL(WBA)* Sam Serrano (PR) PTS–15 Ben Villaflor (Phi) San Juan, Puerto Rico

16 Oct 1976 *B(WBA)* Alfonso Zamora (Mex) RSF–12 Soo-Hwan Hong (S. Kor) Inchon, South Korea

27 Oct 1976 *W(WBA)* Jose Pipino Cuevas (Mex) KO–6 Shoji Tsujimoto (Jap) Kanazawa, Japan

29 Oct 1976 *LW(WBC)* Saensak Muangsurin (Tha) RSF–2 Miguel Velasquez (Spa) Segovia, Spain

5 Nov 1976 *Fe(WBC)* Danny Lopez (USA) PTS–15 David Kotey (Gha) Accra, Ghana

13 Nov 1976 *B(WBC)* Carlos Zarate (Mex) KO–4 Waruinge Nakayama (Ken) Culiacan, Mexico

19 Nov 1976 *Fl(WBC)* Miguel Canto (Mex) PTS–15 Orlando Javierto (Phi) Los Angeles, USA

21 Nov 1976 *LF(WBC)* Luis Estaba (Ven) RSF–10 Valentin Martinez (Mex) Caracas, Venezuela

24 Nov 1976 *SB(WBC)* Dong-Kyun Yum (S. Kor) PTS–15 Royal Kobayashi (Jap) Seoul, South Korea

30 Nov 1976 *JL(WBC)* Alfredo Escalera (PR) PTS–15 Tyrone Everett (USA) Philadelphia, USA

1 Jan 1977 *Fl(WBA)* Guty Espadas (Mex) RTD–7 Jiro Takada (Jap) Tokyo, Japan

15 Jan 1977 *LW(WBC)* Saensak Muangsurin (Tha) RSF–15 Monroe Brooks (USA) Chian-Mai, Thailand

15 Jan 1977 *JL(WBA)* Sam Serrano (PR) KO–11 Alberto Herrera (Ecu) Guayaquil, Ecuador

15 Jan 1977 *Fe(WBA)* Rafael Ortega (Pan) PTS–15 Francisco Coronado (Nic) Panama City, Panama

22 Jan 1977 *W(WBC)* Carlos Palomino (Mex) RSF–15 Armando Muniz (Mex) Los Angeles, USA

29 Jan 1977 *L(WBA)* Roberto Duran (Pan) KO–13 Vilomar Fernandez (Dom) Miami, USA

30 Jan 1977 *LF(WBA)* Yoko Gushiken (Jap) PTS–15 Jaime Rios (Pan) Tokyo, Japan

5 Feb 1977 *B(WBC)* Carlos Zarate (Mex) RSF–3 Fernando Cabanela (Phi) Mexico City, Mexico

12 Feb 1977 *L(WBC)* Esteban de Jesus (PR) RSF–4 Buzzsaw Yamabe (Jap) Bayamon, Puerto Rico

13 Feb 1977 *SB(WBC)* Dong-Kyun Yum (S. Kor) PTS–15 Jose Cervantes (Col) Seoul, South Korea

5 Mar 1977 *LH(WBC)* John Conteh (GB) RSF–3 Len Hutchins (USA) Liverpool, England

6 Mar 1977 *LM(WBA)* Eddie Gazo (Nic) PTS–15 Miguel Angel Castellini (Arg) Managua, Nicaragua

12 Mar 1977 *W(WBA)* Jose Pipino Cuevas (Mex) RSF–2 Miguel Campanino (Arg) Mexico City, Mexico

15 Mar 1977 *LM(WBC)* Eckhard Dagge (FRG) D–15 Maurice Hope (Ant) Berlin, West Germany

17 Mar 1977 *JL(WBC)* Alfredo Escalera (PR) RSF–6 Ron McGarvey (USA) San Juan, Puerto Rico

2 Apr 1977 *LW(WBC)* Saensak Muangsurin (Tha) KO–6 Guts Ishumatsu (Jap) Tokyo, Japan

24 Apr 1977 *Fl(WBC)* Miguel Canto (Mex) PTS–15 Reyes Arnal (Ven) Caracas, Venezuela

30 Apr 1977 *Fl(WBA)* Guty Espadas (Mex) RSF–13 Alfonso Lopez (Pan) Merida, Mexico

15 May 1977 *LF(WBC)* Luis Estaba (Ven) PTS–15 Rafael Pedroza (Pan) Caracas, Venezuela

16 May 1977 *H* Muhammad Ali (USA) PTS–15 Alfredo Evangelista (Uru) Landover, USA

16 May 1977 *JL(WBC)* Alfredo Escalera (PR) KO–8 Carlos Becceril (Mex) Landover, USA

21 May 1977 *LH(WBC)* Miguel Cuello (Arg) KO–9 Jesse Burnett (USA) Monte Carlo, Monaco

21 May 1977 *SB(WBC)* Wilfredo Gomez (PR) KO–12 Dong-Kyun Yum (S. Kor) San Juan, Puerto Rico

22 May 1977 *LF(WBA)* Yoko Gushiken (Jap) PTS–15
    Rigoberto Marcano (Ven) Sapporo, Japan
29 May 1977 *Fe(WBA)* Rafael Ortega (Pan) PTS–15 Flipper
    Uehara (Jap) Okinawa, Japan
7 Jun 1977 *LM(WBA)* Eddie Gazo (Nic) RSF–11 Koichi
    Wajima (Jap) Tokyo, Japan
14 Jun 1977 *W(WBC)* Carlos Palomino (Mex) KO–11 Dave
    'Boy' Green (GB) London, England
15 Jun 1977 *L(WBC)* Esteban de Jesus (PR) KO–11 Vicente
    Saldivar Mijares (Mex) Bayamon, Puerto Rico
15 Jun 1977 *Fl(WBC)* Miguel Canto (Mex) PTS–15 Kimio
    Furesawa (Jap) Tokyo, Japan
17 Jun 1977 *LW(WBC)* Saensak Muangsurin (Tha) PTS–15
    Perico Fernandez (Spa) Madrid, Spain
18 Jun 1977 *LH(WBA)* Victor Galindez (Arg) PTS–15 Richie
    Kates (USA) Rome, Italy
25 Jun 1977 *LW(WBA)* Antonio Cervantes (Col) RSF–5
    Carlos Maria Giminez (Arg) Maracaibo, Venezuela
26 Jun 1977 *JL(WBA)* Sam Serrano (PR) PTS–15 Leonel
    Hernandez (Ven) Puerto de la Cruz, Venezuela
11 Jul 1977 *SB(WBC)* Wilfredo Gomez (PR) KO–5 Raul
    Tirado (Mex) San Juan, Puerto Rico
17 Jul 1977 *LF(WBC)* Luis Estaba (Ven) PTS–15 Ricardo
    Estupinan (Col) Puerto de la Cruz, Venezuela
30 Jul 1977 *M* Carlos Monzon (Arg) PTS–15 Rodrigo Valdez
    (Col) Monte Carlo, Monaco
6 Aug 1977 *LM(WBC)* Rocky Mattioli (Ita) KO–5 Eckhard
    Dagge (FRG) Berlin, West Germany
6 Aug 1977 *W(WBA)* Jose Pipino Cuevas (Mex) KO–2
    Clyde Gray (Can) Los Angeles, USA
20 Aug 1977 *LW(WBC)* Saensak Muangsurin (Tha) RSF–6
    Mike Everett (USA) Roi-Et, Thailand
27 Aug 1977 *JL(WBA)* Sam Serrano (PR) PTS–15 Apollo
    Yoshio (Jap) San Juan, Puerto Rico
28 Aug 1977 *LF(WBC)* Luis Estaba (Ven) RSF–11 Juan
    Alvarez (Mex) Puerto de la Cruz, Venezuela
10 Sep 1977 *JL(WBC)* Alfredo Escalera (PR) PTS–15 Sigfrido
    Rodriguez (Mex) San Juan, Puerto Rico
13 Sep 1977 *LM(WBA)* Eddie Gazo (Nic) PTS–15 Kenji
    Shibata (Jap) Tokyo, Japan
13 Sep 1977 *W(WBC)* Carlos Palomino (Mex) PTS–15
    Everaldo Costa Azevedo (Bra) Los Angeles, USA
13 Sep 1977 *Fe(WBC)* Danny Lopez (USA) RSF–7 Jose
    Torres (Mex) Los Angeles, USA
15 Sep 1977 *L(WBA)* Roberto Duran (Pan) PTS–15 Edwin
    Viruet (PR) Philadelphia, USA
17 Sep 1977 *LH(WBA)* Victor Galindez (Arg) PTS–15 Alvaro
    Lopez (Mex) Rome, Italy
17 Sep 1977 *Fl(WBC)* Miguel Canto (Mex) PTS–15 Martin
    Vargas (Chi) Merida, Mexico
18 Sep 1977 *LF(WBC)* Luis Estaba (Ven) KO–15 Orlando
    Hernandez (CR) Caracas, Venezuela
29 Sep 1977 *H* Muhammad Ali (USA) PTS–15 Earnie
    Shavers (USA) New York, USA
9 Oct 1977 *LF(WBA)* Yoko Gushiken (Jap) KO–4
    Montsayarm Mahachai (Tha) Oita, Japan
22 Oct 1977 *LW(WBC)* Saensak Muangsurin (Tha) PTS–15
    Saoul Mamby (Jam) Bangkok, Thailand
29 Oct 1977 *B(WBC)* Carlos Zarate (Mex) RSF–6 Danilo
    Batista (Bra) Los Angeles, USA
29 Oct 1977 *LF(WBC)* Luis Estaba (Ven) PTS–15 Netrnoi
    Vorasingh (Tha) Caracas, Venezuela
5 Nov 1977 *M* Rodrigo Valdez (Col) PTS–15 Bennie Briscoe
    (USA) Campione d'Italia, Switzerland
5 Nov 1977 *LW(WBA)* Antonio Cervantes (Col) PTS–15
    Adriano Marrero (Dom) Maracay, Venezuela
19 Nov 1977 *LH(WBA)* Victor Galindez (Arg) PTS–15 Eddie
    Gregory (USA) Turin, Italy

Wilfredo Gomez (right) of Puerto Rico is about to unleash a left to the head of Juan Antonio Lopez during the third defence of his super-bantamweight title in 1978 (AP)

19 Nov 1977 *W(WBA)* Jose Pipino Cuevas (Mex) RSF–11 Angel Espada (PR) San Juan, Puerto Rico

19 Nov 1977 *JL(WBA)* Sam Serrano (PR) RSF–10 Tae-Ho Kim (S. Kor) San Juan, Puerto Rico

19 Nov 1977 *B(WBA)* Jorge Lujan (Pan) KO–10 Alfonso Zamora (Mex) Los Angeles, USA

19 Nov 1977 *Fl(WBA)* Guty Espadas (Mex) KO–8 Alex Santana (Nic) Los Angeles, USA

26 Nov 1977 *SB(WBA)* Soo-Hwan Hong (S. Kor) KO–3 Hector Carrasquilla (Pan) Panama City, Panama

30 Nov 1977 *Fl(WBC)* Miguel Canto (Mex) PTS–15 Martin Vargas (Chi) Santiago, Chile

2 Dec 1977 *B(WBC)* Carlos Zarate (Mex) RSF–5 Juan Francisco Rodriguez (Spa) Madrid, Spain

10 Dec 1977 *W(WBC)* Carlos Palomino (Mex) KO–13 Jose Palacios (Mex) Los Angeles, USA

17 Dec 1977 *Fe(WBC)* Cecilio Lastra (Spa) PTS–15 Rafael Ortega (Pan) Torrelavega, Spain

18 Dec 1977 *LM(WBA)* Eddie Gazo (Nic) PTS–15 Lim-Jao Keun (S. Kor) Inchon, South Korea

30 Dec 1977 *LW(WBC)* Saensak Muangsurin (Tha) RTD–13 Jo Kimpuani (Zai) Chantaburi, Thailand

2 Jan 1978 *Fl(WBA)* Guty Espadas (Mex) RSF–7 Kimio Furesawa (Jap) Tokyo, Japan

4 Jan 1978 *Fl(WBC)* Miguel Canto (Mex) PTS–15 Shoji Oguma (Jap) Koriyama, Japan

7 Jan 1978 *LH(WBC)* Mate Parlov (Yug) KO–9 Miguel Cuello (Arg) Milan, Italy

19 Jan 1978 *SB(WBC)* Wilfredo Gomez (PR) KO–3 Royal Kobayashi (Jap) Kitakyushu, Japan

21 Jan 1978 *L* Roberto Duran (Pan) KO–12 Esteban de Jesus (PR) Las Vegas, USA

28 Jan 1978 *JL(WBC)* Alexis Arguello (Nic) RSF–13 Alfredo Escalera (PR) San Juan, Puerto Rico

29 Jan 1978 *LF(WBA)* Yoko Gushiken (Jap) KO–14 Anecito Vargas (Phi) Nagoya, Japan

1 Feb 1978 *SB(WBA)* Soo-Hwan Hong (S. Kor) PTS–15 Yu Kasahara (Jap) Tokyo, Japan

11 Feb 1978 *W(WBC)* Carlos Palomino (Mex) KO–7 Ryu Sorimachi (Jap) Las Vegas, USA

15 Feb 1978 *Fe(WBC)* Danny Lopez (USA) RSF–6 David Kotey (Gha) Las Vegas, USA

18 Feb 1978 *H* Leon Spinks (USA) PTS–15 Muhammad Ali (USA) Las Vegas, USA

18 Feb 1978 *JL(WBA)* Sam Serrano (PR) PTS–15 Mario Martinez (Nic) San Juan, Puerto Rico

19 Feb 1978 *LF(WBC)* Freddie Castillo (Mex) RSF–14 Luis Estaba (Ven) Caracas, Venezuela

25 Feb 1978 *B(WBC)* Carlos Zarate (Mex) RSF–8 Albert Davila (USA) Los Angeles, USA

4 Mar 1978 *W(WBA)* Jose Pipino Cuevas (Mex) RSF–10 Harold Weston (USA) Los Angeles, USA

11 Mar 1978 *LM(WBC)* Rocky Mattioli (Ita) KO–7 Elisha Obed (Bah) Melbourne, Australia

18 Mar 1978 *W(WBC)* Carlos Palomino (Mex) RSF–9 Mimoun Mohatar (Mor) Las Vegas, USA

18 Mar 1978 *B(WBA)* Jorge Lujan (Pan) RTD–11 Roberto Rubaldino (Mex) San Antonio, USA

8 Apr 1978 *LW(WBC)* Saensak Muangsurin (Tha) RSF–13 Francis Moreno (Ven) Hat Yai, Thailand

8 Apr 1978 *SB(WBC)* Wilfredo Gomez (PR) RSF–7 Juan Antonio Lopez (Mex) Bayamon, Puerto Rico

16 Apr 1978 *Fe(WBA)* Eusebio Pedroza (Pan) KO–13 Cecilio Lastra (Spa) Panama City, Panama

18 Apr 1978 *Fl(WBC)* Miguel Canto (Mex) PTS–15 Shoji Oguma (Jap) Tokyo, Japan

22 Apr 1978 *M* Hugo Corro (Arg) PTS–15 Rodrigo Valdez (Col) San Remo, Italy

22 Apr 1978 *B(WBC)* Carlos Zarate (Mex) RSF–13 Andres Hernandez (PR) San Juan, Puerto Rico

25 Apr 1978 *Fe(WBC)* Danny Lopez (USA) RSF–6 Jose Paula (Bra) Los Angeles, USA

28 Apr 1978 *LW(WBA)* Antonio Cervantes (Col) KO–6 Tongta Kiatvayupak (Tha) Udon-Thani, Thailand

29 Apr 1978 *JL(WBC)* Alexis Arguello (Nic) RSF–5 Rey Tam (Phi) Los Angeles, USA

6 May 1978 *LH(WBA)* Victor Galindez (Arg) PTS–15 Alvaro Lopez (Mex) Via Reggio, Italy

6 May 1978 *SB(WBA)* Ricardo Cardona (Col) RSF–12 Soo-Hwan Hong (S. Kor) Seoul, South Korea

6 May 1978 *LF(WBC)* Netrnoi Vorasingh (Tha) PTS–15 Freddie Castillo (Mex) Bangkok, Thailand

7 May 1978 *LF(WBA)* Yoko Gushiken (Jap) RSF–13 Jaime Rios (Mex) Tokyo, Japan

14 May 1978 *LM(WBC)* Rocky Mattioli (Ita) RSF–5 Jose Duran (Spa) Pescara, Italy

20 May 1978 *W(WBA)* Jose Pipino Cuevas (Mex) RSF–2 Billy Backus (USA) Los Angeles, USA

27 May 1978 *W(WBC)* Carlos Palomino (Mex) PTS–15 Armando Muniz (Mex) Los Angeles, USA

2 Jun 1978 *SB(WBC)* Wilfredo Gomez (PR) RSF–3 Sakad Porntavee (Tha) Korat, Thailand

3 Jun 1978 *JL(WBC)* Alexis Arguello (Nic) KO–1 Diego Alcala (Pan) San Juan, Puerto Rico

10 Jun 1978 *H(WBC)* Larry Holmes (USA) PTS–15 Ken Norton (USA) Las Vegas, USA

10 Jun 1978 *B(WBC)* Carlos Zarate (Mex) KO–4 Emilio Hernandez (Ven) Las Vegas, USA

17 Jun 1978 *LH(WBC)* Mate Parlov (Yug) PTS–15 John Conteh (GB) Belgrade, Yugoslavia

2 Jul 1978 *Fe(WBA)* Eusebio Pedroza (Pan) RSF–12 Ernesto Herrera (Mex) Panama City, Panama

8 Jul 1978 *JL(WBA)* Sam Serrano (PR) RSF–9 Yung-Ho Oh (S. Kor) San Juan, Puerto Rico

29 Jul 1978 *LF(WBC)* Netrnoi Vorasingh (Tha) KO–5 Luis Estaba (Ven) Caracas, Venezuela

5 Aug 1978 *M* Hugo Corro (Arg) PTS–15 Ronnie Harris (USA) Buenos Aires, Argentina

9 Aug 1978 *LM(WBA)* Masashi Kudo (Jap) PTS–15 Eddie Gazo (Nic) Akita, Japan

13 Aug 1978 *Fl(WBA)* Betulio Gonzalez (Ven) PTS–15 Guty Espadas (Mex) Maracay, Venezuela

26 Aug 1978 *LW(WBA)* Antonio Cervantes (Col) KO–9 Norman Sekgapane (SA) Mmabatho, South Africa

2 Sep 1978 *SB(WBA)* Ricardo Cardona (Col) PTS–15 Ruben Valdes (Col) Cartagena, Colombia

9 Sep 1978 *W(WBA)* Jose Pipino Cuevas (Mex) RSF–2 Pete Ranzany (USA) Sacramento, USA

9 Sep 1978 *SB(WBC)* Wilfredo Gomez (PR) RSF–13 Leonardo Cruz (Dom) San Juan, Puerto Rico

15 Sep 1978 *H(WBA)* Muhammad Ali (USA) PTS–15 Leon Spinks (USA) New Orleans, USA

15 Sep 1978 *LH(WBA)* Mike Rossman (USA) RSF–13 Victor Galindez (Arg) New Orleans, USA

15 Sep 1978 *Fe(WBC)* Danny Lopez (USA) KO–2 Juan Malvarez (Arg) New Orleans, USA

15 Sep 1978 *B(WBA)* Jorge Lujan (Pan) PTS–15 Albert Davila (USA) New Orleans, USA

30 Sep 1978 *LF(WBC)* Sung-Jun Kim (S. Kor) KO–3 Netrnoi Vorasingh (Tha) Seoul, South Korea

15 Oct 1978 *LF(WBA)* Yoko Gushiken (Jap) KO–5 Sang-Il Chung (S. Kor) Tokyo, Japan

21 Oct 1978 *Fe(WBC)* Danny Lopez (USA) DIS–4 Pel Clemente (Phi) Pessaro, Italy

29 Oct 1978 *SB(WBC)* Wilfredo Gomez (PR) RSF–5 Carlos Zarate (Mex) San Juan, Puerto Rico

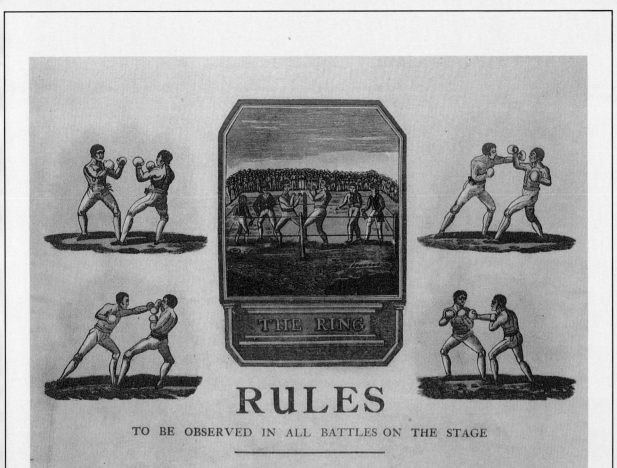

RULES

TO BE OBSERVED IN ALL BATTLES ON THE STAGE

I. THAT a ſquare of a Yard be chalked in the middle of the Stage; and on every freſh ſet-to after a fall, or being parted from the rails, each Second is to bring his Man to the ſide of the ſquare, and place him oppoſite to the other, and till they are fairly ſet-to at the Lines, it ſhall not be lawful for one to ſtrike at the other.

II. That, in order to prevent any Diſputes, the time a Man lies after a fall, if the Second does not bring his Man to the ſide of the ſquare, within the ſpace of half a minute, he ſhall be deemed a beaten Man.

III. That in every main Battle, no perſon whatever ſhall be upon the Stage, except the Principals and their Seconds; the ſame rule to be obſerved in bye-battles, except that in the latter, Mr. Broughton is allowed to be upon the Stage to keep decorum, and to aſſiſt Gentlemen in getting to their places, provided always he does not interfere in the Battle; and whoever pretends to infringe theſe Rules to be turned immediately out of the houſe. Every body is to quit the Stage as ſoon as the Champions are ſtripped, before the ſet-to.

IV. That no Champion be deemed beaten, unleſs he fails coming up to the line in the limited time, or that his own Second declares him beaten. No Second is to be allowed to aſk his man's Adverſary any queſtions, or adviſe him to give out.

V. That in bye-battles, the winning man to have two-thirds of the Money given, which ſhall be publicly divided upon the Stage, notwithſtanding any private agreements to the contrary.

VI. That to prevent Diſputes, in every main Battle the Principals ſhall, on coming on the Stage, chooſe from among the gentlemen preſent two Umpires, who ſhall abſolutely decide all Diſputes that may ariſe about the Battle; and if the two Umpires cannot agree, the ſaid Umpires to chooſe a third, who is to determine it.

VII. That no perſon is to hit his Adverſary when he is down, or ſeize him by the ham, the breeches, or any part below the waiſt: a man on his knees to be reckoned down.

As agreed by ſeveral Gentlemen at Broughton's Amphitheatre, Tottenham Court Road, Auguſt 16, 1743.

The first set of boxing rules as drawn up by Jack Broughton (Mary Evans Picture Library)

PREMIERLAND FRANÇAIS
72, Bd Rochechouart (Elysée-Montmartre)
DIRECTION ROTH & MAITROT

VENDREDI
19
DÉCEMBRE
LE PLUS
GRAND COMBAT
DE L'ANNÉE

Jack JOHNSON CONTRE Jim JOHNSON
Le seul véritable CHAMPION DU MONDE   Le Vainqueur de JOE JEANETTE

PRIX DES PLACES : RING .150 .125 .100 .85 .75 .50 .40! Premières réservées numérotées 30 & 20!
Estrade et Tribune non numérotées .15! - Promenoir 8! (10% en plus pour le droit des Pauvres)

Above *How the French billed the Jack Johnson versus Jim Johnson contest in 1913. It was the first all-negro world heavyweight contest (Explorer Archives)*

Below *Two Joe Louis'... the last thing any heavyweight wanted to see in the 1930s! (FPG International)*

Larry Holmes carved his name into the list of all-time heavyweight greats with his impressive unbeaten record from 1973–85. His run was eventually ended by Michael Spinks (All Sport/Holly Stein)

Above *Boxing in London c. 1820*
(Mary Evans)

*Jeff Fenech (right) is one of several
Australians to have made an impact
on the world scene in the 1980s. He
has won world titles at
bantamweight, super-bantamweight,
and featherweight (All Sport/Roger
Gould)*

Arms raised in triumph, Scotland's world lightweight champion Ken Buchanan (All Sport)

Right *Two of the best known fighters of the 1980s, Sugar Ray Leonard (left) and Marvin Hagler. They were also two of the biggest earners of the decade (All Sport/Mike Powell)*

Below *Barry McGuigan (left) on the way to losing his world featherweight crown to the American Steve Cruz in 1986. The Las Vegas heat played a big part in McGuigan's defeat (All Sport/Mike Powell)*

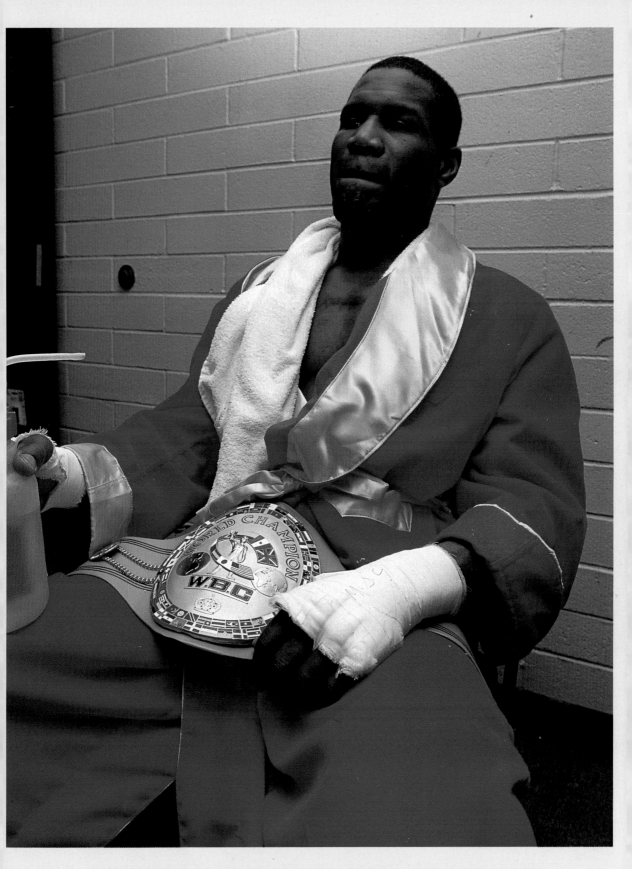

Britain's Dennis Andries has twice won the world light-heavyweight title. In 1986 he beat the American JB Williamson to first win the crown, and in 1989 he recaptured it by beating Tony Willis, also of the United States (Sporting Pictures)

Mike Tyson throws a powerful left to the head of Tony Tucker. Tyson won on points to become the youngest ever undisputed heavyweight champion (All Sport/Duomo)

Inset, bottom left Frank Bruno (left) with his manager Terry Lawless. Bruno has had two cracks at the world heavyweight title and despite two losses, has come out of both contests with credibility, his pride intact, and a lot of affection from the British public (All Sport)

Above *They didn't just graze cattle and breed pigs at New Park Farm, near Bicester, Oxfordshire; in 1841 they also staged famous boxing contests. This one between Broome and Hannan was won by the former after 47 rounds which lasted 79 minutes. A round in those days ended when a fighter was knocked down (ET Archive)*

Below *The man behind Muhammad Ali, and so many other great champions, Angelo Dundee (All Sport)*

Tommy Hearns (facing camera) and Sugar Ray Leonard (striped trunks) fought a re-match in Las Vegas in 1989. A draw saw Leonard retain his WBC super-middleweight title (All Sport/Mike Powell)

Alexis Arguello of Nicaragua, holder of three different world titles (All Sport/Tony Duffy)

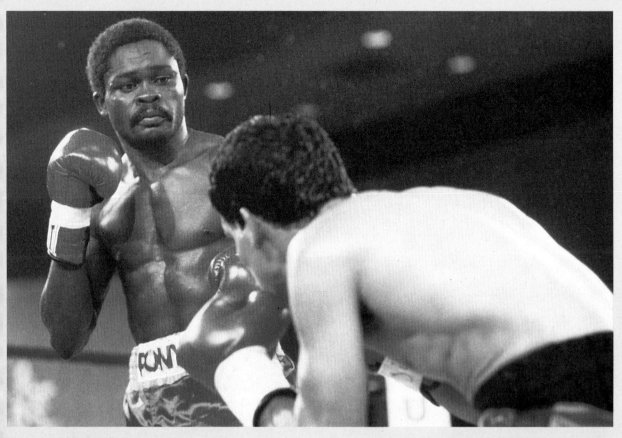

Above *Azumah Nelson (facing camera) on his way to making the first successful defence of his WBC super-featherweight title against Lupe Suarez in 1988 (All-Sport/Simon Bruty)*

Below *John Conteh (left) won the world light-heavyweight title in 1974. However, when he tried to regain the title against Yugoslavia's Mate Parlov (right) in 1978 he was past his best (Sporting Pictures)*

Above *Eusebio Pedroza of Panama, whose seven-year reign as world featherweight champion was ended by Barry McGuigan in 1985 (All Sport/ Mike Powell)*

Right *Britain's Glenn McCrory took the IBF cruiserweight title in 1989. He made one successful defence before losing his title in March 1990 (All Sport/Dan Smith)*

Mike Tyson. No longer invincible (All Sport/Bob Martin)

Above *Now if it was football, I could understand opposing players fighting . . . but cricket, my word! (ET Archive)*

Left *Britain's former world middleweight champion Terry Downes outside one of his betting shops in 1964, shortly before his retirement (All Sport)*

2 Nov 1978 *SB(WBA)* Ricardo Cardona (Col) PTS–15 Soon-Hyun Chung (S. Kor) Seoul, South Korea

4 Nov 1978 *Fl(WBA)* Betulio Gonzalez (Ven) RSF–12 Martin Vargas (Chi) Maracay, Venezuela

10 Nov 1978 *H(WBC)* Larry Holmes (USA) KO–7 Alfredo Evangelista (Uru) Las Vegas, USA

10 Nov 1978 *JL(WBC)* Alexis Arguello (Nic) PTS–15 Arturo Leon (Mex) Las Vegas, USA

11 Nov 1978 *M* Hugo Corro (Arg) PTS–15 Rodrigo Valdez (Col) Buenos Aires, Argentina

20 Nov 1978 *Fl(WBC)* Miguel Canto (Mex) PTS–15 Tacomron Viboonchai (Tha) Houston, USA

27 Nov 1978 *Fe(WBA)* Eusebio Pedroza (Pan) PTS–15 Enrique Solis (PR) San Juan, Puerto Rico

29 Nov 1978 *JL(WBA)* Sam Serrano (PR) PTS–15 Takeo Maruki (Jap) Nagoya, Japan

2 Dec 1978 *LH(WBC)* Marvin Johnson (USA) RSF–10 Mate Parlov (Yug) Marsala, Italy

5 Dec 1978 *LH(WBA)* Mike Rossman (USA) RSF–6 Aldo Traversaro (Ita) Philadelphia, USA

14 Dec 1978 *LM(WBA)* Masashi Kudo (Jap) PTS–15 Ho-In Joo (S. Kor) Osaka, Japan

30 Dec 1978 *LW(WBC)* Sang-Hyun Kim (S. Kor) RSF–13 Saensak Muangsurin (Tha) Seoul, South Korea

7 Jan 1979 *LF(WBA)* Yoko Gushiken (Jap) KO–7 Rigoberto Marcano (Ven) Kawasaki, Japan

9 Jan 1979 *Fe(WBA)* Eusebio Pedroza (Pan) RTD–13 Royal Kobayashi (Jap) Tokyo, Japan

14 Jan 1979 *W(WBC)* Wilfred Benitez (USA) PTS–15 Carlos Palomino (Mex) San Juan, Puerto Rico

26 Jan 1979 *LW(WBA)* Antonio Cervantes (Col) PTS–15 Miguel Montilla (Dom) New York, USA

29 Jan 1979 *W(WBA)* Jose Pipino Cuevas (Mex) RSF–2 Scott Clark (USA) Los Angeles, USA

29 Jan 1979 *Fl(WBA)* Betulio Gonzalez (Ven) D–15 Shoji Oguma (Jap) Hamamatsu, Japan

4 Feb 1979 *JL(WBC)* Alexis Arguello (Nic) KO–13 Alfredo Escalera (PR) Rimini, Italy

10 Feb 1979 *Fl(WBC)* Miguel Canto (Mex) PTS–15 Antonio Avelar (Mex) Merida, Mexico

18 Feb 1979 *JL(WBA)* Sam Serrano (PR) PTS–15 Julio Valdez (Dom) San Juan, Puerto Rico

4 Mar 1979 *LM(WBC)* Maurice Hope (Ant) RTD–8 Rocky Mattioli (Ita) San Remo, Italy

9 Mar 1979 *SB(WBC)* Wilfredo Gomez (PR) RSF–5 Nestor Jiminez (Col) New York, USA

10 Mar 1979 *Fe(WBC)* Danny Lopez (USA) KO–2 Roberto Castanon (Spa) Salt Lake City, USA

10 Mar 1979 *B(WBC)* Carlos Zarate (Mex) KO–3 Mensah Kpalongo (Ton) Los Angeles, USA

14 Mar 1979 *LM(WBA)* Masashi Kudo (Jap) PTS–15 Manuel Gonzalez (Arg) Tokyo, Japan

18 Mar 1979 *Fl(WBC)* Chan-Hee Park (S. Kor) PTS–15 Miguel Canto (Mex) Pusan, South Korea

25 Mar 1979 *W(WBC)* Wilfred Benitez (USA) PTS–15 Harold Weston (USA) San Juan, Puerto Rico

29 Mar 1979 *H(WBC)* Larry Holmes (USA) RSF–7 Ossie Ocasio (PR) Las Vegas, USA

31 Mar 1979 *LF(WBC)* Sung-Jun Kim (S. Kor) D–15 Hector Ray Melendez (Dom) Seoul, South Korea

8 Apr 1979 *Fe(WBA)* Eusebio Pedroza (Pan) RSF–11 Hector Carrasquilla (Pan) Panama City, Panama

8 Apr 1979 *B(WBA)* Jorge Lujan (Pan) RSF–15 Cleo Garcia (Nic) Las Vegas, USA

8 Apr 1979 *LF(WBA)* Yoko Gushiken (Jap) KO–7 Alfonso Lopez (Pan) Tokyo, Japan

15 Apr 1979 *LH(WBA)* Victor Galindez (Arg) RTD–9 Mike Rossman (USA) New Orleans, USA

15 Apr 1979 *JL(WBA)* Sam Serrano (PR) RSF–8 Nkosana 'Happy Boy' Mgxaji (SA) Cape Town, South Africa

17 Apr 1979 *L(WBC)* Jim Watt (GB) RSF–12 Alfredo Pitalua (Col) Glasgow, Scotland

22 Apr 1979 *LH(WBC)* Matt Franklin (USA) RSF–8 Marvin Johnson (USA) Indianapolis, USA

19 May 1979 *Fl(WBC)* Chan-Hee Park (S. Kor) PTS–15 Tsutomo Igerishi (Jap) Seoul, South Korea

1 Jun 1979 *LW(WBC)* Sang-Hyun Kim (S. Kor) PTS–15 Fitzroy Guisseppi (Tri) Seoul, South Korea

3 Jun 1979 *B(WBC)* Lupe Pintor (Mex) PTS–15 Carlos Zarate (Mex) Las Vegas, USA

16 Jun 1979 *L(WBA)* Ernesto Espana (Ven) KO–13 Claude Noel (Tri) San Juan, Puerto Rico

16 Jun 1979 *SB(WBC)* Wilfredo Gomez (PR) KO–5 Julio Hernandez (Nic) San Juan, Puerto Rico

17 Jun 1979 *Fe(WBC)* Danny Lopez (USA) KO–15 Mike Ayala (USA) San Antonio, USA

20 Jun 1979 *LM(WBA)* Masashi Kudo (Jap) RTD–12 Manuel Gonzalez (Arg) Yokkaichi, Japan

22 Jun 1979 *H(WBC)* Larry Holmes (USA) RSF–12 Mike Weaver (USA) New York, USA

23 Jun 1979 *SB(WBA)* Ricardo Cardona (Col) PTS–15 Soon-Hyun Chung (S. Kor) Seoul, South Korea

30 Jun 1979 *M* Vito Antuofermo (Ita) PTS–15 Hugo Corro (Arg) Monte Carlo, Monaco

6 Jul 1979 *Fl(WBA)* Betulio Gonzalez (Ven) KO–12 Shoji Oguma (Jap) Utsonomiya, Japan

8 Jul 1979 *JL(WBC)* Alexis Arguello (Nic) RSF–11 Rafael Limon (Mex) New York, USA

21 Jul 1979 *Fe(WBA)* Eusebio Pedroza (Pan) RSF–12 Ruben Olivares (Mex) Houston, USA

28 Jul 1979 *LF(WBC)* Sung-Jun Kim (S. Kor) PTS–15 Siony Carupo (Phi) Seoul, South Korea

29 Jul 1979 *LF(WBA)* Yoko Gushiken (Jap) PTS–15 Rafael Pedroza (Pan) Kitakyashu, Japan

30 Jul 1979 *W(WBA)* Jose Pipino Cuevas (Mex) PTS–15 Randy Shields (USA) Chicago, USA

4 Aug 1979 *L(WBA)* Ernesto Espana (Ven) RSF–9 Johnny Lira (USA) Chicago, USA

18 Aug 1979 *LH(WBC)* Matt Franklin (USA) PTS–15 John Conteh (GB) Atlantic City, USA

25 Aug 1979 *LW(WBA)* Antonio Cervantes (Col) PTS–15 Kwang-Min Kim (S. Kor) Seoul, South Korea

6 Sep 1979 *SB(WBA)* Ricardo Cardona (Col) PTS–15 Yukio Segawa (Jap) Hacinohe, Japan

9 Sep 1979 *Fl(WBC)* Chan-Hee Park (S. Kor) D–15 Miguel Canto (Mex) Seoul, South Korea

25 Sep 1979 *LM(WBC)* Maurice Hope (Ant) RSF–7 Mike Baker (USA) London, England

25 Sep 1979 *Fe(WBC)* Danny Lopez (USA) KO–3 Jose Caba (Dom) Los Angeles, USA

28 Sep 1979 *H(WBC)* Larry Holmes (USA) RSF–11 Earnie Shavers (USA) Las Vegas, USA

28 Sep 1979 *SB(WBC)* Wilfredo Gomez (PR) KO–10 Carlos Mendoza (Pan) Las Vegas, USA

3 Oct 1979 *LW(WBC)* Sang-Hyun Kim (S. Kor) KO–11 Masahiro Yokai (Jap) Tokyo, Japan

6 Oct 1979 *B(WBA)* Jorge Lujan (Pan) RSF–15 Roberto Rubaldino (Mex) McAllen, USA

20 Oct 1979 *H(WBA)* John Tate (USA) PTS–15 Gerrie Coetzee (SA) Johannesburg, South Africa

21 Oct 1979 *LF(WBC)* Sung-Jun Kim (S.Kor) PTS–15 Hector Ray Melendez (Dom) Seoul, South Korea

24 Oct 1979 *LM(WBA)* Ayub Kalule (Uga) PTS–15 Masashi Kudo (Jap) Akita, Japan

26 Oct 1979 *SB(WBC)* Wilfredo Gomez (PR) KO–5 Nicky Perez (USA) New York, USA

28 Oct 1979 *LF(WBA)* Yoko Gushiken (Jap) RSF–7 Tito Abbella (Phi) Tokyo, Japan

3 Nov 1979 *L(WBC)* Jim Watt (GB) RSF–9 Roberto Vasquez (USA) Glasgow, Scotland

16 Nov 1979 *JL(WBC)* Alexis Arguello (Nic) RTD–7 Bobby Chacon (USA) Los Angeles, USA

16 Nov 1979 *Fl(WBA)* Luis Ibarra (Pan) PTS–15 Betulio Gonzalez (Ven) Maracay, Venezuela

17 Nov 1979 *Fe(WBA)* Eusebio Pedroza (Pan) KO–11 Johnny Aba (NG) Port Moresby, New Guinea

30 Nov 1979 *LH(WBA)* Marvin Johnson (USA) KO–11 Victor Galindez (Arg) New Orleans, USA

30 Nov 1979 *M* Vito Antuofermo (Ita) D–15 Marvin Hagler (USA) Las Vegas, USA

30 Nov 1979 *W(WBC)* Sugar Ray Leonard (USA) RSF–15 Wilfredo Benitez (USA) Las Vegas, USA

6 Dec 1979 *LM(WBA)* Ayub Kalule (Uga) PTS–15 Steve Gregory (USA) Copenhagen, Denmark

8 Dec 1979 *W(WBA)* Jose Pipino Cuevas (Mex) RSF–10 Angel Espada (PR) Los Angeles, USA

8 Dec 1979 *C(WBC)* Marvin Camel (USA) D–15 Mate Parlov (Yug) Split, Yugoslavia

15 Dec 1979 *SB(WBA)* Ricardo Cardona (Col) PTS–15 Sergio Palma (Arg) Barranquilla, Colombia

16 Dec 1979 *Fl(WBC)* Chan-Hee Park (S.Kor) KO–2 Guty Espadas (Mex) Seoul, South Korea

3 Jan 1980 *LF(WBC)* Shigeo Nakajima (Jap) PTS–15 Sung-Jun Kim (S. Kor) Tokyo, Japan

20 Jan 1980 *JL(WBC)* Alexis Arguello (Nic) RSF–11 Ruben Castillo (USA) Tucson, USA

22 Jan 1980 *Fe(WBA)* Eusebio Pedroza (Pan) PTS–15 Shig 'Spider' Nemoto (Jap) Tokyo, Japan

27 Jan 1980 *LF(WBA)* Yoko Gushiken (Jap) PTS–15 Yung-Hyun Kim (S. Kor) Osaka, Japan

2 Feb 1980 *Fe(WBC)* Salvador Sanchez (Mex) RSF–13 Danny Lopez (USA) Phoenix, USA

2 Feb 1980 *SF(WBC)* Rafael Orono (Ven) PTS–15 Seung-Hoon Lee (S. Kor) Caracas, Venezuela

3 Feb 1980 *H(WBC)* Larry Holmes (USA) KO–6 Lorenzo Zanon (Ita) Las Vegas, USA

3 Feb 1980 *SB(WBC)* Wilfredo Gomez (PR) KO–6 Ruben Valdez (Col) Las Vegas, USA

9 Feb 1980 *B(WBC)* Lupe Pintor (Mex) RSF–12 Alberto Sandoval (USA) Los Angeles, USA

10 Feb 1980 *Fl(WBC)* Chan-Hee Park (S. Kor) PTS–15 Arnel Arrozal (Phi) Seoul, South Korea

16 Feb 1980 *Fl(WBA)* Tae-Shik Kim (S. Kor) KO–2 Luis Ibarra (Pan) Seoul, South Korea

2 Mar 1980 *L(WBA)* Hilmer Kenty (USA) RSF–9 Ernesto Espana (Ven) Detroit, USA

14 Mar 1980 *L(WBC)* Jim Watt (GB) RSF–4 Charlie Nash (GB) Glasgow, Scotland

16 Mar 1980 *M* Alan Minter (GB) PTS–15 Vito Antuofermo (Ita) Las Vegas, USA

23 Mar 1980 *LW(WBC)* Saoul Mamby (Jam) RSF–14 Sang-Hyun Kim (S. Kor) Seoul, South Korea

23 Mar 1980 *LF(WBC)* Hilario Zapata (Pan) PTS–15 Shigeo Nakajima (Jap) Tokyo, Japan

29 Mar 1980 *LH(WBC)* Matt Saad Muhammad (USA) RSF–4 John Conteh (GB) Atlantic City, USA

29 Mar 1980 *LW(WBA)* Antonio Cervantes (Col) RSF–7 Miguel Montilla (Dom) Cartagena, Colombia

29 Mar 1980 *Fe(WBA)* Eusebio Pedroza (Pan) KO–9 Juan D. Malvares (Arg) Panama City, Panama

31 Mar 1980 *H(WBC)* Larry Holmes (USA) RSF–8 Leroy Jones (USA) Las Vegas, USA

31 Mar 1980 *H(WBA)* Mike Weaver (USA) KO–15 John Tate (USA) Knoxville, USA

31 Mar 1980 *C(WBC)* Marvin Camel (USA) PTS–15 Mate Parlov (Yug) Las Vegas, USA

31 Mar 1980 *LH(WBA)* Eddie Gregory (USA) RSF–11 Marvin Johnson (USA) Knoxville, USA

31 Mar 1980 *W(WBC)* Sugar Ray Leonard (USA) KO–4 Dave 'Boy' Green (GB) Landover, USA

2 Apr 1980 *B(WBA)* Jorge Lujan (Pan) RSF–9 Shuichi Isogami (Jap) Tokyo, Japan

3 Apr 1980 *JL(WBA)* Sam Serrano (PR) RSF–13 Kiyoshi Kazama (Jap) Nara, Japan

6 Apr 1980 *W(WBA)* Jose Cuevas (Mex) KO–5 Harold Volbrecht (SA) Houston, USA

12 Apr 1980 *Fe(WBC)* Salvador Sanchez (Mex) PTS–15 Ruben Castillo (USA) Tucson, USA

12 Apr 1980 *SF(WBC)* Rafael Orono (Ven) PTS–15 Ramon Soria (Arg) Caracas, Venezuela

12 Apr 1980 *Fl(WBC)* Chan-Hee Park (S. Kor) PTS–15 Alberto Morales (Mex) Taegu, South Korea

18 Apr 1980 *LM(WBA)* Ayub Kalule (Uga) RSF–11 Emilianno Villa (Col) Copenhagen, Denmark

27 Apr 1980 *JL(WBC)* Alexis Arguello (Nic) RSF–4 Rolando Navarrete (Phi) San Juan, Nicaragua

4 May 1980 *SB(WBA)* Leo Randolph (USA) RSF–15 Ricardo Cardona (Col) Seattle, USA

11 May 1980 *LH(WBC)* Matt Saad Muhammad (USA) RSF–5 Louis Pergaud (Cam) Halifax, Canada

18 May 1980 *Fl(WBC)* Shoji Oguma (Jap) KO–9 Chan-Hee Park (S. Kor) Seoul, South Korea

1 Jun 1980 *LF(WBA)* Yoko Gushiken (Jap) RSF–8 Martin Vargas (Chi) Kochi, Japan

7 Jun 1980 *L(WBC)* Jim Watt (GB) PTS–15 Howard Davis (USA) Glasgow, Scotland

7 Jun 1980 *LF(WBC)* Hilario Zapata (Pan) PTS–15 Chi-Bok Kim (S. Kor) Seoul, South Korea

11 Jun 1980 *B(WBC)* Lupe Pintor (Mex) D–15 Eijiro Murata (Jap) Tokyo, Japan

13 Jun 1980 *LM(WBA)* Ayub Kalule (Uga) PTS–15 Marijan Benes (Yug) Randers, Denmark

20 Jun 1980 *W(WBC)* Roberto Duran (Pan) PTS–15 Sugar Ray Leonard (USA) Montreal, Canada

21 Jun 1980 *Fe(WBC)* Salvador Sanchez (Mex) RSF–14 Danny Lopez (USA) Las Vegas, USA

28 Jun 1980 *M* Alan Minter (GB) KO–8 Vito Antuofermo (Ita) London, England

29 Jun 1980 *Fl(WBA)* Tae-Shik Kim (S. Kor) PTS–15 Arnel Arrozal (Phi) Seoul, South Korea

7 Jul 1980 *H(WBC)* Larry Holmes (USA) RSF–7 Scott Ledoux (USA) Minneapolis, USA

7 Jul 1980 *LW(WBC)* Saoul Mamby (Jam) KO–13 Esteban de Jesus (PR) Minneapolis, USA

12 Jul 1980 *LM(WBC)* Maurice Hope (Ant) RSF–11 Rocky Mattioli (Ita) London, England

13 Jul 1980 *LH(WBC)* Matt Saad Muhammad (USA) RSF–14 Alvaro Lopez (Mex) Great George, USA

20 Jul 1980 *LH(WBA)* Eddie Mustaffa Muhammad (USA) RSF–10 Jerry Martin (Ant) McAfee, USA

20 Jul 1980 *Fe(WBA)* Eusebio Pedroza (Pan) KO–9 Sa-Wang Kim (S.Kor) Seoul, South Korea

28 Jul 1980 *SF(WBC)* Rafael Orono (Ven) D–15 Willie Jensen (USA) Caracas, Venezuela

28 Jul 1980 *Fl(WBC)* Shoji Oguma (Jap) PTS–15 Sun-Jung Kim (S. Kor) Tokyo, Japan

2 Aug 1980 *W(WBA)* Thomas Hearns (USA) RSF–2 Jose Cuevas (Mex) Detroit, USA

2 Aug 1980 *LW(WBA)* Aaron Pryor (USA) KO–4 Antonio Cervantes (Col) Cincinnati, USA

2 Aug 1980 *L(WBA)* Hilmer Kenty (USA) RSF–9 Yung-Ho Oh (S. Kor) Detroit, USA

2 Aug 1980 *JL(WBA)* Yasatsune Uehara (Jap) KO–6 Sam
    Serrano (PR) Detroit, USA

4 Aug 1980 *LF(WBC)* Hilario Zapata (Pan) PTS–15 Hector
    Ray Melendez (Dom) Caracas, Venezuela

9 Aug 1980 *SB(WBA)* Sergio Palma (Arg) KO–5 Leo
    Randolph (USA) Spokane, USA

22 Aug 1980 *SB(WBC)* Wilfredo Gomez (PR) RSF–5
    Derrick Holmes (USA) Las Vegas, USA

29 Aug 1980 *B(WBA)* Julian Solis (PR) PTS–15 Jorge Lujan
    (Pan) Miami, USA

5 Sep 1980 *LM(WBA)* Ayub Kalule (Uga) PTS–15 Bushy
    Bester (SA) Aarhus, Denmark

13 Sep 1980 *Fe(WBC)* Salvador Sanchez (Mex) PTS–15 Pat
    Ford (Guy) San Antonio, USA

15 Sep 1980 *SF(WBC)* Rafael Orono (Ven) KO–3 Jovita
    Rengifo (Ven) Barquisimento, Venezuela

17 Sep 1980 *LF(WBC)* Hilario Zapata (Pan) RSF–11 Shigeo
    Nakajima (Jap) Tokyo, Japan

19 Sep 1980 *B(WBC)* Lupe Pintor (Mex) KO–12 Johnny
    Owen (GB) Los Angeles, USA

20 Sep 1980 *L(WBA)* Hilmer Kenty (USA) KO–4 Ernesto
    Espana (Ven) San Juan, Puerto Rico

27 Sep 1980 *M* Marvin Hagler (USA) RSF–3 Alan Minter
    (GB) London, England

2 Oct 1980 *H(WBC)* Larry Holmes (USA) RTD–10
    Muhammad Ali (USA) Las Vegas, USA

2 Oct 1980 *LW(WBC)* Saoul Mamby (Jam) PTS–15 Maurice
    'Termite' Watkins (USA) Las Vegas, USA

4 Oct 1980 *Fe(WBA)* Eusebio Pedroza (Pan) PTS–15 Rocky
    Lockridge (USA) Great George, USA

12 Oct 1980 *LF(WBA)* Yoko Gushiken (Jap) PTS–15 Pedro
    Flores (Mex) Kanazawa, Japan

18 Oct 1980 *Fl(WBC)* Shoji Oguma (Jap) PTS–15
    Chan-Hee Park (S. Kor) Tokyo, Japan

25 Oct 1980 *H(WBA)* Mike Weaver (USA) KO–13 Gerrie
    Coetzee (SA) Sun City, South Africa

1 Nov 1980 *L(WBC)* Jim Watt (GB) RSF–12 Sean O'Grady
    (USA) Glasgow, Scotland

3 Nov 1980 *L(WBA)* Hilmer Kenty (USA) PTS–15 Vilomar
    Fernandez (Dom) Detroit, USA

8 Nov 1980 *SB(WBA)* Sergio Palma (Arg) KO–9 Ulisses
    Morales (Pan) Buenos Aires, Argentina

14 Nov 1980 *B(WBA)* Jeff Chandler (USA) RSF–14 Julian
    Solis (PR) Miami, USA

20 Nov 1980 *JL(WBA)* Yasatsune Uehara (Jap) PTS–15
    Leonel Hernandez (Ven) Tokyo, Japan

22 Nov 1980 *LW(WBA)* Aaron Pryor (USA) RSF–6 Gaetan
    Hart (Can) Cincinnati, USA

26 Nov 1980 *C(WBC)* Carlos de Leon (PR) PTS–15 Marvin
    Camel (USA) New Orleans, USA

26 Nov 1980 *LM(WBC)* Maurice Hope (Ant) PTS–15 Carlos
    Herrera (Mex) London, England

28 Nov 1980 *LH(WBC)* Matt Saad Muhammad (USA) KO–3
    Lotte Mwale (Zam) San Diego, USA

28 Nov 1980 *W(WBC)* Sugar Ray Leonard (USA) RTD–8
    Roberto Duran (Pan) New Orleans, USA

29 Nov 1980 *LH(WBA)* Eddie Mustaffa Muhammad (USA)
    RSF–3 Rudi Koopmans (Hol) Los Angeles, USA

1 Dec 1980 *LF(WBC)* Hilario Zapata (Pan) PTS–15
    Reinaldo Beccerra (Ven) Caracas, Venezuela

5 Dec 1980 *W(WBA)* Thomas Hearns (USA) KO–6 Luis
    Primera (Ven) Detroit, USA

11 Dec 1980 *JL(WBC)* Rafael Limon (Mex) RSF–15
    Idefonso Bethelmy (Ven) Los Angeles, USA

13 Dec 1980 *Fe(WBC)* Salvador Sanchez (Mex) PTS–15
    Juan Laporte (PR) El Paso, USA

13 Dec 1980 *SB(WBC)* Wilfredo Gomez (PR) KO–3 Jose
    Cervantes (Col) Miami, USA

13 Dec 1980 *Fl(WBA)* Peter Mathebula (SA) PTS–15
    Tae-Shik Kim (S. Kor) Los Angeles, USA

19 Dec 1980 *B(WBC)* Lupe Pintor (Mex) PTS–15 Albert
    Davila (USA) Los Angeles, USA

17 Jan 1981 *M* Marvin Hagler (USA) RSF–8 Fulgencio
    Obelmejias (Ven) Boston, USA

24 Jan 1981 *SF(WBC)* Chul-Ho Kim (S. Kor) KO–9 Rafael
    Orono (Ven) San Cristobal, Venezuela

31 Jan 1981 *B(WBA)* Jeff Chandler (USA) PTS–15 Jorge
    Lujan (Pan) Philadelphia, USA

3 Feb 1981 *Fl(WBC)* Shoji Oguma (Jap) PTS–15 Chan-Hee
    Park (S. Kor) Tokyo, Japan

8 Feb 1981 *LF(WBC)* Hilario Zapata (Pan) RTD–13 Joey
    Olivo (USA) Panama City, Panama

14 Feb 1981 *Fe(WBA)* Eusebio Pedroza (Pan) KO–13 Pat
    Ford (Guy) Panama City, Panama

22 Feb 1981 *B(WBC)* Lupe Pintor (Mex) PTS–15 Jose Uziga
    (Arg) Houston, USA

28 Feb 1981 *LH(WBC)* Matt Saad Muhammad (USA) RSF–
    11 Vonzell Johnson (USA) Atlantic City, USA

8 Mar 1981 *JL(WBC)* Cornelius Boza-Edwards (Uga) PTS–
    15 Rafael Limon (Mex) Stockton, USA

8 Mar 1981 *LF(WBA)* Pedro Flores (Mex) TKO–12 Yoko
    Gushiken (Jap) Nama, Japan

22 Mar 1981 *Fe(WBC)* Salvador Sanchez (Mex) RSF–10
    Roberto Castanon (Spa) Las Vegas, USA

28 Mar 1981 *W(WBC)* Sugar Ray Leonard (USA) RSF–10
    Larry Bonds (USA) Syracuse, USA

28 Mar 1981 *Fl(WBA)* Santos Laciar (Arg) KO–7 Peter
    Mathebula (SA) Johannesburg, South Africa

4 Apr 1981 *SB(WBA)* Sergio Palma (Arg) PTS–15 Leonardo
    Cruz (Dom) Buenos Aires, Argentina

4 Apr 1981 *B(WBA)* Jeff Chandler (USA) D–15 Eijiro
    Murata (Jap) Tokyo, Japan

9 Apr 1981 *JL(WBA)* Sam Serrano (PR) PTS–15 Yasatsune
    Uehara (Jap) Wakayama, Japan

11 Apr 1981 *H(WBC)* Larry Holmes (USA) PTS–15 Trevor
    Berbick (Can) Las Vegas, USA

12 Apr 1981 *L(WBA)* Sean O'Grady (USA) PTS–15 Hilmer
    Kenty (USA) Atlantic City, USA

22 Apr 1981 *SF(WBC)* Chul-Ho Kim (S. Kor) PTS–15 Jiro
    Watanabe (Jap) Seoul, South Korea

24 Apr 1981 *LF(WBC)* Hilario Zapata (Pan) PTS–15 Rudy
    Crawford (USA) San Francisco, USA

25 Apr 1981 *LH(WBC)* Matt Saad Muhammad (USA) KO–9
    Murray Sutherland (GB) Atlantic City, USA

25 Apr 1981 *W(WBA)* Thomas Hearns (USA) RSF–12 Randy
    Shields (USA) Phoenix, USA

12 May 1981 *Fl(WBC)* Antonio Avelar (Mex) KO–7 Shoji
    Oguma (Jap) Tokyo, Japan

23 May 1981 *LM(WBC)* Wilfred Benitez (USA) KO–12
    Maurice Hope (Ant) Las Vegas, USA

30 May 1981 *JL(WBC)* Cornelius Boza-Edwards (Uga)
    RTD–13 Bobby Chacon (USA) Las Vegas, USA

6 Jun 1981 *Fl(WBA)* Luis Ibarra (Pan) PTS–15 Santos Laciar
    (Arg) Buenos Aires, Argentina

12 Jun 1981 *H(WBC)* Larry Holmes (USA) RSF–3 Leon
    Spinks (USA) Detroit, USA

12 Jun 1981 *LW(WBC)* Saoul Mamby (Jam) PTS–15 Jo
    Kimpuani (Zai) Detroit, USA

13 Jun 1981 *M* Marvin Hagler (USA) RTD–4 Vito
    Antuofermo (Ita) Boston, USA

20 Jun 1981 *JL(WBA)* Sam Serrano (PR) PTS–15 Leonel
    Hernandez (Ven) Caracas, Venezuela

21 Jun 1981 *L(WBC)* Alexis Arguello (Nic) PTS–15 Jim Watt
    (GB) London, England

25 Jun 1981 *LM(WBA)* Sugar Ray Leonard (USA) KO–9
    Ayub Kalule (Uga) Houston, USA

25 Jun 1981 *W(WBA)* Thomas Hearns (USA) KO–4 Juan Pablo Baez (Dom) Houston, USA

27 Jun 1981 *LW(WBA)* Aaron Pryor (USA) RSF–2 Lennox Blackmore (Guy) Las Vegas, USA

18 Jul 1981 *LH(WBA)* Michael Spinks (USA) PTS–15 Eddie Mustaffa Muhammad (USA) Las Vegas, USA

19 Jul 1981 *LF(WBA)* Hwan-Jim Kim (S. Kor) RSF–13 Pedro Flores (Mex) Seoul, South Korea

25 Jul 1981 *B(WBA)* Jeff Chandler (USA) KO–7 Julian Solis (PR) Atlantic City, USA

26 Jul 1981 *B(WBC)* Lupe Pintor (Mex) RSF–8 Jovito Rengifo (Ven) Las Vegas, USA

29 Jul 1981 *SF(WBC)* Chul-Ho Kim (S. Kor) KO–13 Willie Jensen (USA) Pusan, South Korea

1 Aug 1981 *Fe(WBA)* Eusebio Pedroza (Pan) KO–7 Carlos Pinango (Ven) Caracas, Venezuela

15 Aug 1981 *SB(WBA)* Sergio Palma (Arg) RSF–12 Ricardo Cardona (Col) Buenos Aires, Argentina

15 Aug 1981 *LF(WBC)* Hilario Zapata (Pan) PTS–15 German Torres (Phi) Panama City, Panama

21 Aug 1981 *Fe(WBC)* Salvador Sanchez (Mex) RSF–8 Wilfredo Gomez (PR) Las Vegas, USA

29 Aug 1981 *LW(WBC)* Saoul Mamby (Jam) PTS–15 Thomas Americo (Ina) Djakarta, Indonesia

29 Aug 1981 *JL(WBC)* Rolando Navarrete (Phi) KO–5 Cornelius Boza-Edwards (Uga) Via Reggio, Italy

30 Aug 1981 *Fl(WBC)* Antonio Avelar (Mex) KO–2 Tae-Shik Kim (S. Kor) Seoul, South Korea

12 Sep 1981 *L(WBA)* Claude Noel (Tri) PTS–15 Rodolfo Gonzalez (Mex) Atlantic City, USA

12 Sep 1981 *SF(WBA)* Gustavo Ballas (Arg) RSF–8 Suk-Chul Bae (S. Kor) Buenos Aires, Argentina

16 Sep 1981 *W* Sugar Ray Leonard (USA) RSF–14 Thomas Hearns (USA) Las Vegas, USA

22 Sep 1981 *B(WBC)* Lupe Pintor (Mex) KO–15 Hurricane Teru (Jap) Tokyo, Japan

26 Sep 1981 *LH(WBC)* Matt Saad Muhammad (USA) RSF–11 Jerry Martin (Ant) Atlantic City, USA

26 Sep 1981 *Fl(WBA)* Juan Herrera (Mex) KO–11 Luis Ibarra (Pan) Mexico City, Mexico

3 Oct 1981 *H(WBA)* Mike Weaver (USA) PTS–15 James Tillis (USA) Rosemont, USA

3 Oct 1981 *M* Marvin Hagler (USA) RSF–11 Mustapha Hamsho (Syr) Rosemont, USA

3 Oct 1981 *L(WBC)* Alexis Arguello (Nic) RSF–14 Ray Mancini (USA) Atlantic City, USA

3 Oct 1981 *SB(WBA)* Sergio Palma (Arg) PTS–15 Vichit Muangroi-Et (Tha) Buenos Aires, Argentina

11 Oct 1981 *LF(WBA)* Hwan-Jim Kim (S. Kor) PTS–15 Alphonso Lopez (Pan) Seoul, South Korea

6 Nov 1981 *H(WBC)* Larry Holmes (USA) RSF–11 Renaldo Snipes (USA) Pittsburgh, USA

7 Nov 1981 *LH(WBA)* Michael Spinks (USA) KO–7 Vonzell Johnson (USA) Atlantic City, USA

7 Nov 1981 *LM(WBA)* Tadashi Mihara (Jap) PTS–15 Rocky Fratto (USA) Rochester, USA

7 Nov 1981 *LF(WBC)* Hilario Zapata (Pan) RSF–10 Netrnoi Vorasingh (Tha) Korat, Thailand

14 Nov 1981 *LW(WBA)* Aaron Pryor (USA) RSF–7 Dujuan Johnson (USA) Cleveland, USA

15 Nov 1981 *LM(WBC)* Wilfred Benitez (USA) PTS–15 Carlos Santos (USA) Las Vegas, USA

18 Nov 1981 *SF(WBC)* Chul-Ho Kim (S. Kor) RSF–9 Ryotsu Maruyama (Jap) Pusan, South Korea

21 Nov 1981 *L(WBC)* Alexis Arguello (Nic) KO–7 Roberto Elizondo (USA) Las Vegas, USA

5 Dec 1981 *L(WBA)* Arturo Frias (USA) KO–8 Claude Noel (Tri) Las Vegas, USA

5 Dec 1981 *Fe(WBA)* Eusebio Pedroza (Pan) KO–5 Bashew Sibaca (SA) Panama City, Panama

5 Dec 1981 *SF(WBA)* Rafael Pedroza (Pan) PTS–15 Gustavo Ballas (Arg) Panama City, Panama

10 Dec 1981 *JL(WBA)* Sam Serrano (PR) RSF–12 Hikaru Tomonari (Jap) San Juan, Puerto Rico

10 Dec 1981 *B(WBA)* Jeff Chandler (USA) RSF–13 Eijiro Murata (Jap) Atlantic City, USA

12 Dec 1981 *Fe(WBC)* Salvador Sanchez (Mex) PTS–15 Pat Cowdell (GB) Houston, USA

16 Dec 1981 *LF(WBA)* Katsuo Tokashiki (Jap) PTS–15 Hwan-Jim Kim (S. Kor) Sendai, Japan

19 Dec 1981 *LH(WBC)* Dwight Braxton (USA) RSF–10 Matt Saad Muhammad (USA) Atlantic City, USA

19 Dec 1981 *LW(WBC)* Saoul Mamby (Jam) PTS–15 Obisia Nwankpa (Ngr) Lagos, Nigeria

20 Dec 1981 *Fl(WBA)* Juan Herrera (Mex) RSF–7 Betulio Gonzalez (Ven) Mexico City, Mexico

15 Jan 1982 *SB(WBA)* Sergio Palma (Arg) PTS–15 Jorge Lujan (Pan) Cordoba, Argentina

16 Jan 1982 *JL(WBC)* Rolando Navarrete (Phi) KO–11 Chung-Il Choi (S. Kor) Manila, Philippines

24 Jan 1982 *Fe(WBC)* Eusebio Pedroza (Pan) PTS–15 Juan Laporte (PR) Atlantic City, USA

30 Jan 1982 *LM(WBC)* Wilfred Benitez (USA) PTS–15 Roberto Duran (Pan) Las Vegas, USA

30 Jan 1982 *L(WBA)* Arturo Frias (USA) TKO–9 Ernesto Espana (Ven) Los Angeles, USA

2 Feb 1982 *LM(WBA)* Davey Moore (USA) RSF–6 Tadashi Mihara (Jap) Tokyo, Japan

6 Feb 1982 *LF(WBC)* Amado Ursua (Mex) KO–2 Hilario Zapata (Pan) Panama City, Panama

10 Feb 1982 *SF(WBC)* Chul-Ho Kim (S. Kor) KO–8 Koki Ishii (Jap) Taegu, South Korea

13 Feb 1982 *C(WBA)* Ossie Ocasio (PR) PTS–15 Robbie Williams (SA) Johannesburg, South Africa

13 Feb 1982 *LH(WBA)* Michael Spinks (USA) RSF–6 Mustapha Wasajja (Uga) Atlantic City, USA

13 Feb 1982 *L(WBC)* Alexis Arguello (Nic) RSF–6 James Busceme (USA) Beaumont, USA

15 Feb 1982 *W(WBC)* Sugar Ray Leonard (USA) RSF–3 Bruce Finch (USA) Reno, USA

24 Feb 1982 *C(WBC)* Carlos de Leon (PR) RSF–7 Marvin Camel (USA) Atlantic City, USA

7 Mar 1982 *M* Marvin Hagler (USA) RSF–1 William 'Caveman' Lee (USA) Atlantic City, USA

20 Mar 1982 *Fl(WBC)* Prudencio Cardona (Col) KO–1 Antonio Avelar (Mex) Tampico, Mexico

21 Mar 1982 *LH(WBC)* Dwight Braxton (USA) RSF–6 Jerry Martin (Ant) Las Vegas, USA

21 Mar 1982 *LW(WBA)* Aaron Pryor (USA) RSF–12 Miguel Montilla (Dom) Atlantic City, USA

27 Mar 1982 *SB(WBC)* Wilfredo Gomez (PR) RSF–6 Juan 'Kid' Meza (Mex) Atlantic City, USA

27 Mar 1982 *B(WBA)* Jeff Chandler (USA) RSF–6 Johnny Carter (USA) Philadelphia, USA

4 Apr 1982 *LF(WBA)* Katsuo Tokashiki (Jap) PTS–15 Lupe Madera (Mex) Sendai, Japan

8 Apr 1982 *SF(WBA)* Jiro Watanabe (Jap) PTS–15 Rafael Pedroza (Pan) Osaka, Japan

11 Apr 1982 *LH(WBA)* Michael Spinks (USA) KO–8 Murray Sutherland (GB) Atlantic City, USA

13 Apr 1982 *LF(WBC)* Tadashi Tomori (Jap) PTS–15 Amado Ursua (Mex) Tokyo, Japan

26 Apr 1982 *LM(WBA)* Davey Moore (USA) KO–5 Charlie Weir (SA) Johannesburg, South Africa

1 May 1982 *Fl(WBA)* Santos Laciar (Arg) RSF–13 Juan Herrera (Mex) Merida, Mexico

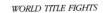

8 May 1982 *L(WBA)* Ray Mancini (USA) RSF–1 Arturo Frias (USA) Las Vegas, USA

8 May 1982 *Fe(WBC)* Salvador Sanchez (Mex) PTS–15 Jorge 'Rocky' Garcia (Mex) Dallas, USA

22 May 1982 *L(WBC)* Alexis Arguello (Nic) KO–5 Andy Ganigan (USA) Las Vegas, USA

29 May 1982 *JL(WBC)* Rafael Limon (Mex) KO–12 Rolando Navarrete (Phi) Las Vegas, USA

3 Jun 1982 *B(WBC)* Lupe Pintor (Mex) RSF–11 Seung-Hoon Lee (S. Kor) Los Angeles, USA

5 Jun 1982 *JL(WBA)* Sam Serrano (PR) TKO–10 Ben Villablanca (Chi) Santiago, Chile

11 Jun 1982 *SB(WBC)* Wilfredo Gomez (PR) KO–10 Juan Antonio Lopez (Mex) Las Vegas, USA

11 Jun 1982 *H(WBC)* Larry Holmes (USA) RTD–13 Gerry Cooney (USA) Las Vegas, USA

12 Jun 1982 *LH(WBA)* Michael Spinks (USA) RSF–8 Jerry Celestine (USA) Atlantic City, USA

12 Jun 1982 *SB(WBA)* Leonardo Cruz (Dom) PTS–15 Sergio Palma (Arg) Miami, USA

26 Jun 1982 *LW(WBC)* Leroy Haley (USA) PTS–15 Saoul Mamby (Jam) Highland Heights, USA

27 Jun 1982 *C(WBC)* S. T. Gordon (USA) RSF–2 Carlos de Leon (PR) Ohio, USA

4 Jul 1982 *LW(WBA)* Aaron Pryor (USA) RSF–6 Akio Kameda (Jap) Cincinnati, USA

4 Jul 1982 *SF(WBC)* Chul-Ho Kim (S. Kor) D–15 Raul Valdez (Mex) Taejon, South Korea

7 Jul 1982 *LF(WBA)* Katsuo Tokashiki (Jap) KO–8 Masaharu Inami (Jap) Tokyo, Japan

17 Jul 1982 *LM(WBA)* Davey Moore (USA) RSF–10 Ayub Kalule (Uga) Atlantic City, USA

20 Jul 1982 *LF(WBC)* Hilario Zapata (Pan) PTS–15 Tadashi Tomori (Jap) Kamazawa, Japan

21 Jul 1982 *Fe(WBC)* Salvador Sanchez (Mex) RSF–15 Azumah Nelson (Gha) New York, USA

24 Jul 1982 *L(WBA)* Ray Mancini (USA) RSF–6 Ernesto Espana (Ven) Warren, USA

25 Jul 1982 *Fl(WBC)* Freddie Castillo (Mex) PTS–15 Prudencio Cardona (Col) Merida, Mexico

29 Jul 1982 *SF(WBA)* Jiro Watanabe (Jap) RSF–9 Gustavo Ballas (Arg) Osaka, Japan

8 Aug 1982 *LH(WBC)* Dwight Braxton (USA) RSF–6 Matt Saad Muhammad (USA) Philadelphia, USA

14 Aug 1982 *Fl(WBA)* Santos Laciar (Arg) PTS–15 Betulio Gonzalez (Ven) Maracaibo, Venezuela

18 Aug 1982 *SB(WBC)* Wilfredo Gomez (PR) RTD–7 Roberto Rubaldino (Mex) San Juan, Puerto Rico

15 Sep 1982 *Fe(WBC)* Juan Laporte (PR) RSF–10 Mario Miranda (Col) New York, USA

18 Sep 1982 *LH(WBA)* Michael Spinks (USA) KO–9 Johnny Davis (USA) Atlantic City, USA

18 Sep 1982 *JL(WBC)* Rafael Limon (Mex) KO–7 Chung-Il Choi (S. Kor) Los Angeles, USA

18 Sep 1982 *LF(WBC)* Hilario Zapata (Pan) PTS–15 Jung-Koo Chang (S. Kor) Seoul, South Korea

10 Oct 1982 *LF(WBA)* Katsuo Tokashiki (Jap) PTS–15 Sung-Nam Kim (S. Kor) Tokyo, Japan

16 Oct 1982 *Fe(WBA)* Eusebio Pedroza (Pan) D–15 Bernard Taylor (USA) Charlotte, USA

20 Oct 1982 *LW(WBC)* Leroy Haley (USA) PTS–15 Juan Jose Giminez (Arg) Cleveland, USA

27 Oct 1982 *B(WBA)* Jeff Chandler (USA) RSF–9 Miguel Iriarte (Pan) Atlantic City, USA

31 Oct 1982 *M* Marvin Hagler (USA) KO–5 Fulgencio Obelmejias (Ven) San Remo, Italy

5 Nov 1982 *Fl(WBA)* Santos Laciar (Arg) RSF–13 Steve Muchoki (Ken) Copenhagen, Denmark

7 Nov 1982 *Fl(WBC)* Eleoncio Mercedes (Dom) PTS–15 Freddie Castillo (Mex) Los Angeles, USA

11 Nov 1982 *SF(WBA)* Jiro Watanabe (Jap) RTD–12 Shoji Oguma (Jap) Hamamatsu, Japan

12 Nov 1982 *LW(WBA)* Aaron Pryor (USA) RSF–14 Alexis Arguello (Nic) Miami, USA

13 Nov 1982 *L(WBA)* Ray Mancini (USA) RSF–14 Duk-Koo Kim (S. Kor) Las Vegas, USA

13 Nov 1982 *SB(WBA)* Leonardo Cruz (Dom) KO–8 Benito Badilla (Chi) San Juan, Puerto Rico

20 Nov 1982 *LH(WBC)* Dwight Muhammad Qawi (USA) RSF–11 Eddie Davis (USA) Atlantic City, USA

25 Nov 1982 *H(WBC)* Larry Holmes (USA) PTS–15 Randall Cobb (USA) Houston, USA

28 Nov 1982 *SF(WBC)* Rafael Orono (Ven) RSF–6 Chul-Ho Kim (S. Kor) Seoul, South Korea

30 Nov 1982 *LF(WBC)* Hilario Zapata (Pan) RSF–8 Tadashi Tomori (Jap) Tokyo, Japan

3 Dec 1982 *LM(WBC)* Thomas Hearns (USA) PTS–15 Wilfred Benitez (USA) New Orleans, USA

3 Dec 1982 *SB(WBC)* Wilfredo Gomez (PR) RSF–14 Lupe Pintor (Mex) New Orleans, USA

10 Dec 1982 *H(WBA)* Mike Dokes (USA) RSF–1 Mike Weaver (USA) Las Vegas, USA

11 Dec 1982 *JL(WBC)* Bob Chacon (USA) PTS–15 Rafael Limon (Mex) Sacramento, USA

15 Dec 1982 *C(WBA)* Ossie Ocasio (PR) PTS–15 Young Joe Louis (USA) Chicago, USA

9 Jan 1983 *LF(WBA)* Katsuo Tokashiki (Jap) PTS–15 Hwan-Jim Kim (S. Kor) Kyoto, Japan

19 Jan 1983 *JL(WBA)* Roger Mayweather (USA) KO–8 Sam Serrano (PR) San Juan, Puerto Rico

29 Jan 1983 *LM(WBA)* Davey Moore (USA) KO–4 Gary Guiden (USA) Atlantic City, USA

1 Feb 1983 *SF(WBC)* Rafael Orono (Ven) KO–4 Pedro Romero (Pan) Caracas, Venezuela

11 Feb 1983 *M* Marvin Hagler (USA) RSF–6 Tony Sibson (GB) Worcester, USA

13 Feb 1983 *W(WBA)* Don Curry (USA) PTS–15 Jun-Sok Hwang (S. Kor) Fort Worth, USA

13 Feb 1983 *LW(WBA)* Leroy Haley (USA) PTS–12 Saoul Mamby (Jam) Cleveland, USA

17 Feb 1983 *C(WBC)* S. T. Gordon (USA) RSF–8 Jesse Burnett (USA) New Jersey, USA

20 Feb 1983 *Fe(WBC)* Juan Laporte (PR) PTS–12 Ruben Castillo (USA) San Juan, Puerto Rico

24 Feb 1983 *SF(WBA)* Jiro Watanabe (Jap) KO–8 Luis Ibanez (Peru) Hamamatsu, Japan

4 Mar 1983 *Fl(WBA)* Santos Laciar (Arg) KO–9 Ramon Neri (Dom) Cordoba, Argentina

13 Mar 1983 *B(WBA)* Jeff Chandler (USA) PTS–15 Jose Canizales (USA) Atlantic City, USA

15 Mar 1983 *Fl(WBC)* Charlie Magri (Tun) RSF–7 Eleoncio Mercedes (Dom) London, England

16 Mar 1983 *SB(WBA)* Leonardo Cruz (Dom) PTS–15 Soon-Hyun Chung (S. Kor) San Juan, Puerto Rico

19 Mar 1983 *LH* Michael Spinks (USA) PTS–15 Dwight Muhammad Qawi (USA) Atlantic City, USA

19 Mar 1983 *W(WBC)* Milton McCrory (USA) D–12 Colin Jones (GB) Reno, USA

26 Mar 1983 *H(WBC)* Larry Holmes (USA) PTS–12 Lucien Rodriguez (Mor) Scranton, USA

26 Mar 1983 *LF(WBC)* Chang-Jung Ko (S. Kor) RSF–3 Hilario Zapata (Pan) Seoul, South Korea

2 Apr 1983 *LW(WBA)* Aaron Pryor (USA) RSF–3 San-Hyun Kim (S. Kor) Atlantic City, USA

9 Apr 1983 *LF(WBA)* Katsuo Tokashiki (Jap) D–15 Lupe Madera (Mex) Tokyo, Japan

21 Apr 1983 *JL(WBA)* Roger Mayweather (USA) RSF–8 Jorge Alvarado (Pan) San Juan, Costa Rica
24 Apr 1983 *Fe(WBA)* Eusebio Pedroza (Pan) PTS–15 Rocky Lockridge (USA) San Remo, Italy
2 May 1983 *L(WBC)* Edwin Rosario (PR) PTS–12 Jose Luis Ramirez (Mex) San Juan, Puerto Rico
5 May 1983 *Fl(WBA)* Santos Laciar (Arg) RSF–2 Shuichi Hozumi (Jap) Shizuoka, Japan
9 May 1983 *SF(WBC)* Rafael Orono (Ven) PTS–12 Raul Valdez (Mex) Caracas, Venezuela
18 May 1983 *LW(WBC)* Bruce Curry (USA) PTS–12 Leroy Haley (USA) Las Vegas, USA
20 May 1983 *H(WBC)* Larry Holmes (USA) PTS–12 Tim Witherspoon (USA) Las Vegas, USA
20 May 1983 *H(WBA)* Mike Dokes (USA) D–15 Mike Weaver (USA) Las Vegas, USA
20 May 1983 *C(WBA)* Ossie Ocasio (PR) PTS–15 Randy Stephens (USA) Las Vegas, USA
27 May 1983 *M* Marvin Hagler (USA) KO–4 Wilford Scypion (USA) Rhode Island, USA

11 Jun 1983 *LF(WBC)* Chang-Jung Ko (S. Kor) RSF–2 Masaharu Iha (Jap) Taegu, South Korea
15 Jun 1983 *SB(WBC)* Jaime Garza (USA) RSF–2 Bobby Berna (Phi) Los Angeles, USA
16 Jun 1983 *LM(WBA)* Roberto Duran (Pan) RSF–8 Davey Moore (USA) New York, USA
23 Jun 1983 *SF(WBA)* Jiro Watanabe (Jap) PTS–15 Roberto Ramirez (Mex) Miyagi-Kew, Japan
25 Jun 1983 *Fe(WBC)* Juan Laporte (PR) PTS–12 Johnny De La Rosa (Dom) San Juan, Puerto Rico
7 Jul 1983 *LW(WBC)* Bruce Curry (USA) KO–7 Hidekazu Akai (Jap) Osaka, Japan
10 Jul 1983 *LF(WBA)* Lupe Madera (Mex) RSF–4 Katsuo Tokashiki (Jap) Tokyo, Japan
16 Jul 1983 *Fl(WBA)* Santos Laciar (Arg) RSF–1 Shin-Hi Sop (S. Kor) Cheju, South Korea
17 Jul 1983 *C(WBC)* Carlos de Leon (PR) PTS–12 S. T. Gordon (USA) Las Vegas, USA
8 Aug 1983 *JL(WBC)* Hector Camacho (PR) RSF–5 Rafael Limon (Mex) San Juan, Puerto Rico

Tommy Hearns is buckling after taking a right from Wilfred Benitez. However, at the end of 15 rounds the decision went to Hearns and he was the new WBC super-welterweight champion in 1982 (AP)

g 1983 *W(WBC)* Milton McCrory (USA) PTS–12 Colin Jones (GB) Las Vegas, USA

g 1983 *JL(WBA)* Roger Mayweather (USA) KO–1 Ben Villablanca (Chi) Las Vegas, USA

g 1983 *SB(WBA)* Leonardo Cruz (Dom) PTS–15 Cleo Garcia (Nic) Santo Domingo, Dominican Republic

g 1983 *B(WBC)* Albert Davila (USA) KO–12 Kiko Bejines (Mex) Los Angeles, USA

1983 *W(WBA)* Don Curry (USA) KO–1 Roger Stafford (USA) Sicily, Italy

1983 *LW(WBA)* Aaron Pryor (USA) KO–10 Alexis Arguello (Nic) Las Vegas, USA

1983 *H(WBC)* Larry Holmes (USA) RSF–5 Scott Frank (USA) Atlantic City, USA

1983 *B(WBA)* Jeff Chandler (USA) RSF–10 Eijiro Murata (Jap) Tokyo, Japan

1983 *LF(WBC)* Chang-Jung Ko (S. Kor) PTS–12 German Torres (Phi) Taejon, South Korea

1983 *L(WBA)* Ray Mancini (USA) KO–9 Orlando Romero (Peru) New York, USA

21 Sep 1983 *C(WBC)* Carlos de Leon (PR) RSF–4 Alvaro Lopez (Mex) San Jose, USA

24 Sep 1983 *H(WBA)* Gerrie Coetzee (SA) KO–10 Mike Dokes (USA) Cleveland, USA

27 Sep 1983 *Fl(WBC)* Frank Cedeno (Phi) RSF–6 Charlie Magri (Tun) London, England

5 Oct 1983 *SF(WBA)* Jiro Watanabe (Jap) TKO–11 Chung-Soon Kwon (S. Kor) Osaka, Japan

20 Oct 1983 *LW(WBC)* Bruce Curry (USA) PTS–12 Leroy Haley (USA) Las Vegas, USA

22 Oct 1983 *Fe(WBA)* Eusebio Pedroza (Pan) PTS–15 Jose Caba (Dom) St Vincent, West Indies

23 Oct 1983 *LF(WBA)* Lupe Madera (Mex) PTS–15 Katsuo Tokashiki (Jap) Saporro, Japan

29 Oct 1983 *SF(WBC)* Rafael Orono (Ven) KO–5 Orlando Maldonado (PR) Caracas, Venezuela

10 Nov 1983 *M* Marvin Hagler (USA) PTS–15 Roberto Duran (Pan) Las Vegas, USA

18 Nov 1983 *JL(WBC)* Hector Camacho (PR) KO–5 Rafael Solis (PR) San Juan, Puerto Rico

25 Nov 1983 *H(WBC)* Larry Holmes (USA) TKO–1 Marvis Frazier (USA) Las Vegas, USA

25 Nov 1983 *LH* Michael Spinks (USA) RSF–10 Oscar Rivadeneyra (USA) Vancouver, Canada

26 Nov 1983 *SF(WBC)* Payao Poontarat (Tha) PTS–12 Rafael Orono (Ven) Bangkok, Thailand

4 Dec 1983 *SB(IBF)* Bobby Berna (Phi) KO–9 Seung-In Suh (S. Kor) Seoul, South Korea

10 Dec 1983 *SF(IBF)* Joo-Do Chun (S. Kor) RSF–5 Ken Kasugai (Jap) Osaka, Japan

10 Dec 1983 *LF(IBF)* Dodie Penalosa (Phi) RSF–12 Satoshi Shingaki (Jap) Osaka, Japan

13 Dec 1983 *C(IBF)* Marvin Camel (USA) KO–5 Roddy McDonald (Can) Halifax, Canada

17 Dec 1983 *B(WBA)* Jeff Chandler (USA) RSF–7 Oscar Muniz (USA) Atlantic City, USA

24 Dec 1983 *Fl(IBF)* Soo-Chun Kwon (S. Kor) KO–5 Rene Busayong (Phi) Seoul, South Korea

14 Jan 1984 *L(WBA)* Ray Mancini (USA) RSF–3 Bobby Chacon (USA) Reno, USA

15 Jan 1984 *W(WBC)* Milton McCrory (USA) RSF–6 Milton Guest (USA) Detroit, USA

18 Jan 1984 *Fl(WBC)* Koji Kobayashi (Jap) RSF–2 Frank Cedeno (Phi) Tokyo, Japan

21 Jan 1984 *LW(WBA)* Johnny Bumphus (USA) PTS–15 Lorenzo Garcia (Arg) Atlantic City, USA

28 Jan 1984 *SF(IBF)* Joo-Do Chun (S. Kor) KO–12 Prayurasak Muangsurin (Tha) Seoul, South Korea

28 Jan 1984 *Fl(WBA)* Santos Laciar (Arg) PTS–15 Juan Herrera (Mex) Marsala, Italy

29 Jan 1984 *LW(WBC)* Billy Costello (USA) RSF–10 Bruce Curry (USA) Beaumont, USA

30 Jan 1984 *L(IBF)* Charlie 'Choo Choo' Brown (USA) PTS–15 Melvin Paul (USA) Atlantic City, USA

4 Feb 1984 *W(WBA)* Don Curry (USA) PTS–15 Marlon Starling (USA) Atlantic City, USA

11 Feb 1984 *LM(WBC)* Thomas Hearns (USA) PTS–12 Luigi Minchillo (Ita) Detroit, USA

22 Feb 1984 *SB(WBA)* Loris Stecca (Ita) RSF–12 Leonardo Cruz (Dom) Milan, Italy

25 Feb 1984 *LH* Michael Spinks (USA) PTS–12 Eddie Davis (USA) Atlantic City, USA

25 Feb 1984 *JL(WBA)* Rocky Lockridge (USA) KO–1 Roger Mayweather (USA) Beaumont, USA

25 Feb 1984 *Fl(IBF)* Soo-Chun Kwon (S. Kor) PTS–15 Roger Castillo (Phi) Seoul, South Korea

4 Mar 1984 *Fe(IBF)* Min-Keum Oh (S. Kor) KO–2 Joko Arter (Phi) Seoul, South Korea

9 Mar 1984 *H(WBC)* Tim Witherspoon (USA) PTS–12 Greg
    Page (USA) Las Vegas, USA

9 Mar 1984 *C(WBC)* Carlos de Leon (PR) PTS–12 Anthony
    Davis (USA) Las Vegas, USA

11 Mar 1984 *LM(IBF)* Mark Medal (USA) RSF–5 Earl
    Hargrove (USA) Atlantic City, USA

15 Mar 1984 *SF(WBA)* Jiro Watanabe (Jap) RSF–15 Celso
    Chavez (Pan) Osaka, Japan

17 Mar 1984 *L(WBC)* Edwin Rosario (PR) RSF–1 Roberto
    Elizondo (USA) San Juan, Puerto Rico

17 Mar 1984 *SF(IBF)* Joo-Do Chun (S. Kor) KO–1 Diego de
    Villa (Phi) Kwangju, South Korea

27 Mar 1984 *SF(WBC)* Payao Poontarat (Tha) TKO–10
    Gustavo Espadas (Mex) Bangkok, Thailand

28 Mar 1984 *SM(IBF)* Murray Sutherland (GB) PTS–15
    Ernie Singletary (USA) Atlantic City, USA

30 Mar 1984 *M* Marvin Hagler (USA) RSF–10 Juan
    Domingo Roldan (Arg) Las Vegas, USA

31 Mar 1984 *Fe(WBC)* Wilfredo Gomez (PR) PTS–12 Juan
    Laporte (PR) San Juan, Puerto Rico

31 Mar 1984 *LF(WBC)* Chang-Jung Ko (S. Kor) PTS–12 Sot
    Chitalada (Tha) Pusan, South Korea

7 Apr 1984 *B(WBA)* Richard Sandoval (USA) RSF–15 Jeff
    Chandler (USA) Atlantic City, USA

9 Apr 1984 *Fl(WBC)* Gabriel Bernal (Mex) RSF–2 Koji
    Kobayashi (Jap) Tokyo, Japan

15 Apr 1984 *W(WBC)* Milton McCrory (USA) RSF–6 Gilles
    Elbilla (Fra) Detroit, USA

15 Apr 1984 *L(IBF)* Harry Arroyo (USA) RSF–4 Charlie
    'Choo Choo' Brown (USA) Atlantic City, USA

15 Apr 1984 *SB(IBF)* Seung-In Suh (S. Kor) KO–10 Bobby
    Berna (Phi) Seoul, South Korea

15 Apr 1984 *B(IBF)* Satoshi Shingaki (Jap) KO–8 Elmer
    Magallano (USA) Kashiwara, Japan

21 Apr 1984 *W(WBA)* Don Curry (USA) RTD–7 Elio Diaz
    (Ven) Fort Worth, USA

22 Apr 1984 *JL(IBF)* Hwan-Kil Yuh (S.Kor) PTS–15 Rod
    Sequenan (Phi) Seoul, South Korea

5 May 1984 *C(WBA)* Ossie Ocasio (PR) RSF–15 John
    Odhiambo (Uga) San Juan, Puerto Rico

13 May 1984 *LF(IBF)* Dodie Penalosa (Phi) KO–9 Jae-Hong
    Kim (S. Kor) Seoul, South Korea

19 May 1984 *Fl(IBF)* Soo-Chun Kwon (S. Kor) PTS–15 Ian
    Clyde (USA) Taejon, South Korea

19 May 1984 *LF(WBA)* Francisco Quiroz (Dom) KO–9
    Lupe Madera (Mex) Maracaibo, Venezuela

26 May 1984 *SB(WBC)* Jaime Garza (USA) KO–3 Felipe
    Orozco (Col) Miami, USA

26 May 1984 *SF(IBF)* Joo-Do Chun (S. Kor) KO–6 Felix
    Marquez (PR) Chonju, South Korea

27 May 1984 *Fe(WBA)* Eusebio Pedroza (Pan) PTS–15
    Angel Levy Meyor (Ven) Maracaibo, Venezuela

27 May 1984 *SB(WBA)* Victor Callejas (PR) KO–8 Loris
    Stecca (Ita) San Juan, Puerto Rico

27 May 1984 *B(WBC)* Albert Davila (USA) RSF–11 Enrique
    Sanchez (Dom) Miami, USA

1 Jun 1984 *LW(WBA)* Gene Hatcher (USA) RSF–11 Johnny
    Bumphus (USA) Buffalo, USA

1 Jun 1984 *L(WBA)* Livingstone Bramble (VI) RSF–14 Ray
    Mancini (USA) Buffalo, USA

1 Jun 1984 *Fl(WBC)* Gabriel Bernal (Mex) RSF–11 Antoine
    Montero (Fra) Nimes, France

3 Jun 1984 *C(WBC)* Carlos de Leon (PR) PTS–12 Bashiru
    Ali (Nig) Oakland, USA

10 Jun 1984 *Fe(IBF)* Min-Keum Oh (S. Kor) PTS–15 Kelvin
    Lampkin (USA) Seoul, South Korea

12 Jun 1984 *JL(WBA)* Rocky Lockridge (USA) RSF–11 Tae-
    Jin Moon (S. Kor) Anchorage, USA

16 Jun 1984 *LM(WBC)* Thomas Hearns (USA) RSF–2
    Roberto Duran (Pan) Las Vegas, USA

22 Jun 1984 *LW(IBF)* Aaron Pryor (USA) PTS–15 Nicky
    Furlano (Can) Toronto, Canada

23 Jun 1984 *L(WBC)* Edwin Rosario (PR) PTS–12 Howard
    Davis (USA) San Juan, Puerto Rico

5 Jul 1984 *SF(WBC)* Jiro Watanabe (Jap) PTS–12 Payao
    Poontarat (Tha) Osaka, Japan

8 Jul 1984 *SB(IBF)* Seung-In Suh (S. Kor) KO–4 Cleo
    Garcia (Nic) Seoul, South Korea

16 Jul 1984 *LW(WBC)* Billy Costello (USA) PTS–12 Ronnie
    Shields (USA) New York, USA

20 Jul 1984 *SF(IBF)* Joo-Do Chun (S. Kor) KO–7 William
    Develos (Phi) Pusan, South Korea

22 Jul 1984 *SM(IBF)* Chong-Pal Park (S. Kor) KO–11
    Murray Sutherland (GB) Seoul, South Korea

4 Aug 1984 *B(IBF)* Satoshi Shingaki (Jap) PTS–15 Horves
    de la Puz (Phi) Naha, Japan

18 Aug 1984 *LF(WBA)* Francisco Quiroz (Dom) KO–2
    Victor Sierra (Pan) Panama City, Panama

18 Aug 1984 *LF(WBC)* Chang-Jung Ko (S. Kor) RSF–9
    Katsuo Tokashiki (Jap) Pohang, South Korea

31 Aug 1984 *H(WBC)* Pinklon Thomas (USA) PTS–12 Tim
    Witherspoon (USA) Las Vegas, USA

1 Sep 1984 *L(IBF)* Harry Arroyo (USA) RSF–8 Charlie 'White
    Lightning' Brown (USA) Youngstown, USA

7 Sep 1984 *Fl(IBF)* Soo-Chun Kwon (S. Kor) RSF–12
    Joaquin Caraballo (Col) Seoul, South Korea

13 Sep 1984 *JL(WBC)* Julio Cesar Chavez (Mex) RSF–8
    Mario Martinez (Mex) Los Angeles, USA

15 Sep 1984 *LM(WBC)* Thomas Hearns (USA) RSF–3 Fred
    Hutchings (USA) Saginaw, USA

15 Sep 1984 *Fl(WBA)* Santos Laciar (Arg) KO–10 Prudencio
    Cardona (Col) Cordoba, Argentina

16 Sep 1984 *JL(IBF)* Hwan-Kil Yuh (S. Kor) KO–6 Sakda
    Galexi (Tha) Pohang, South Korea

22 Sep 1984 *W(WBA)* Don Curry (USA) KO–6 Nino La
    Rocca (Mau) Monte Carlo, Monaco

22 Sep 1984 *B(WBA)* Richard Sandoval (USA) PTS–15
    Edgar Roman (Ven) Monte Carlo, Monaco

6 Oct 1984 *C(IBF)* Leroy Murphy (USA) RSF–14 Marvin
    Camel (USA) Billings, USA

8 Oct 1984 *Fl(WBC)* Sot Chitalada (Tha) PTS–12 Gabriel
    Bernal (Mex) Bangkok, Thailand

20 Oct 1984 *M* Marvin Hagler (USA) RSF–3 Mustapha
    Hamsho (Syr) New York, USA

20 Oct 1984 *LM(WBA)* Mike McCallum (Jam) PTS–15 Sean
    Mannion (USA) New York, USA

2 Nov 1984 *JM(IBF)* Carlos Santos (PR) PTS–15 Mark Medal
    (USA) New York, USA

3 Nov 1984 *LW(WBC)* Billy Costello (USA) PTS–12 Saoul
    Mamby (Jam) New York, USA

3 Nov 1984 *L(WBC)* Jose Luis Ramirez (Mex) RSF–4 Edwin
    Rosario (PR) San Juan, Puerto Rico

3 Nov 1984 *SB(WBC)* Juan 'Kid' Meza (Mex) KO–1 Jaime
    Garza (USA) New York, USA

9 Nov 1984 *H(IBF)* Larry Holmes (USA) RSF–12 James
    'Bonecrusher' Smith (USA) Las Vegas, USA

16 Nov 1984 *LF(IBF)* Dodie Penalosa (Phi) PTS–15 Chun-
    Hwan Choi (S. Kor) Manila, Philippines

21 Nov 1984 *SF(WBA)* Kaosai Galaxy (Tha) KO–6 Eusebio
    Espinal (Dom) Bangkok, Thailand

29 Nov 1984 *SF(WBC)* Jiro Watanabe (Jap) RSF–11 Payao
    Poontarat (Tha) Kumamoto, Japan

1 Dec 1984 *H(WBA)* Greg Page (USA) KO–8 Gerrie
    Coetzee (SA) Sun City, South Africa

1 Dec 1984 *C(WBA)* Piet Crous (SA) PTS–15 Ossie Ocasio
    (PR) Sun City, South Africa

2 Dec 1984 *LM(WBA)* Mike McCallum (Jam) TKO–13 Luigi Minchillo (Ita) Milan, Italy

3 Dec 1984 *Fe(WBC)* Azumah Nelson (Gha) RSF–11 Wilfredo Gomez (PR) San Juan, Puerto Rico

3 Dec 1984 *Fl(WBA)* Santos Laciar (Arg) PTS–15 Hilario Zapata (Pan) Buenos Aires, Argentina

15 Dec 1984 *LW(WBA)* Gene Hatcher (USA) PTS–15 Ubaldo Sacco (Arg) Fort Worth, USA

15 Dec 1984 *B(WBA)* Richard Sandoval (USA) RSF–8 Gardeno Villoa (Chi) Miami, USA

15 Dec 1984 *LF(WBC)* Chang-Jung Ko (S. Kor) PTS–12 Tadashi Kuromochi (Jap) Pusan, South Korea

20 Dec 1984 *C(IBF)* Leroy Murphy (USA) RSF–12 Young Joe Louis (USA) Chicago, USA

2 Jan 1985 *SM(IBF)* Chong-Pal Park (S. Kor) KO–2 Roy Gumbs (Jam) Seoul, South Korea

2 Jan 1985 *SB(IBF)* Chi-Won Kim (S. Kor) KO–10 Seung-In Suh (S. Kor) Seoul, South Korea

5 Jan 1985 *SF(IBF)* Joo-Do Chun (S. Kor) KO–15 Park-Kwang Gu (S. Kor) Ulsan, South Korea

12 Jan 1985 *L(IBF)* Harry Arroyo (USA) RSF–11 Terence Alli (Guy) Atlantic City, USA

19 Jan 1985 *W(WBA)* Don Curry (USA) RSF–4 Colin Jones (GB) Birmingham, England

25 Jan 1985 *Fl(IBF)* Chong-Kwan Chung (S. Kor) D–15 Soo-Chun Kwon (S. Kor) Taejon, South Korea

26 Jan 1985 *JL(WBA)* Rocky Lockridge (USA) RSF–6 Kamel Bou Ali (Tun) Riva Del Garda, Italy

2 Feb 1985 *Fe(WBA)* Eusebio Pedroza (Pan) PTS–15 Jorge Lujan (Pan) Panama City, Panama

2 Feb 1985 *SB(WBA)* Victor Callejas (PR) PTS–15 Seung-Hoon Lee (S. Kor) San Juan, Puerto Rico

16 Feb 1985 *LW(WBC)* Billy Costello (USA) PTS–12 Leroy Haley (USA) New York, USA

16 Feb 1985 *L(WBA)* Livingstone Bramble (VI) PTS–15 Ray Mancini (USA) Reno, USA

16 Feb 1985 *JL(IBF)* Lester Ellis (Aus) PTS–15 Hwan-Kil Yuh (S. Kor) Melbourne, Australia

20 Feb 1985 *Fl(WBC)* Sot Chitalada (Tha) RSF–4 Charlie Magri (Tun) London, England

23 Feb 1985 *LH* Michael Spinks (USA) RSF–3 David Sears (USA) Atlantic City, USA

2 Mar 1985 *LW(IBF)* Aaron Pryor (USA) PTS–15 Garry Hinton (USA) Atlantic City, USA

5 Mar 1985 *SF(WBA)* Kaosai Galaxy (Tha) KO–7 Dong-Chun Lee (S. Kor) Bangkok, Thailand

9 Mar 1985 *W(WBC)* Milton McCrory (USA) PTS–12 Pedro Vilella (USA) Paris, France

15 Mar 1985 *H(IBF)* Larry Holmes (USA) RSF–10 David Bey (USA) Las Vegas, USA

29 Mar 1985 *LF(WBA)* Joey Olivo (USA) PTS–15 Francisco Quiroz (Dom) Miami, USA

30 Mar 1985 *C(WBA)* Piet Crous (SA) RSF–3 Randy Stephens (USA) Sun City, South Africa

30 Mar 1985 *SB(IBF)* Chi-Won Kim (S. Kor) PTS–15 Dario Palacios (USA) Suwon, South Korea

6 Apr 1985 *L(IBF)* Jimmy Paul (USA) PTS–15 Harry Arroyo (USA) Atlantic City, USA

7 Apr 1985 *Fe(IBF)* Min-Keum Oh (S. Kor) PTS–15 Irving Mitchell (USA) Seoul, South Korea

14 Apr 1985 *Fl(IBF)* Soo-Chun Kwon (S. Kor) KO–3 Shinobu Kawashima (Jap) Seoul, South Korea

15 Apr 1985 *M* Marvin Hagler (USA) RSF–3 Thomas Hearns (USA) Las Vegas, USA

19 Apr 1985 *JL(WBC)* Julio Cesar Chavez (Mex) RSF–6 Ruben Castillo (USA) Los Angeles, USA

19 Apr 1985 *SB(WBC)* Juan 'Kid' Meza (Mex) RSF–6 Mike Ayala (USA) Los Angeles, USA

26 Apr 1985 *JL(IBF)* Lester Ellis (Aus) RSF–13 Rod Sequenan (Phi) Melbourne, Australia

26 Apr 1985 *B(IBF)* Jeff Fenech (Aus) RSF–9 Satoshi Shingaki (Jap) Sydney, Australia

27 Apr 1985 *LF(WBC)* Chang-Jung Ko (S. Kor) PTS–12 German Torres (Phi) Ulsan, South Korea

29 Apr 1985 *H(WBA)* Tony Tubbs (USA) PTS–15 Greg Page (USA) Buffalo, USA

3 May 1985 *SF(IBF)* Ellyas Pical (Ina) KO–8 Joo-Do Chun (S. Kor) Djakarta, Indonesia

4 May 1985 *B(WBC)* Daniel Zaragoza (Mex) DIS–7 Freddie Jackson (USA) Aruba, Dutch West Indies

6 May 1985 *Fl(WBA)* Santos Laciar (Arg) PTS–15 Antoine Montero (Fra) Grenoble, France

9 May 1985 *SF(WBC)* Jiro Watanabe (Jap) PTS–12 Juliosoto Solano (Dom) Tokyo, Japan

19 May 1985 *JL(WBA)* Wilfredo Gomez (PR) PTS–15 Rocky Lockridge (USA) San Juan, Puerto Rico

20 May 1985 *H(IBF)* Larry Holmes (USA) PTS–15 Carl Williams (USA) Reno, USA

1 Jun 1985 *JM(IBF)* Carlos Santos (PR) PTS–15 Louis Acaries (Fra) Paris, France

6 Jun 1985 *C(WBC)* Alphonso Ratliff (USA) PTS–12 Carlos de Leon (PR) Las Vegas, USA

6 Jun 1985 *LH* Michael Spinks (USA) RSF–8 Jim McDonald (USA) Las Vegas, USA

8 Jun 1985 *Fe(WBA)* Barry McGuigan (Ire) PTS–15 Eusebio Pedroza (Pan) London, England

15 Jun 1985 *H(WBC)* Pinklon Thomas (USA) RSF–8 Mike Weaver (USA) Las Vegas, USA

22 Jun 1985 *Fl(WBC)* Sot Chitalada (Tha) D–12 Gabriel Bernal (Mex) Bangkok, Thailand

28 Jun 1985 *SB(IBF)* Chi-Won Kim (S. Kor) KO–4 Bobby Berna (Phi) Pusan, South Korea

29 Jun 1985 *SM(IBF)* Chong-Pal Park (S. Kor) PTS–15 Vinnie Curto (USA) Seoul, South Korea

30 Jun 1985 *L(IBF)* Jimmy Paul (USA) RSF–14 Robin Blake (USA) Las Vegas, USA

2 Jul 1985 *LF(WBA)* Joey Olivo (USA) PTS–15 Mun-Jin Choi (S. Kor) Seoul, South Korea

6 Jul 1985 *JL(WBC)* Julio Cesar Chavez (Mex) RSF–2 Roger Mayweather (USA) Las Vegas, USA

12 Jul 1985 *JL(IBF)* Barry Michael (GB) PTS–15 Lester Ellis (Aus) Melbourne, Australia

14 Jul 1985 *W(WBC)* Milton McCrory (USA) KO–3 Carlos Trujillo (Pan) Monte Carlo, Monaco

17 Jul 1985 *SF(WBA)* Kaosai Galaxy (Tha) RSF–5 Rafael Orono (Ven) Bangkok, Thailand

17 Jul 1985 *Fl(IBF)* Soo-Chun Kwon (S. Kor) D–15 Chang-Kwan Chung (S. Kor) Masan, South Korea

21 Jul 1985 *LW(WBA)* Ubaldo Sacco (Arg) RSF–9 Gene Hatcher (USA) Campione de Italia, Italy

28 Jul 1985 *C(WBA)* Dwight Muhammad Qawi (USA) KO–11 Piet Crous (SA) Sun City, South Africa

28 Jul 1985 *LM(WBA)* Mike McCallum (Jam) RSF–8 David Braxton (USA) Miami, USA

4 Aug 1985 *LF(WBC)* Chang-Jung Ko (S. Kor) PTS–12 Francisco Montiel (Mex) Seoul, South Korea

9 Aug 1985 *B(WBC)* Miguel 'Happy' Lora (Col) PTS–12 Daniel Zaragoza (Mex) Miami, USA

10 Aug 1985 *L(WBC)* Hector Camacho (PR) PTS–12 Jose Luis Ramirez (Mex) Las Vegas, USA

19 Aug 1985 *SB(WBC)* Lupe Pintor (Mex) PTS–15 Juan 'Kid' Meza (Mex) México City, Mexico

22 Aug 1985 *LW(WBC)* Lonnie Smith (USA) RSF–8 Billy Costello (USA) New York, USA

23 Aug 1985 *B(IBF)* Jeff Fenech (Aus) RSF–3 Satoshi Shingaki (Jap) Sydney, Australia

After 19 defences of his world featherweight title, Panama's Eusebio Pedroza lost his title to Ireland's Barry McGuigan (back to camera) in 1985 (Steve Powell)

25 Aug 1985 *SF(IBF)* Ellyas Pical (Ind) RSF–3 Wayne Mulholland (Aus) Djakarta, Indonesia

6 Sep 1985 *Fe(WBC)* Azumah Nelson (Gha) KO–5 Juvenal Ordenes (Chi) Miami, USA

17 Sep 1985 *SF(WBC)* Jiro Watanabe (Jap) RSF–7 Kazuo Katsuma (Jap) Osaka, Japan

20 Sep 1985 *H(IBF)* Michael Spinks (USA) PTS–15 Larry Holmes (USA) Las Vegas, USA

20 Sep 1985 *JL(WBC)* Julio Cesar Chavez (Mex) PTS–15 Dwight Pratchett (USA) Las Vegas, USA

22 Sep 1985 *C(WBC)* Bernard Benton (USA) PTS–12 Alphonso Ratliff (USA) Las Vegas, USA

28 Sep 1985 *Fe(WBA)* Barry McGuigan (Ire) RTD–7 Bernard Taylor (USA) Belfast, Ireland

5 Oct 1985 *Fl(WBA)* Hilario Zapata (Pan) PTS–15 Alonso Gonzalez (USA) Panama City, Panama

9 Oct 1985 *SB(IBF)* Chi-Won Kim (S. Kor) KO–1 Seung-In Suh (S. Kor) Seoul, South Korea

12 Oct 1985 *Fe(WBC)* Azumah Nelson (Gha) KO–1 Pat Cowdell (GB) Birmingham, England

12 Oct 1985 *LF(IBF)* Dodie Penalosa (Phi) RSF–3 Yani Dokolamo (Ina) Djakarta, Indonesia

18 Oct 1985 *JL(IBF)* Barry Michael (GB) RSF–4 Jin-Sik Choi (S. Kor) Darwin, Australia

19 Oct 1985 *C(IBF)* Leroy Murphy (USA) KO–12 Chisanda Mutti (Zam) Monte Carlo, Monaco

9 Nov 1985 *SB(WBA)* Victor Callejas (PR) RSF–6 Loris Stecca (Ita) Rimini, Italy

10 Nov 1985 *LF(WBC)* Chang-Jung Ko (S. Kor) PTS–12 Jorge Cano (Mex) Taejon, South Korea

29 Nov 1985 *Fe(IBF)* Chung-Ki Yung (S. Kor) KO–15 Min-Keum Oh (S. Kor) Seoul, South Korea

1 Dec 1985 *B(IBF)* Jeff Fenech (Aus) PTS–15 Jerome Coffee (USA) Sydney, Australia

6 Dec 1985 *W* Don Curry (USA) KO–2 Milton McCrory (USA) Las Vegas, USA

8 Dec 1985 *LF(WBA)* Myung-Woo Yuh (S. Kor) PTS–15 Joey Olivo (USA) Taeku, South Korea

11 Dec 1985 *LH(WBC)* J. B. Williamson (USA) PTS–12 Prince Mohammed (Gha) Inglewood, USA

12 Dec 1985 *SF(WBC)* Jiro Watanabe (Jap) RSF–5 Suk-Huan Yun (S. Kor) Seoul, South Korea

20 Dec 1985 *Fl(IBF)* Chong-Kwan Chung (S. Kor) RSF–4 Soo-Chun Kwon (S. Kor) Pusan, South Korea

21 Dec 1985 *LH(IBF)* Slobodan Kacar (Yug) PTS–15 Eddie Mustafa Mohammad (USA) Pesaro, Italy

23 Dec 1985 *SF(WBA)* Kaosai Galaxy (Tha) KO–2 Edgar Monserrat (Pan) Bangkok, Thailand

17 Jan 1986 *H(WBA)* Tim Witherspoon (USA) PTS–15 Tony Tubbs (USA) Atlanta, USA

18 Jan 1986 *SB(WBC)* Samart Payakaroon (Tha) KO–5 Lupe Pintor (Mex) Bangkok, Thailand

31 Jan 1986 *Fl(WBA)* Hilario Zapata (Pan) PTS–15 Javier Lucas (Mex) Panama City, Panama

8 Feb 1986 *B(WBC)* Miguel Lora (Col) PTS–12 Wilfredo Vasquez (PR) Miami, USA

9 Feb 1986 *LH(WBA)* Marvin Johnson (USA) RSF–7 Leslie Stewart (Tri) Indianapolis, USA

15 Feb 1986 *Fe(WBA)* Barry McGuigan (Ire) RSF–14 Danilo Cabrera (Dom) Dublin, Ireland

15 Feb 1986 *SF(IBF)* Cesar Polonco (Dom) PTS–15 Ellyas Pical (Ina) Djakarta, Indonesia

16 Feb 1986 *L(WBA)* Livingstone Bramble (VI) RSF–13 Tyrone Crawley (USA) Reno, USA

16 Feb 1986 *Fe(IBF)* Chung-Ki Young (S. Kor) KO–6 Tyrone Jackson (USA) Ulsan, South Korea

22 Feb 1986 *Fl(WBC)* Sot Chitalada (Tha) PTS–12 Freddie Castillo (Mex) Kuwait

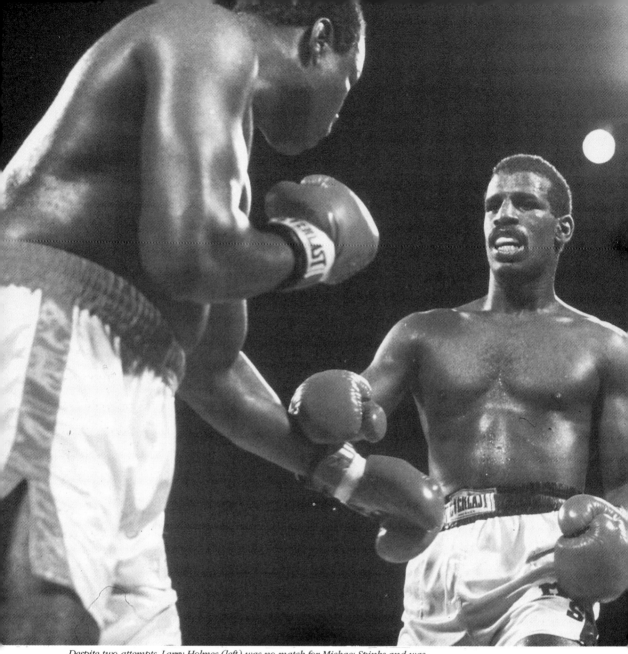

Despite two attempts, Larry Holmes (left) was no match for Michael Spinks and was beaten on points in both their meetings (All Sport/ R Mackson)

25 Feb 1986 *Fe(WBC)* Azumah Nelson (Gha) PTS–12 Marcos Villasana (Mex) Inglewood, USA

3 Mar 1986 *W* Don Curry (USA) KO–2 Eduardo Rodriguez (Pan) Fort Worth, USA

9 Mar 1986 *LF(WBA)* Myung-Woo Yuh (S. Kor) PTS–15 Jose de Jesus (PR) Suwon, South Korea

10 Mar 1986 *M* Marvin Hagler (USA) KO–11 John Mugabi (Uga) Las Vegas, USA

10 Mar 1986 *B(WBA)* Gaby Canizales (USA) KO–7 Richie Sandoval (USA) Las Vegas, USA

15 Mar 1986 *LW(WBA)* Patrizio Oliva (Ita) PTS–15 Ubaldo Sacco (Arg) Monte Carlo, Monaco

20 Mar 1986 *SF(WBC)* Gilberto Roman (Mex) PTS–12 Jiro Watanabe (Jap) Osaka, Japan

22 Mar 1986 *H(WBC)* Trevor Berbick (Jam) PTS–12 Pinklon Thomas (USA) Las Vegas, USA

22 Mar 1986 *C(WBC)* Carlos de Leon (PR) PTS–12 Bernard Benton (USA) Las Vegas, USA

23 Mar 1986 *C(WBA)* Dwight Muhammad Qawi (USA) RSF–6 Leon Spinks (USA) Reno, USA

7 Apr 1986 *Fl(WBA)* Hilario Zapata (Pan) PTS–15 Shuichi Hozumi (Jap) Hirosaki, Japan

11 Apr 1986 *SM(IBF)* Chong-Pal Park (S. Kor) KO–15 Vinnie Curto (USA) Los Angeles, USA

13 Apr 1986 *LF(WBC)* Chang-Jung Koo (S. Kor) PTS–12 German Torres (Mex) Seoul, South Korea

19 Apr 1986 *H(IBF)* Michael Spinks (USA) PTS–15 Larry Holmes (USA) Las Vegas, USA

19 Apr 1986 *C(IBF)* Leroy Murphy (USA) KO–9 Dorcy Gaymon (USA) San Remo, USA

26 Apr 1986 *LW(IBF)* Garry Hinton (USA) PTS–15 Antonio Reyes (Mex) Lucca, Italy

27 Apr 1986 *Fl(IBF)* Chung-Bi Won (S. Kor) PTS–15 Chong-Kwan Chung (S. Kor) Pusan, South Korea

30 Apr 1986 *LH(WBC)* Dennis Andries (Guy) PTS–12 J.B. Williamson (USA) London, England

5 May 1986 *LW(WBC)* Rene Arredondo (Mex) KO–5 Lonnie Smith (USA) Los Angeles, USA

15 May 1986 *JL(WBC)* Julio Cesar Chavez (Mex) RSF–5 Faustino Barrios (Arg) Paris, France

15 May 1986 *SF(WBC)* Gilberto Roman (Mex) PTS–12 Edgar Montserrat (Pan) Paris, France

18 May 1986 *Fe(IBF)* Chung-Ki Yung (S. Kor) PTS–15 Richard Savage (USA) Seoul, South Korea

22 May 1986 *JL(IBF)* Barry Michael (GB) RSF–4 Mark Fernandez (USA) Melbourne, Australia

24 May 1986 *JL(WBA)* Alfredo Layne (Pan) RSF–9 Wilfredo Gomez (PR) San Juan, Puerto Rico

1 Jun 1986 *SB(IBF)* Chi-Won Kim (S. Kor) RSF–2 Rudy Casicas (Phi) Inchon, South Korea

4 Jun 1986 *LM(IBF)* Buster Drayton (USA) PTS–15 Carlos Santos (PR) New Jersey, USA

4 Jun 1986 *L(IBF)* Jimmy Paul (USA) PTS–15 Irleis Perez (USA) New Jersey, USA

4 Jun 1986 *B(WBA)* Bernardo Pinango (Ven) PTS–15 Gaby Canizales (USA) New Jersey, USA

13 Jun 1986 *L(WBC)* Hector Camacho (PR) PTS–12 Edwin Rosario (PR) New York, USA

13 Jun 1986 *JL(WBC)* Julio Cesar Chavez (Mex) RSF–7 Raul Rojas (USA), New York, USA

14 Jun 1986 *LF(WBA)* Myung-Woo Yuh (S. Kor) KO–12 Tomohiri Kiyuna (Jap) Inchon, South Korea

22 Jun 1986 *F(WBC)* Azumah Nelson (Gha) RSF–10 Danilo Cabrera (Dom) San Juan, Puerto Rico

23 Jun 1986 *LM(WBC)* Thomas Hearns (USA) RSF–8 Mark Medal (USA) Las Vegas, USA

23 Jun 1986 *Fe(WBA)* Steve Cruz (USA) PTS–15 Barry McGuigan (Ire) Las Vegas, USA

5 Jul 1986 *Fl(WBA)* Hilario Zapata (Pan) PTS–15 Dodie Penalosa (Phi) Manila, Philippines

6 Jul 1986 *SM(IBF)* Chong-Pal Park (S. Kor) TD–12 Lindell Holmes (USA) Seoul, South Korea

6 Jul 1986 *SF(IBF)* Ellyas Pical (Ina) KO–3 Cesar Polonco (Dom) Djakarta, Indonesia

12 Jul 1986 *C(WBA)* Evander Holyfield (USA) PTS–15 Dwight Muhammad Qawi (USA) Atlanta, USA

18 Jul 1986 *B(IBF)* Jeff Fenech (Aus) RSF–14 Steve McCrory (USA) Sydney, Australia

18 Jul 1986 *JB(WBC)* Gilberto Roman (Mex) PTS–12 Ruben Condori (Arg) Salta, Argentina

20 Jul 1986 *H(WBA)* Tim Witherspoon (USA) KO–11 Frank Bruno (GB) London, England

24 Jul 1986 *LW(WBC)* Tsuyoshi Hamada (Jap) KO–1 Rene Arredondo (Mex) Tokyo, Japan

2 Aug 1986 *Fl(IBF)* Hi-Sop Shin (S. Kor) KO–15 Chung-Bi Won (S. Kor) Inchon, South Korea

3 Aug 1986 *JL(WBC)* Julio Cesar Chavez (Mex) PTS–12 Rocky Lockridge (USA) Monte Carlo, Monaco

10 Aug 1986 *C(WBC)* Carlos de Leon (PR) RSF–8 Michael Greer (USA) Giardini Naxos, Italy

15 Aug 1986 *L(IBF)* Jimmy Paul (USA) PTS–15 Darryl Tyson (USA) Detroit, USA

23 Aug 1986 *LM(WBA)* Mike McCallum (Jam) RSF–2 Julian Jackson (VI) Miami Beach, USA

23 Aug 1986 *JL(IBF)* Barry Michael (GB) PTS–15 Najib Daho (Mor) Manchester, England

23 Aug 1986 *B(WBC)* Miguel Lora (Col) RSF–6 Enrique Sanchez (Dom) Miami Beach, USA

24 Aug 1986 *LM(IBF)* Buster Drayton (USA) RSF–10 Davey Moore (USA) Juan les Pins, France

30 Aug 1986 *SF(WBC)* Gilberto Roman (Mex) D–12 Santos Laciar (Arg) Cordoba, Mexico

30 Aug 1986 *Fe(IBF)* Antonio Rivera (PR) RET–10 Chung-Ki Yung (S. Kor) Seoul, South Korea

6 Sep 1986 *H(IBF)* Michael Spinks (USA) RSF–4 Steffen Tangstad (Nor) Las Vegas, USA

6 Sep 1986 *LH(IBF)* Bobby Czyz (USA) RSF–5 Slobodan Kacar (Yug) Las Vegas, USA

6 Sep 1986 *LW(WBA)* Patrizio Oliva (Ita) RSF–3 Brian Brunette (USA) Naples, Italy

10 Sep 1986 *LH(WBC)* Dennis Andries (Guy) RSF–9 Tony Sibson (GB) London, England

12 Sep 1986 *Fl(WBA)* Hilario Zapata (Pan) PTS–15 Alberto Castro (Col) Panama City, Panama

13 Sep 1986 *LF(WBC)* Chang-Jung Koo (S. Kor) PTS–12 Francisco Montiel (Mex) Seoul, South Korea

14 Sep 1986 *SM(IBF)* Chong-Pal Park (S. Kor) PTS–15 Marvin Mack (USA) Seoul, South Korea

20 Sep 1986 *LH(WBA)* Marvin Johnson (USA) RSF–13 Jean Marie Emebe (Cam) Indianapolis, USA

26 Sep 1986 *L(WBA)* Edwin Rosario (PR) KO–2 Livingstone Bramble (VI) Miami Beach, USA

27 Sep 1986 *W* Lloyd Honeyghan (Jam) RET–6 Don Curry (USA) Atlantic City, USA

27 Sep 1986 *L(WBC)* Hector Camacho (PR) PTS–12 Cornelius Boza-Edwards (Uga) Miami Beach, USA

27 Sep 1986 *JL(WBA)* Brian Mitchell (SA) RSF–10 Alfredo Layne (Pan) Sun City, South Africa

4 Oct 1986 *B(WBA)* Bernardo Pinango (Ven) RET–10 Ciro de Leva (Ita) Turin, Italy

25 Oct 1986 *C(IBF)* Rickey Parkey (USA) RSF–10 Leroy Murphy (USA) Marsala, Italy

25 Oct 1986 *LM(WBA)* Mike McCallum (Jam) KO–9 Said Skouma (Fra) Paris, France

30 Oct 1986 *LW(IBF)* Joe Louis Manley (USA) KO–10 Gary Hinton (USA) Hartford, USA

1 Nov 1986 *SF(WBA)* Kaosai Galaxy (Tha) KO–5 Israel Contreras (Ven) Willemstad, Dutch Antilles

15 Nov 1986 *B(WBC)* Miguel Lora (Col) PTS–12 Albert Davila (USA) Barranquilla, Colombia

22 Nov 1986 *H(WBC)* Mike Tyson (USA) RSF–2 Trevor Berbick (Jam) Las Vegas, USA

22 Nov 1986 *B(WBA)* Bernardo Pinango (Ven) RSF–15 Simon Skosana (SA) Johannesburg, South Africa

22 Nov 1986 *Fl(IBF)* Hi-Sop Shin (S. Kor) KO–13 Henry Brent (USA) Chunchon, South Korea

30 Nov 1986 *LF(WBA)* Myung-Woo Yuh (S. Kor) PTS–15 Mario DeMarco (Arg) Seoul, South Korea

2 Dec 1986 *LW(WBC)* Tsuyoshi Hamada (Jap) PTS–12 Ronnie Shields (USA) Tokyo, Japan

3 Dec 1986 *SF(IBF)* Ellyas Pical (Ina) KO–10 Lee-Dong Choon (S. Kor) Djakarta, Indonesia

5 Dec 1986 *LM(WBC)* Duane Thomas (USA) RSF–3 John Mugabi (Uga) Las Vegas, USA

6 Dec 1986 *L(IBF)* Greg Haugen (USA) PTS–15 Jimmy Paul (USA) Las Vegas, USA

6 Dec 1986 *Fl(WBA)* Hilario Zapata (Pan) PTS–15 Claudemir Dias (Bra) Salvador, Brazil

7 Dec 1986 *LF(IBF)* Jum-Hwan Choi (S. Kor) PTS–15 Choo-Woon Park (S. Kor) Seoul, South Korea

10 Dec 1986 *SB(WBC)* Samart Payakaroon (Tha) KO–12 Juan Meza (Mex) Bangkok, Thailand

10 Dec 1986 *Fl(WBC)* Sot Chitalada (Tha) PTS–12 Gabriel Bernal (Mex) Bangkok, Thailand

12 Dec 1986 *H(WBA)* James Smith (USA) RSF–1 Tim Witherspoon (USA) New York, USA

12 Dec 1986 *JL(WBC)* Julio Cesar Chavez (Mex) PTS–12 Juan Laporte (PR) New York, USA

14 Dec 1986 *LF(WBC)* Chang-Jung Koo (S. Kor) RSF–5 Hideyuki Ohashi (Jap) Inchon, South Korea

15 Dec 1986 *SF(WBC)* Gilberto Roman (Mex) PTS–12 Kongtoranee Payakaroon (Tha) Bangkok, Thailand

26 Dec 1986 *LH(IBF)* Bobby Czyz (USA) KO–1 David Sears (USA) West Orange, USA

10 Jan 1987 *LW(WBA)* Patrizio Oliva (Ita) PTS–15 Rodolfo Gonzalez (Mex) Agrigento, Italy

16 Jan 1987 *SB(WBA)* Louie Espinoza (USA) RSF–4 Tommy Valoy (Dom) Phoenix, USA

18 Jan 1987 *SB(IBF)* Seung-Hoon Lee (S. Kor) KO–9 Prayurasak Muangsurin (Tha) Pohang, South Korea

25 Jan 1987 *SM(IBF)* Chong-Pal Park (S. Kor) RSF–15 Doug Sam (Aus) Seoul, South Korea

31 Jan 1987 *SF(WBC)* Gilberto Roman (Mex) RSF–9 Antoine Montero (Fra) Montpellier, France

3 Feb 1987 *B(WBA)* Bernardo Pinango (Ven) PTS–15 Frankie Duarte (USA) Los Angeles, USA

6 Feb 1987 *W(WBA)* Mark Breland (USA) KO–7 Harold Volbrecht (SA) Atlantic City, USA

13 Feb 1987 *Fl(WBA)* Fidel Bassa (Col) PTS–15 Hilario Zapata (Pan) Barranquilla, Colombia

14 Feb 1987 *C(WBA)* Evander Holyfield (USA) RSF–7 Henry Tillman (USA) Reno, USA

21 Feb 1987 *C(WBC)* Carlos de Leon (PR) RSF–4 Angelo Rottoli (Ita) Bergamo, Italy

21 Feb 1987 *LH(IBF)* Bobby Czyz (USA) KO–2 Willie Edwards (USA) Atlantic City, USA

22 Feb 1987 *W(WBC/IBF)* Lloyd Honeyghan (Jam) RSF–2 Johnny Bumphus (USA) London, England

22 Feb 1987 *Fl(IBF)* Dodie Penalosa (Phi) KO–5 Hi-Sop Shin (S. Kor) Inchon, South Korea

28 Feb 1987 *SF(WBA)* Kaosai Galaxy (Tha) KO–14 Ellyas Pical (Ina) Djakarta, Indonesia

1 Mar 1987 *LF(WBA)* Myung-Woo Yuh (S. Kor) KO–1 Eduardo Tunon (Pan) Seoul, South Korea

4 Mar 1987 *LW(IBF)* Terry Marsh (GB) RSF–10 Joe Louis Manley (USA) Basildon, England

6 Mar 1987 *Fe(WBA)* Antonio Esparragoza (Ven) RSF–12 Steve Cruz (USA) Fort Worth, USA

7 Mar 1987 *H(WBC/WBA)* Mike Tyson (USA) PTS–12 James Smith (USA) Las Vegas, USA

7 Mar 1987 *LH(WBC)* Thomas Hearns (USA) RSF–10 Dennis Andries (Guy) Detroit, USA

7 Mar 1987 *Fe(WBC)* Azumah Nelson (Gha) KO–6 Mauro Gutierrez (Mex) Las Vegas, USA

19 Mar 1987 *SF(WBC)* Gilberto Roman (Mex) PTS–12 Frank Cedeno (Phi) Mexicali, Mexico

27 Mar 1987 *JL(WBA)* Brian Mitchell (SA) D–15 Jose Rivera (PR) San Juan, Puerto Rico

28 Mar 1987 *C(IBF)* Rickey Parkey (USA) RSF–12 Chisanda Mutti (Zam) Lido di Camiore, Italy

29 Mar 1987 *B(WBA)* Takuya Muguruma (Jap) KO–5 Azael Moran (Pan) Moriguchi, Japan

29 Mar 1987 *LF(IBF)* Jum-Hwan Choi (S. Kor) PTS–15 Tracy Macalas (Phi) Seoul, South Korea

5 Apr 1987 *SB(IBF)* Seung-Hoon Lee (S. Kor) KO–10 Jorge Urbina Diaz (Mex) Seoul, South Korea

6 Apr 1987 *M(WBC)* Sugar Ray Leonard (USA) PTS–12 Marvin Hagler (USA) Las Vegas, USA

18 Apr 1987 *W(WBC/IBF)* Lloyd Honeyghan (Jam) PTS–12 Maurice Blocker (USA) London, England

18 Apr 1987 *JL(WBC)* Julio Cesar Chavez (Mex) RSF–4 Francisco da Cruz (Bra) Nimes, France

19 Apr 1987 *LM(WBA)* Mike McCallum (Jam) RSF–10 Milton McCrory (USA) Phoenix, USA

19 Apr 1987 *LF(WBC)* Chang-Jung Koo (S. Kor) RSF–6 Efren Pinto (Mex) Seoul, South Korea

25 Apr 1987 *Fl(WBA)* Fidel Bassa (Col) RSF–13 Dave McAuley (GB) Belfast, N. Ireland

2 May 1987 *SM(IBF)* Chong-Pal Park (S. Kor) PTS–15 Lindell Holmes (USA) Inchon, South Korea

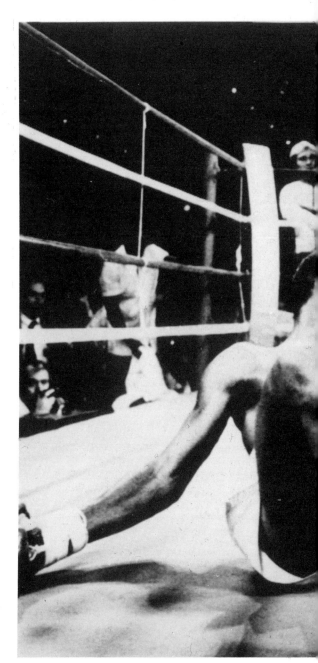

4 May 1987 *LH(IBF)* Bobby Czyz (USA) RSF–6 Jim McDonald (USA) Atlantic City, USA

8 May 1987 *SB(WBC)* Jeff Fenech (Aus) RSF–4 Samart Payakaroon (Tha) Sydney, Australia

16 May 1987 *C(IBF)* Evander Holyfield (USA) RSF–3 Rickey Parkey (USA) Las Vegas, USA

16 May 1987 *B(IBF)* Kelvin Seabrooks (USA) KO–5 Miguel Maturana (Col) Cartagena, Colombia

16 May 1987 *SF(WBC)* Santos Laciar (Arg) RSF–11 Gilberto Roman (Mex) Reims, France

17 May 1987 *JL(WBA)* Brian Mitchell (SA) RSF–2 Aurelio Benitez (Ven) Sun City, South Africa

17 May 1987 *SF(IBF)* Tae-Il Chang (S. Kor) PTS–15 Kwon-Sun Chon (S. Kor) Seoul, South Korea

23 May 1987 *LH(WBA)* Leslie Stewart (Tri) RSF–8 Marvin Johnson (USA) Port of Spain, Trinidad

24 May 1987 *B(WBA)* Chang-Yung Park (S. Kor) RSF–11 Takuya Muguruma (Jap) Osaka, Japan

Mills Lane counts out Milton McCrory after less than two minutes of the second round of his world welterweight title defence in 1985. The victor, Donald Curry, standing on the opposite side of the ring, became the division's first undisputed champion since Ray Leonard in 1981 (AP)

30 May 1987 *H(WBC/WBA)* Mike Tyson (USA) RSF–6 Pinklon Thomas (USA) Las Vegas, USA

30 May 1987 *H(IBF)* Tony Tucker (USA) RSF–10 James Douglas (USA) Las Vegas, USA

7 Jun 1987 *L(IBF)* Vinny Pazienza (USA) PTS–15 Greg Haugen (USA) Providence, USA

7 Jun 1987 *LF(WBA)* Myung-Woo Yuh (S. Kor) RSF–15 Benedicto Murillo (Pan) Pusan, South Korea

14 Jun 1987 *MF(IBF)* Kyung-Yun Lee (S. Kor) RSF–2 Masaharu Kawakami (Jap) Bukok, South Korea

27 Jun 1987 *LM(IBF)* Matthew Hilton (Can) PTS–15 Buster Drayton (USA) Montreal, Canada

28 Jun 1987 *LF(WBC)* Chang-Jung Koo (S. Kor) KO–10 Agustin Garcia (Col) Inchon, South Korea

1 Jul 1987 *LW(IBF)* Terry Marsh (GB) RSF–6 Akio Kameda (Jap) London, England

4 Jul 1987 *LW(WBA)* Juan Martin Coggi (Arg) KO–3 Patrizio Oliva (Ita) Ribera, Italy

4 Jul 1987 *B(IBF)* Kelvin Seabrooks (USA) RTD–9 Thierry Jacob (Fra) Calais, France

4 Jul 1987 *LF(IBF)* Jum-Hwan Choi (S. Kor) KO–4 Toshihiko Matsuda (Jap) Seoul, South Korea

10 Jul 1987 *SB(WBC)* Jeff Fenech (Aus) RSF–5 Greg Richardson (USA) Sydney, Australia

12 Jul 1987 *LM(WBC)* Lupe Aquino (Mex) PTS–12 Duane Thomas (USA) Bordeaux, France

15 Jul 1987 *SM(IBF)* Chong-Pal Park (S. Kor) KO–4 Emmanuel Otti (Uga) Kwangju, South Korea

15 Jul 1987 *SB(WBA)* Louie Espinoza (USA) RSF–15 Manuel Vilchez (Ven) Phoenix, USA

18 Jul 1987 *LM(WBA)* Mike McCallum (Jam) KO–5 Don Curry (USA) Las Vegas, USA

18 Jul 1987 *SB(IBF)* Seung-Hoon Lee (S. Kor) KO–5 Leo Collins (Phi) Pohang, South Korea

19 Jul 1987 *L(WBC)* Jose Luis Ramirez (Mex) PTS–12 Terrence Alli (Guy) St. Tropez, France

22 Jul 1987 *LW(WBC)* Rene Arredondo (Mex) RSF–6
Tsuyoshi Hamada (Jap) Tokyo, Japan
25 Jul 1987 *B(WBC)* Miguel Lora (Col) RSF–4 Antonio
Avelar (Mex) Miami, USA

---

*The Miguel 'Happy' Lora v Antonio Avelar
fight for the WBC bantamweight title on
25 July 1987 took place on a barge in
Miami's Marine Stadium. Despite being
anchored to the ocean bed the ring was still
bobbing up and down during the fight.*

---

26 Jul 1987 *Fe(WBA)* Antonio Esparragoza (Ven) KO–10
Pascual Aranda (Mex) Houston, USA
1 Aug 1987 *JL(WBA)* Brian Mitchell (SA) RSF–14 Francisco
Fernandez (Pan) Panama City, Panama
2 Aug 1987 *H* Mike Tyson (USA) PTS–12 Tony Tucker
(USA) Las Vegas, USA
8 Aug 1987 *SF(WBC)* Jesus Rojas (Col) PTS–12 Santos
Laciar (Arg) Miami, USA
9 Aug 1987 *JL(IBF)* Rocky Lockridge (USA) RET–8 Barry
Michael (GB) Windsor, England
9 Aug 1987 *LF(IBF)* Jum-Hwan Choi (S. Kor) KO–3 Azadin
Anhar (Ina) Djakarta, Indonesia
11 Aug 1987 *L(WBA)* Edwin Rosario (PR) RSF–8 Juan
Nazario (PR) Chicago, USA
15 Aug 1987 *C(WBA/IBF)* Evander Holyfield (USA) RSF–11
Osvaldo Ocasio (PR) St. Tropez, France

Another Mike Tyson win brings the usual barrage of interviewers and well-wishers into the ring (All Sport/Mike Powell)

6 Sep 1987 *Fl(IBF)* Chang-Ho Choi (S. Kor) KO–11 Dodie Penalosa (Phi) Manila, Philippines

20 Sep 1987 *LF(WBA)* Myung-Woo Yuh (S. Kor) KO–8 Ricardo Blanco (Col) Pohang, South Korea

2 Oct 1987 *LM(WBC)* Gianfranco Rosi (Ita) PTS–12 Lupe Aquino (Mex) Perugia, Italy

3 Oct 1987 *JL(WBA)* Brian Mitchell (SA) PTS–15 Daniel Londas (Fra) Gravelines, France

4 Oct 1987 *B(WBA)* Wilfredo Vasquez (PR) RTD–10 Chan-Yung Park (S. Kor) Seoul, South Korea

10 Oct 1987 *L(WBC)* Jose-Luis Ramirez (Mex) KO–5 Cornelius Boza-Edwards (Uga) Paris, France

10 Oct 1987 *M(IBF)* Frank Tate (USA) PTS–15 Michael Olajide (GB) Las Vegas, USA

12 Oct 1987 *SF(WBA)* Kaosai Galaxy (Tha) KO–3 Chung Byong-Kwan (S. Kor) Bangkok, Thailand

16 Oct 1987 *H* Mike Tyson (USA) KO–7 Tyrrell Biggs (USA) Atlantic City, USA

16 Oct 1987 *SB(WBC)* Jeff Fenech (Aus) TD–4 Carlos Zarate (Mex) Sydney, Australia

16 Oct 1987 *LM(IBF)* Matt Hilton (Can) RTD–3 Jack Callahan (USA) Atlantic City, USA

17 Oct 1987 *SF(IBF)* Ellyas Pical (Ina) PTS–15 Tae-Il Chang (S. Kor) Djakarta, Indonesia

18 Oct 1987 *MF(WBC)* Hiroki Ioka (Jap) PTS–12 Mai Thornburifarm (Ina) Osaka, Japan

23 Oct 1987 *M(WBA)* Sumbu Kalambay (Zai) PTS–15 Iran Barkley (USA) Livorno, Italy

24 Oct 1987 *SF(WBC)* Jesus Rojas (Col) RSF–4 Gustavo Ballas (Arg) Miami, USA

25 Oct 1987 *JL(IBF)* Rocky Lockridge (USA) RSF–10 Johnny De La Rosa (Dom) Tucson, USA

28 Oct 1987 *W(WBC)* Jorge Vaca (Mex) TD–8 Lloyd Honeyghan (Jam) London, England

29 Oct 1987 *M(WBC)* Thomas Hearns (USA) KO–4 Juan Roldan (Arg) Las Vegas, USA

29 Oct 1987 *LH(IBF)* Charles Williams (USA) RSF–9 Bobby Czyz (USA) Las Vegas, USA

12 Nov 1987 *LW(WBC)* Roger Mayweather (USA) KO–6 Rene Arredondo (Mex) Los Angeles, USA

18 Nov 1987 *B(IBF)* Kelvin Seabrooks (USA) RSF–4 Ernie Cataluna (Phi) San Cataldo, Philippines

21 Nov 1987 *LM(WBA)* Julian Jackson (VI) RSF–3 In-Chul Baek (S. Kor) Las Vegas, USA

22 Nov 1987 *L(WBA)* Julio Cesar Chavez (Mex) RSF–11 Edwin Rosario (PR) Las Vegas, USA

22 Nov 1987 *LH(WBA)* Virgil Hill (USA) PTS–12 Rufino Angulo (Fra) Paris, France

27 Nov 1987 *LH(WBC)* Donny Lalonde (USA) RSF–2 Eddie Davis (USA) Port of Spain, Trinidad

27 Nov 1987 *B(WBC)* Miguel Lora (Col) PTS–12 Ray Minus Jnr (Bah) Miami, USA

28 Nov 1987 *SB(WBA)* Julio Gervacio (Dom) PTS–12 Louie Espinosa (USA) San Juan, Puerto Rico

5 Dec 1987 *C(IBF)* Evander Holyfield (USA) KO–4 Dwight Muhammad Qawi (USA) Atlantic City, USA

6 Dec 1987 *SM(IBF)* Chong-Pal Park (S. Kor) KO–2 Jesus Gallardo (Mex) Pusan, South Korea

13 Dec 1987 *LF(WBC)* Chang-Jung Koo (S. Kor) PTS–12 Isidro Perez (Mex) Taejon, South Korea

15 Aug 1987 *Fl(WBA)* Fidel Bassa (Col) D–15 Hilario Zapata (Pan) Panama City, Panama

15 Aug 1987 *SB(WBA)* Louie Espinoza (USA) KO–9 Mike Ayala (USA) San Antonio, USA

21 Aug 1987 *JL(WBC)* Julio Cesar Chavez (Mex) PTS–12 Danilo Cabrera (Dom) Tijuana, Mexico

22 Aug 1987 *W(WBA)* Marlon Starling (USA) RSF–11 Mark Breland (USA) Columbia, USA

30 Aug 1987 *W(WBC/IBF)* Lloyd Honeyghan (Jam) KO–1 Gene Hatcher (USA) Marbella, Spain

30 Aug 1987 *Fe(WBC)* Azumah Nelson (Gha) PTS–12 Marcos Vilasana (Mex) Los Angeles, USA

5 Sep 1987 *LH(WBA)* Virgil Hill (USA) RSF–4 Leslie Stewart (Tri) New Jersey, USA

6 Sep 1987 *Fl(WBC)* Sot Chitalada (Tha) KO–4 Rae-Ki Ahn (S. Kor) Bangkok, Thailand

18 Dec 1987 *Fl(WBA)* Fidel Bassa (Col) PTS–12 Felix Marti (Mex) Cartagena, Colombia

19 Dec 1987 *JL(WBA)* Brian Mitchell (SA) RTD–9 Salvatore Curcetti (Ita) Capo Orlando, Italy

27 Dec 1987 *SB(IBF)* Lee-Sung Hoon (S. Kor) PTS–15 Jose Sanabria (Ven) Pohang, South Korea

3 Jan 1988 *LM(WBC)* Gianfranco Rosi (Ita) RSF–7 Duane Thomas (USA) Genoa, Italy

10 Jan 1988 *MF(WBA)* Leo Gamez (Dom) PTS–12 Kim-Bong Jun (S. Kor) Pusan, South Korea

16 Jan 1988 *Fl(IBF)* Rolando Bohol (Phi) PTS–15 Chang-Ho Choi (S. Kor) Manila, Philippines

17 Jan 1988 *B(WBA)* Wilfredo Vasquez (PR) D–12 Takuya Muguruma (Jap) Osaka, Japan

22 Jan 1988 *H* Mike Tyson (USA) RSF–4 Larry Holmes (USA) Atlantic City, USA

22 Jan 1988 *C(WBC)* Carlos De Leon (PR) PTS–12 Jose Maria Flores (Uru) Atlantic City, USA

23 Jan 1988 *Fe(IBF)* Calvin Grove (USA) RSF–4 Antonio Rivera (PR) Gamaches, France

26 Jan 1988 *SF(WBA)* Kaosai Galaxy (Tha) PTS–12 Kontoranee Payakarun (Tha) Bangkok, Thailand

31 Jan 1988 *Fl(WBC)* Sot Chitalada (Tha) RSF–7 Hideaki Kamishiro (Jap) Osaka, Japan

31 Jan 1988 *MF(WBC)* Hiroki Ioka (Jap) RSF–12 Lee-Kyung Yung (S. Kor) Osaka, Japan

6 Feb 1988 *W(WBA)* Marlon Starling (USA) PTS–12 Fujio Ozaki (Jap) Atlantic City, USA

6 Feb 1988 *L(IBF)* Greg Haugen (USA) PTS–15 Vinny Pazienza (USA) Atlantic City, USA

6 Feb 1988 *B(IBF)* Kelvin Seabrooks (USA) RSF–2 Fernando Beltran (Mex) Paris, France

7 Feb 1988 *M(IBF)* Frank Tate (USA) KO–10 Tony Sibson (GB) Stafford, England

7 Feb 1988 *LF(WBA)* Myung-Woo Yuh (S. Kor) PTS–12 Wilibardo Salazar (Mex) Seoul, South Korea

14 Feb 1988 *LW(IBF)* James Buddy McGirt (USA) RSF–14 Frankie Warren (USA) Corpus Christi, USA

20 Feb 1988 *SF(IBF)* Ellyas Pical (Ina) PTS–15 Raul Diaz (Col) Pontianak, Colombia

27 Feb 1988 *SB(WBA)* Bernardo Pinango (Ven) PTS–12 Julio Gervacio (Dom) San Juan, Puerto Rico

29 Feb 1988 *JL(WBC)* Azumah Nelson (Gha) PTS–12 Mario Martinez (Mex) Los Angeles, USA

29 Feb 1988 *SB(WBC)* Daniel Zaragoza (Mex) RSF–10 Carlos Zarate (Mex) Los Angeles, USA

1 Mar 1988 *SM(WBA)* Chong-Pal Park (S. Kor) KO–5 Polly Pesireron (Ina) Chonju, South Korea

5 Mar 1988 *M(WBA)* Sumbu Kalambay (Zai) PTS–12 Mike McCallum (Jam) Pesaro, Italy

7 Mar 1988 *Fe(WBC)* Jeff Fenech (Aus) RSF–10 Victor Callejas (PR) Sydney, Australia

12 Mar 1988 *SM(IBF)* Graciano Rocchigiani (FRG) RSF–3 Vincent Boulware (USA) Dusseldorf, West Germany

12 Mar 1988 *L(WBC)* Jose Luis Ramirez (Mex) PTS–12 Pernell Whitaker (USA) Paris, France

21 Mar 1988 *H* Mike Tyson (USA) RSF–2 Tony Tubbs (USA) Tokyo, Japan

24 Mar 1988 *LW(WBC)* Roger Mayweather (USA) KO–3 Mauricio Aceves (Mex) Los Angeles, USA

24 Mar 1988 *MF(IBF)* Samuth Sithnaruepol (Tha) RSF–11 Pretty Boy Lucas (Phi) Bangkok, Thailand

26 Mar 1988 *Fl(WBA)* Fidel Bassa (Col) PTS–12 Dave McAuley (GB) Belfast, Northern Ireland

28 Mar 1988 *W(WBC)* Lloyd Honeyghan (Jam) KO–3 Jorge Vaca (Mex) London, England

2 Apr 1988 *JL(IBF)* Rocky Lockridge (USA) PTS–15 Harold Knight (USA) Atlantic City, USA

3 Apr 1988 *LH(WBA)* Virgil Hill (USA) RSF–11 Jean-Marie Emebe (Fra) Bismark, USA

8 Apr 1988 *SF(WBC)* Gilberto Roman (Mex) PTS–12 Sugar Rojas (Col) Miami, USA

9 Apr 1988 *C* Evander Holyfield (USA) RSF–8 Carlos De Leon (PR) Las Vegas, USA

11 Apr 1988 *L(IBF)* Greg Haugen (USA) TD–11 Miguel Santana (PR) Tacoma, USA

16 Apr 1988 *W(WBA)* Marlon Starling (USA) D–12 Mark Breland (USA) Las Vegas, USA

16 Apr 1988 *L(WBA)* Julio Cesar Chavez (Mex) RSF–6 Rodolfo Aguilar (Pan) Las Vegas, USA

17 Apr 1988 *Fe(IBF)* Calvin Grove (USA) PTS–15 Myron Taylor (USA) Atlantic City, USA

23 April 1988 *W(IBF)* Simon Brown (Jam) RSF–14 Tyrone Trice (USA) Berck-sur-Mer, France

24 Apr 1988 *MF(WBA)* Leo Gamez (Dom) RSF–3 Kenji Yokozawa (Jap) Tokyo, Japan

26 Apr 1988 *JL(WBA)* Brian Mitchell (SA) PTS–12 Jose Rivera (PR) Madrid, Spain

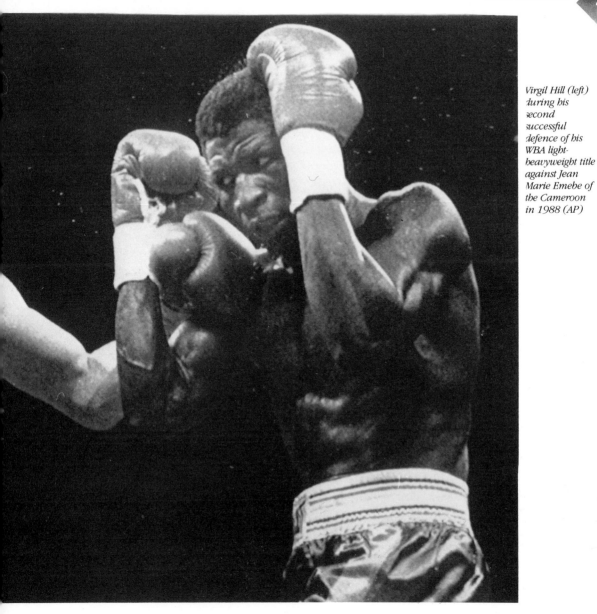

Virgil Hill (left) during his second successful defence of his WBA light-heavyweight title against Jean Marie Emebe of the Cameroon in 1988 (AP)

30 Apr 1988 *B(WBC)* Miguel Lora (Col) PTS–12 Lucio Lopez (Arg) Cartagena, Colombia

6 May 1988 *Fl(IBF)* Rolando Bohol (Phi) PTS–15 Cho-Woon Park (S. Kor) Manila, Philippines

7 May 1988 *LW(WBA)* Juan Martin Coggi (Arg) KO–2 Sang-Ho Lee (S. Kor) Roseto Degli Abruzzi, Italy

9 May 1988 *B(WBA)* Kaokar Galaxy (Tha) PTS–12 Wilfredo Vasquez (PR) Bangkok, Thailand

21 May 1988 *SB(IBF)* Jose Sanabria (Ven) KO–5 Moises Fuentes (Col) Bucaramanga, Venezuela

23 May 1988 *SM(WBA)* Fulgencio Obelmejias (Ven) PTS–12 Chong-Pal Park (S. Kor) Suanbao, Venezuela

28 May 1988 *SB(WBA)* Juan Jose Estrada (Mex) PTS–12 Bernard Pinango (Ven) Tijuana, Mexico

29 May 1988 *LH(WBC)* Donny Lalonde (Can) RSF–5 Leslie Stewart (Tri) Port of Spain, Trinidad

29 May 1988 *SB(WBC)* Daniel Zaragoza (Mex) D–12 Seung-Hoon Lee (S. Kor) Seoul, South Korea

3 Jun 1988 *SM(IBF)* Graciano Rocchigiani (FRG) PTS–15 Nicky Walker (USA) Berlin, West Germany

5 Jun 1988 *MF(WBC)* Hiroki Ioka (Jap) D–12 Napa Kiatwanchai (Tha) Osaka, Japan

5 Jun 1988 *LH(WBA)* Virgil Hill (USA) PTS–12 Ramzi Hassan (Jor) Las Vegas, USA

6 Jun 1988 *M(WBC)* Iran Barkley (USA) RSF–3 Thomas Hearns (USA) Las Vegas, USA

6 Jun 1988 *LW(WBC)* Roger Mayweather (USA) PTS–12 Harold Brazier (USA) Las Vegas, USA

10 Jun 1988 *LH(IBF)* Prince Charles Williams (USA) RTD–11 Richard Caramanolis (Fra) Annecy, France

12 Jun 1988 *M(WBA)* Sumbu Kalambay (Zai) PTS–12 Robbie Sims (USA) Ravenna, Italy

12 Jun 1988 *LF(WBA)* Myung-Woo Yuh (S. Kor) PTS–12 Jose De Jesus (PR) Seoul, South Korea

23 Jun 1988 *Fe(WBA)* Antonio Esparragoza (Ven) D–12 Marcos Villasana (Mex) Los Angeles, USA

25 Jun 1988 *JL(WBC)* Azumah Nelson (Gha) RSF–9 Lupe Suarez (USA) Atlantic City, USA

27 Jun 1988 *H* Mike Tyson (USA) KO–1 Michael Spinks (USA) Atlantic City, USA

27 Jun 1988 *LF(WBC)* Jung-Koo Chang (S. Kor) RSF–8 Hideyuki Ohashi (Jap) Tokyo, Japan

8 Jul 1988 *LM(WBC)* Don Curry (USA) RTD–9 Gianfranco Rosi (Ita) San Remo, Italy

9 Jul 1988 *B(IBF)* Orlando Canizales (USA) RSF–15 Kelvin Seabrooks (USA) Atlantic City, USA

9 Jul 1988 *SF(WBC)* Gilberto Roman (Mex)) RSF–5 Yoshiyuki Uchida (Jap) Kawagoe, Japan

16 Jul 1988 *W(IBF)* Simon Brown (Jam) RSF–3 Jorge Vaca (Mex) Kingston, Jamaica

23 Jul 1988 *Fl(WBC)* Yung-Kang Kim (S. Kor) PTS–12 Sot Chitalada (Tha) Pohang, South Korea

27 Jul 1988 *JL(IBF)* Tony Lopez (USA) PTS–12 Rocky Lockridge (USA) Sacramento, USA

28 Jul 1988 *M(IBF)* Michael Nunn (USA) RSF–9 Frank Tate (USA) Las Vegas, USA

29 Jul 1988 *W(WBA)* Tomas Molinares (Col) KO–6 Marlon Starling (USA) Atlantic City, USA

29 Jul 1988 *W(WBC)* Lloyd Honeyghan (Jam) TKO–5 Young-Kil Chung (S. Kor) Atlantic City, USA

30 Jul 1988 *LM(IBF)* Julian Jackson (VI) KO–3 Buster Drayton (USA) Atlantic City, USA

31 Jul 1988 *LW(IBF)* James Buddy McGirt (USA) KO–1 Howard Davis (USA) New York, USA

1 Aug 1988 *B(WBC)* Miguel Lora (Col) PTS–12 Albert Davila (USA) Los Angeles, USA

4 Aug 1988 *Fe(IBF)* Jorge Paez (Mex) PTS–15 Calvin Grove (USA) Mexicali, Mexico

8 Aug 1988 *Fe(WBC)* Jeff Fenech (Aus) RSF–5 Tyrone Downes (Tri) Melbourne, Australia

14 Aug 1988 *B(WBA)* Sung-Kil Moon (S. Kor) TD–6 Kaokar Galaxy (Tha) Pusan, South Korea

21 Aug 1988 *SB(IBF)* Jose Sanabria (Ven) PTS–12 Vincenzo Belcastro (Ita) Capo D'Orlando, Italy

28 Aug 1988 *LF(WBA)* Myung-Woo Yuh (S. Kor) KO–6 Putt Ohyuthanakorn (Tha) Pusan, South Korea

29 Aug 1988 *MF(IBF)* Samuth Sithnaruepol (Tha) PTS–15 Inkyu Hwang (S. Kor) Bangkok, Thailand

3 Sep 1988 *LW(IBF)* Meldrick Taylor (USA) RSF–12 James Buddy McGirt (USA) Atlantic City, USA

3 Sep 1988 *SF(WBC)* Gilberto Roman (Mex) PTS–12 Kiyoshi Hatanaka (Jap) Nagoya, Japan

9 Sep 1988 *SF(IBF)* Ellyas Pical (Ina) PTS–12 Chang-Ki Kim (S. Kor) Surabaya, Indonesia

22 Sep 1988 *LW(WBC)* Roger Mayweather (USA)) RSF–12 Rodolfo Gonzalez (Mex) Los Angeles, USA

26 Sep 1988 *SB(IBF)* Jose Sanabria (Ven) RSF–10 Fabrice Benichou (Spa) Nogent-sur-Marne, France

2 Oct 1988 *Fl(IBF)* Fidel Bassa (Col) PTS–12 Ray Medel (USA) San Antonio, USA

5 Oct 1988 *Fl(IBF)* Duke McKenzie (GB) KO–11 Rolando Bohol (Phi) London, England

7 Oct 1988 *SM(IBF)* Graciano Rocchigiani (FRG) RSF–11 Chris Reid (USA) Berlin, West Germany

9 Oct 1988 *SF(WBA)* Kaosai Galaxy (Tha) KO–8 Chang-Ho Choi (S. Kor) Seoul, South Korea

14 Oct 1988 *W(IBF)* Simon Brown (Jam) PTS–12 Mauro Martelli (Swi) Lausanne, Switzerland

15 Oct 1988 *SB(WBA)* Juan Jose Estrada (Mex) RSF–11 Takuya Muguruma (Jap) Moriguchi, Japan

21 Oct 1988 *LH(IBF)* Prince Charles Williams (USA) RSF–3 Rufino Angulo (Fra) Villenave D'Ornon, France

27 Oct 1988 *JL(IBF)* Tony Lopez (USA) PTS–12 Juan Molina (PR) Sacramento, USA

28 Oct 1988 *L(IBF)* Greg Haugen (USA) RSF–10 Gert Bo Jacobsen (Den) Copenhagen, Denmark

29 Oct 1988 *L(WBA/WBC)* Julio Cesar Chavez (Mex) TD–11 Jose Luis Ramirez (Mex) Las Vegas, USA

29 Oct 1988 *B(WBC)* Raul Perez (Mex) PTS–12 Miguel Lora (Col) Las Vegas, USA

2 Nov 1988 *JL(WBA)* Brian Mitchell (SA) PTS–12 Jim McDonnell (GB) Southwark, England

4 Nov 1988 *M(IBF)* Michael Nunn (USA) KO–8 Juan Domingo Roldan (Arg) Las Vegas, USA

4 Nov 1988 *LM(IBF)* Robert Hines (USA) PTS–12 Matt Hilton (Can) Las Vegas, USA

5 Nov 1988 *Fe(WBA)* Antonio Esparragoza (Ven) KO–8 Jose Marmolejo (Pan) Marsala, Italy

5 Nov 1988 *LF(IBF)* Tacy Macalos (Phi) PTS–12 Jum-Hwan Choi (S. Kor) Manila, Philippines

6 Nov 1988 *LF(WBA)* Myung-Woo Yuh (S. Kor) KO–7 Bahar Udin (Ina) Seoul, South Korea

7 Nov 1988 *LH(WBC)/SM(WBC)* Sugar Ray Leonard (USA) RSF–9 Donny Lalonde (Can) Las Vegas, USA

Britain's Lloyd Honeyghan (left) lost his WBC welterweight title to Marlon Starling in Las Vegas in 1989. Honeyghan had held the title for less than a year (AP)

27 Nov 1988 *B(WBA)* Sung-Kil Moon (S. Kor) KO–7 Edgar Montserrat (Pan) Seoul, South Korea

29 Nov 1988 *B(IBF)* Orlando Canizales (USA) KO–1 Jimmy Navarro (USA) San Antonio, USA

30 Nov 1988 *Fe(WBC)* Jeff Fenech (Aus) RSF–5 George Navarro (USA) Melbourne, Australia

10 Dec 1988 *JL(WBC)* Azumah Nelson (Gha) RSF–3 Sydney Dal Rovere (Bra) Accra, Ghana

11 Dec 1988 *LF(WBC)* German Torres (Mex) PTS–12 Soon-Joon Kang (S. Kor) Seoul, South Korea

15 Jan 1989 *SF(WBA)* Kaosai Galaxy (Tha) KO–2 Tae-Il Chang (S. Kor) Bangkok, Thailand

21 Jan 1989 *LW(IBF)* Meldrick Taylor (USA) RSF–7 John Meekins (USA) Atlantic City, USA

21 Jan 1989 *LW(WBA)* Juan Martin Coggi (Arg) PTS–12 Harold Brazier (USA) Vasto, Italy

27 Jan 1989 *SM(IBF)* Graciano Rocchigiani (FRG) PTS–12 Tulane Malinga (SA) Berlin, West Germany

4 Feb 1989 *LM(IBF)* Darrin Van Horn (USA) PTS–12 Robert Hines (USA) Atlantic City, USA

4 Feb 1989 *W(WBA)* Mark Breland (USA) RSF–1 Seung-Soon Lee (S. Kor) Las Vegas, USA

4 Feb 1989 *W(WBC)* Marlon Starling (USA) RSF–9 Lloyd Honeyghan (Jam) Las Vegas, USA

10 Feb 1989 *JL(WBA)* Brian Mitchell (SA) KO–8 Salvatore Bottiglieri (Ita) Capo D'Orlando, Italy

11 Feb 1989 *LM(WBC)* Rene Jacquot (Fra) PTS–12 Don Curry (USA) Grenoble, France

11 Feb 1989 *MF(WBC)* Napa Kiatwanchai (Tha) PTS–12 John Arief (Ina) Korat, Indonesia

12 Feb 1989 *LF(WBA)* Myung-Woo Yuh (S. Kor) RSF–10 Katsumi Komiyama (Jap) Chongju, South Korea

18 Feb 1989 *W(IBF)* Simon Brown (Jam) RSF–3 Jorge Maysonet (PR) Budapest, Hungary

18 Feb 1989 *B(WBA)* Sung-Kil Moon (S. Kor) KO–5 Giaki Kobayashi (Jap) Seoul, South Korea

20 Feb 1989 *L(IBF)* Pernell Whitaker (USA) PTS–12 Greg Haugen (USA) Hampton, USA

22 Feb 1989 *LH(WBC)* Dennis Andries (Guy) RSF–5 Tony Willis (USA) Tucson, USA

24 Feb 1989 *M(WBC)* Roberto Duran (Pan) PTS–12 Iran Barkley (USA) Atlantic City, USA

24 Feb 1989 *LM(WBA)* Julian Jackson (VI) KO–8 Francisco De Jesus (Bra) Las Vegas, USA

25 Feb 1989 *H* Mike Tyson (USA) RSF–5 Frank Bruno (GB) Las Vegas, USA

25 Feb 1989 *JL(WBC)* Azumah Nelson (Gha) RSF–12 Mario Martinez (Mex) Las Vegas, USA

25 Feb 1989 *SF(IBF)* Ellyas Pical (Ina) PTS–12 Mike Phelps (USA) Singapore City, Singapore

4 Mar 1989 *LH(WBA)* Virgil Hill (USA) PTS–12 Bobby Czyz (USA) Bismark, USA

5 Mar 1989 *JL(IBF)* Tony Lopez (USA) PTS–12 Rocky Lockridge (USA) Sacramento, USA

5 Mar 1989 *Fl(WBC)* Yung-Kang Kim (S. Kor) PTS–12 Yukhito Tamakuma (Jap) Aomori, Japan

9 Mar 1989 *Fl(IBF)* Duke McKenzie (GB) RSF–4 Tony DeLuca (USA) London, England

10 Mar 1989 *SB(IBF)* Fabrice Benichou (Spa) PTS–12 Jose Sanabria (Ven) Limoges, France

10 Mar 1989 *B(WBC)* Raul Perez (Mex) PTS–12 Lucio Lopez (Arg) Los Angeles, USA

7 Nov 1988 *LW(WBC)* Roger Mayweather (USA) PTS–12 Vinny Pazienza (USA) Las Vegas, USA

7 Nov 1988 *SF(WBC)* Gilberto Roman (Mex) PTS–12 Sugar Rojas (Col) Las Vegas, USA

8 Nov 1988 *M(WBA)* Sumbu Kalambay (Zai) KO–7 Doug De Witt (USA) Monte Carlo, Monaco

11 Nov 1988 *LH(WBA)* Virgil Hill (USA) RSF–10 Willy Featherstone (Can) Bismark, USA

11 Nov 1988 *SB(IBF)* Jose Sanabria (Ven) RSF–6 Thierry Jacob (Fra) Gravelines, France

13 Nov 1988 *Fl(WBC)* Yung-Kang Kim (S. Kor) PTS–12 Emil Matsushima (Jap) Chongju, Japan

13 Nov 1988 *MF(WBC)* Napa Kiatwanchai (Tha) PTS–12 Hiroki Ioka (Jap) Osaka, Japan

26 Nov 1988 *SB(WBC)* Daniel Zaragoza (Mex) KO–5 Valerio Nàti (Ita) Forli, Italy

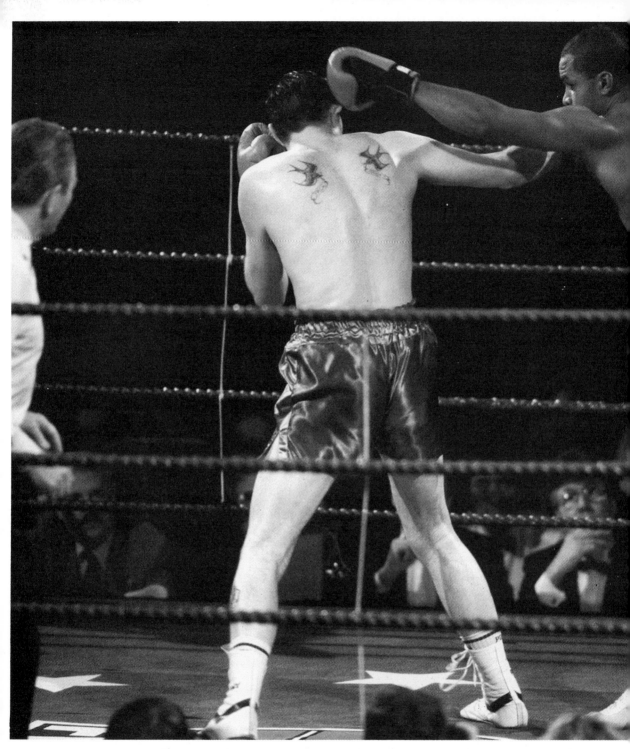

19 Mar 1989 *LF(WBC)* Yol-Woo Lee (S. Kor) RSF–9
German Torres (Mex) Seoul, South Korea
23 Mar 1989 *MF(IBF)* Samuth Sithnaruepol (Tha) D–12
Nico Thomas (Ina) Djakarta, Indonesia
25 Mar 1989 *C(WBA)* Taoufik Belbouli (Fra) RSF–8 Michael
Greer (USA) Casablanca, Morocco
25 Mar 1989 *M(IBF)* Michael Nunn (USA) KO–1 Sumbu
Kalambay (Zai) Las Vegas, USA
25 Mar 1989 *Fe(WBA)* Antonio Esparragoza (Ven) KO–10
Mitsuru Sugiya (Jap) Kawasaki, Japan
30 Mar 1989 *Fe(IBF)* Jorge Paez (Mex) KO–11 Calvin
Grove (USA) Mexicali, Mexico

5 Apr 1989 *SB(WBA)* Juan Jose Estrada (Mex) RSF–10 Jesus
Poll (Ven) Los Angeles, USA
8 Apr 1989 *Fe(WBC)* Jeff Fenech (Aus) PTS–12 Marcos
Villasana (Mex) Melbourne, Australia
8 Apr 1989 *SF(WBA)* Kaosai Galaxy (Tha) PTS–12 Kenji
Matsumura (Jap) Yokohama, Japan
15 Apr 1989 *Fl(WBA)* Fidel Bassa (Col) RSF–6 Julio Gudino
(Pan) Barranquilla, Colombia
16 Apr 1989 *MF(WBA)* Kim-Bong Jun (S. Kor) RSF–7
Agustin Garcia (Col) Pohang, South Korea
22 Apr 1989 *W(WBA)* Mark Breland (USA) RTD–5 Rafael
Pineda (Col) Atlantic City, USA

Carlos De Leon of Puerto Rico (right) created history in 1989 when he captured the crusierweight title for the fourth time by stopping Britain's Sammy Reeson in the 9th round at London's Docklands Arena (All Sport/John Gichigi)

17 May 1989 *C(WBC)* Carlos De Leon (PR) RSF–9 Sammy Reeson (GB) London, England

22 May 1989 *Fe(IBF)* Jorge Paez (Mex) D–12 Louie Espinoza (USA) Phoenix, USA

27 May 1989 *LH(WBA)* Virgil Hill (USA) RSF–7 Joe Lasisi (Nig) Bismark, USA

27 May 1989 *SM(WBA)* In-Chul Baek (S. Kor) RSF–11 Fulgencio Obelmejias (Ven) Seoul, South Korea

3 Jun 1989 *C(IBF)* Glenn McCrory (GB) PTS–12 Patrick Lumumba (Ken) Co. Durham, England

3 Jun 1989 *Fe(WBA)* Antonio Esparragoza (Ven) KO–6 Jean-Marc Renard (Bel) Manur, Belgium

3 Jun 1989 *Fl(WBC)* Sot Chitalada (Tha) PTS–12 Yung-Kang Kim (S. Kor) Trang, Thailand

5 Jun 1989 *SF(WBC)* Gilberto Roman (Mex) PTS–12 Juan Carazo (PR) Los Angeles, USA

7 Jun 1989 *Fl(IBF)* Dave McAuley (GB) PTS–12 Duke McKenzie (GB) London, England

10 Jun 1989 *MF(WBC)* Napa Kiatwanchai (Tha) RSF–11 Hiroki Ioka (Jap) Osaka, Japan

11 Jun 1989 *LF(WBA)* Myung-Woo Yuh (S. Kor) PTS–12 Mario DeMarco (Arg) Inchon, South Korea

11 Jun 1989 *SB(IBF)* Fabrice Benichou (Spa) KO–5 Frans Cornelius Badenhorst (SA) Frosinone, Italy

12 Jun 1989 *SM(WBC)* Sugar Ray Leonard (USA) D–12 Thomas Hearns (USA) Las Vegas, USA

17 Jun 1989 *MF(IBF)* Nico Thomas (Ina) PTS–12 Samuth Sithanaruepol (Tha) Djakarta, Indonesia

21 Jun 1989 *JL(IBF)* Tony Lopez (USA) RSF–8 Tyrone Jackson (USA) Nevada, USA

24 Jun 1989 *LH(WBC)* Jeff Harding (Aus) RSF–12 Dennis Andries (Guy) Atlantic City, USA

24 Jun 1989 *SB(WBC)* Daniel Zaragoza (Mex) PTS–12 Paul Banke (USA) Los Angeles, USA

24 Jun 1989 *B(IBF)* Orlando Canizales (USA) RSF–11 Kelvin Seabrooks (USA) Atlantic City, USA

25 Jun 1989 *LH(IBF)* Prince Charles Williams (USA) TKO–10 Bobby Czyz (USA) Atlantic City, USA

25 Jun 1989 *LF(WBC)* Humberto Gonzalez (Mex) PTS–12 Yol-Woo Lee (S. Kor) Chongju, South Korea

1 Jul 1989 *JL(WBA)* Brian Mitchell (SA) TKO–9 Jackie Beard (USA) Crotone, Italy

7 Jul 1989 *B(WBA)* Kaokar Galaxy (Tha) PTS–12 Sung-Kil Moon (S. Kor) Bangkok, Thailand

8 Jul 1989 *LM(WBC)* John Mugabi (Uga) KO–1 Rene Jacquot (Fra) Miraplis, France

9 Jul 1989 *L(WBA)* Edwin Rosario (USA) RSF–6 Anthony 'Baby' Jones (USA) Atlantic City, USA

12 Jul 1989 *SB(WBA)* Juan Jose Estrada (Mex) PTS–12 Luis Mendoza (Col) Tijuana, Mexico

25 Apr 1989 *W(IBF)* Simon Brown (Jam) RSF–7 Al Long (USA) Washington, USA

29 Apr 1989 *LW(WBA)* Juan Martin Coggi (Arg) PTS–12 Akinobu Hiranaka (Jap) Vasto, Italy

1 May 1989 *L(IBF)* Pernell Whitaker (USA) RSF–3 Louie Lomeli (Ita) Norfolk, USA

2 May 1989 *LF(IBF)* Muangchai Kittikasem (Tha) PTS–12 Tacy Macalos (Phi) Bangkok, Thailand

10 May 1989 *M(WBA)* Mike McCallum (USA) PTS–12 Herol Graham (GB) London, England

13 May 1989 *LW(WBC)* Julio Cesar Chavez (Mex) RSF–10 Roger Mayweather (USA) Los Angeles, USA

In a sport that requires maximum physical stamina, it is strange to find vegetarians. Yet two world champions are known to have been vegetarians – Freddie Welsh (Wal) and Eder Jofre (Bra).

16 Jul 1989 *LM(IBF)* Gianfranco Rosi (Ita) PTS–12 Darrin van Horn (USA) Atlantic City, USA

21 Jul 1989 *H* Mike Tyson (USA) RSF–1 Carl 'The Truth' Williams (USA) Atlantic City, USA

29 Jul 1989 *SF(WBA)* Kaosai Galaxy (Tha) RTD–10 Alberto Castro (Col) Surin, Thailand

30 Jul 1989 *LM(WBA)* Julian Jackson (VI) RSF–2 Terry Norris (USA) Atlantic City, USA

6 Aug 1989 *MF(WBA)* Kim-Bong Jun (S. Kor) PTS–12 Lee-Sam Jung (S. Kor) Seoul, South Korea

6 Aug 1989 *Fe(IBF)* Jorge Paez (Mex) PTS–12 Steve Cruz (USA) El Paso, USA

19 Aug 1989 *M(IBF)* Michael Nunn (USA) PTS–12 Iran Barkley (USA) Reno, USA

20 Aug 1989 *L(WBC/IBF)* Pernell Whitaker (USA) PTS–12 Jose Luis Ramirez (Mex) Norfolk, USA

26 Aug 1989 *B(WBC)* Raul Perez (Mex) TKO–8 Cerdenio Ulloa (Chi) Talcahuano, Chile

31 Aug 1989 *SB(WBC)* Daniel Zaragoza (Mex) RSF–10 Frankie Duarte (USA) Los Angeles, USA

11 Sep 1989 *LW(IBF)* Meldrick Taylor (USA) PTS–12 Courtney Hooper (USA) Atlantic City, USA

12 Sep 1989 *SF(WBC)* Gilberto Roman (Mex) PTS–12 Santos Laciar (Arg) Los Angeles, USA

15 Sep 1989 *W(WBC)* Marlon Starling (USA) PTS–12 Yung-Kil Chung (S. Kor) Hartford, USA

16 Sep 1989 *Fe(IBF)* Jorge Paez (Mex) KO–2 Jose Mario Lopez (Arg) Mexico City, Mexico

20 Sep 1989 *W(IBF)* Simon Brown (Jam) KO–2 Bobby Joe Young (USA) New York, USA

21 Sep 1989 *MF(IBF)* Eric Chavez (Phi) KO–4 Nico Thomas (Ina) Djakarta, Indonesia

22 Sep 1989 *Fe(WBA)* Antonio Esparragoza (Ven) KO–5 Eduardo Monotoyo (Mex) Mexicali, Mexico

24 Sep 1989 *LF(WBA)* Myung-Woo Yuh (S. Kor) KO–11 Taiho Kenbun (Jap) Seoul, South Korea

28 Sep 1989 *JL(WBA)* Brian Mitchell (SA) RSF–7 Irving Mitchell (USA) Lewiston, USA

30 Sep 1989 *Fl(WBA)* Jesus Rojas (Ven) PTS–12 Fidel Bassa (Col) Barranquilla, Colombia

6 Oct 1989 *LF(IBF)* Muangchai Kittikasem (Tha) RSF–7 Tacy Macalos (Phi) Bangkok, Thailand

7 Oct 1989 *JL(IBF)* Juan 'John-John' Molina (PR) RSF–10 Tony Lopez (USA) Sacramento, USA

7 Oct 1989 *SB(IBF)* Fabrice Benichou (Spa) PTS–12 Ramon Cruz (Dom) Bordeaux, France

8 Oct 1989 *SM(WBA)* In-Chul Baek (S. Kor) RSF–11 Ron Essett (USA) Seoul, South Korea

13 Oct 1989 *W(WBA)* Mark Breland (USA) RSF–2 Mauro Martelli (Swi) Geneva, Switzerland

14 Oct 1989 *SF(IBF)* Juan Polo Perez (Col) PTS–12 Ellyas Pical (Ina) Roanoke, USA

17 Oct 1989 *B(WBA)* Luisito Espinosa (Phi) RSF–1 Kaokar Galaxy (Tha) Bangkok, Thailand

21 Oct 1989 *C(IBF)* Glenn McCrory (GB) KO–11 Siza Makhatini (SA) Middlesbrough, England

22 Oct 1989 *MF(WBA)* Kim-Bong Jun (S. Kor) RSF–9 John Arief (Ina) Pohang, South Korea

23 Oct 1989 *B(WBC)* Raul Perez (Mex) PTS–12 Diego Avilar (Mex) Los Angeles, USA

24 Oct 1989 *LH(WBC)* Jeff Harding (Aus) TKO–2 Tom Collins (GB) Brisbane, Australia

24 Oct 1989 *LH(WBA)* Virgil Hill (USA) RSF–1 James Kinchen (USA) Bismark, USA

27 Oct 1989 *LM(IBF)* Gianfranco Rosi (Ita) PTS–12 Troy Waters (Aus) St. Vincent

31 Oct 1989 *SF(WBA)* Kaosai Galaxy (Tha) KO–12 Keji Matsumura (Jap) Kobe, Japan

5 Nov 1989 *JL(WBC)* Azumah Nelson (Gha) RSF–12 Jim McDonnell (GB) London, England

7 Nov 1989 *SF(WBC)* Nana Yaw Konadu (Gha) PTS–12 Gilberto Roman (Mex) Mexico City, Mexico

8 Nov 1989 *Fl(IBF)* Dave McAuley (GB) PTS–12 Dodie Penalosa (Phi) London, England

12 Nov 1989 *MF(WBC)* Jeum-Hwan Choi (S. Kor) RSF–12 Napa Kiatwanchai (Tha) Seoul, South Korea

18 Nov 1989 *LW(WBC)* Julio Cesar Chavez (Mex) RTD–10 Sammy Fuentes (PR) Las Vegas, USA

28 Nov 1989 *C(WBA)* Robert Daniels (USA) PTS–12 Dwight Muhammad Qawi (USA) Paris, France

8 Nov 1989 IBF Dave McAuley (GB) PTS–12 Dodie Penalosa (Phi) London, England

9 Nov 1989 *W(IBF)* Simon Brown (Jam) PTS–12 Luis Santana (USA) Springfield, USA

3 Dec 1989 *SB(WBC)* Daniel Zaragoza (Mex) PTS–12 Chan-Young Park (S. Kor) Seoul, South Korea

7 Dec 1989 *SM(WBC)* Sugar Ray Leonard (USA) PTS–12 Roberto Duran (Pan) Las Vegas, USA

9 Dec 1989 *Fe(IBF)* Jorge Paez (Mex) RSF–6 Lupe Gutierrez (USA) Reno, Nevada, USA

9 Dec 1989 *LF(WBC)* Humberto Gonzalez (Mex) PTS–12 Jung-Koo Chang (S. Kor) Seoul, South Korea

10 Dec 1989 *W(WBA)* Mark Breland (USA) RSF–4 Fujio Osaki (Jap) Tokyo, Japan

11 Dec 1989 *SB(WBA)* Jesus Salud (USA) DIS–9 Juan Jose Estrada (Mex) Los Angeles, USA

16 Dec 1989 *LW(WBC)* Julio Cesar Chavez (Mex) KO–3 Alberto Cortes (Arg) Mexico City, Mexico

7 Jan 1990 *LH(IBF)* Prince Charles Williams (USA) RSF–8 Frankie Swindell (USA) Atlantic City, USA

13 Jan 1990 *SM(WBA)* In-Chul Baek (S. Kor) RTD–7 Yoshiaki Tajima (Jap) Ulsan, South Korea

14 Jan 1990 *LF(WBA)* Myung-Woo Yuh (S. Kor) RSF–7 Hisashi Takashima (Jap) Seoul, South Korea

19 Jan 1990 *LF(IBF)* Muangchai Kittikasem (Tha) KO–3 Jeung-Jai Lee (S. Kor) Bangkok, Thailand

20 Jan 1990 *SF(WBC)* Sung-Kil Moon (S. Kor) TD–9 Nana Yaw Konadu (Gha) Seoul, South Korea

22 Jan 1990 *B(WBC)* Raul Perez (Mex) PTS–12 Gaby Canizales (USA) Los Angeles, USA

27 Jan 1990 *C(WBC)* Carlos De Leon (PR) D–12 Johnny Nelson (GB) Sheffield, England

27 Jan 1990 *SM(IBF)* Lindell Holmes (USA) PTS–12 Frank Tate (USA) New Orleans, USA

27 Jan 1990 *JL(IBF)* Juan Molina (PR) RSF–6 Lupe Suarez (USA) Atlantic City, USA

27 Jan 1990 *B(IBF)* Orlando Canizales (USA) PTS–12 Billy Hardy (GB) Sunderland, England

30 Jan 1990 *Fl(WBC)* Sot Chitalada (Tha) PTS–12 Ric Siodoro (Phi) Bangkok, Thailand

3 Feb 1990 *M(WBA)* Mike McCallum (USA) PTS–12 Steve Collins (USA) Boston, USA

3 Feb 1990 *L(WBC/IBF)* Pernell Whitaker (USA) PTS–12 Freddie Pendleton (USA) Atlantic City, USA

4 Feb 1990 *Fe(IBF)* Jorge Paez (Mex) PTS–12 Troy Dorsey (USA) Las Vegas, USA

7 Feb 1990 *MF(WBC)* Hideyuki Ohashi (Jap) KO–9 Jeum-Hwan Choi (S. Kor) Tokyo, Japan

10 Feb 1990 *MF(WBA)* Kim-Bong Jun (S. Kor) KO–4 Petthal Chuvatana (Tha) Seoul, South Korea

11 Feb 1990 *H* James Douglas (USA) KO–10 Mike Tyson (USA) Tokyo, Japan

21 Feb 1990 *MF(IBF)* Falan Lookmingkwan (Tha) RSF–7 Eric Chavez (Phi) Bangkok, Thailand

26 Feb 1990 *LH(WBA)* Virgil Hill (USA) PTS–12 David Vedder (USA) Bismarck, USA

OTHER CLAIMANTS

Over the years there have been many other claimants to world titles apart from the ones listed in Chapter 3, which are regarded as undisputed title claims. The following is a list of claimants to titles, many of whom were never taken seriously.

Welshman Brian Curvis seems to be taking a hammering from Virgin Islander Emile Griffith at Wembley during their world welterweight bout in 1964. Griffith retained his title with a 15-round points decision (Syndication International)

HEAVYWEIGHT

In 1913, during the reign of Jack Johnson (USA), a 'White Heavyweight' championship was held in Los Angeles and Luther McCarty (USA) was proclaimed champion. Arthur Pelkey (Can), Gunboat Smith (USA) and Georges Carpentier (Fra) all subsequently claimed the crown.

In 1950 Lee Savold (USA) beat Bruce Woodcock (GB) in London for the title, which was only recognized by the British Board. Savold's claim was not taken seriously elsewhere.

LIGHT-HEAVYWEIGHT

Jack Dillon (USA) claimed the title in 1912 following his win over Hugo Kelly (Ita). This was two years before his official recognition as champion.

Bob Godwin (USA) made a dubious claim to the NBA version of the title in 1933.

Between 1935 and 1938 Heinz Lazek (Aut), Gustave Roth (Bel) and Adolph Heuser (Ger) were all recognized as world champions by the IBU.

In 1939 and 1942 respectively, the British Boxing Board of Control recognized Len Harvey (GB) and Freddie Mills (GB) as world champions.

Eddie Cotton (USA) was recognized as champion by the Michigan State Athletic Commission in 1963.

MIDDLEWEIGHT

Charles 'Kid' McCoy (USA) staked a claim as champion in 1897 following his victory over Dan Creedon (NZ). McCoy's claim was never taken seriously.

Hugo Kelly (Ita) claimed the title in 1907 after Tommy Ryan (USA) retired, but Kelly's claim was never taken seriously.

The claims of Billy Papke (USA) and Frank Klaus (USA) between 1911 and 1913 are both dubious claims to the title.

Jeff Smith (USA), Mick King (Aus) and Les Darcy (Aus) all claimed the title between 1914 and 1916 but they were only recognized as world champions in Australia.

Frank Mantell (Ger) claimed the title from 1912 to 1915 but he was not recognized outside California.

Marcel Thil (Fra) was recognized as champion in 1937, but only in Europe.

Fred Apostoli (USA) gained European recognition as champion in 1937 after he beat Marcel Thil (Fra). The New York champion Freddie Steele then refused to meet Apostoli and consequently Apostoli also gained their recognition.

Randolph Turpin (GB) also gained European recognition following his victory over Charles Humez (Fra) in 1953.

LIGHT-MIDDLEWEIGHT

Emile Griffith (VI) beat Teddy Wright (USA) in Vienna, Austria in 1962 to become the first claimant to the light-middleweight title. The fight, however, was only recognized by the Austrian Board of Control. After one successful defence, Griffith let his claim lapse.

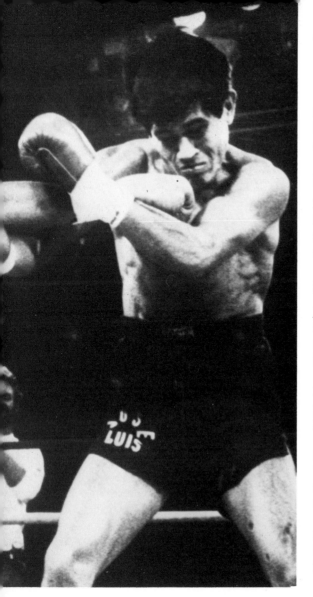

Jose Luis Ramirez (right) takes a punch from Hector Camacho in the opening round of his first defence of the WBC lightweight title in 1985. The fight went the full distance of 12 rounds but Camacho was crowned the new champion (AP)

Hedgemon Lewis (USA) twice beat Billy Backus (USA) in 1972 to gain New York State recognition as champion.

LIGHT-WELTERWEIGHT

Pinkey Mitchell (USA) is often referred to as being the first world light-welterweight champion, but he only assumed that title after being nominated by readers of a boxing magazine in 1922.

LIGHTWEIGHT

Jimmy Britt (USA) claimed the 'White Lightweight' title in 1902 after beating Frank Erne (Swi). He made two successful defences before losing the 'title' to Battling Nelson (Den) in 1905.

Freddie Welsh (GB) claimed the title in 1912, four years before he became officially recognized, following his victory over Hughie Mehegan (Aus).

Following the retirement of Sammy Angott (USA) in 1942 Luther 'Slugger' White (USA) became recognized as world champion, but only by the Maryland State Commission.

Kenny Lane (USA) won recognition by the Michigan State Athletic Commission as world champion in 1963 following his points win over Paul Armstead (USA).

JUNIOR-LIGHTWEIGHT

Sandy Saddler (USA) gained recognition in Cleveland in 1949. He made one successful defence of the title before the weight division fell into disuse.

FEATHERWEIGHT

Ben Jordan (GB) claimed the title in 1898 after he beat George Dixon (Can). Dixon claimed his title was not at stake. Jordan subsequently lost to Eddie Santry (USA) who then claimed the title in 1899.

Tommy Sullivan (USA) claimed the title after beating Abe Attell (USA) in a non-title fight in 1904.

Jim Driscoll (GB) claimed the title in 1909 after he outclassed reigning champion Abe Attell (USA) in a no-decision 10-round contest. Despite Driscoll's claim, most authorities continued to recognize Attell as champion.

WELTERWEIGHT

Joe Walcott (Bar) re-claimed the title in 1904 after Dixie Kid (USA) had outgrown the division. Walcott in his first 'defence' lost to Honey Mellody in 1906.

After Mike 'Twin' Sullivan relinquished the title, the welterweight division was thrown into confusion between 1908 and 1915 with many claimants to the title. None were substantiated until Ted 'Kid' Lewis (GB) became recognized as champion in 1915. The men who claimed the title during the period of uncertainty were: Harry Lewis (USA), Jimmy Gardner (Ire), Jimmy Clabby (USA), Waldemar Holberg (Den), Tom McCormick (Ire), Matt Wells (GB), Mike Glover (USA) and Jack Britton (USA).

Charley Shipes (USA) beat Percy Manning (USA) in 1966 but the contest was recognized as a world title fight only by the Californian State Athletic Commission.

Tommy Noble (GB) was presented with a world-title belt in 1920 after his win over Johnny Murray (USA) but Noble's claim was never taken seriously.

Dick 'Honeyboy' Finnegan (USA) was recognized as world champion in 1926, but only by the Massachusetts State Boxing Commission.

Baby Arizmendi (Mex) claimed the title in 1934 after the New York Commission withdrew its recognition of champion Kid Chocolate.

Maurice Holtzer (Fra) gained IBU recognition as champion in 1937.

Jimmy Perrin (USA) gained Louisiana State recognition as champion in 1940.

While Sandy Saddler was serving in the US Forces (1952–4) Percy Bassett (USA) beat Ray Famechon (Fra) for the 'interim' title in 1952. Bassett subsequently lost the title to Teddy 'Red Top' Davis (USA) in 1953.

SUPER-BANTAMWEIGHT

Although the weight division was introduced by the WBC in 1976, Jack Wolfe (USA) beat Joe Lynch in 1922 in a contest billed as being for the 'world junior featherweight' title. The following year Carl Duane (USA) took the 'title' from Wolfe. No further contests took place until the division was revived by the WBC.

BANTAMWEIGHT

George Dixon (Can) claimed the title in 1888, two years before he was internationally recognized as champion.

Upon Dixon's relinquishment of the title Tommy Kelly (USA) and Chappie Moran (GB) both claimed the title in 1888 and 1889, respectively. Billy Plimmer (GB) also staked a good claim in 1892 as a result of outpointing Kelly over ten rounds.

Jimmy Barry (USA) claimed his title in 1894 following his win over Caspar Leon (Ita). Three years later Barry was internationally recognized as champion, but in the meantime Pedlar Palmer (GB) joined Billy Plimmer as a good claimant to the title.

After Joe Bowker (GB) relinquished the title in 1904 Digger Stanley (GB) and Jimmy Walsh (USA) both claimed the title. Walsh relinquished his claim which left Stanley with the best claim but Walsh then reclaimed his title in 1908. Less than twelve months later he had relinquished it yet again. The division was

thrown into a state of confusion. Stanley reclaimed the title in 1909 but other claimants at this time were: Eddie Campi (USA), Monte Attell (USA), Johnny Coulon (Can), Frankie Conley (Ita), Kid Murphy (USA) and Charles Ledoux (Fra).

Johnny Ertle (Aut) claimed the title in 1915 after he beat the then champion Kid Williams on a foul. Ertle's claim was never taken seriously.

Joe Burman (GB) claimed the title after beating reigning champion Pete Herman (USA) in 1919. Herman, however, claimed his title was not at stake. This was generally accepted and he continued to be recognized as champion.

When the title was declared vacant in 1927 Teddy Baldock (GB) and Willie Smith (SA) claimed the British version of the title.

Pete Sanstol (Nor) was recognized in Canada as the world champion in 1931.

FLYWEIGHT

Although Jimmy Wilde (GB) in 1916 was the first officially recognized world flyweight champion, Sid Smith, Bill Ladbury, Percy Jones and Joe Symonds (all GB) were claimants to the title between 1913 and 1916. Following Pancho Villa's death in 1925 the title was claimed by Frankie Genaro (USA).

Following Fidel La Barba's retirement in 1927 the division was thrown into confusion. Several men claimed the title between 1927 and 1929, including: Johnny McCoy (USA), Newsboy Brown (USSR), Johnny Hill (GB), and Willie Le Morte (USA). Valentin Angelmann (Fra) was recognized as world champion by the IBU for a short while in 1937 but their recognition was withdrawn following the success of Benny Lynch (GB).

'Nonpareil' Jack Dempsey (Ire) retained his world middleweight title in 1887 by knocking out his opponent, Johnny Reagan (USA). The contest took place in two rings. It started at Huntington, Long Island but, in the eighth round, the tide from a nearby river caused the ring to flood. The fighters and spectators boarded a tug and continued the bout some 25 miles away!

WORLD CHAMPIONS IN EACH DIVISION

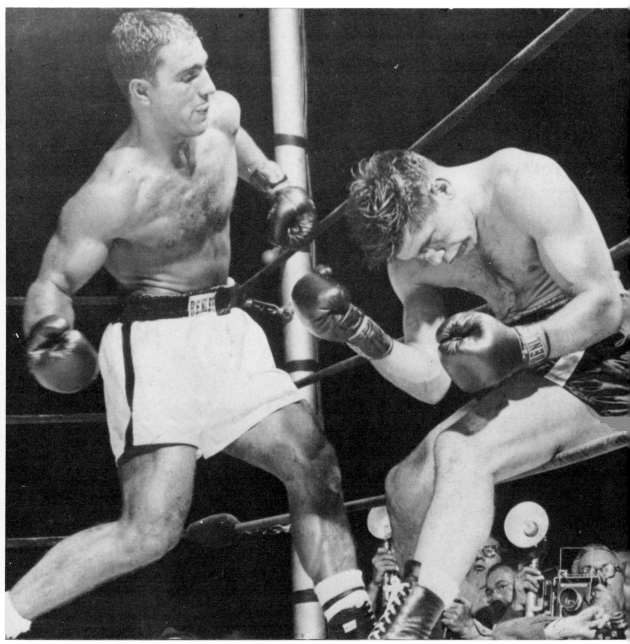

Rocky Marciano's famous right-hand punch known as 'Suzy-Q' is about to be thrown to the head of Roland La Starza in New York in 1953. Marciano retained his world title in the 11th round (Keystone)

HEAVYWEIGHT

UNDISPUTED CHAMPIONS

James J. Corbett	USA	1892
Bob Fitzsimmons	GB	1897
James J. Jeffries	USA	1899
Marvin Hart	USA	1905
Tommy Burns	Can	1906
Jack Johnson	USA	1908
Jess Willard	USA	1915
Jack Dempsey	USA	1919
Gene Tunney	USA	1926
Max Schmeling	Ger	1930
Jack Sharkey	USA	1932
Primo Carnera	Ita	1933
Max Baer	USA	1934
James J. Braddock	USA	1935
Joe Louis	USA	1937
Ezzard Charles	USA	1950
Jersey Joe Walcott	USA	1951
Rocky Marciano	USA	1952
Floyd Patterson	USA	1956
Ingemar Johansson	Swe	1959
Floyd Patterson	USA	1960
Sonny Liston	USA	1962
Cassius Clay	USA	1964
Joe Frazier	USA	1970
George Foreman	USA	1973
Muhammad Ali	USA	1974
(formerly Cassius Clay)		
Leon Spinks	USA	1978
Mike Tyson	USA	1987
James Douglas	USA	1990

WBC

Ken Norton	USA	1978
Larry Holmes	USA	1978
Tim Witherspoon	USA	1984
Pinklon Thomas	USA	1984
Trevor Berbick	Jam	1986
Mike Tyson	USA	1986

WBA

Ernie Terrell	USA	1965
Jimmy Ellis	USA	1968
Muhammad Ali	USA	1978
John Tate	USA	1979
Mike Weaver	USA	1980
Mike Dokes	USA	1982
Gerrie Coetzee	SA	1983
Greg Page	USA	1984
Tony Tubbs	USA	1985
Tim Witherspoon	USA	1986
James Smith	USA	1986
Mike Tyson	USA	1987

IBF

Larry Holmes	USA	1984
Michael Spinks	USA	1985
Tony Tucker	USA	1987
Mike Tyson	USA	1987

NBA

Ezzard Charles	USA	1949

NEW YORK STATE

Joe Frazier	USA	1968

OTHER CLAIMANTS

Luther McCarty	USA	1913
Arthur Pelkey	Can	1913
Gunboat Smith	USA	1914
Georges Carpentier	Fra	1914
Lee Savold	USA	1950

CRUISERWEIGHT

UNDISPUTED

Evander Holyfield	USA	1988

WBC

Marvin Camel	USA	1980
Carlos de Leon	PR	1980
S. T. Gordon	USA	1982
Carlos de Leon	PR	1983
Alfonso Ratliff	USA	1985
Bernard Benton	USA	1985
Carlos de Leon	PR	1986
Carlos de Leon	PR	1989

WBA

Ossie Ocasio	PR	1982
Piet Crous	SA	1984
Dwight Qawi	USA	1985
(formerly Dwight Braxton)		
Evander Holyfield	USA	1986
Taoufik Belbouli	Fra	1989
Robert Daniels	USA	1989

IBF

Marvin Camel	USA	1983
Leroy Murphy	USA	1984
Rickey Parkey	USA	1986
Evander Holyfield	USA	1987
Glenn McCrory	GB	1989

LIGHT-HEAVYWEIGHT

UNDISPUTED CHAMPIONS

Jack Root	Aut	1903
George Gardner	Ire	1903
Bob Fitzsimmons	GB	1903
Philadelphia	USA	1905
Jack O'Brien		
Jack Dillon	USA	1914
Battling Levinsky	USA	1916
Georges Carpentier	Fra	1920
Battling Siki	Sen	1922
Mike McTigue	Ire	1923
Paul Berlenbach	USA	1925
Jack Delaney	Can	1926
Tommy Loughran	USA	1927
Maxie Rosenbloom	USA	1932
Bob Olin	USA	1934
John Henry Lewis	USA	1935
Billy Conn	USA	1939
Gus Lesnevich	USA	1941
Freddie Mills	GB	1948
Joey Maxim	USA	1950
Archie Moore	USA	1952
Harold Johnson	USA	1962
Willie Pastrano	USA	1963
Jose Torres	PR	1965
Dick Tiger	Ngr	1966
Bob Foster	USA	1968
Michael Spinks	USA	1983

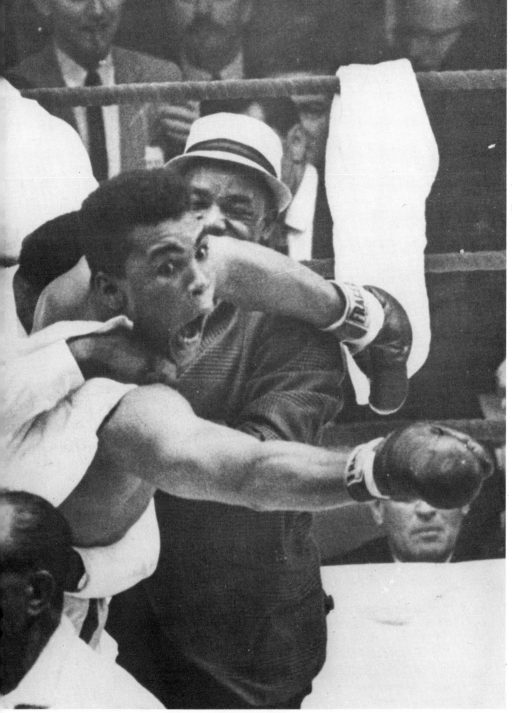

Do you get the impression Cassius Clay has won? He told people he was the greatest even before he had beaten Sonny Liston . . . there was to be no stopping him once he had confirmed it with his capture of the world title in 1964 (Hulton-Deutsch)

WBC			Dennis Andries	Guy	1986	Mike Rossman	USA	1978
			Thomas Hearns	USA	1987	Victor Galindez	Arg	1979
Bob Foster	USA	1970	Donny Lalonde	Can	1988	Marvin Johnson	USA	1979
John Conteh	GB	1974	Sugar Ray Leonard	USA	1988	Eddie Mustaffa	USA	1980
Miguel Cuello	Arg	1977	Dennis Andries	Guy	1989	Muhammad		
Mate Parlov	Yug	1978	Jeff Harding	Aus	1989	(formerly Eddie Gregory)		
Marvin Johnson	USA	1978				Michael Spinks	USA	1981
Matt Saad Muhammad	USA	1979	**WBA**			Marvin Johnson	USA	1986
(formerly Matt Franklin)						Leslie Stewart	Tri	1987
Dwight Braxton	USA	1981	Vicente Rondon	Ven	1971	Virgil Hill	USA	1987
J. B. Williamson	USA	1985	Victor Galindez	Arg	1974			

127

IBF

Slobodan Kacar	Yug	1985
Bobby Czyz	USA	1987
Prince Charles Williams	USA	1987

NBA

Jimmy Slattery	USA	1927
George Nichols	USA	1932
Lou Scozza	USA	1932
Anton Christoforidis	Gre	1941
Harold Johnson	USA	1961

NEW YORK STATE

Jimmy Slattery	USA	1930
Maxie Rosenbloom	USA	1930
Tiger Jack Fox	USA	1938
Melio Bettina	USA	1939

OTHER CLAIMANTS

Jack Dillon	USA	1912
Bob Godwin	USA	1933
Heinz Lazek	Aut	1935
Gustave Roth	Bel	1936
Adolph Heuser	Ger	1938
Len Harvey	GB	1939
Freddie Mills	GB	1942
Eddie Cotton	USA	1963

SUPER-MIDDLEWEIGHT

WBC

Sugar Ray Leonard	USA	1988

WBA

Fulgencio Obelmejias	Ven	1988
In-Chul Baek	S. Kor	1989

IBF

Murray Sutherland	GB	1984
Chong-Pal Park	S. Kor	1984
Graciano Rocchigniani	FRG	1988
Lindell Holmes	USA	1990

MIDDLEWEIGHT

UNDISPUTED CHAMPIONS

Jack Dempsey	Ire	1884
Bob Fitzsimmons	GB	1891
Charles 'Kid' McCoy	USA	1897
Tommy Ryan	USA	1898
Stanley Ketchel	USA	1907
Billy Papke	USA	1908
Stanley Ketchel	USA	1908
Billy Papke	USA	1910
Cyclone Johnny Thompson	USA	1911
George Chip	USA	1913
Al McCoy	USA	1914
Mike O'Dowd	USA	1917
Johnny Wilson	USA	1921
Harry Greb	USA	1923
Tiger Flowers	USA	1926
Mickey Walker	USA	1926
Freddie Steele	USA	1936
Tony Zale	USA	1941
Rocky Graziano	USA	1947
Tony Zale	USA	1948
Marcel Cerdan	Alg	1948
Jake La Motta	USA	1949
Sugar Ray Robinson	USA	1951
Randolph Turpin	GB	1951
Sugar Ray Robinson	USA	1951
Carl 'Bobo' Olson	Haw	1953
Sugar Ray Robinson	USA	1955
Gene Fullmer	USA	1957
Sugar Ray Robinson	USA	1957
Carmen Basilio	USA	1957
Sugar Ray Robinson	USA	1958
Paul Pender	USA	1960
Terry Downes	GB	1961
Paul Pender	USA	1962
Dick Tiger	Ngr	1963
Joey Giardello	USA	1963
Dick Tiger	Ngr	1965
Emile Griffith	VI	1966
Nino Benvenuti	Ita	1967
Emile Griffith	VI	1967
Nino Benvenuti	Ita	1968
Carlos Monzon	Arg	1970
Carlos Monzon	Arg	1976
Rodrigo Valdez	Col	1977
Hugo Corro	Arg	1978
Vito Antuofermo	Ita	1979
Alan Minter	GB	1980
Marvin Hagler	USA	1980
Marvin Hagler	USA	1986

WBC

Rodrigo Valdez	Col	1974
Sugar Ray Leonard	USA	1987
Thomas Hearns	USA	1987
Iran Barkley	USA	1988
Roberto Duran	Pan	1989

WBA

Carlos Monzon	Arg	1974
Sambu Kalambay	Zai	1987
Mike McCallum	Jam	1989

IBF

Frank Tate	USA	1987
Michael Nunn	USA	1988

NBA

Gorilla Jones	USA	1931
Marcel Thil	Fra	1932
Gorilla Jones	USA	1933
Marcel Thil	Fra	1933
Al Hostak	USA	1938
Sol Kreiger	USA	1938
Al Hostak	USA	1939
Tony Zale	USA	1940
Gene Fullmer	USA	1959
Dick Tiger	Ngr	1962

NEW YORK STATE

Dave Rosenberg	USA	1922
Mike O'Dowd	USA	1922
Ben Jeby	USA	1932
Lou Brouillard	Can	1933
Vince Dundee	Ita	1933
Teddy Yarosz	USA	1934
Ed 'Babe' Risko	USA	1935
Freddie Steele	USA	1936
Fred Apostoli	USA	1938
Ceferino Garcia	Phi	1939
Ken Overlin	USA	1940
Billy Soose	USA	1941

OTHER CLAIMANTS

Hugo Kelly	Ita	1907
Billy Papke	USA	1911
Frank Mantell	USA	1912
Frank Klaus	USA	1912
Jeff Smith	USA	1914
Mick King	Aus	1914
Les Darcy	Aus	1915
Marcel Thil	Fra	1937
Fred Apostoli	USA	1937
Randolph Turpin	GB	1953

LIGHT-MIDDLEWEIGHT/ JUNIOR-MIDDLEWEIGHT

UNDISPUTED CHAMPIONS

Denny Moyer	USA	1962
Ralph Dupas	USA	1963
Sandro Mazzinghi	Ita	1963
Nino Benvenuti	Ita	1965
Ki-Soo Kim	S. Kor	1966
Sandro Mazzinghi	Ita	1968
Freddie Little	USA	1969
Carmelo Bossi	Ita	1970
Koichi Wajima	Jap	1971
Oscar Albarado	USA	1974
Koichi Wajima	Jap	1975

WBC

Miguel de Oliveira	Bra	1975
Elisha Obed	Bah	1975
Eckhard Dagge	FRG	1976
Rocky Mattioli	Ita	1977
Maurice Hope	Ant	1979
Wilfred Benitez	USA	1981
Thomas Hearns	USA	1982
Duane Thomas	USA	1986
Lupe Aquino	Mex	1987
Gianfranco Rosi	Ita	1988
Don Curry	USA	1988
Rene Jacquot	Fra	1989
John Mugabi	Uga	1989

WBA

Jae-Do Yuh	S. Kor	1975
Koichi Wajima	Jap	1976
Jose Duran	Spa	1976
Miguel Castellini	Arg	1976
Eddie Gazo	Nic	1977
Masashi Kudo	Jap	1978
Ayub Kalule	Uga	1979
Sugar Ray Leonard	USA	1981
Tadashi Mihara	Jap	1981

Davey Moore	USA	1982				Jack Britton	USA	1916	
Roberto Duran	Pan	1983	**WELTERWEIGHT**			Ted 'Kid' Lewis	GB	1917	
Mike McCallum	Jam	1984				Jack Britton	USA	1919	
Julian Jackson	VI	1988	**UNDISPUTED CHAMPIONS**			Mickey Walker	USA	1922	
			Paddy Duffy	USA	1888	Pete Latzo	USA	1926	
IBF			Mysterious Bill Smith	USA	1892	Joe Dundee	Ita	1927	
			Tommy Ryan	USA	1894	Jackie Fields	USA	1929	
Mark Medal	USA	1984	Charles 'Kid' McCoy	USA	1896	Young Jack Thompson	USA	1930	
Carlos Santos	PR	1984	Mysterious Bill Smith	USA	1898	Tommy Freeman	USA	1930	
Buster Drayton	USA	1986	Rube Ferns	USA	1900	Young Jack Thompson	USA	1931	
Matthew Hilton	Can	1987	Matty Matthews	USA	1900	Lou Brouillard	Can	1931	
Robert Hines	USA	1988	Rube Ferns	USA	1901	Jackie Fields	USA	1932	
Darrin Van Horn	USA	1989	Joe Walcott	Bar	1901	Young Corbett III	Ita	1933	
Gianfranco Rosi	Ita	1989	Dixie Kid	USA	1904	Jimmy McLarnin	Ire	1933	
			Honey Mellody	USA	1906	Barney Ross	USA	1934	
OTHER CLAIMANTS			Mike 'Twin' Sullivan	USA	1907	Jimmy McLarnin	Ire	1934	
Emile Griffith	VI	1962	Ted 'Kid' Lewis	GB	1915	Barney Ross	USA	1935	

Henry Armstrong	USA	1938
Fritzie Zivic	USA	1940
Freddie 'Red' Cochrane	USA	1941
Marty Servo	USA	1946
Sugar Ray Robinson	USA	1946
Kid Gavilan	Cuba	1951
Johnny Saxton	USA	1954
Tony de Marco	USA	1955
Carmen Basilio	USA	1955
Johnny Saxton	USA	1956
Carmen Basilio	USA	1956
Virgil Atkins	USA	1958
Don Jordan	USA	1958
Benny 'Kid' Paret	Cuba	1960
Emile Griffith	VI	1961
Benny 'Kid' Paret	Cuba	1961
Emile Griffith	VI	1962
Luis Rodriguez	Cuba	1963
Emile Griffith	VI	1963
Curtis Cokes	USA	1967
Jose Napoles	Cuba	1969
Billy Backus	USA	1970
Jose Napoles	Cuba	1971
Sugar Ray Leonard	USA	1981
Don Curry	USA	1985
Lloyd Honeyghan	Jam	1986

WBC

John H. Stracey	GB	1975
Carlos Palomino	Mex	1976
Wilfred Benitez	USA	1979
Sugar Ray Leonard	USA	1979
Roberto Duran	Pan	1980
Sugar Ray Leonard	USA	1980
Milton McCrory	USA	1983
Lloyd Honeyghan	Jam	1987
Jorge Vaca	Mex	1987
Lloyd Honeyghan	Jam	1988
Marlon Starling	USA	1989

WBA

Curtis Cokes	USA	1966
Angel Espada	PR	1975
Jose Cuevas	Mex	1976
Thomas Hearns	USA	1980
Don Curry	USA	1983
Mark Breland	USA	1987
Marlon Starling	USA	1987
Tomas Molinares	Col	1988
Mark Breland	USA	1989

IBF

Don Curry	USA	1984
Lloyd Honeyghan	Jam	1987
Simon Brown	Jam	1988

NBA

Johnny Bratton	USA	1951

OTHER CLAIMANTS

Harry Lewis	USA	1908
Jimmy Gardner	Ire	1908
Jimmy Clabby	USA	1910
Waldemar Holberg	Den	1914

Tom McCormick	Ire	1914
Matt Wells	GB	1914
Mike Glover	USA	1915
Jack Britton	USA	1915
Charley Shipes	USA	1966
Hedgemon Lewis	USA	1972

JUNIOR-WELTERWEIGHT/ SUPER-LIGHTWEIGHT

UNDISPUTED CHAMPIONS

Mushy Callahan	USA	1926
Jack 'Kid' Berg	GB	1931
Tony Canzoneri	USA	1931
Johnny Jaddick	USA	1932
Battling Shaw	Mex	1933
Tony Canzoneri	USA	1933
Barney Ross	USA	1933
Tippy Larkin	USA	1946
Carlos Ortiz	PR	1959
Duilio Loi	Ita	1960
Eddie Perkins	USA	1962
Duilio Loi	Ita	1962
Roberto Cruz	Phi	1963
Eddie Perkins	USA	1963
Carlos Hernandez	Ven	1965
Sandro Lopopolo	Ita	1966
Paul Fuji	Haw	1967

WBC

Pedro Adigue	Phi	1968
Bruno Arcari	Ita	1970
Perico Fernandez	Spa	1974
Saensak Muangsurin	Tha	1975
Miguel Velasquez	Spa	1976
Saensak Muangsurin	Tha	1976
Sang-Hyun Kim	S. Kor	1978
Saoul Mamby	Jam	1980
Leroy Haley	USA	1982
Bruce Curry	USA	1983
Billy Costello	USA	1984
Lonnie Smith	USA	1985
Rene Arredondo	Mex	1986
Tsuyoshi Hamada	Jap	1986
Rene Arredondo	Mex	1987
Roger Mayweather	USA	1988
Julio Cesar Chavez	Mex	1989

WBA

Nicolino Loche	Arg	1968
Alfonso Frazer	Pan	1972
Antonio Cervantes	Col	1972
Wilfred Benitez	USA	1976
Antonio Cervantes	Col	1977
Aaron Pryor	USA	1980
Johnny Bumphus	USA	1984
Gene Hatcher	USA	1984
Ubaldo Sacco	Arg	1985
Patrizio Oliva	Ita	1986
Juan Martin Coggi	Arg	1987

IBF

Aaron Pryor	USA	1984
Gary Hinton	USA	1986
Joe Louis Manley	USA	1986

Terry Marsh	GB	1987
James McGirt	USA	1988
Meldrick Taylor	USA	1988

NEW YORK STATE

Jack 'Kid' Berg	GB	1930

OTHER CLAIMANTS

Pinkey Mitchell	USA	1922

Britain's Lloyd Honeyghan (right) did what few other Britons have done when he captured a world title on US soil. He beat Don Curry to win the welterweight title in Atlantic City in 1986 (All Sport/C Cole)

LIGHTWEIGHT

UNDISPUTED CHAMPIONS

Jack McAuliffe	Ire	1888
George 'Kid' Lavigne	USA	1896
Frank Erne	Swi	1899
Joe Gans	USA	1902
Battling Nelson	Den	1908
Ad Wolgast	USA	1910
Willie Ritchie	USA	1912
Freddie Welsh	GB	1914
Benny Leonard	USA	1917
Jimmy Goodrich	USA	1925
Rocky Kansas	USA	1925
Sammy Mandell	USA	1926
Al Singer	USA	1930
Tony Canzoneri	USA	1930
Barney Ross	USA	1933
Tony Canzoneri	USA	1935
Lou Ambers	USA	1936
Henry Armstrong	USA	1938
Lou Ambers	USA	1939
Sammy Angott	USA	1941
Ike Williams	USA	1947
Jimmy Carter	USA	1951
Lauro Salas	Mex	1952
Jimmy Carter	USA	1952
Paddy de Marco	USA	1954
Jimmy Carter	USA	1954
Wallace 'Bud' Smith	USA	1955
Joe Brown	USA	1956
Carlos Ortiz	PR	1962
Ismael Laguna	Pan	1965
Carlos Ortiz	PR	1965
Carlos Ortiz	PR	1967
Carlos Cruz	Dom	1968
Mando Ramos	USA	1969
Ismael Laguna	Pan	1970
Ken Buchanan	GB	1970
Roberto Duran	Pan	1978

'Little and Large': two world champions, heavyweight Primo Carnera (left) with lightweight Al Singer (Topica

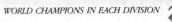

WBC

Pedro Carrasco	Spa	1971
Mando Ramos	USA	1972
Chango Carmona	Mex	1972
Rodolfo Gonzalez	Mex	1972
Guts Ishimatsu	Jap	1974
Esteban de Jesus	PR	1976
Jim Watt	GB	1979
Alexis Arguello	Nic	1981
Edwin Rosario	PR	1983
Jose Luis Ramirez	Mex	1984
Hector Camacho	PR	1985
Jose Luis Ramirez	Mex	1987
Julio Cesar Chavez	Mex	1988
Pernell Whitaker	USA	1989

WBA

Carlos Ortiz	PR	1966
Ken Buchanan	GB	1971
Roberto Duran	Pan	1972
Ernesto Espana	Ven	1979
Hilmer Kenty	USA	1980
Sean O'Grady	USA	1981
Claude Noel	Tri	1981
Arturo Frias	USA	1981
Ray Mancini	USA	1982
Livingstone Bramble	VI	1984
Edwin Rosario	PR	1986
Julio Cesar Chavez	Mex	1987
Edwin Rosario	PR	1989

IBF

Charlie 'Choo Choo' Brown	USA	1984
Harry Arroyo	USA	1984
Jimmy Paul	USA	1985
Greg Haugen	USA	1986
Vinny Pazienza	USA	1987
Greg Haugen	USA	1988
Pernell Whitaker	USA	1989

NBA

Sammy Angott	USA	1940
Sammy Angott	USA	1943
Juan Zurita	Mex	1944
Ike Williams	USA	1945

NEW YORK STATE

Lew Jenkins	USA	1940
Beau Jack	USA	1942
Bob Montgomery	USA	1943
Beau Jack	USA	1943
Bob Montgomery	USA	1944

OTHER CLAIMANTS

Jimmy Britt	USA	1902
Battling Nelson	Den	1905
Freddie Welsh	GB	1912
Luther 'Slugger' White	USA	1942
Kenny Lane	USA	1963

JUNIOR-LIGHTWEIGHT/ SUPER-FEATHERWEIGHT

UNDISPUTED CHAMPIONS

Johnny Dundee	Ita	1921
Jack Bernstein	USA	1923
Johnny Dundee	Ita	1923
Steve 'Kid' Sullivan	USA	1924
Mike Balerino	USA	1925
Tod Morgan	USA	1925
Benny Bass	USSR	1929
Kid Chocolate	Cuba	1931
Frankie Klick	USA	1933
Harold Gomes	USA	1959
Flash Elorde	Phi	1960
Yoshiaki Numata	Jap	1967
Hiroshi Kobayashi	Jap	1967

WBC

Rene Barrientos	Phi	1969
Yoshiaki Numata	Jap	1970
Ricardo Arredondo	Mex	1971
Kuniaki Shibata	Jap	1974
Alfredo Escalera	PR	1975
Alexis Arguello	Nic	1978
Rafael Limon	Mex	1980
Cornelius Boza-Edwards	Uga	1981
Rolando Navarette	Phi	1981
Rafael Limon	Mex	1982
Bobby Chacon	USA	1982
Hector Camacho	PR	1983
Julio Cesar Chavez	Mex	1984
Azumah Nelson	Gha	1988

WBA

Hiroshi Kobayashi	Jap	1969
Alfredo Marcano	Ven	1971
Ben Villaflor	Phi	1972
Kuniaki Shibata	Jap	1973
Ben Villaflor	Phi	1973
Sam Serrano	PR	1976
Yasutsune Uehara	Jap	1980
Sam Serrano	PR	1981
Roger Mayweather	USA	1983
Rocky Lockridge	USA	1984
Wilfredo Gomez	PR	1985
Alfredo Layne	Pan	1986
Brian Mitchell	SA	1986

IBF

Hwan-Kil Yuh	S. Kor	1984
Lester Ellis	Aus	1985
Barry Michael	GB	1985
Rocky Lockridge	USA	1987
Tony Lopez	USA	1988
Juan Molina	PR	1989

OTHER CLAIMANTS

Sandy Saddler	USA	1949

FEATHERWEIGHT

UNDISPUTED CHAMPIONS

Ike Weir	GB	1889
Billy Murphy	NZ	1890
Young Griffo	Aus	1890
George Dixon	Can	1891

Solly Smith	USA	1897
Dave Sullivan	Ire	1898
George Dixon	Can	1898
Terry McGovern	USA	1900
Young Corbett II	USA	1901
Abe Attell	USA	1904
Johnny Kilbane	USA	1912
Eugene Criqui	Fra	1923
Johnny Dundee	Ita	1923
Louis 'Kid' Kaplan	USSR	1925
Benny Bass	USSR	1927
Tony Canzoneri	USA	1928
Andre Routis	Fra	1928
Battling Battalino	USA	1929
Henry Armstrong	USA	1937
Joey Archibald	USA	1939
Willie Pep	USA	1946
Sandy Saddler	USA	1948
Willie Pep	USA	1949
Sandy Saddler	USA	1950
Hogan 'Kid' Bassey	Ngr	1957
Davey Moore	USA	1959
Sugar Ramos	Cuba	1963
Vicente Saldivar	Mex	1964

WBC

Howard Winstone	GB	1968
Jose Legra	Cuba	1968
Johnny Famechon	Fra	1969
Vicente Saldivar	Mex	1970
Kuniaki Shibata	Jap	1970
Clemente Sanchez	Mex	1972
Jose Legra	Cuba	1972
Eder Jofre	Bra	1973
Bobby Chacon	USA	1974
Ruben Olivares	Mex	1975
David Kotey	Gha	1975
Danny Lopez	USA	1976
Salvador Sanchez	Mex	1980
Juan Laporte	PR	1982
Wilfredo Gomez	PR	1984
Azumah Nelson	Gha	1984
Jeff Fenech	Aus	1988

WBA

Raul Rojas	USA	1968
Sho Saijyo	Jap	1968
Antonio Gomez	Ven	1971
Ernesto Marcel	Pan	1972
Ruben Olivares	Mex	1974
Alexis Arguello	Nic	1974
Rafael Ortega	Pan	1977
Cecilio Lastra	Spa	1977
Eusebio Pedroza	Pan	1978
Barry McGuigan	Ire	1985
Steve Cruz	USA	1986
Antonio Esparragoza	Ven	1987

IBF

Min-Keum Oh	S. Kor	1984
Chung-Ki Yung	S. Kor	1985
Antonio Rivera	PR	1986
Calvin Grove	USA	1988
Jorge Paez	Mex	1988

NBA

Name	Country	Year
Tommy Paul	USA	1932
Freddie Miller	USA	1933
Petey Sarron	USA	1936
Leo Rodak	USA	1938
Petey Scalzo	USA	1940
Ritchie Lemos	USA	1941
Jackie Wilson	USA	1941
Jackie Callura	Can	1943
Phil Terranova	USA	1943
Sal Bartolo	USA	1944

NEW YORK STATE

Name	Country	Year
Johnny Dundee	Ita	1922
Tony Canzoneri	USA	1927
Kid Chocolate	Cuba	1932
Baby Arizmendi	Mex	1934
Mike Belloise	USA	1936
Joey Archibald	USA	1938
Harry Jeffra	USA	1940
Joey Archibald	USA	1941
Chalky Wright	Mex	1941
Willie Pep	USA	1942

OTHER CLAIMANTS

Name	Country	Year
Ben Jordan	GB	1898
Eddie Santry	USA	1899
Tommy Sullivan	USA	1904
Jim Driscoll	GB	1909
Tommy Noble	GB	1920
Dick 'Honeyboy' Finnegan	USA	1926
Maurice Holtzer	Fra	1937
Percy Bassett	USA	1952
Teddy 'Red Top' Davis	USA	1953

JUNIOR-FEATHERWEIGHT/ SUPER-BANTAMWEIGHT

UNDISPUTED CHAMPIONS

None

WBC

Name	Country	Year
Rigoberto Riasco	Pan	1976
Royal Kobayashi	Jap	1976
Dong-Kyun Yum	S. Kor	1976
Wilfredo Gomez	PR	1977
Jaime Garza	USA	1983
Juan 'Kid' Meza	Mex	1984
Lupe Pintor	Mex	1985
Samart Payakaroon	Tha	1986
Jeff Fenech	Aus	1987
Daniel Zaragoza	Mex	1988

WBA

Name	Country	Year
Soo-Hwan Hong	S. Kor	1977
Ricardo Cardona	Col	1978
Leo Randolph	USA	1980
Sergio Palma	Arg	1980
Leonardo Cruz	Dom	1982
Loris Stecca	Ita	1984
Victor Callejas	PR	1984
Louie Espinoza	USA	1987
Julio Gervacio	Dom	1987

Name	Country	Year
Bernardo Pinango	Ven	1988
Juan Jose Estrada	Mex	1988
Jesus Salud	USA	1989

IBF

Name	Country	Year
Bobby Berna	Phi	1983
Seung-In Suh	S. Kor	1984
Chi-Wan Kim	S. Kor	1985
Seung-Hoon Lee	S. Kor	1987
Jose Sanabria	Ven	1988
Fabrice Benichou	Spa	1989

OTHER CLAIMANTS

Name	Country	Year
Jack Wolfe	USA	1922
Carl Duane	USA	1923

BANTAMWEIGHT

UNDISPUTED CHAMPIONS

Name	Country	Year
George Dixon	Can	1890
Jimmy Barry	USA	1897
Terry McGovern	USA	1899
Harry Harris	USA	1901
Harry Forbes	USA	1901
Frankie Neil	USA	1903
Joe Bowker	GB	1904
Jimmy Walsh	USA	1905
Johnny Coulon	Can	1911
Kid Williams	Den	1914
Pete Herman	USA	1917
Joe Lynch	USA	1920
Pete Herman	USA	1921
Johnny Buff	USA	1921
Joe Lynch	USA	1922
Abe Goldstein	USA	1924
Eddie Martin	USA	1924
Charley Phil Rosenberg	USA	1925
Panama Al Brown	Pan	1929
Sixto Escobar	PR	1936
Harry Jeffra	USA	1937
Sixto Escobar	PR	1938
Lou Salica	USA	1940
Manuel Ortiz	USA	1942
Harold Dade	USA	1947
Manuel Ortiz	USA	1947
Vic Toweel	SA	1950
Jimmy Carruthers	Aus	1952
Robert Cohen	Alg	1954
Alphonse Halimi	Alg	1957
Joe Becerra	Mex	1959
Eder Jofre	Bra	1962
Fighting Harada	Jap	1965
Lionel Rose	Aus	1968
Ruben Olivares	Mex	1969
Jesus Castillo	Mex	1970
Ruben Olivares	Mex	1971
Rafael Herrera	Mex	1972
Enrique Pinder	Pan	1972

WBC

Name	Country	Year
Rafael Herrera	Mex	1973
Rodolfo Martinez	Mex	1974
Carlos Zarate	Mex	1976
Lupe Pintor	Mex	1979
Albert Davila	USA	1983

Name	Country	Year
Daniel Zaragoza	Mex	1985
Miguel Lora	Col	1985
Raul Perez	Mex	1988

WBA

Name	Country	Year
Romeo Anaya	Mex	1973
Arnold Taylor	SA	1973
Soo-Hwan Hong	S. Kor	1974
Alfonso Zamora	Mex	1975
Jorge Lujan	Pan	1977
Julian Solis	PR	1980
Jeff Chandler	USA	1980
Richard Sandoval	USA	1984
Gaby Canizales	USA	1986
Bernardo Pinango	Ven	1986
Takuya Muguruma	Jap	1987
Chang-Yung Park	S. Kor	1987
Wilfredo Vasquez	PR	1987
Kaokar Galaxy	Tha	1988
Sung-Kil Moon	S. Kor	1988
Kaokar Galaxy	Tha	1989
Luisito Espinosa	Phi	1989

IBF

Name	Country	Year
Satoshi Shingaki	Jap	1984
Jeff Fenech	Aus	1985
Kelvin Seabrooks	USA	1987
Orlando Canizales	USA	1988

NBA

Name	Country	Year
Sixto Escobar	PR	1934
Lou Salica	USA	1935
Sixto Escobar	PR	1935
Georgie Pace	USA	1940
Raton Macias	Mex	1955
Eder Jofre	Bra	1960

NEW YORK STATE

Name	Country	Year
Abe Goldstein	USA	1923
Bud Taylor	USA	1927
Bushy Graham	Ita	1928
Baltazar Sangchilli	Spa	1935
Tony Marino	USA	1936
Robert Cohen	Alg	1955
Mario D'Agata	Ita	1956
Alphonse Halimi	Alg	1957

OTHER CLAIMANTS

Name	Country	Year
George Dixon	Can	1888
Tommy Kelly	USA	1888
Chappie Moran	GB	1889
Billy Plimmer	GB	1892
Jimmy Barry	USA	1894
Pedlar Palmer	GB	1895
Digger Stanley	GB	1904
Jimmy Walsh	USA	1904
Kid Murphy	USA	1907
Jimmy Walsh	USA	1908
Johnny Coulon	Can	1908
Monte Attell	USA	1908
Digger Stanley	GB	1909
Frankie Conley	Ita	1911
Charles Ledoux	Fra	1912
Eddie Campi	USA	1913
Johnny Ertle	Aut	1915

Dick Tiger of Nigeria falls to the canvas as his reign as world light-heavyweight champion comes to an end in 1968. For his conqueror, Bob Foster, it was the start of his six-year reign as the division's 'supremo' (AP)

Joe Burman	GB	1919	Rafael Orono	Ven	1982	Jiro Watanabe	Jap	1982
Teddy Baldock	GB	1927	Payao Poontarat	Tha	1983	Kaosai Galaxy	Tha	1984
Willie Smith	SA	1927	Jiro Watanabe	Jap	1984			
Pete Sanstol	Nor	1931	Gilberto Roman	Mex	1986	**IBF**		
Alphonse Halimi	Alg	1960	Santos Laciar	Arg	1987			
Johnny Caldwell	GB	1961	Jesus Rojas	Col	1987	Joo-Do Chun	S. Kor	1983
			Gilberto Roman	Mex	1988	Ellyas Pical	Ina	1985
			Nana Yaw Konadu	Gha	1989	Cesar Pelonco	Dom	1986
			Sung-Kil Moon	S. Kor	1990	Ellyas Pical	Ind	1986
						Tae-Il Chang	S. Kor	1987
						Ellyas Pical	Ina	1987
						Juan Polo Perez	Col	1989

JUNIOR-BANTAMWEIGHT/ SUPER-FLYWEIGHT

WBC

Rafael Orono	Ven	1980
Chul-Ho Kim	S. Kor	1981

WBA

Gustavo Ballas	Arg	1981
Rafael Pedroza	Pan	1981

WBC

Salvatore Burruni	Ita	1965
Walter McGowan	GB	1966
Chartchai Chionoi	Tha	1966
Efren Torres	Mex	1969
Chartchai Chionoi	Tha	1970
Erbito Salavarria	Phi	1970
Betulio Gonzalez	Ven	1972
Venice Borkorsor	Tha	1972
Betulio Gonzalez	Ven	1973
Shoji Oguma	Jap	1974
Miguel Canto	Mex	1975
Chan-Hee Park	S. Kor	1979
Shoji Oguma	Jap	1980
Antonio Avelar	Mex	1981
Prudencio Cardona	Col	1982
Freddie Castillo	Mex	1982
Eleonceo Mercedes	Dom	1982
Charlie Magri	Tun	1983
Frank Cedeno	Phi	1983
Koji Kobayashi	Jap	1984
Gabriel Bernal	Mex	1984
Sot Chitalada	Tha	1984
Yung-Kang Kim	S. Kor	1988
Sot Chitalada	Tha	1989

WBA

Horacio Accavallo	Arg	1966
Hiroyuki Ebihara	Jap	1969
Bernabe Villacampo	Phi	1969
Berkrerk Chartvanchai	Tha	1970
Masao Ohba	Jap	1970
Chartchai Chionoi	Tha	1973
Susumu Hanagata	Jap	1974
Erbito Salavarria	Phi	1975
Alfonso Lopez	Pan	1976
Gustavo Espadas	Mex	1976
Betulio Gonzalez	Ven	1978
Luis Ibarra	Pan	1979
Tae-Shik Kim	S. Kor	1980
Peter Mathebula	SA	1980
Santos Laciar	Arg	1981
Luis Ibarra	Pan	1981
Juan Herrera	Mex	1981
Santos Laciar	Arg	1982
Hilario Zapata	Pan	1986
Fidel Bassa	Col	1987
Jesus Rojas	Ven	1989

IBF

Soo-Chun Kwon	S. Kor	1983
Chung-Bi Won	S. Kor	1986
Hi-Sop Shin	S. Kor	1986
Dodie Penalosa	Phi	1987
Chang-Ho Choi	S. Kor	1987
Rolando Bohol	Phi	1988
Duke McKenzie	GB	1988
Dave McAuley	GB	1989

FLYWEIGHT

UNDISPUTED CHAMPIONS

Jimmy Wilde	GB	1916
Pancho Villa	Phi	1923
Fidel La Barba	USA	1925
Frankie Genaro	USA	1930
Benny Lynch	GB	1937
Peter Kane	GB	1938
Jackie Paterson	GB	1943
Rinty Monaghan	GB	1948
Terry Allen	GB	1950
Dado Marino	Haw	1950
Yoshio Shirai	Jap	1952
Pascual Perez	Arg	1954
Pone Kingpetch	Tha	1960
Fighting Harada	Jap	1962
Pone Kingpetch	Tha	1963
Hiroyuki Ebihara	Jap	1963
Pone Kingpetch	Tha	1964
Salvatore Burruni	Ita	1965

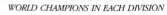

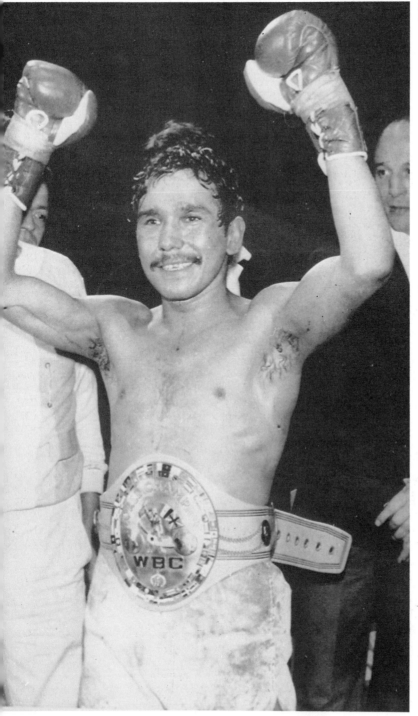

Jackie Brown	GB	1932
Benny Lynch	GB	1935
Valentin Angelmann	Fra	1937

JUNIOR-FLYWEIGHT/ LIGHT-FLYWEIGHT

WBC

Franco Udella	Ita	1975
Luis Estaba	Ven	1975
Freddie Castillo	Mex	1978
Netrnoi Vorasingh	Tha	1978
Sung-Jun Kim	S. Kor	1978
Shigeo Nakajima	Jap	1980
Hilario Zapata	Pan	1980
Amado Ursua	Mex	1982
Tadashi Tomori	Jap	1982
Hilario Zapata	Pan	1982
Chang-Jung Koo	S. Kor	1983
German Torres	Mex	1988
Yul-Woo Lee	S. Kor	1989
Humberto Gonzalez	Mex	1989

WBA

Jaime Rios	Pan	1975
Juan Guzman	Dom	1976
Yoko Gushiken	Jap	1976
Pedro Flores	Mex	1981
Hwan-Jin Kim	S. Kor	1981
Katsuo Tokashiki	Jap	1981
Lupe Madera	Mex	1983
Francisco Quiroz	Dom	1984
Joey Olivo	USA	1985
Myung-Woo Yuh	S. Kor	1985

IBF

Dodie Penalosa	Phi	1983
Chong-Hwan Choi	S. Kor	1986
Tacy Macalos	Phi	1988
Muangchai Kitikasem	Tha	1989

STRAWWEIGHT/ MINI-FLYWEIGHT

WBC

Hiroki Ioka	Jap	1988
Napa Kiatwanchai	Tha	1988
Jeum-Hwan Choi	S. Kor	1989
Hideyuki Ohashi	Jap	1990

WBA

| Leo Gamez | Dom | 1988 |
| Bong-Jun Kim | S. Kor | 1989 |

IBF

Kyung-Yun Lee	S. Kor	1987
Samuth Sithnaruepol	Tha	1988
Nico Thomas	Ina	1989
Eric Chavez	Phi	1989
Falan Lookmingkwan	Tha	1989

NBA

Albert Belanger	Can	1927
Frankie Genaro	USA	1928
Emile Pladner	Fra	1929
Frankie Genaro	USA	1929
Rinty Monaghan	GB	1947

NEW YORK STATE

Izzy Schwartz	USA	1927
Midget Wolgast	USA	1930
Small Montana	Phi	1935

OTHER CLAIMANTS

Sid Smith	GB	1913
Bill Ladbury	GB	1913
Percy Jones	GB	1914
Joe Symonds	GB	1914
Frankie Genaro	USA	1925
Johnny McCoy	USA	1927
Newsboy Brown	USSR	1928
Johnny Hill	GB	1928
Willie Le Morte	USA	1929
Young Perez	Tun	1931

Rocky Lockridge (right) on his way to beating Claude Capelle in the 1978 World Amateur Championships. Lockridge was beaten by the Yugoslav Sacirovic in the next round. Since turning professional in 1978 Lockridge has gone on to win the world junior-lightweight title (AP)

Since the formation of the World Boxing Organisation in 1988, the following have held WBO titles:

Heavyweight: 1989 Francesco Damiani (Ita)
Junior-heavyweight: 1989 Richard Pultz (USA)
Light-heavyweight: 1988 Michael Moorer (USA)
Super-middleweight: 1988 Thomas Hearns (USA)
Middleweight: 1989 Doug De Witt (USA)
Junior-middleweight: 1988 John David Jackson (USA)

Welterweight: 1989 Genaro Leon (Mex)
1989 Manning Galloway
Junior-welterweight: 1989 Hector Camacho (PR)
Lightweight: 1989 Amancio Castro (Col)
1989 Mauricio Aceves (Mex)
Junior-lightweight: 1989 Juan Molina (PR)
1989 Kamel Bou Ali
Featherweight: 1989 Maurizio Stecca (Ita)
1989 Louie Espinoza (USA)
Junior-featherweight: 1989 Kenny Mitchell (USA)
1989 Valerio Nati

Bantamweight: 1989 Israel Contreras (Ven)
Junior-bantamweight: 1989 Jose Ruiz (PR)
Flyweight: 1989 Elvis Alvarez (Col)
Junior-flyweight: 1989 Jose De Jesus (PR)
Mini-flyweight: 1989 Rafael Torres (Dom)

The first WBO champion was Thomas Hearns who beat James Kinchen in Las Vegas on 4 November 1988 to win the super-middleweight title. The first WBO title to change hands was the lightweight title.

BOXING NATIONS

7

Their first champions and world title fights

(First champions are fighters *born* in the country concerned. The first world title fight is the first fight in that particular country. Where there is no nationality after a fighter's name, it indicates he was from the country named.)

ALGERIA

First World Champion: Marcel Cerdan (1948)
First World Title Fight: None

ANTIGUA

First World Champion: Maurice Hope (1979)
First World Title Fight: None

ARGENTINA

First World Champion: Pascual Perez (1954)
First World Title Fight: 11 Jan 1956 *Fl* Pascual Perez v Leo Espinosa (Phi)

AUSTRALIA

First World Champion: Young Griffo (1890)
First World Title Fight: 3 Sep 1890 *Fe* Young Griffo v Billy Murphy (NZ)

AUSTRIA

First World Champion: Jack Root (1903)
First World Title Fight: None

BAHAMAS

First World Champion: Elisha Obed (1975)
First World Title Fight: 28 Feb 1976 *LM (WBC)* Elisha Obed v Tony Gardner (USA)

BARBADOS

First World Champion: Joe Walcott (1901)
First World Title Fight: None

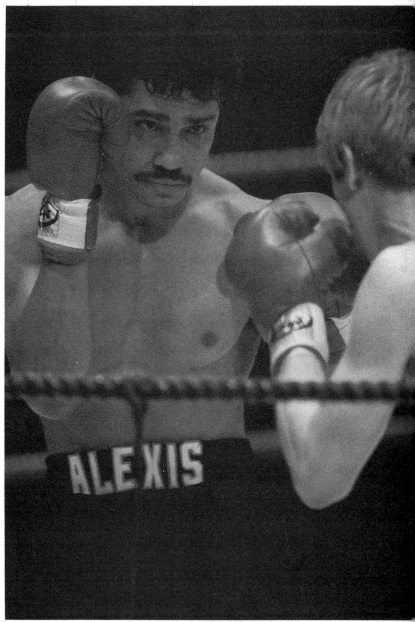

Alexis Arguello of Nicaragua relinquished his WBC super-featherweight title in October 1980 to concentrate on the lightweight division. Eight months later he deposed Jim Watt as champion with a 15-round points win at Wembley (All Sport/Steve Powell)

BELGIUM

First World Champion: None
First World Title Fight: 3 Jun 1989 *Fe*
(WBA) Antonio Esparagoza (Ven) v
Jean-Marc Renard

BRAZIL

First World Champion: Eder Jofre
(1960)
First World Title Fight: 25 Mar 1961 *B*
(NBA) Eder Jofre v Piero Rollo (Ita)

CANADA

First World Champion: George
LaBlanche (1889)
First World Title Fight: 24 Mar 1901 *W*
Rube Ferns (USA) v Matty Matthews
(USA)

CHILE

First World Champion: None
First World Title Fight: 30 Nov 1977 *Fl*
(WBC) Miguel Canto (Mex) v Martin
Vargas

COLOMBIA

First World Champion: Antonio
Cervantes (1972)
First World Title Fight: 27 Nov 1964 *B*
Eder Jofre (Bra) v Bernardo Carabello

COSTA RICA

First World Champion: None
First World Title Fight: 29 Jan 1972 *JL*
(WBC) Ricardo Arredondo (Mex) v
Jose Marin

CUBA

First World Champion: Kid Chocolate
(1931)
First World Title Fight: 5 Apr 1915 *H*
Jess Willard (USA) v Jack Johnson
(USA)

DENMARK

First World Champion: Battling Nelson
(1908)
First World Title Fight: 19 Aug 1972 *M*
Carlos Monzon (Arg) v Tom Bogs

DOMINICAN REPUBLIC

First World Champion: Carlos Cruz
(1968)
First World Title Fight: 29 Jun 1968 *L*
Carlos Cruz v Carlos Ortiz (PR)

DUTCH WEST INDIES

First World Champion: None
First World Title Fight: 4 May 1985 *B*
(WBC) Daniel Zaragoza (USA) v
Freddie Jackson (USA)

ECUADOR

First World Champion: None
First World Title Fight: 15 Jan 1977 *JL*
(WBA) Sam Serrano (PR) v Alberto
Herrera

FINLAND

First World Champion: None
First World Title Fight: 17 Aug 1962 *Fe*
Davey Moore (USA) v Olli Makim

FRANCE

First World Champion: Georges
Carpentier (1920)
First World Title Fight: 18 Apr 1908 *H*
Tommy Burns (Can) v Jewey Smith
(GB)

GERMANY

First World Champion: Max Schmeling
(1930)
First World Title Fight: 23 Jun 1962 *LH*
Harold Johnson (USA) v Gustav Scholz

GHANA

First World Champion: David Khotey
(1975)
First World Title Fight: 9 May 1964 *Fe*
Sugar Ramos (Cuba) v Floyd Robertson

GREECE

First World Champion: Anton
Christoforidis (1941)
First World Title Fight: None

GUYANA

First World Champion: Dennis Andries
(1986)
First World Title Fight: None

HAWAII

First World Champion: Dado Marino
(1950)
First World Title Fight: 30 May 1947 *B*
Manuel Ortiz (USA) v David Kui Kong
Young

HUNGARY

First World Champion: None
First World Title Fight: 18 Feb 1989 *W*
(IBF) Simon Brown (USA) v Jorge
Maysonet (PR)

INDONESIA

First World Champion: Ellyas Pical
(1985)
First World Title Fight: 29 Aug 1981 *LW*
(WBC) Saoul Mamby (Jam) v Thomas
Americo

IRELAND, REPUBLIC

First World Champion: Jack 'Nonpareil'
Dempsey (1884)
First World Title Fight: 17 Mar 1908 *H*
Tommy Burns (Can) v Jem Roche

ITALY

First World Champion: Johnny Dundee
(1921)
First World Title Fight: 18 Mar 1933 *B*
Panama Al Brown (Pan) v Dom
Bernasconi

IVORY COAST

First World Champion: None
First World Title Fight: 24 Apr 1976 *LM*
(WBC) Elisha Obed (Bah) v Sea
Robinson

JAMAICA

First World Champion: Saoul Mamby
(1980)
First World Title Fight: 19 Apr 1964 *LW*
Eddie Perkins (USA) v Bunny Grant

JAPAN

First World Champion: Yoshio Shirai
(1952)
First World Title Fight: 19 May 1952 *Fl*
Yoshio Shirai v Dado Marino (Haw)

KUWAIT

First World Champion: None
First World Title Fight: 22 Feb 1986 *Fl*
(WBC) Sot Chitalada (Tha) v Freddie
Castillo (Mex)

MALAYSIA

First World Champion: None
First World Title Fight: 1 Jul 1975 *H*
Muhammad Ali (USA) v Joe Bugner
(GB)

MEXICO

First World Champion: Battling Shaw
(1933)
First World Title Fight: 1 Mar 1931 *W*
Tommy Freeman (USA) v Alfredo
Gaona

MONACO

First World Champion: None
First World Title Fight: 8 May 1971 *M*
Carlos Monzon (Arg) v Nino Benvenuti
(Ita)

MOROCCO

First World Champion: None
First World Title Fight: 25 Mar 1989 *C*
(WBA) Toufik Belbouli (Fra) v Michael
Greer (USA)

NEW GUINEA

First World Champion: None
First World Title Fight: 17 Nov 1979 *Fe*
(WBA) Eusebio Pedroza (Pan) v
Johnny Aba

England's only world heavyweight champion, the Cornishman Bob Fitzsimmons (ET Archive)

First World Title Fight: 12 Dec 1975 *JL (WBC)* Alfredo Escalera (PR) v Svein-Erik Paulsen

PANAMA

First World Champion: Panama Al Brown (1929)
First World Title Fight: 10 Apr 1965 *L* Ismael Laguna v Carlos Ortiz (PR)

PHILIPPINES

First World Champion: Pancho Villa (1923)
First World Title Fight: 23 Dec 1939 *M (NY)* Ceferino Garcia v Glen Lee (USA)

PUERTO RICO

First World Champion: Sixto Escobar (1934)
First World Title Fight: 21 Feb 1937 *B* Sixto Escobar v Lou Salica (USA)

ST. VINCENT

First World Champion: None
First World Title Fight: 22 Oct 1983 *Fe (WBA)* Eusebio Pedroza (Pan) v Jose Caba (Dom)

SENEGAL

First World Champion: Battling Siki (1922)
First World Title Fight: None

SINGAPORE

First World Champion: None
First World Title Fight: 25 Feb 1989 *SF (IBF)* Ellyas Pical (Ina) v Mike Phelps (USA)

SOUTH AFRICA

First World Champion: Vic Toweel (1950)
First World Title Fight: 4 Sep 1937 *Fe (NBA)* Petey Sarron (USA) v Freddie Miller (USA)

SOUTH KOREA

First World Champion: Ki-Soo Kim (1966)
First World Title Fight: 25 Jun 1966 *LM* Ki-Soo Kim v Nino Benvenuti (Ita)

SPAIN

First World Champion: Baltazar Sangchilli (1935)
First World Title Fight: 7 Jul 1928 *W* Joe Dundee (Ita) v Hilario Martinez

NEW ZEALAND

First World Champion: Billy Murphy (1890)
First World Title Fight: None

NICARAGUA

First World Champion: Alexis Arguello (1974)
First World Title Fight: 31 May 1975 *Fe (WBA)* Alexis Arguello v Rigoberto Riasco (Pan)

NIGERIA

First World Champion: Hogan 'Kid' Bassey (1957)
First World Title Fight: 10 Aug 1963 *M* Dick Tiger v Gene Fullmer (USA)

NORWAY

First World Champion: None

A large crowd flocked to the Oriental Race Track in Havana, Cuba in 1915, to see yet another 'Great White Hope' take on the unpopular coloured world heavyweight champion, Jack Johnson. This time the dreams of many were fulfilled when the giant Jess Willard took the title with a 26th-round knock-out (Hulton)

SWEDEN

First World Champion: Ingemar Johansson (1959)
First World Title Fight: 14 Sep 1968 *H (WBA)* Jimmy Ellis (USA) v Floyd Patterson (USA)

SWITZERLAND

First World Champion: Frank Erne (1899)
First World Title Fight: 27 Apr 1974 *Fl (WBA)* Chartchai Chionoi (Tha) v Fritz Chervet

THAILAND

First World Champion: Pone Kingpetch (1960)
First World Title Fight: 2 May 1954 *B* Jimmy Carruthers (Aus) v Chamrern Songkitrat

TRINIDAD

First World Champion: Claude Noel (1979)
First World Title Fight: 23 May 1987 *LH (WBA)* Leslie Stewart v Marvin Johnson (USA)

TUNISIA

First World Champion: Young Perez (1931)

First World Title Fight: None

UGANDA

First World Champion: Ayub Kalule (1979)
First World Title Fight: None

UNITED KINGDOM

First World Champion: Ike Weir (1889)
First World Title Fight:
England: 27 Jun 1890 *B* George Dixon (Can) v Nunc Wallace
Scotland: 16 Sep 1936 *Fl (IBU)* Benny Lynch v Pat Palmer
Wales: 4 Sep 1946 *L (NBA)* Ike Williams (USA) v Ronnie James
N. Ireland: 23 Mar 1948 *Fl* Rinty Monaghan v Jackie Paterson

UNITED STATES

First World Champion: Paddy Duffy (1888)
First World Title Fight: 30 Jul 1884 *M* Jack Dempsey (Ire) v George Fulljames

URUGUAY

First World Champion: None
First World Title Fight: 30 Jun 1956 *Fl* Pascual Perez (Arg) v Oscar Suarez (Cuba)

USSR

First World Champion: Louis 'Kid' Kaplan (1925)
First World Title Fight: None

VENEZUELA

First World Champion: Carlos Hernandez (1965)
First World Title Fight: 19 Apr 1958 *Fl* Pascual Perez (Arg) v Ramon Arias

VIRGIN ISLANDS

First World Champion: Emile Griffith (1961)
First World Title Fight: None

YUGOSLAVIA

First World Champion: Mate Parlov (1978)
First World Title Fight: 23 May 1970 *M* Nino Benvenuti (Ita) v Tom Bethea (USA)

ZAIRE

First World Champion: Sumbu Kalambay (1987)
First World Title Fight: 30 Oct 1974 *H* Muhammad Ali (USA) v George Foreman (USA)

RECORDS
AND
STATISTICS

The first generally recognised world title bout under Queensberry Rules was on 30 July 1884 and was a middleweight bout, at Great Kills, New York, between Jack Dempsey (Ire) and George Fulljames (USA).

The first black world heavyweight champion was Jack Johnson (USA) who won the title from Tommy Burns (Can) in 1908.

The first all-negro world heavyweight title bout was between Jack Johnson (USA) and Jim Johnson (USA) on 19 December 1913.

The first man to win world titles in two weight divisions was George Dixon (Can) who won the bantamweight title in 1890 and the featherweight title in 1891.

The first man to win world titles at three different weights was Bob Fitzsimmons who won the middleweight title in 1891, the heavyweight in 1897 and the light-heavyweight in 1903.

The first man to regain a world title was Mysterious Billy Smith (USA) who regained the welterweight title on 25 August 1898, five and a half years after first winning the title.

The first former champion to referee a world heavyweight title fight was James J. Jeffries on 3 July 1905 when he took charge of the Marvin Hart (USA)–Jack Root (Aut) bout.

The first referee to officiate inside the ring in England was Eugene Corri (Eng), when he controlled the world heavyweight title fight between Tommy Burns (Can) and Gunner Moir (GB) at the National Sporting Club, London, on 2 December 1907. This was also the first world heavyweight title fight to be held in England.

Boxing's first million-dollar gate was for the Jack Dempsey v Georges Carpentier world heavyweight title fight at Jersey City, USA, on 2 July 1921 (Mary Evans)

The first black world champion was George Dixon of Canada. He beat Nunc Wallace (GB) to win the bantamweight title in 1890.

The first southpaw world champion was Al McCoy (USA), middleweight champion in 1914.

The first million-dollar gate was on 2 July 1921, when 80 183 people paid $1 789 238 to watch the world heavyweight contest between Jack Dempsey (USA) and Georges Carpentier (Fra) in Jersey City, USA.

The first 100 000 crowd was on 23 September 1926 when 120 757 witnessed the Gene Tunney (USA)–Jack Dempsey (USA) world heavyweight contest at the Sesquicentennial Stadium Philadelphia, USA.

The first radio broadcast of a world

title fight in it entirety was of the Jack Dempsey (USA) v Georges Carpentier (Fra) heavyweight bout on 2 July 1921.

The first world title fight to be televised was the Willie Pep (USA)–Chalky Wright (Mex) featherweight contest from New York on 29 September 1944.

The first heavyweight title fight to be televised was the Joe Louis (USA)–Jersey Joe Walcott (USA) bout from New York on 5 December 1947.

The first world title fight to be broadcast in colour was the Emile Griffith (VI)–Manuel Gonzales (USA) welterweight fight from New York on 10 December 1965.

The first world championship fight to be televised from a country other than the United States was the Kid Gavilan (Cuba)–Billy Graham (USA) welterweight bout in Havana, Cuba on 5 October 1952.

The first live televising of a world title fight weigh-in took place on 30 May 1951 when Ezzard Charles (USA) and Joey Maxim (USA) weighed-in for their world heavyweight contest.

The first referee to be replaced during a world title fight was Ruby Goldstein. While refereeing the Ray Robinson (USA)–Joey Maxim (USA) light-heavyweight bout on 25 June 1952 he was overcome by the intense heat and had to be replaced by Ray Miller at the end of the 12th round. Robinson retired two rounds later, also suffering from the excessive heat.

The first stadium to be named after a former world champion was the Escobar Stadium in San Juan, Puerto Rico (opened 1955). It was named after Sixto Escobar, the 1934–9 world bantamweight champion.

The first occasion the same two men engaged in three successive world heavyweight title fights was between 26 June 1959 and 13 March 1961 when Floyd Patterson (USA) and Ingemar Johansson (Swe) engaged in three successive bouts, the American winning two fights to one.

The first time two titles changed hands on the same night was on 21 March 1963 when Luis Rodriguez (Cuba) defeated Emile Griffith (VI) to take the welterweight crown and Sugar Ramos (Cuba) beat Davey Moore (USA) to win the featherweight title.

The first time a four-roped ring was used for a world title fight was at Madison Square Garden, New York, on 8 June 1963 for the Emile Griffith (VI)–Luis Rodriguez (Cuba) welterweight fight. Prior to this either two or three-roped rings were used.

The first WBC title fight was on 2 December 1965. Salvatore Burruni (Ita) knocked out Rocky Gattelleri (Ita) in a flyweight bout in Sydney.

The first WBA title fight was on 5 March 1965. Heavyweight Ernie Terrell (USA) defeated Eddie Machen (USA) on points in Chicago.

The first IBF title fight was on 21 May 1983. Marvin Camel (USA) knocked out Rocky Sekorski (USA) in the 9th round of their cruiserweight fight in Billings, USA.

The first fighter from a communist country to win a world title was Mate Parlov (Yug) who won the world light-heavyweight title in 1978. Benny Bass and 'Kid' Kaplan, world title holders in the 1920s, were both born in Russia but were domiciled in the United States at the time of winning their titles.

The first world title fight to be held in a communist country was the middleweight contest between Nino Benvenuti (Ita) and Tom Bethea (USA) at Umag, Yugoslavia, on 23 May 1970.

The first woman judge to be used in a world heavyweight title fight was Eva Shain who officiated at the Muhammad Ali (USA)–Earnie Shavers (USA) contest on 29 September 1977.

The first time both champion and challenger entered the ring undefeated for a world title fight was on 15 November 1952 in Johannesburg, when the defending champion Vic Toweel (SA) met Jimmy Carruthers (Aus) for the bantamweight title. Carruthers' record remained intact as he won in the 1st round.

New WBC rules in 1987 stated that if a fighter is stopped as a result of cuts then the man ahead on points at the end of the previous round shall be declared the winner. **The first fighter to win a world title under this rule** after being stopped was Jorge Vaca of Mexico who took Lloyd Honeyghan's welterweight title off him on 28 October 1987.

When Kaokar Galaxy (Tha) gained a split decision over Wilfredo Vasquez (PR) to win the WBA bantamweight title in 1989 it created boxing history because his identical twin, Kaosai, was the reigning WBA junior-bantamweight champion at the time. It was **the first time twins had held world titles**.

All three judges for the Juan Martin Coggi (Arg)–Akinobu Hiranaka (Jap) WBA junior-welterweight contest on 29 April 1989 were women. It was **the first time all three judges at a world title fight had been women**.

Archie Moore weighing in for one of his 200-plus professional fights. He is credited with 145 knockouts, more than any other man in professional boxing (Hulton)

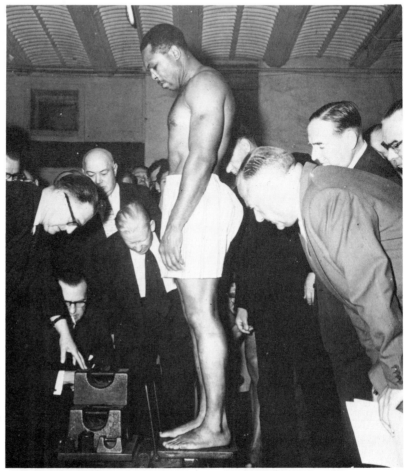

MOST WORLD TITLES

5 Sugar Ray Leonard

WBC Welterweight 1979
WBA Junior-middleweight 1981
WBC Middleweight 1987
WBC Super-middleweight 1988
WBC Light-heavyweight 1988

4 Thomas Hearns

WBA Welterweight 1980
WBC Junior-middleweight 1982
WBC Light-heavyweight 1987
WBC Middleweight 1987

Hearns won a fifth title in 1988 when he won the WBO super-middleweight crown

4 Roberto Duran

WBA Lightweight 1972
WBC Welterweight 1980
WBA Junior-middleweight 1983
WBC Middleweight 1989

3 Bob Fitzsimmons

Middleweight 1891
Heavyweight 1897
Light-heavyweight 1903

3 Tony Canzoneri

NY Featherweight 1927
Lightweight 1930
Junior-welterweight 1931

3 Barney Ross

Lightweight 1933
Junior-welterweight 1933
Welterweight 1934

3 Henry Armstrong

Featherweight 1937
Welterweight 1938
Lightweight 1938

3 Alexis Arguello

WBA Featherweight 1974
WBC Junior-lightweight 1978
WBC Lightweight 1981

3 Wilfredo Gomez

WBC Junior-featherweight 1977
WBC Featherweight 1984
WBA Junior-lightweight 1985

3 Julio Cesar Chavez

WBC Junior-lightweight 1984
WBA Lightweight 1987
WBC Junior-welterweight 1989

3 Jeff Fenech

IBF Bantamweight 1985
WBC Junior-featherweight 1987

WBC Featherweight 1988

Emile Griffith won the welterweight title in 1961 and the middleweight title in 1966. He also claimed to be the first junior-middleweight champion in 1962 but his title was recognised in Australia only.

MOST WORLD TITLE FIGHTS

27 Joe Louis
26 Henry Armstrong
25 Muhammad Ali
24 Larry Holmes
23 Wilfredo Gomez, Manuel Ortiz, Hilario Zapata
22 Alexis Arguello, Tony Canzoneri, George Dixon, Emile Griffith, Eusebio Pedroza, Sugar Ray Robinson
21 Antonio Cervantes, Roberto Duran
18 Miguel Canto, Jose Napoles, Carlos Ortiz, Sam Serrano, Jung-Koo Chang
17 Betulio Gonzalez
16 Bob Foster, Santos Laciar
15 Julio Cesar Chavez, Flash Elorde, Yoko Gushiken, Marvin Hagler, Thomas Hearns, Carlos Monzon, Gilberto Roman, Michael Spinks, Myung-Woo Yuh

MOST WORLD TITLE FIGHT WINS

26 Joe Louis
22 Muhammad Ali, Henry Armstrong
21 Larry Holmes, Manuel Ortiz
20 Wilfredo Gomez
19 Alexis Arguello, Eusebio Pedroza
18 Antonio Cervantes, George Dixon, Hilario Zapata
16 Jung-Koo Chang, Roberto Duran
15 Miguel Canto, Julio Cesar Chavez, Carlos Monzon, Jose Napoles, Sam Serrano, Myung-Woo Yuh
14 Bob Foster, Emile Griffith, Yoko Gushiken, Carlos Ortiz, Sugar Ray Robinson, Michael Spinks
13 Kaosai Galaxy, Marvin Hagler, Azumah Nelson
12 Joe Brown, Tony Canzoneri, Pipino Cuevas, Luis Estaba, Victor Galindez, Santos Laciar, Gilberto Roman, Jiro Watanabe
11 Panama Al Brown, Tommy Burns, Carlos De Leon, Flash Elorde, Jeff Fenech, Thomas Hearns, Eder Jofre, Willie Pep, Aaron Pryor, Barney Ross
10 Bruno Acari, Abe Attell, Jeff Chandler, Alfredo Escalera, Joe Frazier, Joe Gans, Sugar Ray Leonard, Freddie Miller, Brian Mitchell, Saensak Muangsurin, Chong-Pal Park, Salvador Sanchez, Mike Tyson, Carlos Zarate

Between 9–30 October 1939 Henry Armstrong engaged in five world title fights and won them all.

YOUNGEST WORLD CHAMPIONS

The following all won world titles before their 20th birthday:

17 years 176 days Wilfred Benitez (junior-welterweight)
18 years 203 days Pipino Cuevas (welterweight)
18 years 284 days Hiroki Ioka (strawweight)
18 years 352 days Tony Canzoneri (featherweight)
19 years 15 days Netrnoi Vorasingh (junior-flyweight)
19 years 79 days Cesar Polanco (junior-bantamweight)
19 years 95 days Jimmy Walsh (bantamweight)
19 years 167 days Al McCoy (middleweight)
19 years 167 days Ben Villaflor (junior-lightweight)
19 years 188 days Terry McGovern (bantamweight)
19 years 190 days Fighting Harada (flyweight)
19 years 247 days Midget Wolgast (flyweight)
19 years 251 days Lionel Rose (bantamweight)
19 years 320 days Joo-Do Chun (junior-bantamweight)
19 years 326 days Chul-Ho Kim (junior-bantamweight)
19 years 326 days Fidel La Barba (flyweight)
19 years 334 days George Dixon (bantamweight)
19 years 337 days Lester Ellis (junior-lightweight)
19 years 345 days Abe Attell (featherweight)

The youngest world heavyweight champion is Mike Tyson. He was 20 years 144 days when he won the WBC title in 1986.

OLDEST WORLD CHAMPIONS

The following all won their **first** world title over the age of 33:

39 years 4 days* Archie Moore (light-heavyweight)
37 years 168 days Jersey Joe Walcott (heavyweight)
35 years 144 days Fulgencio Obelmejias (super-middleweight)
34 years 236 days Johnny Thompson (middleweight)
34 years 105 days Toufik Belbouli (cruiserweight)
34 years 31 days Luis Estaba (junior-flyweight)
33 years 340 days Dado Marino (flyweight)
33 years 233 days Trevor Berbick (heavyweight)

33 years 144 days Joey Giardello
(middleweight)
33 years 103 days Johnny Buff
(bantamweight)
33 years 97 days Jess Willard
(heavyweight)
33 years 94 days Buster Drayton
(junior-middleweight)
33 years 70 days Dick Tiger
(middleweight)
33 years 50 days Claude Noel
(lightweight)

* Moore might have been 36 years 4
days when he first won the light-
heavyweight title; it has never been
established whether he was born in
1913 or 1916. He is, however,
undisputedly the oldest person to have
held a world title. He was either 48
years 59 days, or 45 years 59 days
when he relinquished his light-
heavyweight title in 1962. No matter
which date is correct both would still
make him the **oldest ever world
champion**.

Bob Fitzsimmons was 27 when he won
the world middleweight title in 1891.
He was 33 when he won the
heavyweight title and when he won the
light-heavyweight title in 1903 he was
40 years 183 days old which makes
him the **oldest person to win a world
title**.

LONGEST REIGNING CHAMPIONS

(longest continuous reigns)

11 years 252 days Joe Louis,
heavyweight, 22 Jun 1937–1 Mar 1949
11 years 103 days Johnny Kilbane,
featherweight, 22 Feb 1912–2 Jun 1923
9 years 285 days Tommy Ryan,
middleweight, 24 Oct 1898–5 Aug 1907
9 years 55 days Archie Moore, light-
heavyweight, 17 Dec 1952–10 Feb 1962
7 years 262 days Benny Leonard,
lightweight, 27 May 1917–15 Jan 1925
7 years 125 days Jimmy Wilde,
flyweight, 14 Feb 1916–18 Jun 1923
7 years 104 days Larry Holmes,
heavyweight, 9 Jun 1978–21 Sep 1985
7 years 91 days Flash Elorde, junior-
ightweight, 16 Mar 1960–15 Jun 1967

SHORTEST REIGNING CHAMPIONS

(excluding fighters who promptly
announced their retirement after
winning a title)

33 days Tony Canzoneri, lightweight,
21 May–23 Jun 1933
46 days Dave Sullivan, featherweight,
26 Sep–11 Nov 1898
45 days Royal Kobayashi, super-
bantamweight, 10 Oct–24 Nov 1976
47 days Emile Pladner, flyweight, 2

Mar–18 Apr 1929

*The shortest reigning heavyweight
champion was Tony Tucker who held
the IBF title for just 64 days between 30
May–2 Aug 1987.*

HEAVIEST WORLD CHAMPIONS

(all heavyweight)

270lb Primo Carnera, 1 Mar 1934
240lb John Tate, 20 Oct 1979
239½lb Greg Page, 29 Apr 1984
238lb Tony Tubbs, 20 Mar 1988
235lb Tim Witherspoon, 20 Jul 1986
232lb Mike Weaver, 31 Mar 1980
230lb Jess Willard, 5 Apr 1915
230lb Muhammad Ali, 30 Apr 1976
230lb James Douglas, 11 Feb 1990

*The heaviest unsuccessful challenger
was Abe Simon who weighed 255½lb
when he fought Joe Louis in 1942.*

*The greatest weight difference in a
world title fight was 86lb between
Primo Carnera (270lb) and Tommy
Loughran (184lb) when they fought on
1 March 1934 for the heavyweight title.*

*The greatest combined weight in a
world heavyweight title fight is 488¾lb
when Primo Carnera (259½lb) and
Paolino Uzcudin (229¼lb) met on 22
October 1933.*

TALLEST WORLD CHAMPIONS

(all heavyweights)

6ft 6in Ernie Terrell
6ft 5¼in Primo Carnera[1]
6ft 5¼in Jess Willard[2]
6ft 5in Tony Tucker
6ft 4in James Smith
6ft 4in John Tate
6ft 4in James Douglas
6ft 3½in Larry Holmes

The following all measured 6ft 3in:
Muhammad Ali, George Foreman, Ken
Norton, Michael Dokes, Greg Page,Tim
Witherspoon, Pinklon Thomas

[1] *Some reports state that Carnera claimed to be
6ft 8½in*
[2] *Willard is often quoted as being 6ft 6¼in*

LIGHTEST AND SHORTEST WORLD CHAMPIONS

With the lightest weight division
getting lighter all the time it is virtually
impossible to keep accurate records as
to the lightest and shortest champions.

Former flyweight champion Jimmy
Wilde never weighed above 96lb and
was regarded as the lightest champion.
He would certainly have been eligible
for the current strawweight division

which has an upper limit of 105lb. The
lightest world heavyweight champion
was Bob Fitzsimmons who weighed
167lb. The shortest world champion is
believed to be Netrnoi Vorasingh who
won the WBC light-flyweight in 1978.
He was 4ft 11in tall. The only other two
champions known to have been under
5ft are Pascual Perez (4ft 11½in) and
Johnny Coulon (4ft 11¾in). The
shortest world heavyweight champion,
at 5ft 7in, was Tommy Burns.

WORLD TITLE FIGHTS THAT ENDED IN ROUND ONE

12 Sep 1899 *B* Terry McGovern (USA)
beat Pedlar Palmer (GB)
12 May 1902 *L* Joe Gans (USA) beat
Frank Erne (Swi)*
4 Jul 1907 *H* Tommy Burns (Can)*
beat Bill Squires (Aus)
22 Feb 1908 *M* Stanley Ketchel (USA)*
beat Mike 'Twin' Sullivan (USA)
17 Mar 1908 *H* Tommy Burns (Can)*
beat Jem Roche (Ire)
7 Apr 1914 *M* Al McCoy (USA) beat
George Chip (USA)*
31 Aug 1917 *W* Ted 'Kid' Lewis (GB)*
beat Albert Badoud (Swe)
11 May 1922 *LH* Georges Carpentier
(Fra)* beat Ted 'Kid' Lewis (GB)
2 Mar 1929 *Fl (NBA)* Emile Pladner
(Fra) beat Frankie Genaro (USA)*
17 Jul 1930 *L* Al Singer (USA) beat
Sammy Mandell (USA)*
14 Nov 1930 *L* Tony Canzoneri (USA)
beat Al Singer (USA)*
19 Sep 1932 *B* Al Brown (Pan)* beat
Emile Pladner (Fra)
29 May 1933 *W* Jimmy McLarnin (GB)
beat Young Corbett III (Ita)*
17 Feb 1935 *Fe (NBA)* Freddie Miller
(USA)* beat Jose Girones (Spa)
13 Oct 1936 *B* Sixto Escobar (PR)*
beat Carlos Quintana (Pan)
22 Jun 1938 *H* Joe Louis (USA)* beat
Max Schmeling (Ger)
26 Jul 1938 *M (NBA)* Al Hostak (USA)
beat Freddie Steele (USA)*
25 Jan 1939 *H* Joe Louis (USA)* beat
John Henry Lewis (USA)
16 Mar 1939 *W* Henry Armstrong
(USA)* beat Lew Feldman (USA)
17 Apr 1939 *H* Joe Louis (USA)* beat
Jack Roper (USA)
11 Dec 1939 *M (NBA)* Al Hostak
(USA)* beat Eric Seelig (Ger)
9 Jan 1942 *H* Joe Louis (USA)* beat
Buddy Baer (USA)
19 Jun 1943 *Fl* Jackie Paterson (GB)
beat Peter Kane (GB)*
18 Sep 1946 *H* Joe Louis (USA)* beat
Tami Mauriello (USA)
5 Mar 1948 *LH* Gus Lesnevich (USA)
beat Billy Fox (USA)
15 Nov 1952 *B* Jimmy Carruthers

Jersey Joe Walcott, the heavyweight division's oldest champion. He was 38 years 235 days when he eventually lost his title

(Ven)* beat Piero del Papa (Ita)
7 May 1972 *LM* Koichi Wajima (Jap)* beat Domenico Tiberia (Ita)
1 Sep 1973 *H* George Foreman (USA)* beat Joe Roman (PR)
17 Oct 1973 *JL (WBA)* Ben Villaflor (Phi) beat Kuniaki Shibata (Jap)*
21 Dec 1974 *L (WBA)* Roberto Duran (Pan)* beat Mastaka Takayama (Jap)
15 Oct 1976 *L (WBA)* Roberto Duran (Pan)* beat Alvaro Rojas (CR)
3 Jun 1978 *JL (WBC)* Alexis Arguello (Nic)* beat Diego Alcala (Pan)
7 Mar 1982 *M* Marvin Hagler (USA)* beat William 'Caveman' Lee (USA)
20 Mar 1982 *Fl (WBC)* Prudencio Cardona (Col) beat Antonio Avelar (Mex)*
8 May 1982 *L (WBA)* Ray Mancini (USA) beat Arturo Frias (USA)*
10 Dec 1982 *H* Mike Dokes (USA) beat Mike Weaver (USA)*
16 Jul 1983 *Fl (WBA)* Santos Laciar (Arg)* beat Shin-Hi Sop (S. Kor)
19 Aug 1983 *JL (WBA)* Roger Mayweather (USA)* beat Ben Villablanca (Chi)
12 Sep 1983 *W (WBA)* Don Curry (USA)* beat Roger Stafford (USA)
25 Nov 1983 *H (WBC)* Larry Holmes (USA)* beat Marvis Frazier (USA)
25 Feb 1984 *JL (WBA)* Rocky Lockridge (USA) beat Roger Mayweather (USA)*
17 Mar 1984 *L (WBC)* Edwin Rosario (PR)* beat Roberto Elizondo (USA)
17 Mar 1984 *SF (IBF)* Joo-Du Chun (S. Kor)* beat Diego de Villa (Phi)
3 Nov 1984 *SB (WBC)* Juan 'Kid' Meza (Mex) beat Jaime Garza (USA)*
8 Oct 1985 *SB (IBF)* Chi-Wan Kim (S. Kor)* beat Song-In Suh (S. Kor)
12 Oct 1985 *Fe (WBC)* Azumah Nelson (Gha)* beat Pat Cowdell (GB)
24 Jul 1986 *LW (WBC)* Tsuyoshi Hamada (Jap) beat Rene Arredondo (Mex)*
12 Dec 1986 *H (WBA)* James Smith (USA) beat Tim Witherspoon (USA)*
26 Dec 1986 *LH (IBF)* Bobby Czyz (USA)* beat David Sears (USA)
1 Mar 1987 *LF (WBA)* Myung-Woo Yuh (S. Kor)* beat Eduardo Tunon (Pan)
30 Aug 1987 *W (WBC/IBF)* Lloyd Honeyghan (Jam)* beat Gene Hatcher (USA)
27 Jun 1988 *H* Mike Tyson (USA)* beat Michael Spinks (USA)
31 Jul 1988 *LW (IBF)* James 'Buddy' McGirt (USA)* beat Howard Davis (USA)

(Aus) beat Vic Toweel (SA)*
15 May 1953 *H* Rocky Marciano (USA)* beat Jersey Joe Walcott (USA)
30 Mar 1957 *Fl* Pascual Perez (Arg)* beat Dai Dower (GB)
17 Aug 1960 *JL* Flash Elorde (Phi)* beat Harold Gomes (USA)
8 Apr 1961 *Fe* Davey Moore (USA)* beat Danny Valdez (USA)
16 Dec 1961 *JL* Flash Elorde (Phi)* beat Sergio Caprari (Ita)
25 Sep 1962 *H* Sonny Liston (USA) beat Floyd Patterson (USA)*
21 Mar 1963 *LW* Roberto Cruz (Phi)

beat Battling Torres (Mex)
22 Jul 1963 *H* Sonny Liston (USA)* beat Floyd Patterson (USA)
18 Sep 1963 *Fl* Hiroyuki Ebihara (Jap) beat Pone Kingpetch (Tha)*
25 May 1965 *H* Muhammad Ali (USA)* beat Sonny Liston (USA)
22 Jan 1969 *LH* Bob Foster (USA)* beat Frank de Paula (USA)
22 Apr 1969 *H (NY)* Joe Frazier (USA)* beat Davy Zyglewicz (USA)
3 Jun 1971 *Fe (WBC)* Kuniaki Shibata (Jap)* beat Raul Cruz (Mex)
5 Jun 1971 *LH (WBA)* Vicente Rondon

29 Nov 1988 *B (IBF)* Orlando Canizales (USA)* beat Jimmy Navarro (USA)
4 Feb 1989 *W (WBA)* Mark Breland (USA) beat Seung-Soon Lee (S. Kor)
25 Mar 1989 *M (IBF)* Michael Nunn (USA)* beat Sumbu Kalambay (Zai)
8 Jul 1989 *LM (WBC)* John Mugabi (Uga) beat Rene Jacquot (Fra)*
21 Jul 1989 *H* Mike Tyson (USA)* beat Carl Williams (USA)
17 Oct 1989 *B (WBA)* Luisito Espinosa (Phi) beat Kaokar Galaxy (Tha)*
24 Oct 1989 *LH (WBA)* Virgil Hill (USA)* beat James Kinchen (USA)

* Defending champion

Joe Louis has stopped more men (5) in the first round of world title fights than any other fighter.

Floyd Patterson is the only man to have been stopped twice in the first round in world title fights, and on both occasions it was by Sonny Liston.

Al Singer holds the unique record of winning and losing a world title in the 1st round. He beat Sammy Mandell to win the lightweight title in July 1930. The fight lasted 1 min 46 sec. Four months later he lost the title to Tony Canzoneri and this time the fight lasted 1 min 6 sec. They were Singer's only world title fights: total length 172 secs!

SHORTEST WORLD TITLE FIGHTS

45 sec Al McCoy v George Chip, middleweight, 7 Apr 1914
45 sec Lloyd Honeyghan v Gene Hatcher, WBC/IBF welterweight, 30 Aug 1987
54 sec Mark Breland v Seung-Soon Lee, WBA welterweight, 4 Feb 1989
58 sec Emile Pladner v Frankie Genaro, NBA flyweight, 2 Mar 1929
61 sec Jackie Paterson v Peter Kane, flyweight, 19 Jun 1943
61 sec Bobby Czyz v David Sears, IBF light-heavyweight, 26 Dec 1986
63 sec Michael Dokes v Mike Weaver, WBA heavyweight, 10 Dec 1982
66 sec Tony Canzoneri v Al Singer, lightweight, 14 Nov 1930
67 sec Marvin Hagler v Caveman Lee, middleweight, 7 Mar 1982
75 sec Terry McGovern v Pedlar Palmer, bantamweight, 12 Sep 1899
79 sec Santos Laciar v Shin-Hi Sop, WBA flyweight, 16 Jul 1983
80 sec Al Hostak v Eric Seelig, NBA middleweight, 11 Dec 1939

Jim Jeffries beat Jack Finnegan in 55 sec in 1900 and this fight is regarded by some sources as being for the world heavyweight title.

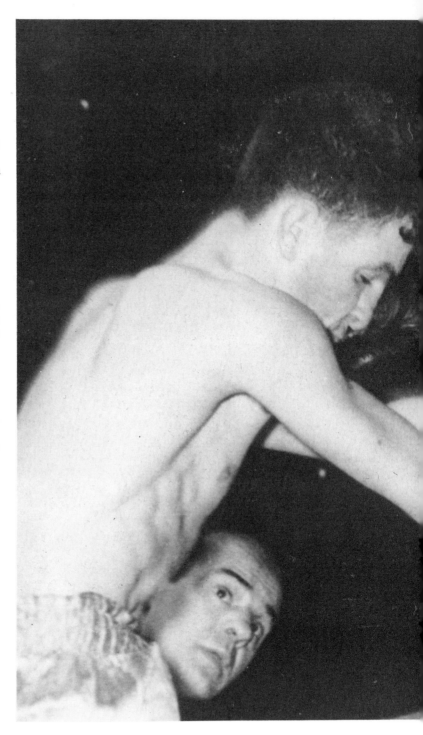

The shortest heavyweight contests have been:

63 sec Mike Dokes v Mike Weaver, 10 Dec 1982
88 sec Tommy Burns v Jem Roche, 17 Mar 1908
91 sec Mike Tyson v Michael Spinks, 27 Jun 1988
93 sec Mike Tyson v Carl Williams, 21 Jul 1989
96 sec Joe Frazier v Dave Zyglewicz, 22 Apr 1969
112 sec Muhammad Ali v Sonny Liston, 25 May 1965
120 sec George Foreman v Joe Roman, 1 Sep 1973

DISQUALIFICATIONS IN WORLD TITLE FIGHTS

29 Mar 1889 *W* Paddy Duffy (USA)

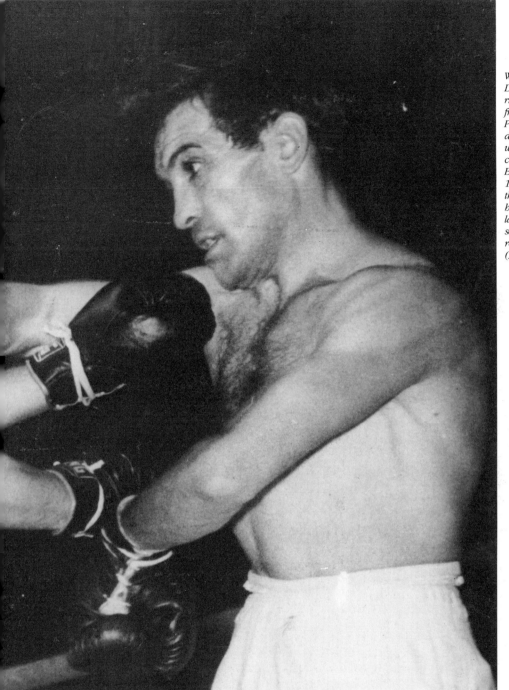

Welshman Dai Dower takes a right to the head from Argentina's Pascual Perez during their world flyweight contest in Buenos Aires in 1957. Sadly for the Welshman his challenge lasted a mere 90 seconds as Perez retained his title (AP)

eat Tom Meadows (Aus)
11 Nov 1898 *Fe* George Dixon (Can)
eat Dave Sullivan (Ire)*
15 Jan 1900 *W* Rube Ferns (USA) beat
Mysterious Billy Smith (USA)
30 Apr 1904 *W* Dixie Kid (USA) beat
oe Walcott (Bar)*
31 Oct 1904 *L* Joe Gans (USA)* beat
immy Britt (USA)
3 Sep 1906 *L* Joe Gans (USA)* beat

Battling Nelson (Den)
28 Nov 1912 *L* Willie Ritchie (USA)
beat Ad Wolgast (USA)*
5 Mar 1913 *M* Frank Klaus (USA) beat
Billy Papke (USA)*
10 Sep 1915 *B* Johnny Ertle (Aut) beat
Kid Williams (Den)*
4 Jul 1916 *L* Freddie Welsh (GB)* beat
Ad Wolgast (USA)
18 Nov 1921 *JL* Johnny Dundee (Ita)

When Mike Tyson knocked out Michael Spinks in 91 seconds in 1988 it earned the champion the equivalent of $221 000 a second!

beat George Chaney (USA)
26 Jun 1922 *W* Jack Britton (USA)*
beat Benny Leonard (USA)
30 Nov 1922 *M (NY)* Mike O'Dowd
(USA) beat Dave Rosenberg (USA)*
9 Jul 1926 *W* Pete Latzo (USA)* beat
George Levine (USA)
20 Jul 1928 *Fl (NY)* Corporal Izzy
Schwartz (USA)* beat Frisco Grande
(Phi)
18 Apr 1929 *Fl (NBA)* Frankie Genaro
(USA) beat Emile Pladner (Fra)*
25 Jul 1929 *W* Jackie Fields (USA)*
beat Joe Dundee (Ita)
12 Jun 1930 *H* Max Schmeling (Ger)
beat Jack Sharkey (USA)
11 Jun 1932 *M (NBA)* Marcel Thil (Fra)
beat Gorilla Jones (USA)*
20 Jan 1936 *M (NBA)* Marcel Thil
(Fra)* beat Lou Brouillard (Can)
23 May 1941 *H* Joe Louis (USA)* beat
Buddy Baer (USA)
16 Nov 1963 *JL* Flash Elorde (Phi)*
beat Love Allotey (Gha)
4 Oct 1969 *M* Nino Benvenuti (Ita)*
beat Fraser Scott (USA)
10 Jul 1970 *LW (WBC)* Bruno Arcari
(Ita)* beat Rene Roque (Fra)
5 Nov 1971 *L (WBC)* Pedro Carrasco
(Spa) beat Mando Ramos (USA)
16 Feb 1974 *LW (WBC)* Bruno Arcari
(Ita)* beat Tony Ortiz (Spa)
4 Apr 1975 *LF (WBC)* Franco Udella
(Ita) beat Valentine Martinez (Mex)
30 Jun 1976 *LW (WBC)* Miguel
Velasquez (Spa) beat Saensak
Muangsurin (Tha)*
21 Oct 1978 *Fe (WBC)* Danny Lopez
(USA)* beat Pel Clemente (Phi)
4 May 1985 *B (WBC)* Daniel Zaragoza
(Mex) beat Freddie Jackson (USA)
11 Dec 1989 *SB(WBA)* Jesus Salud
(USA) beat Juan Jose Estrada (Mex)*

* Defending champion

*Ad Wolgast (USA) is the only person to
have been disqualified in two world
title fights.*

*Joe Gans (USA), Marcel Thil (Fra) and
Bruno Arcari (Ita) have all had two
opponents disqualified in world title
fights.*

MOST KNOCKDOWNS IN WORLD TITLE FIGHTS

Figures in brackets indicate the
number of times the fighter was
floored. Winner of each fight is first
named man.

14 – Vic Toweel (SA–0) v Danny O.
Sullivan (GB–14)
bantamweight: 2 Dec 1950
11 – Mike O'Dowd (USA–2) v Al
McCoy (USA–9)
middleweight: 14 Nov 1917

11 – Jack Dempsey (USA–2) v Luis
'Angel' Firpo (Arg–9)
heavyweight: 14 Sep 1923
11 – Max Baer (USA–0) v Primo
Carnera (Ita–11)
heavyweight: 14 Jun 1934
10 – Benny Lynch (GB–0) v Jackie
Brown (GB–10)
flyweight: 9 Sep 1935
10 – Jimmy Carter (USA–0) v Tommy
Collins (USA–10)
lightweight: 24 Apr 1953

*Bill Ladbury (GB) floored Bill Smith
(GB) 16 times in a flyweight bout in
1913 but the fight was not universally
recognised as being for the world title.*

MOST KNOCKDOWNS IN SINGLE ROUND

Figures in brackets indicate the
number of times fighter was floored.
Winner of each fight is first named
man.

The most successful British trainer, Terry Lawless (All Sport)

6 Dec 1897 Walter Croot (GB) v Jimmy Barry (USA) bantamweight
24 Jun 1947 Jimmy Doyle (USA) v Sugar Ray Robinson (USA) welterweight
24 Mar 1962 Benny Paret (Cuba)* v Emile Griffith (VI) welterweight
21 Mar 1963 Davey Moore (USA)* v Sugar Ramos (Cuba) featherweight
19 Sep 1980 Johnny Owen (GB) v Lupe Pintor (Mex) WBC bantamweight
13 Nov 1982 Duk-Koo Kim (S. Kor) v Ray Mancini (USA) WBA lightweight
31 Aug 1983 Kiko Bejines (Mex) v Albert Davila (USA) WBC bantamweight

* Defending champion

RECORD PURSES

The largest purse for a world title fight was for the Mike Tyson versus Michael Spinks heavyweight contest at Atlantic City, New Jersey, USA on 27 June 1988. Tyson received a reported $22 million and Spinks $13.8 million.

The biggest earner in boxing is Sugar Ray Leonard with career earnings of $105 million. He received a reported $11 million for his clash with Thomas Hearns for the undisputed welterweight title in 1981 and when he came out of retirement to challenge for Marvin Hagler's middleweight crown in 1987 he received around $12 million. Hagler's pay day was $18 million. Leonard collected another big cheque when he fought Roberto Duran in the *Una Mas* super-middleweight contest in 1989, earning $15 million and taking his career earnings beyond the $100 million mark.

The first $100 000 purse was won by Jack Johnson (USA) when he beat Jim Jeffries (USA) on 4 July 1910 in a heavyweight title bout. Johnson actually received $120 000.

The first $1 million purse went to Sonny Liston (USA) and Floyd Patterson (USA). Each received $1 434 000 for their world heavyweight title fight on 22 July 1963 at Las Vegas.

The first $5 million purse was claimed by Muhammad Ali (USA) and George Foreman (USA). Each received $5 million for their heavyweight title fight in Kinshasa, Zaire, on 30 October 1974.

The large purses paid to fighters these days are aided by television rights. **The record purse in pre-television days** was the $990 445 paid to Gene Tunney (USA) for his second meeting with Jack Dempsey (USA) on 22 Sep 1927.

9 – Jack Dempsey (USA–2) v Luis 'Angel' Firpo (Arg–7) heavyweight, 14 Sep 1923, round one
8 – Vic Toweel (SA–0) v Danny O'Sullivan (GB–8) bantamweight, 2 Dec 1950, round five

Floyd Patterson (USA) was floored more times (17) than any other man in world heavyweight title fights.

FATALITIES IN WORLD TITLE FIGHTS

Since the first world title fight under Queensberry Rules in 1884, there have been over 2000 world title fights. The number of fatalities is few in comparison to that number, with just seven men losing their life as a result of injuries received during a world title bout. The following is a full list of such casualties (the fighter concerned appears first):

MISCELLANEA

The following brothers have won world titles:

Joe and Vince Dundee
Leon and Michael Spinks
Ricardo and Prudencio Cardona
Don and Bruce Curry
Kaokar and Kaosai Galaxy

The Curry's and the Galaxy's both held their titles simultaneously. The Galaxy brothers are the only twins to have held world titles.

The last world heavyweight title fight scheduled for 10 rounds was the famous Gene Tunney–Jack Dempsey 'Battle of the Long Count' on 22 September 1927

The last world title fight scheduled for 15 rounds was the IBF strawweight fight between Samuth Sithnaruepol (Tha) and Inkyu Hwang (S. Kor) at Bangkok on 29 August 1988

There have been four instances of world title fights being staged on **Boxing Day** (December 26):

1908 Jack Johnson v Tommy Burns (heavyweight)
1930 Frankie Genaro v Midget Wolgast (flyweight)
1933 Frankie Klick v Kid Chocolate (junior-lightweight)
1986 Bobby Czyz v David Sears (IBF light-heavyweight)

The most world title fights on one bill was at the New Orleans Superdrome on 15 Sep 1978. The bouts were as follows:

Muhammad Ali v Leon Spinks (WBA heavyweight)
Mike Rossman v Victor Galindez (WBA light-heavyweight)
Danny Lopez v Juan Malvarez (WBC featherweight)
Jorge Lujan v Albert Davila (WBA featherweight)

The first time two world title fights were contested on the same day was on 26 Sep 1894 when Bob Fitzsimmons fought Dan Creedon for the heavyweight title in New Orleans,

Freddie Mills (right) doing his bit for the Korean war effort. He is seen discussing plans with Mr Brigwell at the War Office to take British boxers to Korea for a series of exhibition bouts for the troops (Hulton)

USA, and George Dixon and Young Griffo fought for the featherweight title in Boston, USA.

The most world title fights in one year is 117 in 1989.

Four ex-world champions have refereed world heavyweight title fights:

Mushy Callahan (Floyd Patterson v Roy Harris, 12 Aug 1958)
Georges Carpentier (Jack Johnson v Frank Moran, 27 Jun 1914) Carpentier was only 20 at the time.
James J. Jeffries (Marvin Hart v Jack Root, 3 Jul 1905; Tommy Burns v Philadelphia Jack O'Brien, 28 Nov 1906; Tommy Burns v Bill Squires, 4 Jul 1907)

Tommy Loughran (Floyd Patterson v Pete Rademacher, 22 Aug 1957)
Jersey Joe Walcott (Floyd Patterson v Tom McNeeley, 4 Dec 1961; Muhammad Ali v Sonny Liston, 25 May 1965)

Arthur Donovan refereed a record 14 world heavyweight title fights between 1933–46. Next comes Mills Lane with 12 between 1978–87 and then Arthur Mercante who officiated in 8 contests between 1960–86.

The first time both husband and wife officiated at two world title fights on the same bill was at the Trump Plaza, Atlantic City, on 22 January 1988 when Rudy Ortega was a judge for the

Tyson–Holmes heavyweight contest and his wife Joan was a judge for the Carlos De Leon–Jose Maria Flores WBC cruiserweight bout.

Sugar Ray Robinson won the world middleweight title five times. No other man has won any one title as often. Carlos De Leon in 1989 captured the cruiserweight crown for the fourth time. Muhammad Ali won the heavyweight title three times and Jimmy Carter (1950s) and Edwin Rosario (1980s) both won the lightweight title on three occasions.

EIGHT GREAT WORLD CHAMPIONS

Muhammad Ali ·

Born: Louisville, Kentucky, USA, 17 January 1942

What more can be said about Muhammad Ali that hasn't already been said? He simply **was** the greatest. Who said so? Ali himself, of course, countless times. But that was always one of Ali's trademarks, reminding the boxing world how great he was and how insignificant his opponents were.

He brought a new approach to boxing, the like of which had not been seen before. Outside the ring he was extrovert and flamboyant. Inside the ring he was downright outrageous and cheeky. But let's not forget, he was also a brilliant boxer.

Born in Louisville, Kentucky as Cassius Marcellus Clay junior, he won the Olympic light-heavyweight title in Rome in 1960. He is rumoured not to have taken his medal from around his neck for days. He even wore it in the bath. He was that proud of what he had done for the black people of America. He turned professional a few months after his Olympic success and his first professional bout was against Tunney Hunsaker in his home town on 29 October. The man later to be labelled the 'Louisville Lip' won in six rounds.

By 1963 Clay was being tipped as a world-title contender, but at Wembley in June that year he literally suffered the biggest blow of his career to date when Henry Cooper's famous left-hook put him on the canvas. Only the bell and the now-famous split glove incident prevented Clay suffering his first defeat. He came back to win after a bloodied Cooper was forced to quit in the next round.

Eight months later Clay got his first crack at the world champion Sonny Liston and he defied the odds of 8–1 against him to stop the champion, who failed to come out for the 7th round. The boxing world had a new heavyweight champion. In the return bout, Liston was knocked out in the 1st round.

THE WORLD TITLE FIGHTS OF MUHAMMAD ALI

Date	Weight	Opponent	Venue	Result	
25 Feb 1964	H	Sonny Liston	Miami	Won	RTD–6
25 May 1965	H	Sonny Liston	Lewiston, Maine	Won	KO–1
22 Nov 1965	H	Floyd Patterson	Las Vegas	Won	RSF–12
29 Mar 1966	H	George Chuvalo	Toronto	Won	PTS–15
21 May 1966	H	Henry Cooper	London	Won	RSF–6
6 Aug 1966	H	Brian London	London	Won	KO–3
10 Sep 1966	H	Karl Milden-berger	Frankfurt	Won	RSF–12
14 Nov 1966	H	Cleveland Williams	Houston	Won	RSF–3
6 Feb 1967	H	Ernie Terrell	Houston	Won	PTS–15
22 Mar 1967	H	Zora Folley	New York	Won	KO–7
8 Mar 1971	H	Joe Frazier	New York	Lost	PTS–15
30 Oct 1974	H	George Foreman	Kinshasa, Zaire	Won	KO–8
24 Mar 1975	H	Chuck Wepner	Cleveland	Won	RSF–15
16 May 1975	H	Ron Lyle	Las Vegas	Won	RSF–11
1 Jul 1975	H	Joe Bugner	Kuala Lumpur, Malaysia	Won	PTS–15
1 Oct 1975	H	Joe Frazier	Manila, Philippines	Won	RTD–14
20 Feb 1976	H	Jean Pierre Coopman	San Juan, Puerto Rico	Won	KO–5
30 Apr 1976	H	Jimmy Young	Landover	Won	PTS–15
24 May 1976	H	Richard Dunn	Munich	Won	KO–5
28 Sep 1976	H	Ken Norton	New York	Won	PTS–15
16 May 1977	H	Alfredo Evangelista	Landover	Won	PTS–15
29 Sep 1977	H	Earnie Shavers	New York	Won	PTS–15
15 Feb 1978	H	Leon Spinks	Las Vegas	Lost	PTS–15
15 Sep 1978	H (WBA)	Leon Spinks	New Orleans	Won	PTS–15
2 Oct 1980	H (WBA)	Larry Holmes	Las Vegas	Lost	RTD–10

By now Clay had embraced the Muslim faith and changed his name to Muhammad Ali. He was a 'working' champion, and between his first defence against Liston and 1967 he engaged in eight world title

155

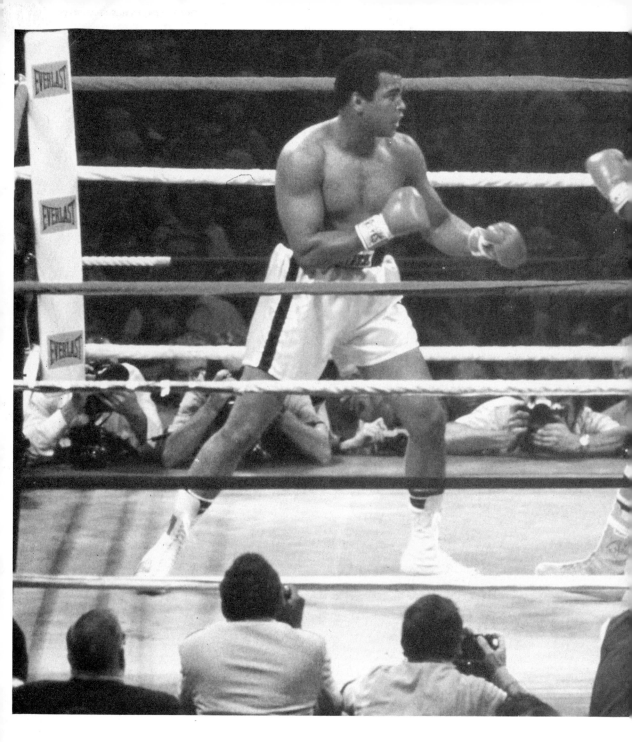

fights, winning them all. He took his skills out of America and into Canada and across Europe so fight fans the world over could revel in his wonderful ring skills.

However, he eventually lost his title, though not in the ring. It was taken away from him for refusing to be drafted into the US Army. He refused to fight in Vietnam and consequently would not be drafted. He faced a term in prison, which he avoided, but was out of the ring for over three years.

After three comeback fights he attempted to regain his world title, but lost on points to Joe Frazier. He gained revenge over 'Smokin' Joe' in 1974 when he retained his NABF heavyweight title. In his very next fight he emulated Floyd Patterson and regained the world title with an 8th round knockout of George Foreman in Kinshasa, Zaire.

He wasn't as nimble on his feet as he had been when he first took the title, but nevertheless, he still managed ten successful defences before Leon Spinks

Muhammad Ali
(left)
on his way to
making boxing history
by beating
Leon Spinks and
regaining the world
heavyweight title
for a second time
(All Sport)

got the better of him over 15 rounds in Las Vegas in 1978. Mind you, Ali was then 36 while Spinks was only 24. Remarkably, in the re-match seven months later, Ali became the first man to recapture the title a second time when he gained the points decision over Spinks in New Orleans.

Ali announced his retirement the following year, rightly choosing to bow out at the top. But unfortunately, he found the temptation to fight his successor, Larry Holmes, too great and he made a comeback, only to suffer a 10th round defeat. After one more contest, a 10-round points defeat by Trevor Berbick in Nassau, Bahamas on 11 December 1981, Muhammad Ali finally called it a day.

Despite an illness which was probably allied to his many years of boxing at the highest level, Ali still attends fights and luncheons, and is still one of the most popular men the sport has ever known.

Henry Armstrong

Born: Columbus, Mississippi, USA, 12 December 1912
Died: Los Angeles, USA, 23 October 1988

Henry Armstrong was one of the most colourful and best of all boxing champions and he earned a place in the record books by becoming the first and, to date, only man to hold world titles at three weights simultaneously. And that was in the days before the countless number of junior weight divisions were introduced.

Armstrong was born as Henry Jackson, the son of a Mississippi cropper. He had a very undistinguished start to his boxing career as Melody Jackson. However, he still wanted to pursue a boxing career despite an unsuccessful start and in order to get fights he changed his name to Henry Armstrong. The rest is history.

Between 29 October 1937 and 17 August 1938, Armstrong won the feather, welter, and lightweight titles by beating Petey Sarron, Barney Ross and Lou Ambers, no mean opponents. In beating Sarron for the featherweight title at Madison Square Garden, Henry, known as 'Homicide Hank', had to shed four pounds in less than a week to make the 9st limit. Seven months later he battled to put weight on to make the welterweight limit. He was successful in achieving his weight and also in beating Barney Ross over 15 gruelling rounds.

Between winning the welterweight crown in 1938 and losing to Fritzie Zivic in 1940, Armstrong engaged in 19 world welterweight contests, and won them all. The only two blemishes on his record were a defeat by Lou Ambers for the lightweight crown in 1939 and a draw against Ceferino Garcia for the middleweight title. Victory would have given him his fourth title.

He carried on fighting until 1943 but was well past his best and drink and drugs plagued the latter part of his career. Sadly, away from the ring, Armstrong could not cope with the pressures. He eventually became an ordained minister but when he died in Los Angeles in 1988, he was virtually blind and living in poverty.

At one time it would have been written that his achievement of holding three world titles simultaneously would never be beaten. But in an age when world titles are often 'manufactured' to fit the needs of fighters, then one has to admit that his record probably will be equalled one day. But whoever

Henry Armstrong holds a unique place in boxing history as the only man to hold world titles at three weights simultaneously (Hulton)

equals his achievement will surely never be held in the same esteem as Henry Armstrong.

THE WORLD TITLE FIGHTS OF HENRY ARMSTRONG

Date	Weight	Opponent	Venue	Result	
29 Oct 1937	Fe	Petey Sarron	New York	Won	KO–6
31 May 1938	W	Barney Ross	New York	Won	PTS–15
17 Aug 1938	L	Lou Ambers	New York	Won	PTS–15
25 Nov 1938	W	Ceferino Garcia	New York	Won	PTS–15
5 Dec 1938	W	Al Manfredo	Cleveland	Won	KO–3
10 Jan 1939	W	Baby Arizmendi	Los Angeles	Won	PTS–10
4 Mar 1939	W	Bobby Pacho	Havana, Cuba	Won	KO–4
16 Mar 1939	W	Lew Feldman	St Louis	Won	KO–1
31 Mar 1939	W	Davey Day	New York	Won	KO–12
25 May 1939	W	Ernie Roderick	London	Won	PTS–15
22 Aug 1939	L	Lou Ambers	New York	Lost	PTS–15
9 Oct 1939	W	Al Manfredo	Des Moines, Iowa	Won	KO–4
13 Oct 1939	W	Howard Scott	Minneapolis	Won	KO–2
20 Oct 1939	W	Ritchie Fontaine	Seattle	Won	KO–3
24 Oct 1939	W	Jimmy Garrison	Los Angeles	Won	PTS–10
30 Oct 1939	W	Bobby Pacho	Denver	Won	KO–4
11 Dec 1939	W	Jimmy Garrison	Cleveland	Won	KO–7
4 Jan 1940	W	Joe Ghnouly	St Louis	Won	KO–5
24 Jan 1940	W	Pedro Montanez	New York	Won	KO–9
1 Mar 1940	M (NY)	Ceferino Garcia	Los Angeles	Drew	PTS–10
26 Apr 1940	W	Paul Junior	Boston	Won	KO–7
24 May 1940	W	Ralph Zanelli	Boston	Won	KO–5
21 Jun 1940	W	Paul Junior	Portland	Won	KO–3
23 Sep 1940	W	Phil Furr	Washington	Won	KO–4
4 Oct 1940	W	Fritzie Zivic	New York	Lost	PTS–15
17 Jan 1941	W	Fritzie Zivic	New York	Lost	KO–12

Henry Armstrong (facing camera) during his world welterweight contest with Barney Ross in 1938. Armstrong added the title to his featherweight title won in 1937. Three months after beating Ross, Armstrong collected the lightweight crown when he beat Lou Ambers. He

Roberto Duran

Born: Guarare, Panama, 16 June 1951

Panamanian Roberto Duran, known as 'Stone Fists' because of his lethal punching, gave early signs that he was going to be one of the great world champions as he dominated the lightweight division in the 1970s. But to come back and win a world title in 1989, at the age of 38, is quite a remarkable feat. Only the great champions are capable of doing that.

Duran turned professional in 1967 and started his career with a 4-round points win over Carlos Mendoza at Colon, Panama. He stopped 23 of his first 29 opponents, and remained undefeated by the time he challenged Scotland's Ken Buchanan for the WBA lightweight title in 1972. The tough-fighting Duran proved too strong for the Scot and the fight was stopped in the 13th round.

He made 12 successful defences of his title, and only one man, Edwin Viruet in 1977, took him the distance. His last fight for the lightweight title was for the unified crown at Las Vegas in January 1978 and Duran beat the WBC champion Esteban De Jesus with a 12th-round knock-out. He relinquished the title after that to try his hand at the welterweight division and at Montreal in 1980 he was successful in his quest when he beat Sugar Ray Leonard on points. In the return five

THE WORLD TITLE FIGHTS OF ROBERTO DURAN

Date	Weight	Opponent	Venue	Result	
26 Jun 1972	L (WBA)	Ken Buchanan	New York	Won	RSF–13
20 Jan 1973	L (WBA)	Jimmy Robertson	Panama City	Won	KO–5
2 Jun 1973	L (WBA)	Hector Thompson	Panama City	Won	RSF–8
8 Sep 1973	L (WBA)	Ishimatsu Suzuki	Panama City	Won	RSF–10
16 Mar 1974	L (WBA)	Estaban De Jesus	Panama City	Won	KO–11
21 Dec 1974	L (WBA)	Mastaka Takayama	San Jose, Costa Rica	Won	RSF–1
2 Mar 1975	L (WBA)	Ray Lampkin	Panama City	Won	KO–14
19 Dec 1975	L (WBA)	Leoncio Ortiz	San Juan, Puerto Rico	Won	KO–15
23 May 1976	L (WBA)	Lou Bizzaro	Erie, USA	Won	KO–14
15 Oct 1976	L (WBA)	Alvaro Rojas	Hollywood, USA	Won	KO–1
29 Jan 1977	L (WBA)	Vilomar Fernandez	Miami	Won	KO–13
15 Sep 1977	L (WBA)	Edwin Viruet	Philadelphia	Won	PTS–15
21 Jan 1978	L	Esteban De Jesus	Las Vegas	Won	KO–12
20 Jun 1980	W	Sugar Ray Leonard	Montreal	Won	PTS–15
25 Nov 1980	W	Sugar Ray Leonard	New Orleans	Lost	RTD–8
30 Jan 1982	LM (WBC)	Wilfred Benitez	Las Vegas	Lost	PTS–15
16 Jun 1983	LM (WBA)	Davey Moore	New York	Won	RSF–8
10 Nov 1983	M	Marvin Hagler	Las Vegas	Lost	PTS–15
16 Jun 1984	LM (WBC)	Thomas Hearns	Las Vegas	Lost	RSF–2
24 Feb 1989	M (WBC)	Iran Barkley	Atlantic City	Won	PTS–12
7 Dec 1989	SM (WBC)	Sugar Ray Leonard	Las Vegas	Lost	PTS–12

months later, however, Leonard regained the title when Duran mysteriously retired in the 8th, after which he made his famous 'No Mas (No more)' statement.

Duran kept on fighting and an attempt to win the WBC super-welterweight title in 1982 was unsuccessful with the decision going the way of the champion, Wilfred Benitez. But the following year, Duran brutally beat Davey Moore to win the WBA version of the title and a few months later he stepped up a division to challenge Marvin Hagler for the middleweight crown. Hagler, though, successfully defended his title by gaining the points decision.

Following a 2nd-round defeat by Thomas Hearns in 1984, Duran decided to quit. But his period of inactivity lasted just 18 months before he was back on the trail of world title number four, and in February 1989 he was matched with Iran Barkley, the man who a few months earlier had beaten Tommy Hearns to take the WBC middleweight crown. Barkley was nine years younger than Duran, but 'Stone Fists' defied his years to win on points over 12 rounds.

Duran turned back the years to beat Barkley and gave a great performance. However in his next fight, against Sugar Ray Leonard for the WBC super-middleweight title billed as *Una Mas*, Duran gave a lacklustre performance and was unanimously beaten on points. Maybe it will now be *No Mas* for Roberto Duran, a great world champion.

Roberto Duran in action against Robbie Sims at Las Vegas in 1986. Sims won on points in this non-title bout (All Sport/Mike Powell)

Sugar Ray Leonard

Born: Wilmington, South Carolina, USA, 17 May 1956

Sugar Ray Leonard has had more retirements than Frank Sinatra. But just like 'Ole Blue Eyes', when he bounces back he is as successful and popular as ever. To listen to Leonard out of the ring it is hard to comprehend that he is a boxer. He is so mellow and mild. But put him in the ring and he finds that mean streak which makes a great champion.

Born at Wilmington, South Carolina, Ray was inspired by Muhammad Ali and the martial arts expert, Bruce Lee. He started boxing at the age of 14 and in 1976 captured the Olympic light-welterweight title. The following year he turned professional and after 23 straight wins he won his first title when he beat Pete Ranzany for the NABF welterweight crown.

The first of his record-equalling five world titles came in 1979 when he beat Wilfred Benitez for the WBC welterweight title. He lost the title to 'Stone Fists' Roberto Duran just six months later, but Leonard gained his revenge later in 1980 when he recaptured the crown after Duran mysteriously retired.

Leonard captured his second world title when he beat Ayub Kalule to win the WBA junior-middleweight title in 1981 and three months later he was crowned the undisputed welterweight king when he beat Tommy Hearns in the 14th round, after being on the brink of defeat. After one more successful defence against Bruce Finch, he had to undergo surgery for a detached retina and announced his first retirement in November 1982.

Twelve months later Leonard made a comeback and in May 1984 he had his first fight in 26

Sugar Ray Leonard relaxes away from the ring, enjoying his latest 'retirement' (All Sport/Mike Powell)

months when he beat Kevin Howard in a non-title bout. But that was it. He was inactive again until April 1987 when he couldn't resist the chance to fight Marvin Hagler for the WBC middleweight title, especially after the pundits said he had no chance. In a controversial points decision, Leonard won over 12 rounds and thus captured his third world title, and then promptly retired again.

Titles four and five came on the same night in Las Vegas in September 1988, when he won both the WBC's light-heavyweight and newly-introduced super-middleweight titles, beating Donny Lalonde in nine rounds.

Leonard retained his super-middleweight title by drawing with his old adversary Hearns in 1988, and had his last world title fight in December 1989 when he beat Duran with a unanimous points decision in a fight that was much less inspiring than the pre-fight hype. Leonard received a reported $15 million for the fight, which was billed as 'Una Mas' – once more – and took his career earnings beyond the $100 million mark. The fight with Duran is supposed to be Leonard's last. But let's wait and see!

THE WORLD TITLE FIGHTS OF SUGAR RAY LEONARD

Date	Weight	Opponent	Venue	Result	
30 Nov 1979	W (WBC)	Wilfred Benitez	Las Vegas	Won	RSF–15
31 Mar 1980	W (WBC)	Dave 'Boy' Green	Landover, USA	Won	KO–4
20 Jun 1980	W (WBC)	Roberto Duran	Montreal	Lost	PTS–15
25 Nov 1980	W (WBC)	Roberto Duran	New Orleans	Won	RTD–8
28 Mar 1981	W (WBC)	Larry Bonds	Syracuse, USA	Won	RSF–10
25 Jun 1981	LM (WBA)	Ayube Kalule	Houston	Won	KO–9
16 Sep 1981	W	Thomas Hearns	Las Vegas	Won	RSF–14
15 Feb 1982	W (WBC)	Bruce Finch	Reno, USA	Won	RSF–3
6 Apr 1987	M (WBC)	Marvin Hagler	Las Vegas	Won	PTS–12
7 Sep 1988	LH (WBC)/ SM (WBC)	Donny Lalonde	Las Vegas	Won	RSF–9
12 Jun 1989	SM (WBC)	Thomas Hearns	Las Vegas	Drew	12
7 Dec 1989	SM (WBC)	Roberto Duran	Las Vegas	Won	PTS–12

Ray Leonard (left) regained the welterweight title which Roberto Duran had taken off him in June 1980. The two did battle a third time in 1989 in a contest billed as 'Una Mas'. However, it can be rightly described as 'Una Farce'. Please, lads . . . 'No Mas' (AP)

Joe Louis

Born: Lafayette, Alabama, USA, 13 May 1914
Died: Las Vegas, Nevada, USA, 12 April 1981
No man has held any world title longer than heavyweight champion Joe Louis, and no man has made as many successful defences. In the 11 years and

9 months between 22 June 1937, when he beat James J. Braddock to win the title in Chicago, and 1 March 1949 when he announced his retirement, Louis

One of the heavyweight division's finest champions, Joe Louis, known as 'The Brown Bomber'. He is flanked by two former world champions, James J. Braddock (left) and Tommy Loughran (Keystone)

successfully defended his title 25 times. He dominated the heavyweight division and his only blemish was in 1950 when he came out of retirement to challenge the new title holder, Ezzard Charles, but was beaten on points over 15 rounds.

The son of an Alabama cotton picker, his real name was Joseph Louis Barrow. After the 1934 national amateur championships he turned professional and beat Jack Kracken with a 1st-round knock-out in Chicago on 4 July 1934, Independence Day.

Nearly two years after turning professional he was still undefeated, and had already scored wins over former world champions Primo Carnera and Max Baer. However, another ex-champion, Max Schmeling, ended his run of success with a 12th-round knock-out in 1936. Louis got back onto the championship trail in his very next fight by beating Jack Sharkey, also an ex-world champion, in the 3rd round. That defeat by Schmeling was to be Louis' last for 14 years.

He got his first crack at the world title in 1937 and he survived an early knockdown to beat James J. Braddock to capture the crown. Louis' first defence was against the gritty Welshman Tommy Farr who took the champion all the way. Only two other men, Arturo Godoy and Jersey Joe Walcott, took Louis the distance during his reign as champion, so it was a great performance by the little-rated Farr.

Although inactive during the war years because of Army service, Joe did a lot for the war effort by raising money from exhibition bouts. He made four successful defences of his title after the war, including two against Jersey Joe Walcott. But shortly after the second, he announced his retirement in March 1949.

Eighteen months later however, he came out of retirement to challenge the new champion Ezzard Charles. The burden of the income tax system forced Joe's return to the ring but it was not a happy one. He lost on points to Charles, but he continued fighting for

THE WORLD TITLE FIGHTS OF JOE LOUIS

Date	Weight	Opponent	Venue	Result	
22 Jun 1937	H	James J Braddock	Chicago	Won	KO–8
30 Aug 1937	H	Tommy Farr	New York	Won	PTS–15
23 Feb 1938	H	Nathan Mann	New York	Won	KO–3
1 Apr 1938	H	Harry Thomas	Chicago	Won	KO–5
22 Jun 1938	H	Max Schmeling	New York	Won	KO–1
25 Jan 1939	H	John Henry Lewis	New York	Won	RSF–1
17 Apr 1939	H	Jack Roper	Los Angeles	Won	KO–1
28 Jun 1939	H	Tony Galento	New York	Won	RSF–4
20 Sep 1939	H	Bob Pastor	Detroit	Won	KO–11
9 Feb 1940	H	Arturo Godoy	New York	Won	PTS–15
29 Mar 1940	H	Johnny Paychek	New York	Won	KO–2
20 Jun 1940	H	Arturo Godoy	New York	Won	RSF–8
16 Dec 1940	H	Al McCoy	Boston	Won	RTD–6
31 Jan 1941	H	Red Burman	New York	Won	KO–5
17 Feb 1941	H	Gus Dorazio	Philadelphia	Won	KO–2
21 Mar 1941	H	Abe Simon	Detroit	Won	KO–13
8 Apr 1941	H	Tony Musto	St Louis	Won	RSF–9
23 May 1941	H	Buddy Baer	Washington	Won	DIS–7
18 Jun 1941	H	Billy Conn	New York	Won	KO–13
29 Sep 1941	H	Lou Nova	New York	Won	RSF–6
9 Jan 1942	H	Buddy Baer	New York	Won	KO–1
27 Mar 1942	H	Abe Simon	New York	Won	KO–6
19 Jun 1946	H	Billy Conn	New York	Won	KO–8
18 Sep 1946	H	Tami Mauriello	New York	Won	KO–1
5 Dec 1947	H	Jersey Joe Walcott	New York	Won	PTS–15
25 Jun 1948	H	Jersey Joe Walcott	New York	Won	KO–11
27 Sep 1950	H	Ezzard Charles	New York	Lost	PTS–15

another year, gaining a few insignificant successes. He was nowhere near good enough to challenge for the world title again and when he suffered a humiliating defeat at the hands of one of the rising stars of the sport, Rocky Marciano, Joe finally quit for good.

The 'Brown Bomber' died in 1981 and the best tribute to him came from Muhammad Ali who said of Louis: 'I idolized him. I just gave lip service to being the greatest. He *was* the greatest.'

Rocky Marciano

Born: Brockton, Massachusetts, USA, 1 September 1923
Died: Newton, Iowa, USA, 31 August 1969

Larry Holmes came close to overhauling Rocky Marciano's record of 49 professional fights undefeated. But he fell at the last 'hurdle' and so the 'Brockton Blockbuster's record remains intact.

Marciano was one of the hardest-hitting heavyweight champions and his famous right-hand, nicknamed 'Suzy-Q', won him many of his contests. The right-hook he delivered to knock out defending champion Jersey Joe Walcott and capture the world title at Philadelphia in 1952 was probably the hardest punch ever thrown by Marciano.

Born in Brockton, Massachusetts, Rocky's real name was Rocco Francis Marchegiano. Perhaps surprisingly, his first professional fight did not come until he was 23, when he knocked out Lee Epperson in the 3rd round at Holyoke, Massachusetts. When Marciano fought for the world title in 1952 he was 29 years of age.

He got his title chance after knocking out former champion Joe Louis in the 8th round of their contest in 1951. Marciano was matched with the champion of just over a year, Jersey Joe Walcott, and despite being put on the canvas in the 1st round, Marciano got up and ended Walcott's reign as champion with that 13th round knock-out punch. Eight months later Walcott was given a chance of regaining his crown but this time Marciano made no mistake and knocked out the challenger in the 1st round. The fight lasted just 145 seconds.

Considering his size (he stood 5ft 11in and weighed 184lb), Marciano had awesome power. Today he would probably be better suited to the cruiserweight division, but how interesting it would have been to see how he would have fared against the heavyweight champions of recent years, and vice versa.

Marciano made five more defences of his world title and shortly after beating Archie Moore in nine rounds despite being put on the canvas, he announced his retirement from the ring. His record read: Fights 49, wins 49, 43 inside the distance. It was an impressive record and was not challenged until Larry Holmes came within one of equalling it.

A wise businessman, Marciano left the ring with his money wisely invested. But it was while flying to a

When Marciano, the 'Brockton Blockbuster', retired in 1956 he was undefeated in 49 professional fights (Hulton-Deutsch)

business convention that his light aircraft crashed at Newton, Iowa, on 31 August 1969. Marciano lost his life the day before his 46th birthday. He was the last great white heavyweight champion.

THE WORLD TITLE FIGHTS OF ROCKY MARCIANO

Date	Weight	Opponent	Venue	Result	
23 Sep 1952	H	Jersey Joe Walcott	Philadelphia	Won	KO–13
15 May 1953	H	Jersey Joe Walcott	Chicago	Won	KO–1
24 Sep 1953	H	Roland La-Starza	New York	Won	RSF–11
17 Jun 1954	H	Ezzard Charles	New York	Won	PTS–15
17 Sep 1954	H	Ezzard Charles	New York	Won	KO–8
16 May 1955	H	Don Cockell	San Francisco	Won	RSF–9
21 Sep 1955	H	Archie Moore	New York	Won	KO–9

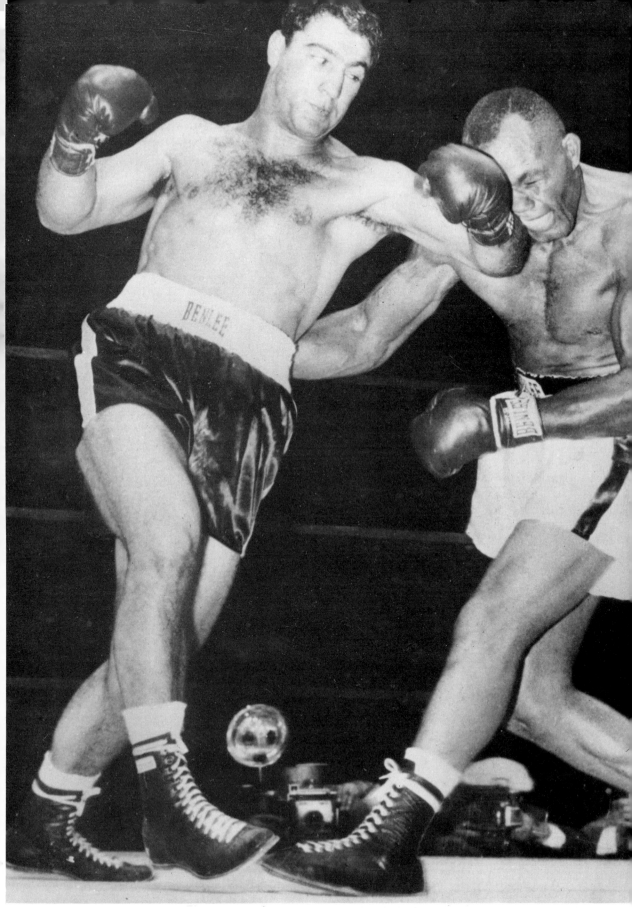

Rocky Marciano (left) beat Jersey Joe Walcott to capture the world heavyweight crown in 1952

Sugar Ray Robinson

Born: Detroit, Michigan, USA, 3 May 1921
Died: Los Angeles, USA, 12 April 1989

Muhammad Ali was the self-styled 'Greatest' boxing world champion. But ask the purists who they believed to be the greatest fighter of all time and it's a good bet they would come up with the same answer: Sugar Ray Robinson. During his 25 year career

Left elbow bent too much, elbows too far apart, left foot bent inwards, right shoulder too high . . . little wonder Sugar Ray Robinson stuck to boxing! (Syndication International)

Robinson engaged in 201 professional fights, including 22 world title bouts. He was probably the best pound-for-pound fighter that boxing has ever seen.

Born as Walker Smith in the back streets of Detroit in 1921, he moved to New York with his mother and two sisters when he was 11. And it was as a youngster in his new home town that he was introduced to the Harlem gym where he took up boxing under the watchful eye of George Gainford, who gave him his first amateur bout when he was only 15, a year younger than the legal age limit. In order to get him the bout, Gainford had to give him an identity card belonging to another fighter by the name of Ray Robinson. The name stuck, and the 'Sugar' part of his name was added when Gainford told a reporter what a sweet boxer Robinson was, and described him as 'sweet as sugar'. And so was born 'Sugar' Ray Robinson.

After winning 85 amateur bouts, including a Golden Gloves title, he turned professional in 1940. He won his first 40 contests before losing to Jake La Motta in 1943. He wasn't to lose again for eight years.

Robinson won the world welterweight crown in 1946 by beating Tommy Bell on points. He made five successful defences before gaining revenge over La Motta to capture the middleweight crown in 1951. Robinson then engaged in a whistle-stop tour of Europe as he beat opponents in France, Belgium, Switzerland, Germany and Italy, all within a couple of months. By the time he arrived in London for his world title fight with Randolph Turpin at Earls Court he had, perhaps, overdone it and Turpin sprang a surprise by winning on points. In New York two months later, Robinson regained his title with a 10th-round revenge win.

Robinson, the man with the best left hand in the business, dominated the middleweight division until dethroned by Gene Fullmer in 1957. He regained the title, lost it again, this time to Carmen Basilio, and then regained it once more. Both battles with Basilio were bloody affairs. When he lost to Paul Pender in 1960, Robinson was nearly 39 years of age and he never regained the title he had proudly held for so long.

THE WORLD TITLE FIGHTS OF SUGAR RAY ROBINSON

Date	Weight	Opponent	Venue	Result	
20 Dec 1946	W	Tommy Bell	New York	Won	PTS–15
24 Jun 1947	W	Jimmy Doyle	Cleveland	Won	KO–8
19 Dec 1947	W	Chuck Taylor	Detroit	Won	KO–6
28 Jun 1948	W	Bernard Docu-sen	Chicago	Won	PTS–15
11 Jul 1949	W	Kid Gavilan	Philadelphia	Won	PTS–15
9 Aug 1950	W	Charley Fusari	Jersey City	Won	PTS–15
14 Feb 1951	M	Jake La Motta	Chicago	Won	RSF–13
10 Jul 1951	M	Randolph Turpin	London	Lost	PTS–15
12 Sep 1951	M	Randolph Turpin	New York	Won	RSF–10
13 Mar 1952	M	Carl 'Bobo' Olson	San Francisco	Won	PTS–15
16 Apr 1952	M	Rocky Graziano	Chicago	Won	KO–3
25 Jun 1952	LH	Joey Maxim	New York	Lost	RTD–14
9 Dec 1955	M	Carl 'Bobo' Olson	Chicago	Won	KO–2
18 May 1956	M	Carl 'Bobo' Olson	Los Angeles	Won	KO–4
2 Jan 1957	M	Gene Fullmer	New York	Lost	PTS–15
1 May 1957	M	Gene Fullmer	Chicago	Won	KO–5
23 Sep 1957	M	Carmen Basilio	New York	Lost	PTS–15
25 Mar 1958	M	Carmen Basilio	Chicago	Won	PTS–15
22 Jan 1960	M	Paul Pender	Boston	Lost	PTS–15
10 Jun 1960	M	Paul Pender	Boston	Lost	PTS–15
3 Dec 1960	M (NBA)	Gene Fullmer	Los Angeles	Drew	15
4 Mar 1961	M (NBA)	Gene Fullmer	Las Vegas	Lost	PTS–15

Sugar Ray had come gallantly close to adding a third title to his name in 1952 when he challenged Joey Maxim for the light-heavyweight title, but sheer exhaustion in the intense heat forced him to retire in the 14th round. Mind you, he did better than referee Ruby Goldstein, who had to retire in the 12th round!

In December 1965, a month after losing to Joey Archer, Robinson called it a day. He made a lot of money out of boxing but bad advisers and too many hangers-on cost him dearly. Also, big demands from the tax-man left him with very little to show for his long career. Robinson died in 1989 and in his case, the legacy wasn't counted in terms of bucks and dimes but in terms of memories. Sugar Ray Robinson left us with plenty of those.

Jimmy Wilde

Born: Tylorstown, Wales, 15 May 1892
Died: Cardiff, Wales, 10 March 1969

For his size, Welshman Jimmy Wilde was one of the most powerful punchers in professional fighting. His boxing weight was often around 96 pounds and he ruled the flyweight division around the time of World War I (Hulton)

To look at Jimmy Wilde you would never have given him a chance of surviving in the tough world of boxing. And you would certainly never have considered him to be a world champion. But despite his frail-looking appearance, he had a lethal punch and one that many fighters in heavier divisions would have been proud of. He stood a little over 5ft 2in, never weighed more than 108lb and is widely acknowledged as the first champion in the flyweight division.

Hailing from the Welsh mining community centred around Pontypridd, Wilde started his boxing

THE WORLD TITLE FIGHTS OF JIMMY WILDE

Date	Weight	Opponent	Venue	Result	
18 Dec 1916	Fl	Young Zulu Kid	London	Won	KO–11
12 Mar 1917	Fl	George Clark	London	Won	RTD–4
18 Jun 1923	Fl	Pancho Villa	New York	Lost	KO–7

as a boy around the miners' club and local boxing booths. His style was unorthodox and he would often not take guard. Instead he would hold his gloves by his side. But when he trapped an opponent he would unleash a *repertoire* of lethal punches. Consequently he was nicknamed 'The Ghost with the Hammer in His Hand'. He was also affectionately known as 'The Mighty Atom', which was an appropriate description of him.

Surprisingly Wilde lost his first title fight when Tancy Lee stopped him in the 17th round of their British flyweight title fight in 1915. But that was to be Wilde's last defeat at the weight for six years.

He served as a physical training instructor during World War I but carried on fighting and in 1916 he captured the British title when he beat Joe Symonds in 12 rounds. After beating Joe Rossner he claimed the world flyweight title. His claim was strengthened when he knocked out Young Zulu Kid in 1916. This is generally regarded as the first official world title fight in the flyweight division.

In 1920 Wilde toured America and took on the best of their flyweights. He engaged in 12 contests and won them all, five by knockouts. Jimmy Wilde was accepted as the world's best flyweight on both sides of the Atlantic. In 1921 he fought bantamweight Pete Herman in a non-title fight, having run out of worthy flyweight challengers, and had to concede a stone to Herman. It proved too much of a handicap and the referee stopped the contest in the 17th round.

The tiny Welshman then announced his retirement, but with the arrival of Filippino Pancho Villa on the flyweight scene in 1923, Wilde accepted a challenge from Villa. The Welshman made the trip to New York but was pounded to defeat by his younger opponent and was counted out in the 7th round. Wilde announced his retirement again, and this time it was for good.

Wilde remained in close contact with the sport he loved until the time of his death in 1969, two months short of his 77th birthday. He was a broken man and spent the last four years of his life in hospital, unaware that his wife had died two years before him.

Jack Dempsey v Gene Tunney

Soldier's Field, Chicago, USA, 22 September 1927

The start of the famous 'Long Count' incident, as referee Dave Barry sends Jack Dempsey to a neutral corner (Syndication International)

On 23 September 1926, Jack Dempsey lost his world heavyweight crown to Gene Tunney at the Sesquicentennial Stadium, Philadelphia in front of 120 757 fans, the sport's first six-figure crowd. Exactly a year later, give or take a day, they did battle again and the outcome was yet another 10-round points win for Tunney. But what drama there was in the 7th round in what has become known as 'The Battle of the Long Count', one of the most controversial incidents in boxing.

Another 100 000 crowd, paying a staggering $2.5 million, packed into Soldier's Field, home of the Chicago football team, for the return bout. As referee Dave Barry called the two fighters together, the rain started pouring down. Tunney had the better of the opening five rounds, but in the 6th Dempsey got on top for the first time. After some exchanges in the next round, a left-hook from former champion Dempsey sent Tunney to the canvas.

The contest was being fought to the Illinois State Athletic Commission's 'neutral corner' rule. In other words, the fighter on his feet at a knock-down had to go to a neutral corner. Dempsey didn't realise this, and stood gloating over the champion who was on the floor for the first time in his career.

Referee Barry waved Dempsey to a neutral corner, and Dempsey went to the one nearest to Tunney. Barry then waved him away to the opposite corner. All this was wasting valuable seconds for Dempsey and giving Tunney much needed breathing space. The count still hadn't started.

When it did start, Tunney eventually got to his feet at the count of nine but the official timekeeper Beeler gave the count as 14 seconds. Other sources say it might have been as long as 18 seconds. If Dempsey had retreated immediately, Tunney would have been counted out and Dempsey would have become the first man to regain the world heavyweight title. Instead, Tunney got to his feet and regained the initiative over the last three rounds to gain a unanimous points decision.

Dempsey lodged a complaint to the Illinois Athletic Commission, but to no avail. Tunney maintained he could have got up at five but was told to 'take a breather' from his corner. The fight aroused so much interest around America that 12 fans died listening to the commentary on the radio, seven of them in the 7th round!

Tunney collected $990 445 for his win. He had asked promoter Tex Rickard for $1 million. Tunney made out a cheque for the difference and thus received his first seven-figure cheque. It was a good pay day for Tunney, but how close he came to losing his world crown in the 'Battle of the Long Count'.

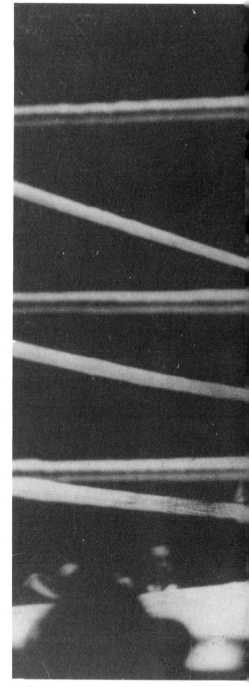

Both men spent time on the canvas but in the end it was Benny Lynch (standing) who won despite a brave effort from Peter Kane (Syndication International)

Shawfield Stadium, Clyde, Scotland, 13 October 1937 *Benny Lynch v Peter Kane*

In the years leading up to World War II, and in the years immediately after it, Great Britain produced some fine flyweights who became world-class fighters. But when promoter George Dingley brought Benny Lynch and Peter Kane together at Clyde Football Club's ground in October 1937, even he couldn't have realised that he was going to be part of one of the greatest flyweight contests of all time, certainly in Britain.

Scottish-born Lynch had captured the NBA and IBU version of the title in 1935 when he beat Jackie Brown in Manchester. But after beating Small Montana at the Empire Pool in 1937 he was universally recognised as the world champion. Nine months after that victory, Lynch was lined up to meet Peter Kane, a blacksmith from Golborne, which is half-way between Liverpool and Manchester. Kane was earning a reputation for himself as a hard puncher and he had the credentials to be a challenger for Lynch's title. However, promoters were so keen to stage the fight that there was a lot of behind-the-scenes wrangling before the fight eventually got under way.

Both men generated a lot of public interest and a crowd of over 30 000 filled the stadium – how Clyde FC would dearly love to have a crowd like that today! Lynch opened with a furious burst and seemed keen to end it quickly. He caught the challenger in the opening seconds and he was down. Surprisingly, he got up at the count of three. A more experienced boxer would have stayed down longer, but Kane wanted to get up and show what he was capable of, and indeed he did. Lynch couldn't take advantage and by the end of the round the scorecards had the two fighters level.

Kane had Lynch of the floor in the 2nd round, although the punch did little damage. As the fight went on, the contrasting styles of the two fighters took control, Kane throwing punches whenever he could and Lynch adopting a more casual approach, letting Kane do all the work. The crowd loved it and spent much of the fight on their feet.

By the 9th round it was obvious that Lynch's tactics were paying off. Kane was beginning to tire. But just as Lynch was about to go in for the kill, Kane caught the champion on the jaw. It rocked him, but thankfully for Lynch the bell was there to save him.

Kane came out full of aggression, but again the champion was prepared to let him do all the work until he felt the time was right, and that time came in the 12th round. Lynch attacked from the bell and continued to pound away at the challenger. Kane eventually fell under the barrage of blows but again, foolishly got up at the count of three. He was met by more blows from Lynch, and now it was Kane's turn to be saved by the bell.

When they came out for the 13th, Kane was a standing target for Lynch and was powerless to do anything about the punches the champion was throwing at him. Kane went down but, unbelievably, was up at seven. However, when he went down the next time he was counted out by the referee, W. Barrington Dalby. It was a courageous performance by Kane, a classy performance by Lynch and certainly a contest that the large Glasgow crowd remembered for a long time.

The former world light-heavyweight champion Bobby Czyz was selected for the US amateur squad to fight Poland in 1980. However, he had to withdraw at the last minute after damaging his nose in a car crash. All the American team and officials were killed when their plane crashed just outside Warsaw.

Polo Grounds, New York, USA,
12 September 1951 *Randolph Turpin v Sugar Ray Robinson*

Having dominated the welterweight division since beating Tommy Bell to win the title in 1946, Sugar Ray Robinson was now keen to do the same in the middleweight division. After beating Jake La Motta for the title in February 1951, Robinson set off on a tour of Europe before making his first defence against Britain's Randolph Turpin at London's Earls Court on 10 July.

Robinson arrived in London having engaged in six fights in 49 days – possibly a contributory factor to what became one of the biggest upsets in boxing. Turpin gave an outstanding display of strength to gain a popular points win. But two months later it was a different story as Robinson gained his revenge in what has often been dubbed 'The Fight of the Century'.

Britain's Randolph Turpin (right) brought off quite a shock in the first meeting with Sugar Ray Robinson in July 1951. But two months later the American put the records straight (Syndication International)

The New York Polo Grounds were packed with 61 437 fans, a record for a non-heavyweight contest, who paid nearly $800 000 for the privilege of being there. Turpin was seven years younger than Robinson but had shown great maturity, as well as strength, in winning the first fight. But would he have the character to do the same again, on US soil, just two months later? Those who suggested Robinson was jaded after his European tour were probably right. He came out for the return like a new man, ready to do business.

But, once more, he found Turpin no pushover. The two men were evenly matched over the opening nine rounds, but then the contest burst into life. They went into the 10th of the 15 scheduled rounds with Robinson marginally ahead on two judges' scorecards and the two men all-square according to referee Ruby Goldstein. But then Robinson was caught during an encounter and came out of it with a badly cut eye. He reacted quickly. He knew that if he didn't do something the fight could, and probably would, have been stopped.

He attacked Turpin and rocked him with a blow to the jaw. The Englishman stayed on his feet, but a second blow put him on the canvas. He got up at nine but was unsteady. There was very little of the round remaining. Robinson hammered Turpin for 30 seconds while he was on the ropes before Goldstein stepped in to stop the contest with just eight seconds remaining.

Today, there would probably have been cries to stop the bout earlier. But back in 1951, the question being asked was: 'Should Goldstein have stopped the fight with only eight seconds remaining?' The referee was only too aware that another fighter, George Flores, had died in a fight at Madison Square Garden a week earlier. Boxing did not want another fatality on its hands, so maybe he was right.

England was proud of her world champion, albeit for 64 days. But who knows, he could have been champion a bit longer had Ruby Goldstein not called a halt to the proceedings in the 10th round. For Robinson, it was a remarkable piece of boxing because the cut would probably have cost **him** the fight if he hadn't acted as quickly as he did.

Robinson went on to dominate the middleweight division just as he had done the welterweight division. For Turpin there was one more crack at the world title, but it ended in defeat by Carl 'Bobo' Olson in 1953.

Caesar's Palace, Las Vegas, USA, 6 April 1987

Sugar Ray Leonard v Marvin Hagler

This was the long-awaited clash between Sugar Ray Leonard, who had ruled the welterweight division between 1979 and 1982, and Hagler, who had dominated the middleweight class since taking the title off Britain's Alan Minter on a stormy night at Wembley in 1980. Since becoming champion, Hagler was gaining a reputation as one of the all-time greats. He had made 12 defences of his title, including wins over two other great fighters of the modern era, Roberto Duran, and Tommy Hearns. Leonard by contrast had been inactive for three years, and had only engaged in one fight since announcing his retirement in November 1982 after a detached retina.

Las Vegas was raring to go for the big fight which had been given the sort of hype that goes hand-in-hand with Leonard fights. Because of his inactivity and Hagler's consistency over the years, Leonard was

given no chance to capture Hagler's crown. But if anybody could respond to a challenge like that then it was Sugar Ray Leonard.

The fight was for the WBC version of the title only. Hagler was the undisputed world champion but, because the WBA and IBF felt he should fight Britain's Herol 'Bomber' Graham, they both withdrew recognition and so only the WBC title was at stake.

From the moment promoter Bob Arum announced the fight was on, all 15 000 Caesar's Palace seats, at an average of $500 each, were sold out six months before the fight. The worldwide television audience was in excess of 300 million. Hardly surprising, then, that it was a bumper pay day for both men with Hagler reputedly receiving $18 million of the

After such a great build up, the Leonard–Hagler fight didn't
quite live up to its billing. The end of the contest, however,
produced some strange judging! (All Sport/Mike Powell)

$30 million on offer. No wonder he preferred to fight Leonard instead of Graham!

Leonard came out with a youthfulness that many thought had long gone. Hagler stalked the ring in prey of the challenger. But the contest was not so much about what happened during the 12 rounds of fighting, but what happened at the end of the contest – the judges scoring.

The fight itself was, perhaps, not one of the best. Leonard did a lot of moving about to avoid Hagler's punches. But Hagler, on the other hand, missed a lot of punches. Age was obviously telling on the two men who were both in their thirties. Leonard gave an expert display of self defence, but in the 9th round got tangled up in a barrage of punches which clearly gave the round to the champion. Hagler set about trying to stop Leonard but the challenger was happy to keep avoiding his punches and capitalise on Hagler's mistakes to pick up points.

For most observers, Hagler had done enough to retain his title, and as the two men touched gloves at the end of the contest Leonard said, 'You beat me'. But when the scoring was announced, judge Dave Moretti scored it 115–113 to Leonard, Lou Fillippo gave it 115–113 to Hagler and the Mexican judge, Jojo Guerra, scored it 118–110 to Leonard. He gave only two rounds to Hagler, and neither of them was round 9, the one conclusive round of the fight!

It may not have been the 'Fight of the Century' despite such a billing, but as the headline in *The Guardian* said at the time, 'Marvellous script, mystifying scoreline'. Funny ole game, boxing!

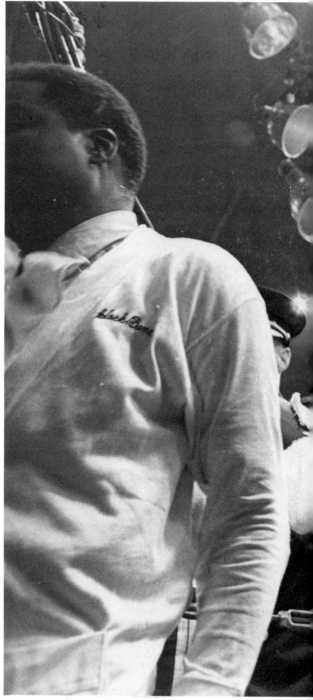

There are just four words coming out of Cassius Clay's mouth after winning the world heavyweight title for the first time. And they are: 'I am the greatest' (Hulton-Deutsch)

Miami Beach Convention Hall, Florida, USA,
25 February 1964

Cassius Clay v Sonny Liston

Just as Floyd Patterson was proving to be a good heavyweight world champion, along came Sonny Liston who needed only two minutes and six seconds to hammer the champion into a 1st round defeat, in Chicago in September 1962. The return bout eight months later was the same: a one round knock-out for Liston.

The new champion from Arkansas weighed in at around 215lb and was the heaviest champion since Primo Carnera. He looked invincible, and after two awesome wins over Patterson one was left wondering if there was a challenger capable of beating him. But nobody is invincible and waiting in the wings was a flamboyant youngster from Louisville, Kentucky. His name was Cassius Marcellus Clay, the 1960 Olympic light-heavyweight champion.

Clay, who later became well known for his pre-fight predictions and barrage of insults towards his opponents, predicted he would beat Liston, whom he described as 'The Big Ugly Bear'. The bookmakers didn't see it that way and they made it 8–1 against a Clay victory.

Despite Clay's attempt at pre-fight hype, the American boxing public shunned the contest and only 8 297 attended the Miami Convention Centre. They, like the bookies, foresaw another easy Liston win and weren't prepared to pay big money for a ringside seat. But how those fans who stayed away must have regretted it because that night saw the arrival of one of boxing's truly great champions.

Clay entered the ring with the words 'The Lip' embroidered on the back of his gown. Liston didn't arrive until five minutes after the challenger and looked as sinister as ever. The possibility of him winning three successive title fights in the 1st round was very real. He had a 7½lb weight advantage over Clay. But the opening round saw the challenger avoiding the famous left hooks of Liston as he danced his way around the ring with pace never before seen from a heavyweight.

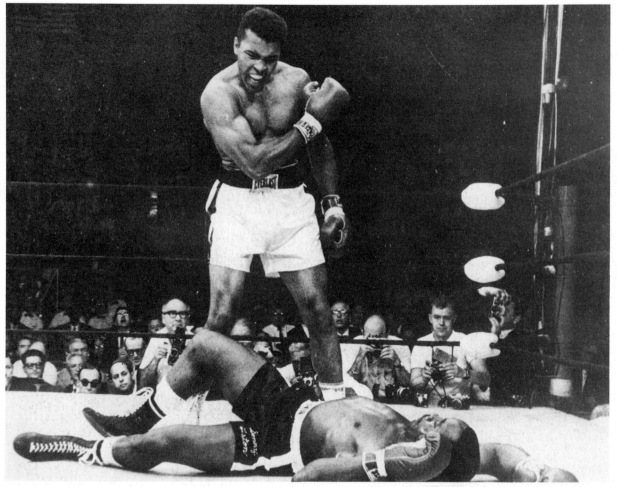

Muhammad Ali has his 'Big Ugly Bear' (Sonny Liston) on the canvas in the first and only round of their return contest in 1965 (AP)

Clay had not only survived the 1st round, which Patterson had failed to do on two occasions, he had actually won it. Liston levelled the score in the second after connecting with a couple of punches, one to the jaw and one to the stomach. But he missed with a lot as Clay kept dancing his way out of trouble. Clay was well on top in the 3rd round and actually cut Liston, but his inexperience showed towards the end of the round when he allowed Liston to connect with three uppercuts.

The challenger was proving to be one of Liston's toughest opponents. Liston took the 4th, but at the end of the round Clay complained to his corner that he couldn't see properly as a result of getting the solution used to stop Liston's cut in his eyes. Clay then spent the 5th round just keeping out of the way of the champion's punches without showing any real aggression. He succeeded and returned to the security of his corner, still complaining about his eyes.

Clay came out for the 6th round rubbing his eye. Referee Barney Felix was about to call a doctor for an examination during the break, but the bell went and he allowed Clay to box on. As Clay moved to the centre of the ring he was still rubbing his eye but a fast right and left to Liston's jaw had the champion rocking.

Cassius connected with three more lefts and rights and Liston was worried. Clay was more sure of himself and as he danced around the tiring Liston he kept throwing jabs to the champion's puffed face. Liston connected with one good blow towards the end of the round but it finished with a couple of stinging jabs from Clay.

As the bell sounded for round 7, Sonny Liston remained on his stool and declared that he could not continue because of an injured shoulder. Cassius Marcellus Clay junior was the new heavyweight champion of the world. But how could Liston retire? Clay hadn't hurt him all that much. The explanations have never been fully accepted. But Liston's retirement didn't take anything away from Clay's great performance.

Municipal Stadium, Philadelphia, USA,
23 September 1952 *Rocky Marciano v Jersey Joe Walcott*

The defending champion Jersey Joe Walcott is sent reeling after Rocky Marciano had hit him with a right described as 'the hardest punch ever thrown in world championship boxing' (AP)

When Jersey Joe Walcott won the world heavyweight title in 1951 it was at the fourth attempt and against odds of 6-1 on the champion Ezzard Charles. Furthermore, Walcott was 37 at the time, which made him the oldest man to win the title.

He had been boxing professionally since 1930 and, in his first title fight, had put Joe Louis on the canvas before losing the 15-round points decision. Louis once more, and Charles twice, had thwarted Walcott in his other attempts to win the title. But after capturing the crown in July 1951 and making a successful defence 11 months later against Charles, Walcott then accepted a challenge from Rocky Marciano, a man nine years his junior and with an impressive professional record of 42 fights, 42 wins, 37 stoppages. Marciano had a lethal punch and that night at the Municipal Stadium, Philadelphia, Walcott had the misfortune to be hit with one of the hardest punches ever thrown in boxing.

Surprisingly the challenger was 7–2 on to win the title, but his record and age difference justified the faith the bookmakers had in him. But Marciano must have wondered what had hit him in the opening round. The champion attacked right from the start and a right and then a left hook put Marciano on the floor for the first time in his career. When he got up there was blood coming from his nose. This wasn't the start Marciano had anticipated, but his strength kept him going until the end of the round and in the latter stages he made a minor comeback and caught Walcott with a couple of punches.

The fans had forgotten the cold of the night; they had warmed to the contest after just one round. Walcott set about Marciano in the same way in the next two rounds with an early flurry, though again Marciano staged a late recovery. Nevertheless, the first three rounds all went to the champion.

Round 4 also went to Jersey Joe, although he must have been impressed with the way Marciano stood up to him under pressure. Marciano was starting to get into the fight and caught Walcott with a blow just under the heart. The round was all square and then Marciano won his first round in the 6th, although he ended it with another cut, this time to his forehead. Walcott came back to take rounds 7 and 8, Marciano took the 9th and the 30 000 fans at ringside knew they had a great fight on their hands.

At the end of the 10th it was apparent that the champion was tiring and the longer the fight progressed, the better it was for Marciano. In the next round both men were showing signs of having gone ten gruelling rounds. Walcott had cuts over both eyes and Marciano was bleeding from his nose, forehead and a new cut near to his right eye. It was causing him lots of problems and surprisingly, in the 12th when many thought he might try to finish it, Marciano seemed unable to get the better of the champion and lost another round.

Walcott was well ahead on points and had to survive just three more rounds to hold on to his title. Both corners had done remarkable jobs in stemming the blood flow from their fighters. Marciano opened the 13th by tearing after Walcott and catching him with a left to the body and then came a right hook which caught Walcott on the jaw. It was delivered with such speed that Walcott never saw it coming. The champion sunk to one knee leaning against the ropes. Referee Daggert counted him out after just 43 seconds of the round.

The blow which won Marciano the title is often regarded as the hardest punch ever seen in boxing. It was delivered with his famous right hand which Marciano nicknamed 'Suzy-Q'; it won him many of his 49 professional fights including the heavyweight championship of the world in 1952. But it was not the punch alone which won him the title; a fair bit of courage also played its part.

Araneta Coliseum, Quezon City, Philippines,
1 October 1975

Muhammad Ali v Joe Frazier

*Muhammad Ali delivers a punishing blow to Joe Frazier during their
'Thrilla in Manila' (AP)*

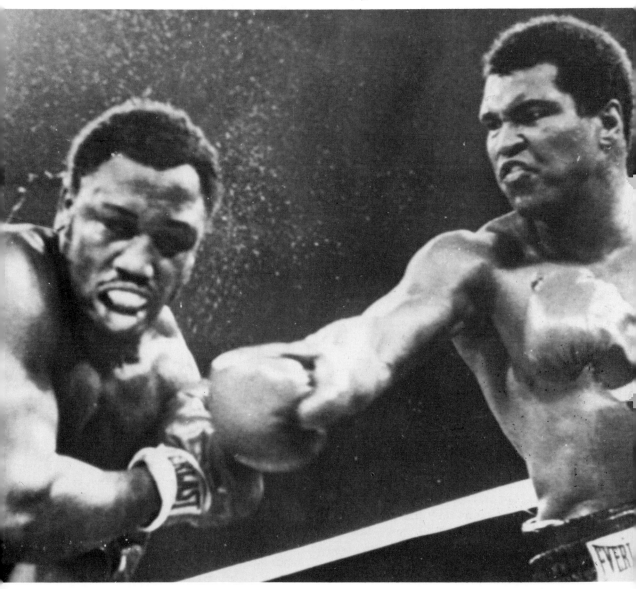

On 1 October 1975 two men engaged in one of the hardest and most unrelenting heavyweight title bouts ever seen. The two central characters were Muhammad Ali, the defending champion, and Joe Frazier, who was trying to win back the crown he had lost to George Foreman more than two years earlier.

This was the third meeting between these two great rivals, and each had a personal score to settle. Frazier had gained a unanimous points decision over Ali when he tried to regain his world title in 1971. But Ali gained revenge by winning on points over 12 rounds to regain his NABF title in 1974.

But this was the needle match and the pre-fight hype was as great as in any of Ali's previous world title fights, even though the contest was taking place in Manila. Ali wanted to win desperately, but so did Frazier. Both men attracted the kind of attention never before seen in the Philippines with more than 100 000 fans paying to watch them prepare for the fight in the weeks leading up to the bout.

Frazier's will to win stemmed from the fact that he disliked Ali, who had humiliated him in public several times. He tried his own piece of 'psyching' by referring to Ali by his pre-Muslim name, Cassius Clay.

Ali, in return, was never short of a retort: 'Frazier's got two chances, slim and none', he said. He further added: 'It's gonna be a chilla and a thrilla when I get the gorilla in Manila.'

The atmosphere was electric at Quezon City's Araneta Coliseum as local referee Carlos Padilla called the fighters together for their pre-fight talk. More than 770 million watched the fight as it was beamed via closed circuit television to cinemas and stadiums all around the world. Ali tipped the scales at 224½lbs, ten pounds heavier than Frazier. Ali gained an early advantage by taking the opening rounds, but Frazier then took control in the middle of the fight. Both men threw everything at each other. Both men took everything the other threw at them. Ali's two-handed ripostes scored points while Frazier's left hooks caused Ali trouble.

Ali regained control in the 12th round and he took the next two rounds, unleashing punch after punch upon the tiring body of his opponent. It was in the 14th round that Ali sent Frazier's gumshield from his mouth, which was followed by a gush of blood.

Frazier was not allowed out of his corner for the final round and an exhausted Muhammad Ali had regained his title. Despite the pre-fight verbal fisticuffs and antagonism, Ali was generous in victory when he had the honesty to acknowledge Frazier as 'one hell of a fighter', and he rightly described the contest as 'one hell of a fight'.

The man credited with Muhammad Ali's 'Float like a butterfly, sting like a bee' line is Drew 'Bundini' Brown, Ali's cornerman and motivator for most of his professional career.

Marvin Hagler v Thomas Hearns

Referee Richard Steels said of this middleweight contest, 'I haven't seen that much action in three rounds ever'; and he's seen a few fights in his lifetime. These two outstanding fighters certainly dished up a treat for the Caesar's Palace fans.

For Hagler it was the 11th defence of the world middleweight title he had held since beating Alan Minter at Wembley in 1980. For Hearns it was his first tilt at the middleweight crown. He had been the dominant welterweight in the early part of the 1980s before stepping up to junior-middleweight, but now he was moving up a division to fight one of the finest middleweights of all time.

In true Caesar's Palace style, the fight was given star billing normally reserved for the likes of Tom Jones, Frank Sinatra and Dean Martin. And in true Las Vegas style, big money bets were being placed on the outcome. Tommy Hearns told his fans he would end it within ten minutes and his fans believed him. He was installed as the pre-fight favourite, which was remarkable considering Hagler was unbeaten in nine years. Both men weighed in at 159lbs and the 15 000 crowd was about to witness one of the most thrilling boxing contests of all time, even though it lasted less than nine minutes.

The opening round was one of the finest and was voted *Ring's* 'Round of the Year'. Hearns was prepared for Hagler's customary slow start and had planned his fight accordingly, but Hagler surprised him by rushing across the ring and attacking from the outset, thus making a mess of Hearns' plans and forcing him backwards. Hearns stunned Hagler with a couple of punches and upon the call of 'Box him, Tommy' from his corner, the contest became a fierce toe-to-toe encounter with both men delivering countless blows to each other.

The opening two rounds saw a relentless exchange of blows, with Hagler withstanding the pressure slightly better than Hearns. But in the 3rd round, Hagler looked as though he was going to pay the price of six minutes' ferocious fighting. His face was bloodied following cuts above and below his right eye. Twice in this round referee Steele called the doctor into the ring to examine the injuries, but on both occasions Hagler was cleared to fight on.

After the second visit from the doctor, Hagler realised that time was running out and that he had to do something very quickly, otherwise he would be stopped and lose his title. There was a feeling of desperation in Hagler's final onslaught as he charged across the ring and caught Hearns with a powerful left

*The fight may have lasted only three rounds but Marvin
Hagler (left) and Tommy Hearns gave the Caesar's Palace
crowd good value for their money (All Sport/Dave Connor)*

and then a right. Hearns was rocking and Hagler pursued him around the ring to land two more rights. Hearns went down and appeared to be out, but at the count of nine he was up. However, his eyes were glassy and his legs crossed, and the referee immediately stopped the contest.

The fight ended within ten minutes as Hearns had predicted, but not the way he wanted. Hagler knew he had to take a gamble after the second visit of the doctor into the ring and it paid off, but where else would you take such a gamble other than in Las Vegas?

APPENDIX: THE BARE-KNUCKLE DAYS

THE BARE-KNUCKLE CHAMPIONS

Names in brackets indicate fighter's nickname

Jem Mace, one of the best known of the bare-knuckle fighters. He was nicknamed 'Gypsy' (Mary Evans)

ENGLISH CHAMPIONS

1720	James Figg
1740	Jack Broughton
1750	Jack Slack
1760	Bill Stevens (*Nailer*)
1761	George Meggs (*Collier*)
1762	George Milsom
1764	Bill Darts
1769	Tom Lyons (*Waterman*)
1771	Peter Corcoran
1776	Harry Sellars
1783	Tom Johnson
1791	Ben Brain (*Big Ben*)
1794	Daniel Mendoza
1795	Gentleman John Jackson
1800	Jim Belcher
1803	Hen Pearce (*Game Chicken*)
1807	John Gully
1808	Tom Cribb
1821	Tom Spring
1824	Tom Cannon (*Great Gun of Windsor*)
1825	Jem Ward (*Black Diamond*)
1827	Peter Crawley (*Young Rump Steak*)
1831	Jem Ward
1833	Deaf James Burke
1839	William Thompson (*Bendigo*)
1840	Nick Ward
1841	Ben Gaunt
1845	Willie Thompson
1850	William Perry (*Tipton Slasher*)
1851	Harry Broome
1856	Tom Paddock
1857	Tom Sayers (*Napolean of the Prize Ring*)
1860	Sam Hurst
1861	Jem Mace (*Gypsy*)
1862	Tom King
1863	Jem Mace
1865	Joe Wormwald
1866	Jem Mace
1873	Tom Allen
1876	Joe Goss
1882	Charlie Mitchell
1885	Jem Smith

OTHER CLAIMANTS

* After Figg's retirement Tom Pipes, Bill Gretting and Jack Broughton all claimed the title
* George Taylor claimed the title in 1734
* Jem Ward made a claim on the title in 1827
* Deaf James Burke claimed the title in 1839

AMERICAN CHAMPIONS

1816	Jacob Hyer
1841	Tom Hyer
1852	John C. Morrissey (Ire)
1859	John C. Heenan (*Benecia Boy*)
1863	Joe Coburn (Ire)

OTHER CLAIMANTS

Mike McCoole (Ire) 1865, Tom Allen (Eng) 1869

UNDISPUTED BARE-KNUCKLE WORLD HEAVYWEIGHT CHAMPIONS

1863	Tom King (GB)
1869	Mike McCoole (Ire)
1870	Jem Mace (GB)
1873	Tom Allen (GB)
1876	Joe Goss (GB)
1880	Paddy Ryan (USA)
1882	John L. Sullivan (USA) (*Boston Strong Boy*)

LONGEST & SHORTEST CONTESTS

The longest recorded bare-knuckle fight was between James Kelly and Jonathan Smith at Dalesford, New South Wales, Australia on 3 December 1855. It lasted 6 hr 15 min. The only other contest to last more than six hours was the Mike Madden–Bill Hayes fight at Edenbridge, Kent, England, on 17 July 1849. It lasted 6 hr 3 min.

The most rounds for a bare-knuckle contest is 276 (in 4 hr 30 min). That is how many rounds Jack Jones and Patsy Tunney had to endure during their contest in Cheshire, England in 1825. It was fought to Broughton's rules which meant a round ended every time a fighter was knocked down.

The shortest bare-knuckle contest lasted a mere 7 seconds. That is all it took for Tom Dow to knock out Ned Kiely in Kansas, USA on 4 January 1868.

SOME BARE-KNUCKLE FIRSTS

The first person to receive a boxing belt was Tom Cribb after beating Tom Molineaux at Copthall Common, England, on 18 December 1810. The belt was presented by King George III.

The first man to regain a title was Jem Ward in 1831. He lost his title to Peter Crawley on 2 January 1827.

Seven days later Crawley announced his retirement, thus making him the shortest reigning bare-knuckle champion. Ward claimed his title back but actually regained it when he beat Simon Byrne on 12 July 1831.

The first brothers to win titles were Jem and Nick Ward who won the English title in 1825 and 1840 respectively.

The first fatality in a Prize Ring contest was at Taylor's Booth, Tottenham Court Road, London on 24 April 1741 when George Stevenson died following a fight with Jack Broughton. It was as a result of this fatality that Broughton set about devising rules to make the sport safer. Bare-knuckle fighting was banned in Australia following the death of Alex Agar in a contest with Jim Lawson who was subsequently imprisoned for manslaughter.

BARE-KNUCKLE TRIVIA

Former English champion Tom Cannon was nicknamed the 'Great Gun of Windsor' which was quite ironic because he shot himself in 1858

INDEX

Page numbers in italics refer to illustrations. Names of title-holders mentioned only in tables are not listed in the index.